COMPETITION AND TRADE POLICIES

Is there an inherent conflict between competition and trade policies, or are the two policy areas complementing each other? The relationship between competition and trade policies, and the development of an effective competition policy for an integrated world economy, is one of the most important and challenging issues policy-makers presently face. This book examines current debates around competition and trade policy interactions, and discusses the need for new policy initiatives in an international context.

The papers in this collection are presented in five parts. Part I contains a discussion of some general principles and issues, while Part II is more specifically related to network industries and telecommunications. Part III examines some development policy aspects. Part IV presents European Economic Area policies and proposals, notably the initiative taken by Commissioner for Competition, Karel van Miert, for developing an EU competition policy for the new trade order. Parts V and VI contain background papers for panel discussions on vertical restraints and business perspectives, respectively, in an international trade and competition policy context.

Einar Hope is Director General of Competition for the Norwegian Competition Authority, and Professor of Economics at the Norwegian School of Economics and Business Administration, Bergen, Norway. His fields of research include industrial organization, energy economics and financial economics. He has founded three research institutions for applied economic research, and has been actively involved in work on regulatory reforms in Norway, especially in the electricity industry.

Per Maeleng has been Head of Division for Information in the Norwegian Competition Authority, and is now editor of a new journal on competition policy, for publication by the Norwegian Competition Authority in 1998. He is preparing a doctorate thesis in comparative literature and has been publishing articles on literature in various publications in Norway and abroad.

ROUTLEDGE STUDIES IN THE MODERN WORLD ECONOMY

COMPETITION AND TRADE POLICIES

Coherence or conflict?

Edited by
Einar Hope and Per Maeleng

London and New York

First published 1998
by Routledge
11 New Fetter Lane, London EC4P 4EE

Simultaneously published in the USA and Canada
by Routledge
29 West 35th Street, New York, NY 10001

Typeset in Garamond by
Keystroke, Jacaranda Lodge, Wolverhampton
Printed and bound in Great Britain by
Biddles Ltd, Guildford and King's Lynn

British Library Cataloguing in Publication Data
A catalogue record for this book is available from the British Library

Library of Congress Cataloguing in Publication Data
Competition and trade policies: coherence or conflict
/ edited by Einar Hope.
'This book documents the proceedings of the conference Competition
Policies for an Integrated World Economy, held in Oslo on 13–14
June 1996, and organized by the Norwegian Competitive Authority.'
– Preface.
Includes bibliographical references and index.
1. European Union countries – Commercial policy – Congresses.
2. Competition – European Union countries – Congresses.
3. International economic relations – Congresses. 4. Competition,
International – Congresses. I. Hope, Einar.
HF1531.C614   1998
382'.3'094 – dc21   97–30045

ISBN 0–415–16783–3

CONTENTS

CONTENTS

CONTENTS

ILLUSTRATIONS

Figures

Tables

CONTRIBUTORS

Knut Almestad, President, EFTA Surveillance Authority, Brussels

Milos Barutciski, Partner at Davies, Ward & Beck, Baristers and Solicitors, Toronto

Philippe Brusick, Officer in Charge, Competition and Trade Policies Branch, UNCTAD, Geneva

Stephen Calkins, Professor of Law, Wayne State University, Detroit

Henry Ergas, Economic Adviser, Trade Practices Commission, Australia, and Professor, University of Auckland

Richard J. Gilbert, Professor of Economics, University of California at Berkeley

Calvin S. Goldman, Partner at Davies, Ward & Beck, Baristers and Solicitors, Toronto

Bernard Hoekman, Senior Economist, The World Bank, Washington DC

Einar Hope, Director General, Norwegian Competition Authority, Oslo

Martin Howe, Director, Office of Fair Trading, London

Ulrich Immenga, Professor, University of Göttingen

Christopher Jones, Assistant to the Director General, European Commission, Brussels

R. Shyam Khemani, Principal Industrial Economist and Manager, Competition and Strategy Group, The World Bank, Washington DC

Hideaki Kobayashi, Deputy Secretary General, Fair Trade Commission, Tokyo

Patrick Low, Director of the Economic and Research Analysis Unit, World Trade Organization, Geneva

Petros C. Mavroidis, Legal Advisor, World Trade Organization, Geneva

CONTRIBUTORS

Victor D. Norman, Professor, Norwegian School of Economics and Business Administration, Bergen

P. M. A. L. Plompen, Director, Philips International B.V., Eindhoven

Michael J. Reynolds, Resident Partner, Allen & Overy, Brussels

Frederic M. Scherer, Professor, Graduate School of Government, Harvard University

Carl Shapiro, Professor of Business Administration, Haas School of Business, University of California at Berkeley

Karel van Miert, Commissioner for Competition, European Commission, Brussels

Leonard Waverman, Professor, University of Toronto, and Director, Global Forum for Competition and Trade Policy

Dieter Wolf, President of the Federal Cartel Office, Bundeskartellamt, Berlin

PREFACE

This book documents the proceedings of the conference 'Competition Policies for an Integrated World Economy', held in Oslo on 13–14 June 1996, and organized by the Norwegian Competition Authority.

The conference was intended as a meeting place for practitioners of competition policy in competition authorities and representatives for the academic and research communities and the business community. The proceedings include invited contributions from leading experts within each field. The contributions consist partly of plenary session papers and partly of background documentation for panel discussions. Some panellists have prepared full-length papers for their panel presentations while others have written shorter statements. This implies that the level and style of presentation of the articles in the book may vary somewhat more than one normally finds in proceedings from purely scientific conferences. Hopefully, this variety of approaches makes the book the more interesting and accessible to a broader readership than would otherwise have been the case with a more narrow approach.

The Norwegian Competition Authority is grateful to the Norwegian Ministries of Government Administration and Foreign Affairs, respectively, for financial support to the conference. A number of my colleagues at the Authority rendered invaluable assistance in connection with the arrangement; I would like especially to mention Unni Bache, Øyvind Christensen, Anne Sofie Gjestrum, Per Mæleng, Laila Rundtom, Knut Wettermark and Ellen Aas. Per Mæleng's skills and patience have also been invaluable in the editorial process.

The subject of the book – interlinkages between competition and trade policies and the development of an effective competition policy for an integrated world economy – is one of the most important and challenging questions competition policy-makers presently face. It is also a fertile research area. I hope that the book will contribute to this policy debate with new knowledge and insights, and that it will stimulate further analytical and policy-oriented work.

Einar Hope
Director General
Oslo, December 1996

1

INTRODUCTION

Einar Hope

A number of developments have taken place in recent years in the international economy which have changed fundamentally the conditions for competition. This imposes new requirements and demands on policy-makers developing an effective competition policy for the efficient use of resources in an international context. The globalization of economic activity and relations, rapid technological developments, and the progressive elimination of trade restraints are some of the most important factors to be mentioned. As a consequence, markets have become more open and interconnected, and competition is increasingly transcending national boundaries and penetrating deeply into national markets. The process of trade liberalization has to some extent shifted the emphasis from trade restraints to competition restraints as obstacles to international investment and trade flows. This has led to an increased awareness of inter-linkages between trade and competition policies and their consequences for the international trade system.

Attention is being increasingly devoted to these issues around the world; at the political level as well as from an institutional and analytical perspective. The World Trade Organization (WTO) decided at its First Ministerial Conference in Singapore in December 1996 to 'establish a working group to study issues raised by Members relating to the interaction between trade and competition policy, including anti-competitive practices, in order to identify any areas that may merit further consideration in the WTO framework'.[1] The Organization for Economic Cooperation and Development (OECD) has done a considerable amount of analytical and policy-oriented work in this area, both separately in the Trade Committee and the Competition Law and Policy Committee, and jointly between the two committees. A decision has recently been taken by the OECD to create a Joint Group on Trade and Competition.[2] The UNCTAD has recently reviewed and revised its set of 'Multilaterally Agreed Equitable Principles and Rules for the Control of Restrictive Business Practices'.[3] Within the EU, Commissioner for Competition, Karel van Miert, took the initiative in 1994 to produce the van Miert Report,[4] and this has been followed up with further work.

1

In addition, interested parties have taken the initiative to form private, politically independent bodies, like, e.g., the Global Forum for Competition and Trade Policy[5] and the International Antitrust Code Working Group.[6] Influential individuals have also come up with suggestions or proposals for solutions on policy issues.[7]

The work and the initiatives referred to above are represented, directly or indirectly, in this volume. The issues are primarily approached from a competition and competition policy perspective, while at the same time emphasizing the need for developing a coherent policy framework for a consistent treatment of competition enforcement principles and trade remedies in an international context.

Coherence or conflict?

In the ideal world one would expect to find a high degree of coherence or complementarity between trade and competition policies, rather than conflict. Both policy areas have the same basic objectives for policy decisions: the attainment of economic efficiency in resource utilization and the advancement of overall economic welfare. They also have a common theoretical foundation – the theory of free trade and the theory of perfectly competitive markets – as reference point for realizing these objectives. The analysis typically starts from there by identifying possible sources of market failures or imperfections and their consequences for achieving the economic welfare and resource utilization goals. The nature of such distortions is different, though. In the trade policy area they typically consist of trade restraints created by policy decisions by governments of nations in the form of tariffs, quotas, export subsidies on traded goods and services, anti-dumping duties, voluntary export restraint agreements, etc., while in the competition policy area they typically consist of market imperfections in the form of monopolization, collusion, various forms of restrictive business practices etc., instigated by acts of private market agents.

Methodologically, there is also 'coherence', in the sense that the same analytical tools or models are being applied in both policy fields. This is at least the case for the modern strategic trade policy analysis[8] and the analysis of strategic interactions in oligopoly markets. Thus, an integrated treatment of policy options and effects should, in principle, be possible.

There is, however, still a considerable gap or divergence of focus with regard to analytical approaches under the present state of the art of policy research. The literature on strategic trade policy is almost void of explicit treatment of competition policy issues, basing the analysis to a large extent on the 'third country model', although there have been some recent attempts to extend the analysis to include effects on consumers in the home country of trade strategic measures. Similarly, competition policy analysis has been almost void of explicit treatment of strategic trade policy issues, concentrating the analysis on welfare effects for domestic consumers of market strategic behaviour of, e.g., a national oligopoly.[9]

Further theoretical work to bridge this gap is needed in order to develop a coherent framework for an integrated analysis of (strategic) trade and competition policy issues.

Even though trade and competition policies have similar basic objectives, the instruments to achieve those objectives are radically different. Trade policy enforcers try to obtain collective, cooperative solutions through international negotiations to reduce the adverse effects on international trade of unilaterally imposed trade restraints by individual countries or groups of countries, while competition policy enforcers try to prevent firms under their jurisdictions from behaving collectively or collusively, if such behaviour is likely to jeopardize the economic efficiency goal.[10] Competition policy enforcers have quite powerful policy instruments at their disposal, in the form of *per se* prohibitions or interventions on a rule of reason basis against market behaviour and practices which can be considered detrimental to the stated goal. The trade policy enforcers find themselves in a quite different situation in this respect, with much weaker policy instruments and typically based on some form of international consensus in order to be applied.

The performance criteria for evaluating the outcome of the use of policy instruments are also somewhat different. In competition policy, performance is measured directly as an increase in economic efficiency of improved competition following a policy intervention. Under trade policy an increase in international trade flows often seems to be considered as a performance criterion in itself, or at least as a proxy for the efficiency enhancing effect on the international division of labour of a given trade policy instrument.[11]

The welfare function for the assessment of welfare improvements of policy measures may also be weighted somewhat differently across interest groups under the two policy regimes. Generally speaking, competition policy emphasizes consumer interests over producer interests, to the effect that efficiency gains should be passed on to consumers in the form of lower prices, better quality, improved accessibility to products and services etc., and not accrue as increased profits with the producers. A protectionistic trade policy measure would therefore be met with general scepticism by competition authorities, because this would normally harm consumers and favour domestic producers. In fact, in many countries competition policy and consumer policy are integrated under the same legal and institutional umbrella. There is, on the other hand, at least a presumption, based on empirical observations, that producer interests tend to be weighted more favourably under trade policy than competition policy in most countries.

This brief exposé indicates that there are close similarities and interlinkages between trade policy and competition policy, but also differences.[12] It is a demanding task to design an optimal policy mix of targets and instruments for the two policy areas under such conditions, even for an 'ideal' world situation. The difficulties multiply as we move to the real world with all the complexities added, because of, for example, quite different legal and institutional systems across countries, for the enforcement of such an optimal policy mix in an international setting.

Anti-competitive practices and trade

The efforts to liberalize trade through successive rounds of trade negotiations have limited the scope for governmental trade policy measures that distort the conditions of international competition. This development has, as already mentioned, gradually shifted the attention of policy-makers and analysts from trade policy remedies to private anti-competitive practices as potential barriers to trade, and thus to the efficacy of competition policy as a possible remedy. Since the focus in this book is on competition policy, let us consider briefly and in a summary fashion some such private anti-competitive practices and trade distortive effects that may result from them. For this purpose we use a simple classification scheme:

1 Anti-competitive practices of private parties in one country affecting the markets of other countries.
2 Anti-competitive practices of private parties in one country affecting the domestic market of the same country.
3 International anti-competitive practices of private parties in several countries affecting the markets of one or more countries.

The prime candidate for a private regulation of the first category is cooperation among exporters in one country in the form of an export cartel. This may distort competition in foreign markets, provided the cartel has a strong enough market position in those markets to influence prices or other parameters. The likely outcome is increased prices in the foreign markets, a negative effect on consumers' welfare in those countries and reduced traded volumes in international trade of the commodities encompassed by the cartel agreement.

A merger between two or more firms in the home country may have similar effects in foreign markets, again provided the merger gives scope for exercising market power in those markets. The effects of a merger compared with an export cartel may be different in the home markets of the country, though, depending on the specific competitive conditions of those markets in relation to the said practices.[13]

Export cartels and similar private practice, anti-competitive arrangements which have their intended effects solely outside the jurisdiction of the country in question, are usually exempted legislatively from competition law enforcement in most countries. An increased awareness of the possible distortive effects of such arrangements on international trade and competition

4

should make this 'effect doctrine' an obvious candidate for review and revision by competition authorities in a joint effort to reduce distortions of this kind.

The second category above encompasses a number of national regulations and practices by domestic firms which may create barriers to market access for foreign competitors to the domestic market. The prime candidates here are vertical restraints and relationships effectuated by a dominant firm, or group of firms, seeking to obtain vertical control of, for example, a distribution system. Vertical restraints come in many forms: exclusive dealing contracts for products or geographical territories, resale price maintenance agreements, franchise arrangements, and vertical control through full vertical integration.

The trade distortive effects of vertical restraints materialize to the extent that domestic firms succeed in preventing foreign competitors from entering the domestic market, e.g. by foreclosing access to distribution channels for goods and services locally. Measures like refusals to deal, boycotts, loyalty discounts, price discrimination, predatory pricing, strategic adjustment of production capacities, control of access to essential facilities such as the domestic electricity network system, and import cartel agreements may also be used as measures to deter entry by foreign competitors to the domestic market.

Private regulations and practices in this category fall normally within the domain and jurisdiction of the national competition authority and can be enforced under its competition law. Whether they will be intervened against or not depends upon how aggressively the competition authority combats such practices.[14] This may vary from country to country, but in view of the increased importance being given in recent years in competition policy analysis to entry conditions in general, and to potential import competition in particular, as a disciplining factor for the market behaviour of incumbent firms – derived from the theory of contestable markets – one would expect to find a more 'interventionistic' approach to those practices in most competition authorities than before. This may particularly be the case for small countries, where potential import competition normally means relatively more for competition and trade than for large countries.

The third category consists first and foremost of anti-competitive practices that are associated with international cartel agreements: price or quota cartels, market sharing arrangements, bid-rigging, etc. Such practices are normally prohibited *per se* in the competition laws of most countries. The competition and trade distortive effects are obvious, as several national markets are normally affected. Enforcement is difficult, partly because of information problems and partly because of the multinational nature of the agreements, and therefore requires some form of international agreement among the competition authorities of the countries where the parties to the cartel agreement are localized.

Policy options

Competition and trade policy officials seem to agree generally about the need to develop a more coherent framework for the analysis of competition and trade policy issues, and a more consistent approach to an effective application of policy instruments. There is, however, much less consensus about the specific structure of the framework and the policy options. Several schools of thought or divergences of opinion can be distinguished.

Some question the very position or hypothesis that private anti-competitive practices necessarily have substantive distortive effects on trade and competition that require corrective measures in an international context, and emphasize the need for empirical documentation before policy solutions are set forth. Others seem to be more inclined to go directly to solution concepts.

Another dividing line is between those who favour voluntary agreements of cooperation among countries or authorities to find policy solutions. Others advocate more binding commitments to an organized international policy enforcement cooperation, with dispute settlement procedures or other mechanisms for the imposition of common enforcement rules and principles for the participating countries.

A third divergence of opinion exists between those who maintain that policy interventions to correct for trade and competition distortions are best pursued by a policy area by policy area approach, attacking trade restraints with trade policy remedies and competition restraints with competition policy instruments. Others argue for an integrated approach within a common framework for policy decisions, where trade and competition policy measures can support and reinforce each other.

In spite of some differences of opinion on policy issues, a number of policy options have been proposed for a more effective application of competition policy measures in an international context, and work is in progress of implementing some of them. One can distinguish between three main approaches:[15]

1   harmonizing national competition law and practices (convergence), and extending the scope and coverage of competition laws;
2   improving cooperation among national competition authorities; and
3   creating a multilateral framework for competition law enforcement and dispute settlement.

The work on convergence of competition laws has been pursued most actively by the Committee on Competition Law and Policy of the OECD. It has been going on for several years, a number of publications have been produced which have had some influence on policy development,[16] and interim reports have been submitted to the OECD ministerial meetings.[17] The intention is not necessarily to obtain strict uniformity in law and institutions across member countries, but rather to converge on greater similarity in underlying principles, analytical methods, policy objectives and enforcement efforts. This work has also had an impact on non-member countries that are adopting or considering adopting competition laws, and thus securing some degree of 'convergence' from the beginning.

A recent OECD study on scope and coverage of national competition laws has revealed a number of exceptions of various kinds: legal coverage, exclusion of certain sectors or types of activities, deference of general legislation, such as competition law, to specific legislation, etc.[18] This work will be followed up by the Joint Group on Trade and Competition.

Bilateral agreements of cooperation between national competition authorities have been negotiated by a number of countries: the US and the EU, the US and Canada, the EU and Japan, and Australia and New Zealand. The present agreements are modelled more or less on the same basic principles, setting forth rules and procedures of cooperation in specific cases, and for sharing and exchange of information.[19] The confidentiality of information exchange issue has been and remains a major hurdle for further development of such cooperative agreements.

A novel concept of 'comity' has been introduced in connection with the efforts of improving cooperation among competition authorities to reduce international trade and competition restraints. Comity refers generally to factors and issues that a competition authority in one country has to take into account in deciding whether or not to pursue a case involving legal subjects in another jurisdiction. A distinction is made between 'negative' and 'positive' comity, the distinction being more a matter of degree than of substantive content of the concept in the sense that 'positive' refers to more affirmative acts of assistance than 'negative'. Under positive comity, one competition authority can ask another to open a proceeding if the interests of the first country seem to be affected by anti-competitive conduct within the jurisdiction of the second authority. The principle of positive comity is built into the existing bilateral agreements of cooperation as well as in OECD recommendations.

Proposals for creating a multilateral, or plurilateral, framework for competition law enforcement and dispute settlement are primarily associated with the van Miert Report.[20] More radical proposals for working towards the establishment of an international competition authority with some degree of enforcement competence and power have also been made.[21] The WTO has taken up the challenge of advancing this work, with its decision in Singapore to establish a working group on trade and competition policy.

NOTES

1 Singapore Ministerial Declaration of the World Trade Organization, adopted on 13 December 1996. It was also decided to establish a working group to examine the relationship between trade and investment.
2 OECD, *Strengthening the Coherence between Trade and Competition Policies, Joint Report by the Trade Committee and the Committee on Competition Law and Policy*, Paris, 1996.
3 See appendix to the paper by P. Brusick in this volume.
4 *Competition Policy in the New Trade Order: Strengthening International Cooperation and Rules. Report of the Group of Experts*, Commission of the European Communities, Brussels, 1995.
5 See, for example, its report, *Harmonization of International Competition Law Enforcement*, June 1995, by D. I. Baker, A. N. Campbell, M. J. Reynolds, and J. W. Rowley, also published in L. Waverman, W. Comanor and A. Goto (eds), *Competition Policy in the Global Economy, Modalities for Cooperation*, Routledge, 1996.
6 *Draft International Antitrust Code as a GATT–MTO-Plurilateral Trade Agreement*, Max Planck Institute, Munich, 1993.
7 See, for example, F. M. Scherer, *Competition Policies for an Integrated World Economy*, Brookings Institution, Washington DC, 1994.
8 For a survey, see J. A. Brander, 'Strategic trade policy', in G. M. Grossman and K. Rogoff (eds), *Handbook of International Economics*, vol. 3, Elsevier, Amsterdam, 1995.
9 For an exception, see P. P. Barros and L. M. B. Cabral, 'Merger policy in open economies', *European Economic Review*, 1994.
10 Scherer formulates the difference of the instruments of trade and competition policies in the following way: 'Trade policy seeks to avoid strategic behavior and secure *cooperative* solutions among trading nations; competition policy fosters *non-cooperative* solutions among the business enterprises facing one another in the market place', Scherer, *op. cit.*, p.7.
11 Sometimes 'balanced' trade in the trading relations between two or more countries is put forward as an aim or as a subtarget of trade policy. Such sub-targets will, in general, result in increased inefficiencies in resource utilization, because they imply extra restrictions on the optimal policy mix problem.
12 For a more comprehensive discussion, see J. Gual, 'The three common policies: an economic analysis, and discussion thereof by D. Laussel and C. Monet', in P. Buigues, A. Jacquemin and A. Sapir (eds), *European Policies on Competition, Trade, and Industry: Conflict and Complementarities*, Edward Elgar, Aldershot, 1995.
13 A trade policy restraint often originates from a competition policy issue. For example, most anti-dumping cases start with a complaint from an incumbent firm or firms about foreign competition on the home market, in the form of low import prices. The very threat of raising an anti-dumping case domestically may have a restraining effect on the willingness of foreign competitors to compete actively on the domestic market. The effects on competition of such behaviour may thus be similar to effects of the incumbent firm(s) entering into an implicit cartel agreement with foreign competitors.

In anti-dumping cases incumbent firms invariably use the argument that they are being exposed to collusive or monopolistic behaviour by foreign firms. The results of a recent OECD study seem to indicate, however, that such behaviour is the exception rather than the rule in most anti-dumping cases in practice. The study will not be published by the OECD, but by the individual authors.

A trade policy restraint may also influence the competitive behaviour of the players in a market. For example, voluntary export restraints may induce collusive behaviour by the exporters of the commodities in question.

14 A lax competition enforcement policy may be used deliberately as a substitute for an industrial policy, if the country is prevented, e.g. through international agreements, from pursuing as active an industrial policy as it wants. For a discussion, see, for example, Gual, *op. cit.*

15 See OECD 1996, *op. cit.*

16 For an early contribution, see *Competition and Trade Policies: Their Interaction*, OECD, Paris, 1984.

17 The next interim report on convergence will be provided for the 1997 ministerial meeting.

18 *Coverage on Competition Law and Policies*, OECD, Paris, 1996.

19 The OECD Council adopted in 1995 a *Revised Recommendation Concerning Cooperation between Member Countries on Anti-competitive Practices Affecting International Trade*, where principles of such information sharing are set forth.

20 See n. 4 above and the contribution of van Miert in this volume.

21 See, for example, Scherer, *op. cit.*, and his article in this volume.

Part I

COMPETITION AND TRADE

2

INTERNATIONAL TRADE AND COMPETITION POLICY

Frederic M. Scherer

Introduction

Since the ratification of the GATT Agreement in 1947–8 and the several rounds of tariff reductions that followed it, there has been a remarkable expansion of international trade. Foreign direct investment has grown even more rapidly, as business enterprises have established an immediate competitive presence not only in their home territories but also in numerous other nations' markets. The 1995 Treaty of Marrakesh, finalizing the Uruguay Round of international trade negotiations, extended the compass of GATT to agriculture, some service industries, intellectual property, and significant facets of foreign direct investment.

After the Uruguay Round negotiations were concluded at Geneva in December 1993, attention turned to unfinished items on the agenda for deeper integration of the world's economies. Four have gained pride of place: environmental protection rules, labour standards, continuing liberalization of trade in services, and competition policy. This paper explores the rationale for measures to harmonize and/or integrate competition policies across national boundaries.[1]

The principal function of competition policy is to keep markets open and undistorted by monopolistic practices, thereby satisfying three more fundamental goals: fostering an allocation of resources that best satisfies consumer demands, sustaining pressure on business enterprises to run a taut ship and innovate, and permitting market participants to pursue the opportunities that maximize their individual productive and creative potential.

Monopolistic distortions of international trade

The exercise of monopoly power that spills over across national boundaries can distort international trade in numerous ways. Buyer cartels and vertical restraints that constrict distribution channels against imported goods have effects directly analogous to the import tariffs which repeated GATT rounds

13

have sought to dismantle.[2] Seller cartels and the exercise of unilateral monopoly power in international trade introduce distortions essentially equivalent to those associated with export tariffs. Here one encounters an interesting asymmetry. Import tariffs have been imposed almost ubiquitously upon international trade, whereas export tariffs are rare. This asymmetry is probably explained by the relative ease with which cartelization can be substituted for export tariffs as an instrument of national policy and by the skill of monopolistic interest groups in persuading legislators to let cartel rents be captured by the cartel members, whose efforts can be said to create the rents, rather than by the general public fisc. When monopolies and cartels extend their reach across multiple nations, their discriminatory pricing and the re-exportation restrictions they impose upon middlemen can frustrate arbitrage and prevent the law of one price from operating. A firm or group of jointly acting oligopolists with monopoly power in the home market but facing competition abroad has incentives to dump the output from surplus capacity in foreign markets – a traditional bugaboo of international trade policy.

The responses authorized under GATT to dumping that injures target nation industries engender further conflicts between competition policy and international trade policy. A common remedy for dumping (and also in export subsidy cases) is to negotiate with the offending exporters a Voluntary Restraint Agreement (VRA), under which the exporters agree to raise their prices and/or reduce their export volume. Raising prices and restricting output are the classic behavioural traits of monopolists. When multiple sellers consent to such export restraints, they must find some way to divide up shares of their reduced output and to enforce agreed-upon prices – in other words, to form what amounts to an export cartel. Or if the firms do not assume these collective responsibilities, the government of the exporting nation must step in as *de facto* cartel master.[3]

The internationalization of competition policy

As international trade and investment have grown, so also has the acceptance by the world's nations of active competition policies, national and – to a much more limited degree – international.

At the end of the Second World War a half-century ago, only one nation – the US – had a pro-competition policy that was enforced assiduously. A few nations such as Canada and Australia had competition laws analogous to those of the US, but they were scarcely enforced. Other nations had laws that generally permitted cartels but subjected them to weak regulatory oversight in the hope of inhibiting abuses. The first strengthened post-war competition laws were imposed upon defeated Germany and Japan by the occupying powers. In Japan, this forced move in a new and unfamiliar direction engendered a reaction that left the Japanese Fair Trade Commission unpopular and largely ineffective during the first two decades of its existence. A similar

14

reaction might have been expected in Germany, but one of history's accidents intervened. Prominent in the first democratically elected German government were members of the liberal Freiburg School, who believed passionately in free market processes, in part as an antidote to the traditions of government control and business–government collaboration that had supported fascism under Hitler. As a result, a fairly tough anti-cartel law was passed in 1957 and enforced with great seriousness, if not always with adequate resources, by the newly organized Bundeskartellamt. The British government, which had long pursued a *laissez-faire* policy toward cartels, feared that monopolistic price raising could interfere with achieving full employment after the war. In 1948 it established a Monopolies and Restrictive Practices Commission to perform investigative and advisory functions. In 1956 a Restrictive Practices Court with the power to prohibit cartels was created. To the surprise of many, its first decisions took a rather strong anti-cartel line.

An even more important step occurred with the formation of the European Common Market. As tariff barriers were reduced within the Common Market, anti-dumping mechanisms were phased out, beginning in 1970. But to ensure that trade among Common Market member nations was not distorted, an active competition policy was considered necessary. As an EC commissioner stated in the 1961 debate over a draft regulation implementing a competition policy:

> It is beyond dispute – and the authors of the Treaty of Rome were fully aware of this – that it would be useless to bring down the trade barriers between the member states if the governments or private industry were to remain free through economic or fiscal legislation, through subsidies or cartel-like restrictions on competition, virtually to undo the opening of the markets and to prevent, or at least unduly to delay, the action needed to adapt them to the Common Market.[4]

To guard against this danger, the Treaty of Rome included firm language declaring inconsistent with the Common Market inter-firm agreements and concerted practices likely to affect trade between member states. Also prohibited were abuses of dominant market positions affecting trade between member states. After the slow start that seems typical of virtually all new competition laws, enforcement became increasingly vigorous. Formal mechanisms for restraining large competition-impeding mergers within the Common Market were added in 1990. As time passed, all Common Market member nations (excepting Luxembourg) and affiliated European Free Trade Association member nations have seen fit to pass their own internal competition laws.

These developments have been widely emulated, and as a result, most nations within the industrialized and rapidly industrializing world and many fragments of the former Soviet Union have adopted pro-competition laws, which have been enforced with widely varying consistency, competence, and enthusiasm.

In addition to the harmonization of policies achieved within the EC, the compass of competition policy has been extended across national borders in several ways.

Perhaps most important thus far, individual nations have reached out to attack under their domestic competition laws restrictive practices (such as export and import cartels) pursued by foreign-based business enterprises whose effects have spilled over national boundaries, especially when the perpetrating firms have had local branch offices from which evidence could be subpoenaed, and assets that could be seized in payment of fines and other penalties. These exercises of 'extraterritorial jurisdiction', led initially by the US, have triggered angry defensive reactions from some nations within which the target enterprises resided. Nevertheless, they appear to have gained increasing acceptance as a policy instrument, following a successful European Community prosecution against an international wood pulp cartel[5] and a similar case against a Japanese cartel by Canada,[6] which had previously protested vigorously a US action against a cartel exporting uranium yellow-cake to the US from its Canadian base.[7]

To mitigate the hostility that extraterritorial cases can provoke and to increase the effectiveness of domestic competition policies toward international business activities, individual nations and trading blocs have negotiated agreements to cooperate in the mutual pursuit of competition policy actions. One of the first such protocols was between the US and West Germany, initiated in 1976. Since then cooperation agreements have been signed, *inter alia*, between the US and Australia (1982), the US and Canada (1984), France and Germany (1987), Australia and New Zealand (1990), and the US and the European Community (1991). The EC–US agreement calls for information exchanges, mutual assistance in enforcement actions, and the exercise of comity in potential enforcement action conflicts without obliging cooperation when the interests of the parties diverge.

Over the past half century there have been sporadic attempts, thus far unsuccessful, to harmonize and perhaps to enforce competition policies on a world-wide plane. The first significant effort was embodied in the draft Havana Charter Treaty of 1948, which would have made a new International Trade Organization (ITO) responsible for promulgating tariff reductions, arbitrating international trade disputes, *and* fostering adherence to international competition policy rules. On the competition policy dimension, the Havana Charter stipulated that:

> Each Member shall take appropriate measures and shall cooperate with the (ITO) to prevent, on the part of private or public commercial enterprises, business practices affecting international trade which

restrain competition, limit access to markets, or foster monopolistic control, whenever such practices have harmful effects on the expansion of production or trade and interfere with the achievement of any of the other objectives (of the Charter).[8]

The Havana Charter Treaty was not ratified – in no small measure because the US Congress viewed it as too great an infringement on American sovereignty. Its provisions for tariff reduction and a mechanism for adjudicating dumping and subsidy disputes in international trade were carved out and embodied in the GATT system. Several subsequent efforts to adopt multinational competition policy codes and institutions to enforce them have met with equally little success. However, proposals continue to be brought forward – one by myself,[9] and another which is described in Professor Immenga's contribution to the conference proceedings.

Is the time now ripe for bolder steps toward the world-wide harmonization of competition policies and the creation of institutions to adjudicate cross-border competition policy disputes? With the continuing growth of international trade and investment and completion of the Uruguay Round, competition policy moves toward the top of the agenda of still-unsettled but important issues. But objections remain on at least three counts. For one, although there has been considerable convergence of national competition policies, huge differences remain between nations in both the substance and philosophical foundations of national laws. These differences might be seen as a positive reason for harmonization. But if harmonization is attempted, the differences testify that the task will not be an easy one. Second, some participants in the debate, including the US antitrust enforcement agencies, argue that the progress made toward harmonization through the exercise of extraterritorial jurisdiction and bilateral cooperation treaties is sufficient to solve the most pressing problems. Third, unwillingness to cede national sovereignty to supranational organizations in matters as important as conduct codes for business enterprise is a serious and perhaps insuperable obstacle. The sovereignty issue is particularly sensitive in the US, both because the US is jealous of its leading role in world affairs, and because the real or perceived impact of foreign competition on the wages and welfare of many American workers, especially less-skilled workers, has evoked much anxiety.

Having only one vote and at best a faint voice to cry out in the wilderness, I can do nothing about the reluctance of nations, including my own, to accept possible infringements on their sovereignty. I therefore devote the remainder of this paper to questioning the second argument against multinational measures: that existing extraterritorial enforcement efforts, leavened through bilateral cooperation agreements, suffice to eliminate the most important monopoly distortions to international trade. I advance my argument through three case studies of important recent cases in which existing institutions failed: the industrial diamond case, the Canadian potash case, and the European cement case.

Industrial diamond price-setting

The international diamond cartel, orchestrated by the De Beers–Oppenheimer organizations, has been one of the most durable and successful cartels in world history.[10] Despite new entry by Russian, Indian, and Australian producers, the cartel has maintained remarkable control over the prices of jewel-grade diamonds. Its influence on the price of industrial-grade diamonds has been less complete, in part because attempting to control the sales of lower-quality stones could overstrain even the substantial financial resources of the De Beers group, and partly because synthetic diamonds – produced using a process pioneered by General Electric – compete with natural stones.

During the 1990s, General Electric and De Beers together controlled 80 to 90 per cent of the world's industrial diamond supply. In December 1991, with a recession affecting much of the world economy, putting downward pressure on industrial diamond prices, General Electric announced synthetic diamond price increases of approximately 12 per cent. The price adjustments were essentially followed by De Beers in February 1992. In November of 1991 Edward Russell, the manager of General Electric's synthetic diamond production unit in Ohio, was fired. He claimed in a law suit that he was dismissed for complaining to General Electric's top management that members of the General Electric diamond sales organization were violating the US antitrust laws through meetings with, and the transmission of advance pricing information to, De Beers representatives in Europe. General Electric asserted in reply that it had fired Russell because of his poor performance, even though, the evidence showed, it had awarded Russell a substantial salary increase shortly before the firing.[11]

Evidence in a US government antitrust suit against General Electric revealed that General Electric employees had in fact discussed the stabilization of prices with officials of De Beers affiliates in Europe and had provided information on contemplated price increases to them.[12] There were, however, two serious weaknesses in the government's case.

First, the key person on the De Beers side of the communications was a French citizen, Philippe Liotier. However, M. Liotier's connection with De Beers was, to say the least, organizationally complex.[13] Liotier held several jobs. He was managing director of the Diamant Boart, a diamond purchase and sales intermediary, which was owned by an organization whose board of directors (on which Liotier also served) had three De Beers members, and which shared ownership 50–50 with De Beers in UHPU (Ultra High Pressure Units), the company manufacturing synthetic diamonds in Europe for De Beers. In another of his directorships, Liotier reported to Viscount

Etienne Davignon (previously commissioner of the European Community for industrial policy), who sat on the board of still another De Beers affiliate.[14] The question on which the US Antitrust Division's case foundered was whether, in his communications with General Electric over prices and impending price changes, Liotier was serving as representative of the Diamant Boart, a *buyer* of industrial diamonds from General Electric and De Beers, or as a representative of the De Beers interests as *sellers* of industrial diamonds. If he represented buyer interests only, the discussions were not subject to antitrust prosecution; but if he represented seller interests, they violated the law.

The US government's second problem was that three individuals who could have been representing De Beers interests in the discussions with General Electric personnel were European citizens who could not be compelled to provide testimony on the nature and intent of their representations. Belgian authorities cooperated with the US in searching the premises of the Diamant Boart in Brussels for relevant documents in November 1993, but the evidence produced in this way was inconclusive. An American citizen who worked for Diamant Boart was subpoenaed during a trip to the US for grand jury testimony. He testified again as a witness for General Electric, but the two sets of testimony were contradictory and therefore given little weight by the trial court. Without live testimony from the other individuals linked to De Beers, the Antitrust Division could not prove that those individuals were orchestrating a horizontal price-fixing scheme and not merely securing information useful to diamond buying organizations. Therefore, the government's case was dismissed.

Discussing the government's defeat in what it had proclaimed to be a major extraterritorial antitrust initiative, US Attorney General Janet Reno acknowledged that the government suffered from 'some difficulties in obtaining documents'.[15] She added, however, that only a few weeks earlier President Clinton had signed into law the International Antitrust Enforcement Assistance Act of 1994, which would permit US antitrust agencies to share confidential information with competition policy authorities overseas.[16] The new law, Attorney General Reno predicted in her commentary on the General Electric case, would help in the development of evidence for similar future cases.

Here a note of scepticism must be injected. Foreign competition policy authorities are likely to cooperate in the provision of evidence only when it is in their interest to do so. The De Beers organization, like many multinational enterprises, has affiliates in many nations. Its operations are relatively foot-loose. It has chosen to locate key subsidiaries in nations with a demonstrated willingness to tolerate its cartel activities. It is known for its alacrity in punishing diamond cutters who fail to exhibit the expected degree of cooperation with the cartel, providing to them only diamonds of inferior quality, or sometimes, no supplies at all.[17] Would one national cartel authority assist another nation's authority in a competition policy case when the subject enterprise threatens to withdraw its production and employment from the first nation, or to deprive independent producers in the first nation of needed raw materials or components? In my opinion, cooperation is unlikely. Courage in such matters is almost as scarce as gem-quality diamonds.

Canadian potash

Potassium is an essential nutrient for plant growth. Its application as a fertilizer component is particularly important in the cultivation of high-yielding corn, soyabean, and wheat varieties. Among the naturally occurring mineral salts and oxides of potassium (generically called potash) that can be applied as fertilizers, the most common is potassium chloride, which is extracted from sedimentary deposits laid down ages ago when oceans receded from the earth's surface and also from high-salt lakes such as the Dead Sea and America's Great Salt Lake.

The Canadian province Saskatchewan is the OPEC of world potash markets. Its vast sedimentary deposits of potassium chloride comprise nearly half of known and extractible world reserves, and in recent years, it has originated roughly a fourth of total world potash supplies.[18] Russia has reserves almost as large as those of Saskatchewan, but as in crude oil, the inefficiency of its mines and transportation network allows it to export only a disproportionately small fraction of its production potential. Within Saskatchewan during the late 1980s, six companies produced nearly all of the province's output. The largest of these was the Potash Corporation of Saskatchewan (PCS), an enterprise owned by the government of Saskatchewan. The other leading producers were privately owned. An export cartel, Canpotex, brokered sales and set prices for potash exported to parts of the world (especially Asia) other than the US. Because of US antitrust laws, Canpotex did not participate in marketing potash to US customers.

During the mid-1980s, PCS sought to increase its share of a stagnant North American potash market, thereby utilizing its substantial excess capacity and employing additional Saskatchewan workers, by cutting prices to selected US customers. Other members of the Saskatchewan oligopoly responded in kind, leading to a price war and losses of more than C$100 million by PCS in 1986. The sharp reduction in prices spread to the potash producers of New Mexico, who mined severely depleted reserves at high cost to supply 10 per cent of US potash requirements. On 10 February 1987, two New Mexico companies filed a petition with the US Department of Commerce accusing the Saskatchewan industry of dumping potash in the US. While the Department of Commerce was collecting data to ascertain the extent to which prices were below 'fair market value', the US International Trade Commission ruled preliminarily on 23 March 1987, that US potash producers had been materially injured by Canadian imports.

At about the same time, the government of Saskatchewan fired the top management of PCS and installed new leaders hired away from a privately owned potash producer. The new management was given explicit instructions to cease its price-cutting and to restore PCS to profitability, among other things to enhance the province's severance tax revenues and to secure a higher sale price in the planned future privatization of PCS. PCS began to assert its traditional price leadership upward from the $29–$35 range in which prices had hovered during 1986. See Figure 2.1, which traces average f.o.b. mine list prices per short ton of granular potash (in US dollars) for shipments from Saskatchewan to North American customers.[19] Year markers are placed at the beginning of each year. The first vertical dashed line marks the filing of a dumping action against Saskatchewan producers and the second vertical line the ITC's preliminary injury determination.

On 21 August 1987, the US International Trade Administration announced preliminary dumping margins against the leading Saskatchewan producers ranging from 9 to 85 per cent, including a 52 per cent margin for PCS and a weighted industry average margin of 37 per cent. The decision is marked by the third vertical dashed line in Figure 2.1. Industry members would be required to post bonds on all future sales in the amount of their preliminarily assessed dumping margins. PCS had tried to reduce its ultimate dumping margin liability by leading a substantial price increase in June. Two weeks after the preliminary dumping margins were announced, it added a further $35 per ton surcharge to its prices to cover the bonds that would have to be posted, accompanying its announcement with a statement that the increase would be rescinded if dumping margins did not have to be paid. Other producers followed its lead, and potash prices soared. See again Figure 2.1.

In addition to the impending imposition of substantial dumping duties, the Canadian producers were subjected to another constraint. Spurred by the threat of substantial duties on potash exported to the US, the Saskatchewan parliament passed in September 1987 a new law authorizing pro-rationing of individual provincial potash producers' output if circumstances were deemed by the lieutenant governor to warrant such a step. Thus, a stand-by cartel mechanism compelled by state action, and consequently exempt from US antitrust prohibitions, was put in place. The Saskatchewan government was in a position to act swiftly if potash producers' net (after-duty) price and profit realizations deteriorated.

In the closing days of December, the Saskatchewan potash producers negotiated with the US government a 'suspension agreement' under which each firm committed itself for five years to sell potash in the US at prices undercutting its calculated fair market value by no more than a small fraction. The agreement was validated on 8 January 1988 (fourth dashed vertical line). Three days later PCS announced that it would rebate the previous $35 surcharge, at the same time setting a new f.o.b. list price of $85

(US) per ton. Others followed suit, although there was considerable discounting of actual transaction prices below the list prices recorded in Figure 2.1. The discounting tended to increase as the potash producers gradually grew more confident that the dumping duty threat had abated.

During 1993 law firms claiming to represent thousands of US farm supply cooperatives and other dealers that purchased potash and distributed it to farmers, either in pure form or blended with other fertilizers, filed in federal courts diverse complaints alleging that the price increases of 1987 were effected conspiratorially in violation of the Sherman Antitrust Act, and seeking substantial treble damages.[20] In August of 1993, twelve such suits brought by various collections of plaintiff groups were consolidated into a single class action suit before the US federal district court in Minneapolis. In September 1996, a magistrate recommended summary judgment in favour of the potash producer defendants.

As a participant in the proceedings, I have attempted to report the historical facts with as little embellishment as possible. Now I add my interpretation, to be taken with the appropriate grain of potassium (not sodium) chloride. Although the change in PCS management would probably have led to a cessation of the price war, it seems almost certain that prices would not have been raised along the steep trajectory shown in Figure 2.1 had there been no anti-dumping action by the US government.

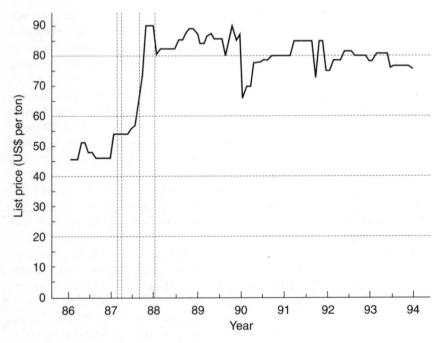

Figure 2.1 Movement of Saskatchewan potash prices, 1986–93

Given Saskatchewan's powerful position as the dominant source of potash to the US and the reliance of the government on revenue from price-dependent potash severance taxes, state-induced price increases would have been in the provincial government's interest even without anti-dumping threats from the US. But the anti-dumping action was clearly a precipitating impetus, leading the government of Saskatchewan to take legislative action that it had not seen fit to take during the preceding eighteen years.[21] As such, it represents a serious failure of harmonization between international trade policies and international competition policies, left unresolved *inter alia* by a subsequent free trade agreement between the US and Canada. The treble damages suit by potash merchants is a further case of failed policy coordination. A better resolution of such conflicts is critically needed.

European Community cement and 'the Greek problem'

On 30 November 1994, the European Community Commission levied against forty-two Portland cement producers and their trade associations the largest collection of fines, totalling Ecu 248 million, ever assessed under Article 85 of the Treaty of Rome.[22] The Commission's decision, which is being appealed before EC judicial authorities, concluded that cement producers had engaged in numerous collusive understandings aimed at limiting cement shipments across national borders within the Community. Many of the arrangements castigated in the EC decision cannot detain us here. I focus on one facet of the allegations, involving the so-called 'Greek problem'.

During the 1970s Greek cement producers added 7 million tons of annual cement-making capacity, nearly doubling their combined capacity, largely to serve the exploding demand for construction materials from Middle Eastern oil-producing nations enriched by the increase in oil prices from $3 to $34 per barrel between 1973 and 1981. As oil prices subsequently eroded and then collapsed in 1985 and 1986, the Middle Eastern demand for cement fell sharply. Greek producers were left with capacity to produce 16.2 million metric tons of cement per year, far in excess of domestic consumption (6.1 million tons). Cement prices in Greece – kept down in part by government price controls and subsidies – were much lower than in other EC nations (see Figure 2.2). Important EC markets could be reached easily by water transportation from production sites on the coast of Greece.

The Greek producers began positioning themselves to ship substantial quantities of cement to Italy, France, and (especially) the UK, where prices were held at high levels under the umbrella of a cartel that had escaped censure by Britain's Restrictive Trade Practices Court.

Other European cement producers were alarmed by the threat of rapidly rising Greek penetration into their home markets. At a series of meetings during mid-1986, representatives of the leading British, French, German, Italian, Spanish, and (non-EC) Swiss companies discussed a portfolio of

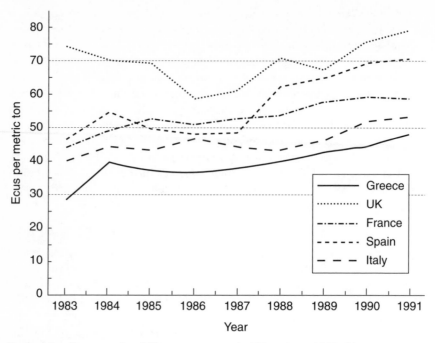

Figure 2.2   Cement price differences among six EC nations, 1983–91

'carrot' and 'stick' actions to deal with countries 'who disrupt by exporting surplus tonnage'.[23] Most of the 'stick' measures, such as penalizing customers who purchased Greek cement, counterattacking with exports to Greece, triggering price wars in remaining Greek export markets, and boycotting shipping companies that transported Greek cement, proved to be infeasible. However, a proposed 'carrot' measure – purchasing excess cement from the Greek producers and channelling it to markets outside the EC – was implemented. Northern European enterprises entered into bilateral arrangements with the principal Greek producers to purchase substantial amounts of cement from them, disposing of it in ways that caused minimal disruption to the buyers' home markets. Whether these purchases, which resembled the 'dancing partner' arrangements orchestrated by US petroleum refiners during the 1930s,[24] were carried out individually, or as part of a concerted scheme, will probably be contested in appeals before the European Court of Justice. It is also unclear whether a *quid pro quo* for the purchases was an agreement by Greek producers to restrain the export of additional cement into Northern Europe and Italy. What is clear is that the purchases and their disposal were discussed by the multi-company 'European Task Force' and were effected by leading producers. Some of the cement acquired in this way was resold through the buyers' normal distribution networks within the Community and some was exported to Egypt, West Africa, the Bahamas, and Canada. The

24

'first priority' target, however, was said at a June 1986 meeting to be the US,[25] and beginning in July of 1986, the first of numerous substantial shipments moved from Greece through a Northern European middleman to the US. Deliveries of Greek cement in the US rose steadily from zero in 1984 to a peak of 2.27 million short tons in 1988 before declining, first gradually and then sharply.[26]

As the first Greek shipments arrived, the US was experiencing booming demand for cement, causing domestic mills to operate at virtually full capacity while leaving a growing gap to be filled by imports (which rose from 10.3 per cent of US consumption in 1984 to 18.7 per cent in 1987).[27] Thus, the additional cement from Greece helped alleviate a tight market situation. Its entry into the US market was facilitated by the fact that in 1986, 53 per cent of all US cement-making capacity was owned by foreign firms – most of it by firms that were meeting to discuss the Greek problem in Europe.[28] The UK's Blue Circle group, Ciments Français and Lafarge of France, Holderbank of Switzerland, and Heidelberger of Germany all owned substantial cement mills near the US eastern seaboard and were therefore in a position to work the imports from Greece into their normal distribution systems. The first purchases of Greek cement were at f.o.b. prices in the range of $27–$29 per metric ton. Since the dollar was trading at near parity to the Ecu at the time, and since (subsidized) Greek home prices were approximately Ecu 36 per ton (see Figure 2.2), the origin prices were at dumping levels. The Greek imports induced a reduction of US prices, but not enough to trigger the second criterion for actionable dumping under GATT – material injury.[29] Plants located in eastern Pennsylvania, Maryland, and on the Hudson River reallocated their shipments away from coastal cities and toward the west, while coastal locations were served to an increasing extent through Greek imports. Thus, international trade with third-party nations was very clearly affected by arrangements implemented to reduce competition within the EC. Whether, given the tight market situation in the US, trade can be said to have been *distorted* is debatable. The most one can say is that if the Greek producers had tried to sell an equivalent amount of cement in the US without moving it through the friendly hands of Northern European dancing partners, they almost surely would have had to do so at lower, more disruptive, prices. And at lower prices, more Greek cement would have displaced cement from the highest-cost US mills.

Between 1985 and 1991, annual cement consumption in twelve member nations of the European Community grew by nearly 30 per cent.[30] In the US, the 1989–91 recession reduced cement demand appreciably. The US international trade authorities ruled in 1990 that Mexican producers had been dumping their cement in the US. In early 1991, Japanese producers, whose domestic cartel sustained very high prices while keeping out most imports,[31] were found to have been dumping in the US, and dumping margins of 48 to 85 per cent were assessed.[32] It is unclear what relative weights the growth of

European demand, the temporary slump in US demand, the prosecution of anti-dumping cases against Mexican and Japanese sources, and the initiation of EC competition policy proceedings against cement makers in November 1991, carried in the decline of Greek exports to the US East Coast. Since the sharpest drop occurred during 1990 and 1991, the EC action seems an improbable cause.

To the extent that the dancing partner arrangement affected the flow of Greek cement to the US (as well as Egypt, Canada, West Africa, and the Bahamas), one may assume that the EC's competition action thwarted its continuation. During the several years when the arrangement was active, however, one can conclude again that arguably anti-competitive activities in one competition policy jurisdiction spilled over to affect international trade flows within another jurisdiction. The same conclusion holds *a fortiori* with respect to the cartel-induced dumping of cement from Japan into the US and other nations. To the best of my knowledge, the US antitrust enforcers were unaware of these influences on their home market, or at least, they took no enforcement actions against them. It is doubtful whether the EC would have acted against its domestic producers had their conduct not distorted competition within the Community.[33] Since the arrangement probably permitted Greek cement to move to the US at prices higher than those that would have been sustainable had Greek producers acted independently, and since it reduced the risk of anti-dumping countermeasures by the US, the EC authorities might rationally have ignored a similar export cartel whose motivation was less visibly the frustration of intra-EC competition. Here too, therefore, we find a significant lacuna in the integration of international trade and competition policies.

Conclusion

That such gaps exist, and that they are important, is the broader moral of this paper. Coordination of price changes between General Electric and De Beers affiliates arguably permitted a counter-cyclical price increase for industrial diamonds sold in world markets. Under existing institutions, the US antitrust authorities were powerless to obtain the information they needed to determine what actually happened. Clumsy anti-dumping actions by the US government forced price increases by Saskatchewan potash producers and induced the Saskatchewan government to pass a standby cartelization law with long-term consequences for the supply of fertilizer and hence the supply of basic grain products. Until the EC authorities intervened to enhance competition within their home jurisdiction, coordinated producer measures to alleviate 'the Greek problem' affected the supply of Portland cement into the US and other nations. It was left to US trade authorities to act against Japanese dumping that stemmed from ineffective enforcement of the Japanese anti-monopoly law toward cement producers and their distributors within the Japanese home market. Surely, there is room for improvement.

Whether improvement will come through more aggressive unilateral enforcement actions (unsuccessful in the diamond case), better bilateral cooperation (unsuccessful in all of the cases reviewed here), or (more radical) measures to move toward multilateral coordination of competition policies remains to be debated and determined.

In my monograph, *Competition Policy for an Integrated World Economy*, I advanced a modest proposal for a transition to multilateral coordination under the auspices of the World Trade Organization (WTO). Recognizing the reticence of nations to surrender their sovereignty and the other difficult problems that would attend such a change, modesty is essential. If progress is to occur, some important limitations must be clearly recognized.[34]

First, there remain enormous differences across nations in the substance of national competition policies. Any multilateral accord will have to be on some limited subset of core principles governing only transactions with significant implications for international trade and/or investment. The most likely candidates are export and import cartels, serious abuses of dominant positions in the world market, and merger approval procedures.

Second, even in these core areas, many nations will be unwilling to go all the way to a flat prohibition. Brazil is unlikely to surrender its (usually unsuccessful) right to orchestrate an international coffee cartel, Saudi Arabia and other oil-producing nations their participation (however dispirited of late) in OPEC, Canada its right to restrain exports of potash, Russia its cooperation with the De Beers diamond syndicate, and the US the dominance of Boeing in large turbojet airliner markets. Thus, exceptions will be necessary. Under my proposal, each nation would be allowed three four-digit SITC industry exceptions from an otherwise general ban on export cartels. As experience is gained, the number of exemptions might be progressively reduced to two and then one per nation.

Third, it must be recognized that historically, a considerable time interval passed before national competition policy enforcement agencies learned how to do their work effectively. Seven years elapsed between passage of the US Sherman Act and the first Supreme Court prohibition of a price-fixing ring; twelve years between the Treaty of Rome and the first imposition of fines against EC cartels; eleven years between the creation of the UK Monopolies and Restrictive Practices Commission and the first prohibition of a cartel by the Restrictive Practices Court; and twenty years between the post-occupation amendment of Japan's Anti-Monopoly Law and a Fair Trade Commission attack on illegal cartels, including the Commission's first criminal price-fixing indictment.[35] Before serious enforcement can proceed, much learning must occur, and political support must be built. Therefore, I propose that an international body with competition policy responsibilities begin by confining its activities to investigation and the publication of informative reports on alleged border-spanning restrictive practices. Only in the seventh year of its existence would I have the agency assume actual enforcement responsibilities.

Finally, even after a considerable shakedown period, an international competition policy agency would have to tread warily, according considerable respect to national sovereignty. It would use the good offices of national competition authorities to support its investigations, and it would entrust national authorities with implementing recommended corrective actions. Only in cases of national intransigence would conventional WTO enforcement sanctions be set in motion.

This, to repeat, is a modest proposal. Despite that, it may be more than the community of nations is willing to swallow. Yet the time when such measures must be considered seriously has arrived. I offer it in that spirit to help focus the debate.

NOTES

1 There is of course a vast literature on this subject, to which justice cannot be done here. This paper is based loosely on my own contribution, *Competition Policies for an Integrated World Economy*, Brookings Institution, Washington DC, 1994.

2 On the latter, see my 'Retail distribution channel barriers to international trade', forthcoming in the proceedings of a November 1995 Columbia University School of Law conference on 'The Multilateral Trade Regime in the 21st Century'.

3 On the important and controversial case of dynamic random access memory chips (DRAMs), see K. Flamm, *Mismanaged Trade? Strategic Policy and the Semiconductor Industry*, Brookings Institution, Washington DC, 1996. Many other examples exist. On the European experience, see P. A. Messerlin, 'The EC antidumping regulations: A first economic appraisal', *Weltwirtschaftliches Archiv*, 1989, vol. 125, pp. 563–87.

4 Speech by H. von der Groeben, quoted in US Senate, Committee on the Judiciary, Subcommittee on Antitrust and Monopoly, Hearings, Antitrust Developments in the European Common Market, USGPO, 1963, p. 96.

5 A. *Åhlström Osakeyhtiö et al. v. Commission of the European Communities* [1988] ECR 5193.

6 See 'Canadian court fines Japanese firm $900,000 for anti-competitive conspiracy', *Antitrust and Trade Regulation Report*, 25 November 1993, pp. 691–2.

7 The Canadian cartel was in effect a restriction against a restriction, since US law prohibited the sale within the US of uranium imported to the US from Canada for enrichment (a process on which the US had a dominant free world position). Thus, the enriched Canadian uranium had to be re-exported.

8 US Department of State, *Havana Charter for an International Trade Organization*, 24 March 1948.

9 Scherer, *op. cit.*, chapter 5.

10 See S. Kanter, *The Last Empire: De Beers, Diamonds and the World*, Farrar, Straus & Giroux, New York, 1993; E. J. Epstein, *The Rise and Fall of Diamonds*, Simon & Schuster, New York, 1982; D. E. Koskoff, *The Diamond World*, Harper & Row, New York, 1981; G. Lenzen, *Prokuktions- und Handelsgeschichte des Diamanten*, Duncker & Humblot, Berlin, 1966 (English translation, Praeger, London, 1970); and D. Spar, *The International Diamond Cartel*, John F. Kennedy School of Government case study C15-89-878.0, Harvard University, 1989.

11 'For GE, A time bomb in Ohio?', *Business Week*, 14 February 1994, p. 30.

12 *United States v. General Electric Co., et al.*, CCH 1994–2 Trade Cases, para. 70,806 (December 1994).

13 For a chart showing some of the complex interrelationships among De Beers affiliates, see 'The Oppenheimer empire', *The Economist*, 1 July 1989, p. 60.

14 Davignon participated with Liotier in a meeting with General Electric employees on 12 February 1991, at which a General Electric executive suggested to Davignon that GE's European sales head and Liotier could work together to help 'stabilize prices'.

15 'General Electric is exonerated of industrial diamond price-fixing', *Antitrust & Trade Regulation Report*, 1994, vol. 67, p. 696. See also US Department of Justice, Antitrust Division, 'Opening markets and protecting competition for America's business and consumers', 27 March 1996, p. 3.

16 'Clinton signs Bill to help enforcers obtain foreign-located antitrust evidence', *Antitrust & Trade Regulation Report*, 1994, vol. 67, pp. 568–9. The Congressional committee reports on that bill can be found in the same journal, pp. 448–53.

17 See Spar, 'International diamond cartel (B)', pp. 2–5.

18 See e.g., B. W. Wilkinson, 'The Saskatchewan potash industry and the 1987 US anti-dumping action', *Canadian Public Policy*, 1989, vol. 15, pp. 145–61; V. J. Picketts, A. Schmitz, and T. Schmitz, 'Rent seeking: The potash dispute between Canada and the United States', *American Journal of Agricultural Economics*, 1991, vol. 73, pp. 255–65; and D. G. Haglund and A. von Bredow, *US Trade Barriers and Canadian Minerals: Copper, Potash and Uranium*, Centre for Resource Studies, Kingston, Ontario, 1990, chapter 3.

19 The data are drawn from weekly surveys published in the Green Markets trade newsletter and compiled in an expert report by A. M. Rosenfield, submitted 18 September 1995, in the Potash Antitrust Litigation. Actual average transaction prices are often lower than list prices. In 1986, for example, off-list discounts were as high as $10–$15 per ton.

20 Potash Antitrust Litigation, MDL Docket No. 981, US District Court for the District of Minnesota, Third Division. The author served as consultant and expert witness for Kalium Chemicals, a leading Saskatchewan potash producer.

21 In 1969 the Saskatchewan government implemented output quotas and floor price controls in response to depressed market conditions, but that action was declared to be unconstitutional by the Canadian High Court. The 1987 law was carefully drafted to take advantage of subsequent changes in the Canadian constitution and to avoid provisions rendering the 1969 actions vulnerable to judicial rebuke.

22 Commission Decision under Cases IV/33.126 and 33.322, reported in the *Official*

Journal of the European Communities, 1994, vol. 37. The discussion here draws heavily upon that document.

23 Commission Decision, p. 57 (quoting a paper, 'Collective response to problems posed by destabilizing cement industry', drafted at a 3–5 June 1986 meeting in Zurich).

24 *United States v. Socony–Vacuum Oil Co. et al.*, 310 US 150 (1940).

25 Commission Decision, p. 70.

26 'Cement imports, by country of origin', October 1990, *Construction Review*, p. viii.

27 For comparative consumption, capacity, and output data, see M. D'Ercole and C. Fortuna, 'Industrial restructuring, regulation and competition: The cement sector in the triad', paper presented at a conference on 'Economic and Corporate Restructuring', in Maastricht, September 1995.

28 See B. T. Allen, 'Foreign owners and American cement: Old cartel hands, or new kids on the block?', *Review of Industrial Organization*, 1993, vol. 8, pp. 697–716.

29 Average f.o.b. mill cement prices in the US were approximately Ecu 50 per metric ton in 1986, Ecu 46 per metric ton in 1987, and Ecu 45 per ton in 1988. US Bureau of the Census, *Statistical Abstract of the United States 1991*, pp. 694–5.

30 D'Ercole and Fortuna, 'Industrial Restructuring', Figure 1.

31 For an analysis of how the Japanese cement cartel works, see M. Tilton, *Restrained Trade: Cartels in Japan's Basic Materials Industries*, Cornell University Press, Ithaca, 1996, chapter 4.

32 See 'ITC clears way for duties on cement from Japan', *Journal of Commerce*, April 1991, p. 4A.

33 In its November 1994 decision, the European Community Commission stated that: 'The concerted practice relating to the channelling of production surpluses for export is also restrictive of competition. Through such practice, members of the WCC waived pursuit of an autonomous commercial policy, setting up a system of solidarity and monitoring aimed at preventing incursions by competitors on respective national markets within the Community', p. 120.

34 This section is drawn with minor revisions from my paper, 'Competition policy convergence: Where next?', delivered at a conference of the Austrian Economic Association in Vienna, 20 June 1996.

35 Tilton, *op.cit.*, pp. 33–55.

3

COMPETITION AND/OR TRADE POLICY?

Leonard Waverman

Introduction

There are a growing number of papers, proposals, meetings and conferences devoted to examining the interface between competition and trade policy.[1] I do not attempt here to summarize all the issues involved in that interface or the arguments, pro and con, of the need for harmonization. The three issues that I would like to address are as follows.

1 Are competition policy and trade policy complements or substitutes; and can one utilize trade policy norms such as national treatment and reciprocity in competition policy and reciprocally? What do reciprocity and conditional most-favoured-nation status imply for competition policy?
2 Will domestic rivalry (no international coordination in competition policy) lead to a 'race to the bottom' or a 'race to the top'?
3 Finally, in the last part of the paper, I will look at the complex issues of the interface between trade in services and competition policy in one example, telecommunications.

Trade and competition policy: complements or substitutes?

A number of clear distinctions between trade policy and competition policy have been raised:

- trade policy addresses issues at the border with other countries; competition policy addresses competition within the border;
- trade policy, in the GATT context, concerns government-imposed barriers to trade and investment; competition policy examines privately erected barriers to competition;
- trade policy is the subject of elaborate multilateral and bilateral

negotiations – to this point, multilateral or bilateral negotiations of competition policy issues are few;

- trade disputes operate under both national and international law, competition policy disputes operate mainly under national law;
- retaliation for alleged trade abuses exists – sanctions, aggressive unilateral action (the US's Super 301), internationally agreed procedures (anti-dumping and countervail), and international dispute resolution now under the WTO. Retaliation for alleged foreign competition policy abuses are few and involve the extra-territorial application of domestic competition law and threatened trade sanctions.

The GATT arose following the Second World War because of the set of tariffs and non-tariff barriers that had been erected in vain attempts to maximize domestic welfare. The GATT recognized that reducing tariffs could improve both domestic and global welfare (but with some income distribution effects within countries). The expansion of the GATT and now the WTO to an expanded set of non-tariff barriers on both trade and investment has created the concern that many domestic policies – competition policy is one such area – act as non-tariff barriers.[2]

Competition law in some countries predates 'modern' trade policy. The US Sherman Act was enacted in 1899. The first Canadian statute establishing an anti-combines policy was in 1898. These domestic policies were aimed at the exercise of undesirable private market power. Thus in the US, private trusts were broken up (American Tobacco, Standard Oil), mergers prevented (the Clayton Act 1914), and sets of coordinated practices condemned. The world of 1899 had been one of substantial free trade, in the GATT sense – tariffs were low, and while governments erected barriers, they were not designed as trade barriers. However, at the turn of the century, both Canada and the US raised trade barriers while implementing domestic competition policy regimes;[3] promoting domestic competition, while preventing foreign competition, was not then viewed as inconsistent. While government monopolies existed in many countries, they were not seen as primarily imposed to reduce trade or prevent imports. It was the exercise of non-publicly condoned market-power that was controlled by competition law.

The trade barriers erected in the first half of the twentieth century clearly affected prices in domestic markets, but not necessarily the degree of domestic competition. The purpose of limiting imports yesterday and today is to raise the price in domestic markets. Whether the instrument is a tariff, a quota or an export subsidy in a Brander–Spencer duopoly world,[4] domestic prices increase. With less foreign competition, the nature of domestic market competition usually, but not always, changes. In agricultural markets, for instance, strong domestic competition has remained even when the Corn Laws, marketing boards, or 300 per cent tariffs have been imposed. The purpose of the protection of textile and apparel industries in western developed economies under the Multi-Fibre Agreement is not to create oligopolies, but to maintain employment. Thus, trade restrictions do not necessarily reduce the degree of competition, in the antitrust sense, in the domestic market, especially in developed economies. In many less developed economies, I suspect, but have no proof, that trade restrictions decrease domestic competition. The 'Voluntary Restraint Agreements' imposed in the car industry (Canada and US in 1982) and in steel did affect price–cost margins, but they were designed to do so. The effects of trade restrictions may be to reduce domestic competition, but not necessarily so.

The introduction of domestic competition law can be consistent with liberalizing trade. Breaking up monopolies, ending the abuse of dominant position, preventing group action, normally increase the ability of foreigners to penetrate the domestic market. Can domestic competition law be consistent with a reduction of imports? The arguments put forward are that the absence of an enforced competition law reduces imports or foreign direct investment. Comanor and Rey[5] argue that a competition law which is not effective against vertical restraints can foreclose foreign competitors; their example is the ability of foreign automobile producers to import into the US in the 1970s because of their ability to share dealerships with US car retailers. On the other hand, they argue that the exclusive distribution outlets and inability to dual-deal in Japan limit the entry of foreign-based car firms. (This will be discussed in greater detail below.) The US has raised the argument, in general, that the existence of Japanese *keiretsu* forecloses their US counterparts. Market access is a euphemism for foreclosure, and trade policy becomes competition policy. Thus, Fox argues for a 'market access rule, contemplating that markets not be blocked by artificial restraints that harm competition'.[6]

It is surely an empirical problem as to whether an absence of a competition law, a competition law different from that of other countries, or a lax enforcement of competition law has as its effect a restriction of imports and/or a lessening of domestic competition in particular cases. The exclusive dealing in the Japanese domestic car sector may foreclose US imports. However, if exclusive dealing does not reduce competition in domestic Japanese car markets, is market access a trade, but not a competition policy issue? The arguments can go either way.

National treatment

M. Trebilcock proposes that instead of the procedural harmonization of domestic competition laws that the GATT principle of 'national treatment' be implemented.[7] Trebilcock provides a detailed cogent analysis of how non-discrimination would operate for both outbound and inbound trade.[8] Equivalent treatment implies that countries cannot adopt 'domestic policies that either explicitly or implicitly discriminate either between foreign trading powers (the 'most favoured nation' principle – MFN), or that discriminate between domestic producers and foreign producers (the 'national treatment' principle).[9] Of course, the major source of difficulty is what constitutes 'discrimination' in the case of competition law. Export and import cartels are the easy cases. What of the alleged differential law on exclusive territories/distribution outlets between the US, Japan and Europe? If we return to the Comanor and Rey case of the car industry, the question is whether the Japanese law (or absence of enforcement) discriminates against foreign car producers. The simple fact that the law is applied in the same way to all producers – i.e. those foreign car producers have equal rights to domestic producers as to the use of exclusive dealers – may be discriminatory. When the Japanese car producers began to export in the late 1960s and 1970s, the Japanese market was much more closed than today, thus foreign car producers found it difficult to export to Japan.[10] The fact that they would have been able to sign up exclusive dealers had they been able to penetrate the Japanese market is of little consequence after the fact. Market structure and rules have hysteresis effects. Once the market became open at the border, the inability to piggyback on existing dealers is, to Comanor and Rey, an entry barrier; to others it is an issue of market access, not competition policy. An entry barrier is an action which raises the costs to entrants. Since incumbents incurred the costs of building these networks, as do entrants, any asymmetry is due to customer inertia, the advantages of being first, etc. Under US law, such asymmetry might be anti-competitive (as in *Kodak v. Independent Service Organizations*). Is it necessarily the same under Japanese law? Trebilcock suggests that as long as the foreign law was not disguised protection, it is not discriminatory. The problem is how to define in a tribunal, court or dispute resolution procedure that the law/enforcement was *intended* to be discriminatory. In competition law, intent has a chequered history. One cannot look at the result of the action/inaction since the effect of exclusive dealerships may be to reduce entry. However, since these dealerships may also increase information/service, etc., consumer welfare can be greater. Finally, if the law is successfully challenged, how are changes to be enforced? Would Japanese car dealers be forced to carry foreign brands? Could they sue for free-riding on their brand name?[11]

Europe has a set of competition policy issues concerning the implementation of the Single Market. While exclusive dealerships are generally not permitted, a block exemption for their use has been given in the car sector. However, foreign car producers do not appear concerned that these distribution arrangements limit entry. Much foreign entry into Europe comes about through the purchase of existing firms or via greenfield plants. In Japan, US car firms (GM and Ford) purchased minority shares in Japanese car producers, and Mazda distributes Ford cars in Japan. While Japanese car markets do have relatively low import shares and relatively high retail prices, there has been no comprehensive analysis of the impact of exclusive dealerships on competition.

Reciprocity

Reciprocity involves one country's lowering of barriers if, and only if, another country reciprocates. Reciprocity is still a relevant trade issue. Free trade agreements such as NAFTA do not involve lowering barriers to all countries and in that sense involve reciprocity. Reciprocity colours the discussions at the Asia-Pacific Economic Co-operation (APEC) organization, where the future path is divided between those who want a formal free trade agreement and those who advocate 'open regionalism', i.e. allowing all nations outside APEC to sell into APEC as insiders. All this concerns goods; when it comes to services, reciprocity is still the dominant trade mechanism, as I will detail below in discussing telecommunications.

How does reciprocity fit with competition policy? First, reciprocity as a trade enhancing vehicle does limit competition in that barriers into industry X in country A will not be removed unless barriers into industry X in country B are removed. In some cases, such as the telecommunications sector, the domestic industry's cries for reciprocity may well be disguised protectionism. Thus, reciprocity may be a competition policy issue if it limits competition. Is reciprocity an interesting issue for the harmonization of competition law? Country A, for example, could agree to recognize another country's competition law as 'functionally equivalent', and vice versa. In this case, perhaps labelled 'national treatment plus', an action could be launched against practices in this other country using either country's competition rules; not a likely scenario. What about 'conditional MFN', in which a country lists those countries whose competition policy laws are so sufficiently similar that it will not engage in extraterritorial application of its own laws and it will engage in positive comity? – unlikely. Perhaps these musings have demonstrated that trade principles are not that useful in competition law and policy and this creates the concern that if principles differ, then the concepts differ.

I began this section by asking whether trade and competition policies are complements or substitutes. The answer requires a much more careful and detailed analysis than I have undertaken here. Another way of asking the question is to see if the competition in competition policies leads to a 'race to the bottom'.

A race to the top, or to the bottom?

The nature of competition in competition policy and trade policy regimes is an interesting topic. Two opposing views exist.

The first view is that without global harmonization, countries will select those internal and external policies that maximize domestic welfare at the expense of global welfare. In terms of competition policy, 'concerning a competition among rules, it can be argued that a race to the bottom could take place, leading to lax competition policies'.[12] Tractman provides the more general view that regulatory competition lowers the level of regulation to render its compliance less costly, that 'a firm will move to other jurisdictions with lower regulatory costs, ceteris paribus' and that:

> regulatory competition appears generally unconstrained by such international regimes as the GATT, the Subsidies Code, and US Trade Law. Therefore, [it] may be a more easily available tool than more overt subsidies and may be the decisive weapon in the international economic warfare of the coming years.[13]

Recently, Ruggerio has suggested:

> If we do not uphold the primacy of the multilateral rules, we risk seeing a form of Gresham's Law operating in dispute settlement, with weaker rules driving out stronger as governments choose the jurisdiction which most favours their case.[14]

Iacabucci provides an opposing view: a 'race to the top' in competition policy can occur because 'nations face strong incentives to implement vigorous competition policies'.[15] In Iacabucci's paper a race to the top occurs out of domestic self-interest:

> Adding a second national firm in a duopoly with each duopolist in a separate country reduces total profits, but shifts rents to the two domestic producers. In striving to earn rents at the expense of the other country, each country will adapt a vigorous competition policy; this will eventually dissipate rents, just as firms striving for rents cause them to disappear, thereby improving global welfare.[16]

Porter adds another reason for a race to the top – strong domestic competition makes firms better globally.[17] Thus, countries should impose strict competition policy regimes in order to promote domestic efficiency and global competitiveness. A strong domestic competition policy is consistent with a strong international showing.

Which view predominates? First, while 120 countries are members of the WTO, only some sixty have domestic competition law regimes (see the attached table for a list of countries which have enacted domestic competition law in the last decades). The number of countries with domestic competition law is increasing, but slowly, and questions of enforcement are important. The ability to observe non-enforcement is easy for tariffs and less obvious for non-tariff barriers, but treaty rights exist, as does a procedure for disputes and enforcement.

Competition laws can be written. However, they are not external treaties, need not be enforced and few avenues for remedies exist. While Mexico in 1985 introduced the largest and fastest unilateral dismantling of trade barriers ever seen, a competition law was only introduced because of NAFTA and questions exist today as to the scope and depth of Mexican competition law.

Trachtman discusses the ability of firms to locate where regulatory compliance costs are lowest.[18] Pollution or tax havens come to mind; however, are 'competition law havens' realistic? Will firms locate or relocate to regimes that have lax competition law?

Competition law havens are unlikely to appear for a number of reasons. First, Ruggerio is quite correct that a choice of governing rules for dispute resolution can lead to firms/nations choosing the weakest rules. However, one does not 'choose' among competition policy regimes to the same degree at all. Second, many factors determine the location of industry, and a lax competition policy regime is unlikely to be an important determinant of the location decisions for new plants. Third, if a company were to locate in such a haven, call it country A, what gains would it exact? Since country A has lax competition rules, entry itself into A may be difficult, since one assumes that the existing domestic firms in A, given the lack of competition policy, will erect barriers to potential entrants, foreign and domestic.[19] If companies X and Y locate in country A in order to collude, the effects doctrine and extraterritorial application of other countries' domestic competition laws bring this conspiracy under attack. The possible gains to companies X and Y colluding in country A are from exporting to other countries with lax competition law, but not to countries which have strong pro-competition policies. Will a merger of companies X and Y in country A benefit the two firms? The answer is no: if the merger is of a sufficient size and if it involves countries outside A then it will be notifiable in a number of jurisdictions. Thus a lax competition policy is unlikely to induce firms to locate in that jurisdiction.

The more important issue is whether a lax competition law provides cost advantages to domestic firms either in the domestic market or in foreign markets, and whether this advantage will lead to a race to the bottom in terms of competition in other jurisdictions. A race to the bottom can involve rewriting domestic laws to weaken them. Some argue that the US's revision to the National Cooperative Research Act to allow production joint ventures and alliances does that.[20] The race to the bottom is more likely to involve reductions in enforcement in countries with stricter competition laws and the reluctance of countries to introduce competition law in the first place. Rather than dismissing the race to the bottom out of hand, it is wiser to consider that complex motivations for government policy and for protectionism exist and that these motivations may impinge on competition.

With reference to the US, Stegemann writes:

> A crucial perceptual factor supporting intense protectionist sentiments in the United States is the feeling that American industries have fallen behind in international competition, not because of lack of effort or ability, but because other countries are using 'unfair' means to propel their own industries. . . . [A]s a result of this grievance, Americans became more interested in scrutinizing the economic policies of their trading partners, especially Japan. Popular writings on the 'Japanese challenge' painted a picture of the US economy becoming the castaway residual of other countries' sectoral planning. To defend its economic property, the United States would have to join the game, would have to implement its own industrial policy, or would at least have to deter other countries from taking advantage of American naiveté and openness.[21]

Tyson argues that:

> . . . aggressive unilateralism is defensible as an interim response to foreign trading practices and structural barriers that harm American economic interests and that are not covered by binding multilateral regulations. The alternative is not a world of free trade; it is a world in which trade and structural barriers can inflict substantial damage on national economic interests, especially in imperfectly competitive technology-intensive industries. In such a world, the United States has three options; accept the damage, try to offset it by promotional or protectionist measures at home, or negotiate to remove its source. Aggressive unilateralism sensibly pursues the third option.[22]

'Joining the game' and 'aggressive unilateralism' might lead to pressures to reduce competition policy constraints on firms operating in 'global' markets. Neven, Nuttall and Seabright review the EU merger regulation and suggest that competition policy decisions on mergers are over-politicized, and that key economic variables, such as the definition of the market, are perhaps chosen to suit the outcome desired.[23] Firms in small open economies, such as Canada, often criticize competition policy concerns as limiting their ability to compete world-wide. Where the dominant political view is that world trade is an unfair, uneven playing field, and that policy regimes abroad, including competition policy, are not 'equivalent', the temptation may be to attempt to fix matters at home, and to create more 'powerful' domestic firms to compete overseas. Thus the unfortunate and inaccurate attention placed on trade, the incorrect view that trade determines the numbers employed rather than their distribution across industries, the increasingly mercantilist view that exports are 'good' and imports 'bad', creates pressure to increase outbound trade. We must be vigilant that domestic competition does not suffer as a result. 'In the Transnational context there is no specific industrial policy so that the temptation is to use competition and trade policy, especially anti-dumping actions, as substitutes'.[24] Thus competition policy may be a substitute for bad trade policy.

Competition policy and trade policy in services[25]

Services represent the major share of GNP in developed economies, the major share of FDI, and a growing share of world trade. Services, however, require the right of establishment in the foreign regime before international trade can occur. A significant number of services are still offered under conditions of monopoly in domestic markets and as this service supply is liberalized, both competition policy and trade policy become intertwined. The service where these issues are most prevalent today is telecommunications.

The principle of market access has been discussed in a number of OECD documents related to liberalization of trade in services in general and in telecommunications services in particular in *Elements of a Conceptual Framework for Trade in Services* and *Trade in Information, Computer and Communication Services*.[26]

The new service provider (the entrant) will be competing with the existing domestic monopoly provider of access in offering certain international services, and it is essential that discrimination by the monopoly not be allowed. This then requires that the right of market access include:

- the right of interconnection at a gateway;
- the provision of non-proprietary 'open network standards' for interconnection;
- the right of equal access;
- the right of non-discrimination – both technical and tariffed;
- the right of establishment (retail office, advertising, etc.).

More detail will not be included here. The reader is referred to the above OECD references.

Some telecommunications is internationally traded; a call from the US to the UK involves the joint provision of service by at least two operators, one on the US end and one on the UK end.

International telecommunications operates under bilateral principles, with competition only slowly emerging and with limited market access. The key barrier preventing competitive offerings of facilities or services is a country's monopoly right to provide permission to operate. For telecommunications under the existing bilateral rules, this means that a potential entrant wishing to provide services from country D to a foreign regime F, must find a correspondent in the foreign country. For transmission cable this permission is to land cable (i.e. connect an underwater cable to the shore). For satellites the crucial right is to up-link messages (i.e. to beam messages from F up to a satellite). In the past, and still today in most countries, domestic monopolies became the sole providers of termination services for an international incoming call (an export of a service for the calling country) and sole providers of outgoing messages terminated in a foreign jurisdiction (an import of foreign termination services for the calling country). This system of two monopolies providing termination services for each other operated in conjunction with the offering of services and facilities jointly by these domestic monopoly providers through consortia for the construction and maintenance of underwater cables and for satellites through non-profit organizations such as INTELSAT and EUTELSAT. The setting of methods to 'settle' for differences in the amount of traffic also became bilateral, since the termination of a call in a foreign country requires agreed upon interconnection.[27]

These imports and exports of services are not established under GATT consistent principles – discrimination is rampant, multilateral principles are weak and national treatment is virtually non-existent.

The Uruguay Round GATT Agreement contains a Telecommunications Annex. A Negotiating Group on Basic Telecommunications consisting of nineteen countries (plus the member countries of the European Community) was established with a final report originally due in April 1996, but delayed until February 1997. At the time of writing, media reports suggested that liberalization of international telecom services was an area of conflict. The participating countries in the current WTO Negotiation Group agreed to a standstill on 'any measure affecting trade in basic telecommunications in such a manner as would improve its negotiating position and leverage'. Some countries consider the Federal Communications Commission November 1995 decision on International Telecom as contrary to the standstill agreement under the GATT.

Since communications is two-way, with an option on who initiates the call, countries with high retail prices for outbound international calls can induce a significant number of calls to be initiated in the regime with the lower retail price, resulting in traffic imbalances whereby the low-priced regimes have to settle with the high-priced regimes for the 'disproportionate' use made of the latter's termination facilities. High prices for outward international calls set by the operator in country F yield inflows of foreign currency from other countries. In any other international regime than telecommunications – for example, the trade in furniture – this ability to transfer resources via a tariff – a tax imposed on international out calls – would have resulted in complaints, investigations and sanctions. However, when the firm so taxed outside country F is a monopoly that still makes enormous profits (the current mark-ups over incremental cost are likely four or five to one),[28] voluble trade disputes do not arise. Rather than complaining about the extraordinarily high price of all international calls, including

AT&T's, the FCC complains about the outflows of dollars from the US through the antiquated settlement process. It is unusual for regulatory agencies such as the FCC to complain about the current aspects of trade.

For trade and competition policy there are two sets of markets to examine – the international telecom market and domestic telecom markets. Liberalization is occurring in both sets of markets, but trade policy and competition policy are often in conflict.

There are minimal entry barriers into international calling if countries allow simple international resale and have rules for open access to the local system. Only five countries at this point allow international simple resale: the US, the UK, Australia, Sweden and Canada – but with significant differences. The UK allows simple resale, but has not had an open access system to British Telecom until recently; the US now conditions simple resale on the conditions of market access in the foreign regime and whether the foreign applicant is dominant in its home market.[29]

This conditionality ensures that applications for resale are fought by incumbents. In 1993, AT&T requested a FCC ruling in the international arena and stated that 'reciprocal market access' be the basis of US policy. In February of 1995, the FCC filed a Notice of Proposed Rule-Making suggesting a new policy called 'effective market access' as the criterion for entry. The December 1995 FCC decision did not incorporate effective market access, but did incorporate 'effective competitive opportunities' as the test as to whether foreign carriers can provide international service in the US. The FCC must approve new facilities, foreign acquisition of control and can also determine that a foreign carrier who applies for resale is a dominant firm (in its own jurisdiction) and thus must file tariffs (section 203 of the Communications Act). Thus, recent 'liberalization' of international telecommunications in the US – the world's most competitive and liberalized telecom market – involves trade issues of reciprocity and market access. National treatment is not the guiding rule. These rules are designed to make foreign markets more competitive and to benefit US consumers. Do they do so and are they the best policies?

The US was the first country to begin to liberalize domestic and international telecommunications. As MCI, Sprint and others began to offer international telecom services, the FCC introduced a set of non-competition rules, since these US competitors faced monopolies overseas. Individual US operators could not negotiate differential accounting rates and their share of traffic incoming to the US was a proportionate return of their outgoing traffic. The view was that if US competitive carriers negotiated with a foreign monopoly telecom operator for traffic, they would bid increasingly high to capture traffic, transferring rents to the foreign monopoly. This was called 'whipsawing' by the FCC and had to be prevented.

The FCC and other jurisdictions also had to deal with requests for service provision by new operators and with the growing set of international alliances among telecom operators. Requests for service provision require FCC certification under section 214. The Department of Justice also analyses purchases of interest in US carriers, such as the BT acquisition of 20 per cent of MCI, and France Telecom's and Deutsche Telekom's 20 per cent acquisition of Sprint.

As noted, new international entrants – resellers or facilities owners – can provide International Message Service (IMTS) only by obtaining a connecting agreement with the foreign monopoly. Entry is possible, but is not likely to be profitable without such an agreement. For example, the entrant could advertise a reverse charge phone number in its home country, as is now the practice of a number of North American IMTS providers. AT&T, MCI, United States Sprint and Bell Canada all provide a service where the caller in the foreign country, say France, obtains a US (or Canadian) operator. These calls are incoming to France, often carrying a surcharge per call and earn France one-half the accounting rate. A new entrant could then offer such a service, but without an agreement from France receives no return traffic. Since this entrant faces competition in collection rates from carriers with return traffic, such entry is unlikely to be profitable.

Thus, effective competition in IMTS service requires the agreement of access to the foreign public switched system and an agreement of return traffic. It appears that many countries which have monopolies on outgoing IMTS calls are not opposed to competition on incoming IMTS calls, assuming that competition will lower retail rates in the other country and stimulate outgoing traffic and thus generate additional profits for their monopoly provider, but are opposed to competition on outgoing calls.

Under the FCC's December 1995 ruling, a foreign dominant facilities-based affiliation must show effective competition opportunities (ECO) in its domestic market on a route-by-route basis.

ECO consists of six factors:

1   US carriers can offer international facilities-based services in the foreign country 'substantially similar' to those to be offered in the US;
2   competitive safeguards to protect against 'anti-competitive and discriminatory practices'; one safeguard – cost-allocation rules to prevent cross-subsidization – is singled out;
3   published, non-discriminatory charges, terms and conditions should exist for interconnection and for the termination and origination of international services;
4   timely and non-discriminatory disclosure of technical information;
5   protection of carrier and customer proprietary information;
6   an independent regulatory body.

De jure prohibition against US carriers in providing facilities-based IMTS is a priori evidence that 'effective competitive opportunities do not exist on that

Table 3.1 Adoption of competition law in selected developing and emerging market economies (May 1996)

Africa and Middle East

Algeria	1995
Côte d'Ivoire	1991
Kenya	1988
Mali	1992
South Africa	1979
Tunisia	1991

Initiatives/drafts: Cameroon, Egypt, Jordan, Gabon, Ghana, Morocco, Senegal, Zambia, Zimbabwe

Asia

China	1993
India	1969
Pakistan	1970
South Korea	1980
Sri Lanka	1987
Taiwan	1991
Thailand	1979

Initiatives/drafts: Indonesia, Malaysia, Philippines

Latin America and the Caribbean

Argentina	1910, 1946, 1980, revisions under way
Brazil	1962, 1994
Chile	1959, 1973
Colombia	1959, 1992
Jamaica	1993
Mexico	1992
Peru	1991, 1994
Venezuela	1992

Initiatives/drafts: Ecuador, El Salvador, Paraguay

Central and Eastern Europe and Former Soviet Union

Belarus	1992
Bulgaria	1991
Czeck/Slovak Republics	1991
Georgia	1992, revisions under way
Hungary	1990
Kazakhstan	1991
Moldova	1992
Poland	1990
Romania	1991
Russia	1991
Ukraine	1992
Uzbekistan	1992, 1994

Initiatives/drafts: Kyrgyzstan

Source: World Bank

particular route';[30] no other factors would be examined, and the application would be denied. This is extremely strong and potentially anti-competitive, since it ties even private line service or simple resale to the ability of US carriers to offer IMTS, not just the equivalent service being applied for. This is inconsistent with the general test of 'effective competitive opportunities' since it makes effective access essentially into reciprocal access – i.e. allowing IMTS competition.

On 15 December 1995,[31] the FCC allowed France Telecom and Deutsche Telekom to purchase 20 per cent of Sprint, subject to a number of conditions. Since neither France nor Germany offers ECO (equivalent competitive opportunities), Sprint will be regulated as a dominant carrier on US–France and US–Germany routes, even though it has only a small share of traffic on those routes. As a 'dominant' carrier, Sprint must meet the reporting and disclosure requirements of dominant carriers. Two specific requirements were added. First, Sprint will not be allowed to operate new circuits on these routes until France and Germany liberalize two markets – basic switched international voice resale, and the ability of alternative international facilities providers to offer services such as data which already had been liberalized in the two countries. Second, France Telecom must lower its accounting rates to the US–UK and US–Germany rate within two years. This approval (subject to the conditions imposed) came a year after Sprint applied for approval (19 October 1994) and despite the objections of AT&T, ACC, BT North American Inc., MCI and others.

Telecommunications is unusual in that the domestic provision in most countries is still the prerogative of domestic monopolies. As competition is introduced, and as foreign firms attempt to enter domestic and international telecom markets, there will continue to be a clash between competition and market access.

NOTES

1 See, for example, P. Buigues, A. Jacquemin and A. Sapir, *European Policies on Competition, Trade and Industry: Conflict and Complementarities*, Edward Elgar, Aldershot, 1995.

2 See R. Ruggiero, 'The road ahead: International trade policy in the era of the WTO', Fourth Annual Sylvia Ostry Lecture, Sylvia Ostry Foundation, Toronto, 1990; E. Katzenback, H. E. Scharrer and L. Waverman (eds), *Competition Policy in an Interdependent World Economy*, Nomos Verlagsgesellschaft, Baden–Baden, 1993.

3 See M. Trebilcock, 'Competition and trade policy: Mediating the interface', Faculty of Law, University of Toronto, 1995.

4 See J. Brander and B. Spencer, 'Export subsidies and international market share rivalry', *Journal of International Economics*, 1985.

5 See W. Comanor and P. Rey, 'Competition policy towards vertical foreclosure in a global economy', in L. Waverman, W. Comanor and A. Goto (eds), *Convergence and Harmonisation of Domestic Competition Policies*, Routledge, London, 1996.

6 See E. Fox, 'Competition law and the next agenda for the WTO', *New Dimensions of Market Access in a Globalizing World Economy*, OECD, Paris, 1995.

7 See Trebilcock, *op. cit.*

8 See also E. Iacabucci, 'The interdependence of trade and competition policies', Faculty of Law, University of Toronto, 1996.

9 Trebilcock, *op. cit.*, p. 44.

10 See W. Ruigrok, R. Van Tulder, G. Bauen, 'Cars and complexes,' *Fast/Monitor*, n. 285, 1991.

11 Market entry into the Japanese car market primarily involves Japanese producers marketing foreign cars (not true for BMW). This itself raises competition policy concerns. See P. Holmes and A. Smith, 'Automobile industry', in P. Buigues, A. Jacquemin and A. Sapir, *op. cit.*, p. 152.

12 P. Buigues, A. Jacquemin, A. Sapir, *op. cit.*, p. 6.

13 J. Tractman, 'International regulatory competition, externalization and jurisdiction', *Harvard International Law Journal*, 1993, vol. 34, Winter, pp. 53, 60.

14 R. Ruggiero, 'The road ahead: International trade policy in the era of the WTO', Fourth Annual Sylvia Ostry Lecture, Ottawa, 28 May 1996, Centre for International Studies Working Paper. Reprinted by permission of the Sylvia Ostry Foundation, Toronto and of Mr Renato Ruggiero, Director-General, WTO.

15 Iacabucci, *op. cit.*, p. 37.

16 *Ibid.*, p. 33.

17 M. Porter, *The Competitive Advantage of Nations*, 1994.

18 Tractman, *op. cit.*

19 This brings us back to national treatment.

20 See C. Shapiro and R. Willig, 'On the antitrust treatment of production joint ventures', *Journal of Economics Perspectives*, 1990, Summer, pp. 113–30.

21 K. Stegemann, 'Policy rivalry among industrial states: what can we learn from models of strategic trade policy?', *International Organization*, 1989, vol. 43, no. 1, Winter, p. 78.

22 L. Tyson, 'Who's bashing whom? Trade conflict in high-technology industries', *Institute for International Economics*, Washington, 1993, p. 258.

23 D. Neven, R. Nuttell, P. Seabright, *Merger Regulation in the EU*, CEPR, London, 1994. See also E. Sirel, 'Strategic alliances and competition policy', *Memoire*, Sorbonne, 1995.

24 P. Buigues, A. Jacquemin, A. Sapir, *op. cit.*, p. xii.

25 This section is based on L. Waverman, *Global Speak, The Political Economy of International Telecommunications*, AEI, Washington, 1996, and L. Waverman, W. Comanor, A. Gato (eds), *Convergence and Harmonization of Domestic Competition Policies*, Routledge, London (forthcoming).

26 *Elements of a Conceptual Framework for Trade in Services*, OECD, Paris, 1987; *Trade in Information, Computer and Communication Services*, OECD, Paris, 1990.

27 H. Ergas and P. Patterson provide an excellent analysis of how bilateral agreements came into effect in 'International Telecommunications Settlement Arrangement. An unsustainable inheritance?', *Telecommunications Policy*, 1991.

28 See L. Waverman, *op. cit.*

29 FCC Order, December 1995.

30 FCC, p. 20.

31 FCC 95–498.

4

BASIC PRINCIPLES FOR AN INTERNATIONAL ANTITRUST CODE[1]

Ulrich Immenga

The idea of a code

The European Parliament has urged the EC Commission to put three issues on the agenda of the WTO meeting next December in Singapore: social policy, environmental policy, competition policy.[2] As to the last point, three questions have to be answered: why has international competition become a widely debated issue? Which are the promising approaches to international competition rules? Which should be the guiding principles for such rules?

The title of my report puts it forward frankly: I opt for a code as an instrument of international competition, though it is quite clear that this instrument will not be for tomorrow. It might serve, however, for several objectives. First of all, it will initiate and support discussions. A code that presents rules in a complete institutional setting should be an efficient means to exchange arguments. Without such a framework, arguments will lose grounds and most likely end up in mere politics. Beyond these objectives a code may initiate the implementation of competition laws in countries which do not yet dispose of such legislation. A code, therefore, appears as a model law. In this function it may also induce a harmonization of existing legislations. Last but not least, sometimes I like to be Utopian: if, surprisingly, politics moves fast, a code presents a basis to start with into the real world of international competition law.

An international competition law as a high-ranking topic

Before describing principles that should determine such a code, economic and legal conditions have to be marked, at least briefly, which tend to internationalize rules of competition.

The Directorate-General IV of the EC Commission started an initiative based on an expert report, entitled *Competition Policy in the New Trade Order: Strengthening International Cooperation and Rules*.[3] The focus was on two points which were considered to be the most relevant. First, due to the progressive disappearance of trade barriers, business activities of companies that may be contrary to the competition rules, for example price-fixing or market-sharing cartels, can affect several countries at the same time. This could lead to conflicts between competition authorities on the remedies to be adopted. It may also be possible that each authority, acting independently, is unable to detect and punish this kind of transnational behaviour. Furthermore, certain competition authorities tend to extend the scope of their competence excessively and/or try to impose solutions likely to create problems with their partners. Second, from a trade policy perspective, the interrelation of private and public trade barriers has to be recognized clearly.[4] The Uruguay Round successfully liberalized tariffs and non-tariff trade barriers, to permit a freer flow of goods and services. These achievements might be seriously diminished if private firms could replace previously existing public barriers to trade by restraints of competition. Cartels or exclusive dealings agreements might establish exactly the same barriers which just had been liberalized.[5] The competition rules of the EC Treaty demonstrate the necessity of competition rules to accomplish an internal market when state regulations which hinder free market access disappeared as a consequence of the application of the four freedoms of the Treaty.

The present status of international competition law

At present, international aspects of competition laws are determined by the effects doctrine. According to this rule national competition laws are applicable to foreign firms if restraints of competition affect national territory. This doctrine is a unilateral measure and might produce some relief. The status of the law, however, does not present satisfactory solutions.[6]

There is no real consensus among nations to recognize the effects doctrine. Where it is acknowledged its definition varies. Furthermore, the validity of the doctrine is controversial. In particular its extraterritorial reach has been questioned.

The application of the effects doctrine also results in legal uncertainties. Jurisdictional conflicts arise, if specific activities are considered under differing national laws. Authorization or prohibition might be applied to the same case. Comity could require a certain respect among nations and, if observed, level down rising tensions. But comity is not a general rule of international law and its application remains uncertain.

Political conflicts will most probably result from a strict application of the effects doctrine. Trade and industry policies might be affected. American courts developed the balancing test, a test to evaluate the conflicting interests and to decide on their impact on the parties involved. Reliable standards to balance, however, have not emerged, and they will not emerge, because of the political nature of the conflict.

One of the major disadvantages of the effects doctrine stems from the fact that it does not apply to anti-competitive restraints on imports. If firms collaborate to prevent imports from abroad, there is no anti-competitive effect on the territory of exporting countries. The doctrine does not apply. The US enacted specific legislation to support its export industry and to combat this kind of restriction.

The effects doctrine lacks internationally applied enforcement rules. This is particularly felt with regard to the need for sufficient information to pursue foreign firms' violations of domestic law. This presents legal problems because international public law does not authorize investigations by competition authorities in foreign countries. Furthermore, there would be practical obstacles to collecting information from foreign firms.

Some of the disadvantages of the effects doctrine might be overcome by bilateral agreements. These exist between several nations and, as one of the most advanced examples, between the EC and the US. By these agreements the application of the effects doctrine might be strengthened. An exchange of information and collaboration between national authorities will provide improved possibilities to act against anti-competitive behaviour. The US–EC agreement, furthermore, provides a new progressive element. Beyond negative comity that restricts the application of domestic laws because of conflicting foreign interests, the agreement requires positive comity. This is an important step: the contracting parties are obliged to enforce their laws as strictly as possible to international activities of their firms. The reach of positive comity, however, is limited. The domestic law must be applicable. This is not the case, for example, if export cartels have no domestic effects or are generally admitted under the domestic law.

In recent years, many bilateral agreements have been signed, particularly by the US with Australia, Canada, Germany, and as mentioned before, with the European Communities. The agreement between Australia and New Zealand even permits the parties to apply mutually their national competition laws to restraints which are affecting both countries. In 1994 the US enacted the International Antitrust Enforcement Assistance Act, which enlarges the competences of US Antitrust Authorities to conclude bilateral agreements in order to promote international cooperations and a convergence of national laws.[7]

The EC expert report emphasizes a strengthening of bilateral cooperation. In its view, in particular the 'positive comity' mechanism makes a significant contribution to attaining the objectives of successive GATT rounds. According to the report it is this approach which makes it possible to pursue the objectives of international action in this area: a more effective enforcement of competition rules which should have the effect of checking trends towards an extra-territorial enforcement of national rules; the creation of conditions favouring the gradual alignment of different laws, which will enhance the legal security for firms and reduce their costs; and the promotion of equal conditions of competition in all countries. Nevertheless, the report admits that international cooperation does not achieve the objectives of an international order for competition law.

Basic considerations to constitute a code

An elaboration of any code has to make clear its basic ideas. The character of a code depends on these ideas, which will determine the institutional framework as well as substantive rules.

As a consequence of the Uruguay Round achievements and the reduction of governmental restrictions of trade, there will be a considerable increase of free movement of goods and services. In contrast to the EC framework, however, the newly developed GATT rules do not regulate private anti-competitive behaviour. This is a disregard of firms' possibilities to restrict cross-border market access. Consequently, there have to be instruments against private actions complementary to the GATT rules. Governmental barriers should not be replaced by private ones.

The WTO system should, to preserve a consistency of rules and institutions and to promote political acceptance, be extended along the lines of the present system in order to develop international competition rules as a plurilateral agreement.

There is a rising consensus of the interrelation of competition and trade issues. The respective rules have to be developed in consistency. It should be considered to what extent trade rules, for example those against dumping, could be substituted by competition rules.

Already at the present stage of developments in competition policy it seems to be possible to achieve a general consensus on lower levels: a ban on clearly anti-competitive behaviour such as price cartels or a misuse of the power of dominant firms.

A cautious approach requires the implementation of international rules as part of national law, which are minimum rules and applicable to international activities only. It would seem necessary to establish an international forum for consultation and information exchange that might serve, furthermore, as an addressee of notifications.

Governments might act like private firms. They own corporations and grant monopolies in certain branches of the economy. Furthermore, state institutions might influence private business actions. Rules against private business actions should be applicable to government actions as well.

Competition issues and even more trade issues are to a large extent influenced by politics. To achieve a more stable framework for international trade the political impact should be diminished. Trade regulation has to be changed from discretionary policies to law. Provisions governing the conditions of market access should be strictly law oriented and governed by a rule of law and due process. This is a condition to restrict politics in trade issues and to ensure efficiency in a liberalized economic system. Lawyers, however, evaluate competition policy not only as a means to achieve economic efficiency, but, furthermore, as a basic value of a market-oriented society that protects individual liberties and equal opportunities of domestic citizens. This perspective of competition law has rightly been described as a 'constitutional perspective'.[8]

Principles of an international antitrust code

A Draft International Antitrust Code (DIAC) has existed since 1993, when it was submitted to the GATT Director General and released to the press.[9] It is based on a private initiative and brought together academic experts from several European countries, including Poland, the US and Japan. The group was completely independent and financed by private foundations. The authors were fully aware that, if they had taken into account the existing policy constraints and protectionist pressures, there would be good reasons for a short, simple framework agreement with no ambitious substantive rules which might have a realistic chance of receiving political support. The majority decided, however, to submit a comprehensive draft as an academic model agreement to stimulate world-wide reflection and debate.

The above-mentioned EC expert report followed a more restricted line, in particular with regard to substantive rules, and proposed enforcement rules in an institutional setting less ambitious than the DIAC. As a co-author of both projects, I feel somewhat uncomfortable to be supporting either the ideas of the Draft Code or of the expert report. It should be permissible, however, for me to present my own views, which do not necessarily reflect the principles of either of the projects.

The institutional framework

Rules of an international character cannot be established in isolation, but have to be integrated into an existing institutional framework. The DIAC clearly favours integration into the WTO system. The expert report does not exclude this view; however, nor does it support it strongly. There are several reasons for proposing this solution.[10]

- The agreements comprised by the WTO (GATT, TRIPS, GATS) are a concept of protecting world trade against public (state) barriers such as tariffs and quotas. International free trade may be affected, however, by private trade barriers in the form of cartels, monopolies, etc. as well. International competition is a trade issue and should be handled by one system.

- The GATT/WTO remedies in case of violations are a second reason to assign a code to this institution. It provides experience in solving conflicts, disposes of a now strengthened dispute settlement system and includes a system of remedial actions (compensatory concessions or countermeasures).

- Finally, rules under the WTO are already directed against anti-competitive behaviour of firms. Article VIII GATS obliges the contracting parties to control monopoly suppliers in their territory, in order to prevent the abuse of a monopoly position. Section 8 of the TRIPS Agreement provides control measures against anti-competitive practices in contractual licences. It follows that the WTO system since the conclusion of the Uruguay Round has adopted the concept of rules against restrictive practices of business firms.

- The WTO system offers the opportunity of plurilateral agreements under Annex 4 to the Agreement establishing the WTO. To implement international competition rules in this way means that the contracting parties are bound by international public law. The agreement does not, however, bind all parties to the WTO as multilateral agreements do, but only those who signed the plurilateral agreement. This procedure offers an evident advantage. The rules will, initially, apply only to those countries that are particularly interested and experienced in matters of international competition. The geographical coverage of the agreement should, therefore, in its beginning include the countries that are already cooperating on a bilateral basis and, in addition, Japan or other highly industrialized Asian countries as main trading partners at world level. An extension might be envisaged gradually according to the development and interests of other countries.

Transformation into national law

The still ruling concept of national sovereignty requires that the rules of the plurilateral agreement are implemented as national law. By way of this transformation the rules have to be qualified legally as national law and, as part of an internationally binding agreement, as connected to public international law. This twofold legal qualification has to be taken into account to solve enforcement issues.

National treatment

A further principle, well known on the international level and part of the GATT, is the requirement of national treatment. In the present context it means that national and international competition has to be treated without differentiation.

Minimum standards

An international code requires equal standards that are internationally applicable. These standards should be minimum standards to ensure that there will be at least a minimum of internationally equivalent provisions. It follows that those countries that are disposing of an anti-competitive legislation might have a two-tiered system, a bottom line of internationally standardized laws, and beyond them diverging national laws. This approach allows countries to develop their own rules for national competition issues.

Transborder cases

As an international code its rules should deal with international cases only. Exclusively national cases are the preserve of national authorities and courts. The code has to apply to transborder situations. The provisions of the DIAC are applicable to restraints of competition that are affecting at least two parties to the agreement. They are considered to be affected whenever there are economic effects in its territory or otherwise on its commerce.[11]

Institutional and enforcement issues

These five principles are basically underlying both the DIAC and the EC expert report. There are some differences, however, with regard to enforcement issues and corresponding institutional requirements.

The EC expert report considers it necessary that an international body be entrusted with three functions:

1   to serve as a forum for drafting and permanently reviewing, adapting, and, insofar as possible, extending the common principles for incorporation in the various national laws and for their enforcement;
2   to establish a register of anti-competitive practices which would initially concern only practices satisfying specific criteria. It follows that some notification requirements have to be established;
3   to provide a structure for settling disputes between participating countries. According to the report the WTO settlement mechanism seems to correspond fairly closely to the structure which might be established to arbitrate on disputes concerning action by competition authorities. In the following the report refers in detail to the functions of such a panel. Violations would trigger international 'secondary obligations' recognized in GATT/WTO law, for example cessation of the illegal act and possibility of authorization of countermeasures pending the withdrawal of the illegal act.

The efficiency of international competition rules depends on their enforcement. While the EC expert report's recommendations are cautiously framed with regard to the limited competences of the WTO, the DIAC develops new institutional means of enforcement which, however, largely respect national authorities.

To deal with enforcement issues, two kinds of problems have to be distinguished:

- violations with regard to the implementation of the Agreement;
- violations with regard to the application of the Agreement's rules.

The first type of disputes between the parties to the Agreement might be resolved according to the existing dispute settlement mechanism of the WTO. If the Agreement has not been implemented into national law, or has been implemented in an inadequate form, any party might call upon the panel of the WTO. There is a breach of international public law in the event of any violation of the Agreement. The remedies provided by the dispute settlement system will be applied. The DIAC comes close to this conception.[12]

The second type of disputes concerns a violation of transformed national law. Two kinds of violations may occur. The national authorities might not enforce their laws. This might happen in international conflicts. A country may refuse to act against domestic restraints of competition, which protect markets against the entry of foreign companies. Or, national authorities might apply the rules of the Agreement in a way that is considered to be wrong. Since the rules of the Agreement are not self-executing, it is necessary to provide an international control of these kinds of violations. The more cautious approach of the EC expert report refers to a specific dispute settlement panel, which has to be set up. The sanctions, however, are limited.

The DIAC presents a really new conception, which is not as strong as a self-executing character of the Agreement, but ensures international enforcement of the transformed national law. The conception is a step beyond the present WTO system, since it requires an International Antitrust Authority (IAA) as a new institution. However, it has to be emphasized that the issuing of administrative orders by the IAA directed against private persons as initiators of a restraint of competition is not possible. Its powers are restricted to bring actions before national courts. This is the so-called international procedural initiative; the new idea which respects national sovereignty while ensuring the application of the rules of the international Agreement in a domestic court system.

Article 19, section 2, of the DIAC provides the right of the IAA to bring actions against national antitrust authorities in individual cases before national law courts, whenever a national antitrust authority refuses to take appropriate measures against individual restraints of competition; the right to sue private persons and undertakings as alleged parties or initiators of a restraint of competition before national law courts asking for injunctions against the execution of the restraint; and, finally, the right to national appeal even when the IAA is not a party to the case but under the same conditions as parties to the case.

This conception offers an appropriate opportunity in the form of a compromise between national and international interests to enforce trans-border competition rules. This system might be completed by additional civil law sanctions such that anti-competitive practices are not enforceable at law.[13] In this way domestic courts will play the decisive role in applying the international rules.

Market access commitments and competition rules

The EC expert report provides for an interesting additional provision based on a linkage between market access commitments as embodied and negotiated in the WTO on the one hand, and rules on anti-competitive practices on the other. The report proposes to include, within a competition framework, provisions by which the 'nullification or impairment' through private practices of market access commitments negotiated under the WTO would be actionable, unless appropriate corrective measures are taken by the country concerned. This proposal refers to the early Havana Charter (Article 46), where an absence of government action to prevent a limitation of access to markets could constitute a violation of its provisions.

The DIAC has not gone so far, because it has explicitly concentrated on mere competition issues and not on the interrelation of trade and competition. Nevertheless, the expert proposal could easily be incorporated into the enforcement system of the DIAC.

Principles of substantive law

The majority of the authors of the DIAC opted for a comprehensive code including detailed substantive rules. This approach is part of the underlying idea to present a broad basis for discussions. Any substantive rules might be discussed at length. Therefore, in my view, it is necessary to focus at this stage of international discussions on the institutional conditions to be provided for an implementation of competition rules.

Nevertheless, it seems to be appropriate to describe areas of potential consensus on substantive rules. Five forms of restraints of competition shall be addressed in this context in a very generalized way.

1   There seems to be a general understanding that so-called hard core cartels should be prohibited. They are employed exclusively to restrict competition as price-fixing, output restraints, market division, customer allocation, and collusive tendering. Of course, export cartels should be included into this list.

2   Other horizontal agreements, which go beyond mere restrictions of competition and include efficiency gains by cooperation, should be evaluated under a rule of reason test. This is in particular true for research and development cooperation.

3   Distribution strategies (vertical restraints) include contractual and economic ties, such as vertical price-fixing, exclusive arrangements and the inducement by economic pressure or influence to behave anti-competitively. National competition policies generally contain a strict prohibition of resale price-fixing. Beyond this common understanding, policies with regard to vertical restraints are controversial because of their contradictory effects. They may be anti- or pro-competitive. The evaluation depends, *inter alia*, on a balance of intra- and interbrand competition. Therefore, in these cases a rule of reason approach seems as well to be appropriate.

4   With regard to market dominance, which is generally accepted by competition policies, an abuse control should be established. Article 86 of the EC Treaty may serve as a model. It might be left open for further discussion whether the abuse control should be strictly conduct-oriented or include exploitation abuses as well. Economists generally rule out a control that focuses on results instead of anti-competitive conduct.

5   As to merger control it might be questioned if the time for a real international merger policy has now come. Merger policy very often comes very close to national industrial policies. Consequently, there are considerable areas of divergence with regard to mergers in competition law. Therefore, developments and progress might be achieved in the area of procedure, but not in substance. This is particularly important with regard to notifications, thresholds, time limits and specifications of information. A close cooperation of competition authorities concerned in a specific case should support an exchange of relevant information, an understanding on appropriate investigations based on mutual assistance, and on harmonized rules on confidentiality.

NOTES

1   This contribution was first published in *Antitrust Report*, August 1997, p. 8, under the title 'An international antitrust code in perspective'.

2   EP Doc. A 4–327/95.

3   COM (95) 359 endg.

4   See Petersmann, 'Proposals for negotiating international competition rules in the GATT–WTO world trade and legal system', *Aussenwirtschaft*, 1994, vols II/III, pp. 231–56.

5   See for more details, E. Fox, 'Competition law and the agenda for the WTO: Forging the links of competition and trade', *Pacific Rim Law & Policy Journal*, 1995, vol. 4, no. 1, p. 1.

6 The leading US case is *United States v. Aluminium Comp. of America*, 148 F.2d 416 (2nd Cir. 1945). The effects doctrine has been codified under German legislation, §98, 2, Law against Restraints of Trade. For the following discussion, see Immenga, 'Comment: The failure of present institutions and rules to respond to the globalization of competition', *Aussenwirtschaft*, 1994, vols II/III, p. 201.

7 103 d Conmg., 2. Sess. 1994 (15. USC. §6201 *et seq.*)

9 Petersmann, *op. cit.*, p. 263.

9 Fikentscher/Immenga (eds), *Draft International Antitrust Code*, 1995.

10 See Jackson, 'Alternative approaches for implementing competition rules in international economic relations', *Aussenwirtschaft*, 1994, vols II/III, p. 177.

11 See in detail Art. 3 s. 1(b) DIAC.

12 Art. 19 s. 2(e); Art. 20, s. 2.

13 See *EC Expert Report*, p. 25.

5

A SMALL OPEN ECONOMY PERSPECTIVE ON INTERNATIONAL COMPETITION POLICY

Victor D. Norman

Introduction

It is an established truth that small economies have more to gain from international trade and competition than large economies. The standard argument is in two parts. First, small economies typically have more skewed resource endowments than large ones, and thus have more marked comparative advantages and correspondingly larger classical gains from trade. Second, economies of scale are larger relative to the domestic market in small than in large economies, so high unit production costs, limited product ranges, and imperfect competition are more severe problems for the small economy, and the gains from becoming part of an international market are correspondingly greater.

The two questions discussed in this paper are (a) whether it follows that small countries have more to gain from international competition policy than large ones, and (b) if so, what the ingredients in a policy for greater international competition should be.

The answer to the first question is yes, but perhaps not for the reasons one might expect. Note first that the answer is not trivial. The fact that a small country gains a lot from international trade and competition does not by itself mean that it gains more from trade in perfectly competitive international markets than from imperfectly competitive trade. In a world of scale economies, product differentiation and imperfect competition, market power is not limited to firms located in large countries. With imperfectly competitive markets for both exports and imports, it could conceivably be the case that the market power that small-country firms exert in foreign markets could be sufficiently large for the gains abroad to more than offset the detrimental effects of imperfect competition in import markets.

Norway may serve as an illustration. With exports heavily concentrated in a few industries – petroleum, shipping services, basic metals, and specialized engineering products – many Norwegian export firms have quite significant market shares abroad. Statoil is a major seller of petrol in Sweden and of natural gas to Germany; individual Norwegian companies are among the three or four dominant firms in the world market for transportation of chemicals and in the international passenger cruise market; two Norwegian firms have traditionally dominated the world market for certain iron alloys; etc. At the same time, Norwegian imports comprise almost all other goods. That, of course, makes Norway vulnerable to foreign market power in a number of specialized product groups. Given the range of products imported, however, it is not at all clear that the degree of market power of foreign firms selling in Norway is higher than the average degree of market power of Norwegian exporters. This being the case, one might argue that successful, global competition policy could, in fact, be detrimental to Norway; or at least less beneficial to Norway than to countries with a more diversified industrial structure.

Is this, then, a correct line of reasoning? As I see it, it is wrong, because it neglects the effects that imperfect competition has on real factor prices. Through factor-price effects, a greater part of the burden of imperfect competition falls on small countries, even if their firms have as much international market power in their particular market segments as the firms of large countries have in theirs.

The point is illustrated in Figure 5.1. Consider a single industry with a particularly simple technology: one unit of output requires one unit of labour, so marginal cost is simply the wage rate. Suppose that the industry is a pure export industry, and that firms have international market power. Let DD be the foreign demand curve. If the industry is a non-negligible part of the domestic economy, the economy wage rate will be affected by industry output, so the industry marginal cost curve will be upward sloping, as illustrated by the WW curve. Prices and output are given where the difference between the international price and the domestic wage equals the monopoly mark-up, as illustrated by the quantity, the price and the wage. Compared to the perfect competition solution, this creates pure profits equal to the shaded area. Of this, however, only A is appropriated from foreign consumers; while B derives from a lower domestic wage, and is thus rents shifted from workers to export firms at home. The deadweight burden of market power is (C+D). The burden is shared by the home country (D) and foreign countries (C). While the export firms derive a total gain from market power of (A+B), therefore, their home country only gains (A – C), which could well be negative.

Both the share of monopoly profits that derives from domestic factor rents (B) and the domestic share of the deadweight burden (C) depend on the relative elasticities of international demand and the domestic industry marginal-cost curve. To focus on the supply side, assume that the slope of the

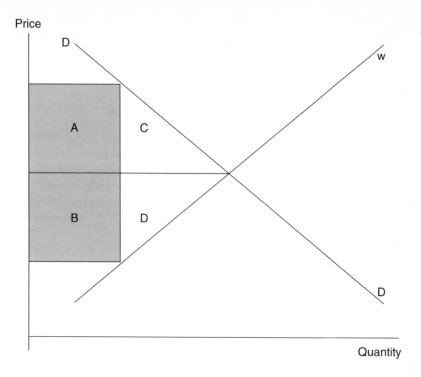

Figure 5.1 Single-industry demand and marginal cost curves

demand curve is the same for small and large country export industries. The question is then whether there are systematic differences between small and large countries in the factor-price elasticity of supply to export industries. The answer would seem to be yes. In order for export firms in small countries to achieve international market power, the firms (and thus the industries) must be larger relative to the economy as a whole than is the case in large countries. As a result, their output levels have a greater impact on domestic factor prices; so a larger fraction of their profits is paid by domestic factor owners and a larger share of the deadweight burden remains in their home country.

This is an important point, particularly in relation to industrial policy. There is a tendency in most countries, and particularly in small ones, to be impressed by large export firms, as if their international market power somehow compensates for the smallness of the country. The corollary, which seems to be taken for granted in most countries, is that market power in export markets is unambiguously good. If the profits that successful exporters obtain largely are rents shifted from domestic factor owners, such a perception is at best misleading. Even if export firms derive substantial monopoly profits, the national gain may be small, or even negative.

The point also shows that small countries do, in fact, have more to gain from universally applied competition policy than larger ones. This brings me to the second question, namely how international competition policy should be designed.

Sources of imperfect competition

Policy design requires a diagnosis. In the case of international competition policy, the question is why international markets are not (close to) perfectly competitive. Given the size of the world economy, there must surely be very few industries that are truly natural world monopolies. Aircraft production may be one, and there may be a few others. For most industries, however, total world demand should be sufficient to combine full exploitation of economies of scale and perfect competition.

There could be world monopolies or cartels even in the absence of natural monopolies. Still, given the size of world markets, the source of market power in most instances must be natural or artificial impediments to international trade. These impediments could be of two types. One is trade-costs imposed by nature or governments. The other is active, international market segmentation by firms.

We do not know very much about the relative importance of trade costs and active market segmentation in restricting competition. What we do seem to know, particularly from work on the effect of the European Single Market, is (a) that market segmentation is quantitatively important in the sense that we observe large international price differences for a number of goods, (b) that trade costs and active segmentation interact, in the sense that trade costs simplify active segmentation and, (c) that in industries with both, elimination of market segmentation will have a much greater impact on competition and national welfare than a reduction in trade costs alone. In simulation studies, a reduction in real trade costs within Europe equivalent to 2.5 per cent of intra-European trade will typically have four to five times as great an impact on real incomes if it is combined with market integration than if segmented national markets persist.[1]

Market segmentation is so important because dominance in home markets seems to be a primary source of market power. If that is the case, the burden of market segmentation should be greater for small than for large economies, since the number of active home-market firms generally is smaller the smaller the economy. There is another reason as well. If there are fixed costs of entering a new market, the number of foreign sellers will also be smaller in a smaller economy. With international price discrimination, therefore, a small economy will suffer from high prices both from domestic and foreign sellers; whereas larger economies at least will have the benefit of foreign firms dumping goods in their market.

This general diagnosis has implications for the relative merits of trade policy, national competition policy, and international competition policy.

Trade policy

There are good reasons, even apart from competition aspects, to advocate free trade. Let us leave these aside, however, and focus on the role of free trade as a competition-enhancing device.

To the extent that domestic market power derives from artificial barriers to trade, it is obvious that freer trade means increased competition from imports and thus more competition in domestic markets. In that sense, policies that ensure as free international trade as possible must be an important element in any set of pro-competitive policies.

There is another reason for free-trade policies to be important, related to the interaction of governments and national export firms. As is known from the theory of so-called strategic trade policy[2] countries can – in markets with imperfect competition – shift profits from foreign firms to their own through active trade policy. By subsidizing exports of commercial aircraft, European governments can ensure that profits that would otherwise be made by Boeing, accrue to Airbus instead. By protecting the Italian market for personal computers, Italy could shift profits from IBM and Apple to Olivetti. Moreover, such policies could be in the national interest, in the sense that the gain to national firms could outweigh any negative effects on domestic consumers.

It should be obvious, however, that such policies could have severely negative effects on competition, for at least three reasons. First, they reinforce existing market structure. Strategic trade policy derives from international market power, and the policies are essentially aimed at strengthening that power. Second, the policies will have the effect of making the profits of domestic monopolists or oligopolists even greater; i.e. raising the return to market power. But that will strengthen the incentives to obtain monopoly power, and thus make firms waste even more resources in attempts at achieving it. Third, strategic trade policy will, if pursued, make national authorities lose credibility as pro-competitive regulators. The credibility of a policy to foster competition in the taxi industry is not exactly enhanced if at the same time the government actively supports the market power of the national airlines that carry passengers to the taxi stand.

For competition policy to be credible, governments must pursue competition systematically, so they must abstain from *ad hoc* collusion with monopolists or oligopolists. Even if free trade had no real function, that by itself would be a sufficient case for free trade as an element in an overall competition-policy package.

As a digression, a brief visit to the Norwegian government's flirtation with OPEC is called for at this point. As a major oil exporter, it is, of course, tempting for Norway to encourage the oil cartel. Still, how one can defend a policy of jail sentences for domestic price-fixing, and at the same time engage in high-level price-fixing talks with OPEC, is beyond me. And an increase in the oil price of 10–20 per cent would, even for Norway, be only a modest compensation if the implication is an all-clear signal to domestic cartels and monopolies.

Returning to the general issue, it is clear from the discussion above that a policy of free trade is important, both directly for the degree of competition, and indirectly because it represents a government commitment to competition-enhancing policies more generally. In this context it might be worth noting that many Scandinavian economists see the economic success of our countries largely as a reflection of the disciplining effects that a long-term commitment to free trade has had on micro and macro agents.

National competition policy

While free trade is important, it is equally clear that it is not sufficient to ensure competition – it must be supplemented by active competition policy both at the national and international level. This conference is on inter-national policy, so it may not be entirely appropriate to stress the importance of purely domestic policy. Nevertheless, I shall risk it.

Even though trade costs are coming down and markets are becoming more international, it is still the case that the bulk of economic transactions are between agents living in the same country. For manufactured goods, more than 80 per cent of all goods produced in the OECD countries are sold in the country of origin. For services the percentage is even higher. In labour markets, international transactions are negligible. Even in the celebrated 'international' capital markets, the correlation between domestic saving and domestic investment remains high.

All of this is changing, but the process is slow, and in some respects countered by other forces. One such counterforce is the growing relative importance of service industries in general, and of health and personal care industries in particular. It is not clear, therefore, that the domestic share of the total number of economic transactions is decreasing.

To a considerable extent the dominance of domestic transactions must reflect natural (rather than artificial) barriers to trade. For some services, those natural barriers are apparent – personal care is the obvious example. For goods they are less apparent. Still they must be there. Even allowing for imperfect competition, studies show that the pattern of market shares seen in European markets for manufactured goods can be made consistent with profit-maximizing firms only if the sum of natural and artificial barriers to trade is equivalent to tariffs of 30–60 per cent, depending on the product.[3] Few would seriously accept that trade barriers of this magnitude, in an area where all tariffs were removed twenty years ago, are entirely due to border formalities, national product standards, or discriminatory government procurement. Most of it must belong in the category of 'natural' trade costs.

We can only speculate as to what these high, 'natural' trade barriers are. For most goods, only a small fraction can be transport costs in the strict sense. One factor that may be important is history, in the sense that sunk costs in product design and distribution systems may give national firms a shelter against foreign firms which would have to incur such costs if they were to enter the market. With historically sheltered markets, domestic firms will have designed their products to suit domestic tastes (compare, for example, the comfort of French cars to the solid engineering of German ones) and built up comprehensive domestic distribution systems. As trade barriers are removed, these investments remain an effective source of natural protection for at least the lifetime of designs and physical investments. Given consumer brand loyalty, they are, in fact, likely to remain a protective shelter for much longer than that.

Whatever the reason, the indications are that in a number of sectors, competition will be a national problem for a long time, even if a free-trade regime is fully implemented. Free trade, international integration, and competition policy at the supranational level are good things, but they do not necessarily ensure competition among taxi drivers, barber shops, retail bankers, high schools, local hospitals, or short-haul airlines. They may not even be sufficient to ensure competition in food processing, household appliances or other product groups where historical product designs and brand loyalties are important.

International competition policy

This does not mean that international competition policy or international coordination of national policies is unimportant. They are important both with respect to increased competition in those markets that are truly international, and in encouraging international competition in markets which are initially dominated by domestic sellers.

The importance of international policy follows directly from the observation made earlier that the gains from freer trade are increased by a factor of four to five if lower trade costs are accompanied by an end to international market segmentation. An end to segmentation does not follow automatically from removal of official trade barriers, so something more is needed. That 'something' is active competition policy at the international level.

Trade theory has little to contribute to the question of how international competition policies should be designed. That should be left to experts on regulation. Trade theory may, however, say something on the appropriate aim of the policies.

The ultimate aim should be market integration, in the strict sense of uniform producer prices across markets. To achieve that, the link between producers and the distribution systems in different countries must be broken. The parallel-import principle established as part of the European Single Market programme goes some way in that direction, but it is not sufficient. In the presence of transport costs, it will generally not be profitable to cross-haul products between markets; so even with parallel imports, firms can charge different f.o.b. prices to different markets.

The aim of competition policy, therefore, should be something like a 'parallel export' system. Arbitrage traders should be permitted to set up shop outside the factory gate and sell to any market in direct competition with the producer – and they should be protected against price discrimination by the producer. Of course, simply permitting parallel exports will not be enough, as producers will charge the domestic f.o.b. price when selling to them; and as domestic f.o.b. prices typically are higher than export f.o.b. prices, the arbitrage exporters will go out of business. Still, the idea of parallel exports captures the flavour of what is needed.

If conduct regulation had been in vogue, it would have been natural to recommend a rule requiring firms to charge uniform f.o.b. prices and the establishment of an international agency to monitor the rule. Alternatively, one could have made sales contracts, at specified f.o.b. prices, freely negotiable; the buyer being free to specify any destination. Again, however, some agency would be needed to monitor such a system. Given the general weaknesses of conduct regulation, such an approach is not attractive.

The essential aim of international competition policy must be to devise structural regulation that has equivalent effects. That ought to be high on the agenda of discussions of competition policy in an integrated world economy.

NOTES

1 See, for example, A. Smith and A. S. Venables, 'Completing the internal market in the EC: Some industry simulations', *European Economic Review*, 1988, vol. 32, pp. 1501–25; M. Gasiorek, M. A. Smith and A. S. Venables, '1992: Trade and welfare – A general equilibrium model', in L. A Winters (ed.), *Trade Flows and Trade Policy After '1992'*, Cambridge University Press, Cambridge, 1992; J. Haaland and V. Norman, 'Global production effects of European integration', in L. A. Winters (ed.), *op. cit.*

2 I. A. Brenda, 'Strategic trade policy', in G. M. Grossman and K. Rogoff, *Handbook of International Economics 3*, Ellesmere, Amsterdam, 1995.

3 A. Smith and A. S. Venables, *op. cit.*, vol. 32, pp. 1501–25.

6

UNILATERAL REFUSALS TO LICENSE INTELLECTUAL PROPERTY AND INTERNATIONAL COMPETITION POLICY

Richard J. Gilbert and Carl Shapiro

Introduction

There is a tension between intellectual property and antitrust policies. Antitrust policy is intended to protect consumers; the intellectual property laws are designed to protect the owners of intellectual property rights. Of course these rights are intended to foster innovation, and innovation ultimately benefits consumers. Technical progress is a crucial determinant of consumer welfare.[1] Thus it is reasonable to conclude, as did the US Court of Appeals for the Federal Circuit (which hears appeals of patent cases) that '[T]he aims and objectives of patent and antitrust laws may seem, at first glance, wholly at odds. However, the two bodies of law are actually complementary, as both are aimed at encouraging innovation, industry and competition.'[2] None the less, even if both legal doctrines are aimed at promoting economic efficiency in the long run, they appear to serve different constituents in the short run.

Intellectual property policies can have substantial impacts on the global economy and are likely to trump the antitrust laws in many circumstances. Consider the recent complaint by the US Department of Justice against the Pilkington Company.[3] Pilkington is a British company that invented the float process for making flat glass in the late 1950s. Although Pilkington's key patents have expired, it retains many trade secrets that relate to the float glass process. Pilkington had licensed both its patents and related know-how. The licences imposed restrictions that prohibited the licensees from using Pilkington's technology outside a defined territory. The Department of Justice challenged these licensing practices, arguing that Pilkington had effectively orchestrated a world-wide glass cartel. The case was settled with a consent decree in which Pilkington agreed not to enforce territorial restrictions with respect to its existing trade secrets. Key to the Department of Justice's case was an allegation that Pilkington's trade secrets were insubstantial relative to the anti-competitive effects of the licences. Had the case gone to trial, Pilkington would have argued that its trade secrets were valid and substantial. If Pilkington had prevailed on that point, it would have established a presumption that its licensing practices are valid. In that situation, the government would have a burden of proof to show that the anti-competitive effects of Pilkington's licensing practices outweigh the presumed rights of the intellectual property rights-holder to employ territorial and other restrictive licensing terms.

Our purpose is to highlight some of the intellectual property issues that we expect will have important consequences for global competition. We will then turn to one particular aspect of the intersection between intellectual property and antitrust policy. This is the obligation to deal, or, by another name, the compulsory licence. A refusal to deal appears, on its surface, to be inherently contrary to consumer interests, because it limits the ability of other firms to introduce new products or achieve lower costs of production. However, a closer inspection shows that an obligation to deal does not necessarily promote consumer welfare, even in the short run. Licensing a high-cost supplier can increase production costs, and compulsory licensing can legitimize arrangements that result in higher prices. Over the longer run, compulsory licensing can reduce the incentives for investment in research and development.

Intellectual property protection regimes

Recently, debate over the intersection of intellectual property and antitrust has focused on the scope of copyright protection, particularly for computer software. Patents generate their share of controversy – a vivid example is the furore over patent protection for genetically engineered species. Moreover, controversy over patent protection is likely to intensify as software patents become more prevalent. However, it is in the use of copyright to protect computer software that intellectual property and competition policies have frequently clashed in the past two decades.

Copyright has been the primary means of protection for computer soft-ware. Copyright protection lasts a long time – the life of the author plus fifty years, or seventy-five years from first publication for works made for hire. Copyright protection also has a low threshold for protection. It is not like a patent, which requires that a work be novel, non-obvious, and useful, to gain patent protection. A copyright protects only the expression, not the under-lying ideas. Copyright protection does not extend to ' . . . an idea, procedure, process, system, method of operation, concept, principle, or discovery, regardless of the form in which it is described, explained, illustrated, or embodied in such work'.[4] Unlike a patent, a copyright does not preclude others from independently creating similar expression.

It would seem that these conditions would severely limit the ability of copyright to prevent imitative efforts, but that need not be so. There are several areas in which copyright has proven to be a potent source of intellectual property protection.

The first is protection of what is called 'structure, sequence, and organization'. Although copyright is limited to expression, one cannot avoid its reach simply by making trivial changes to the original work. For example, take Peter Mayle's popular book *A Year in Provence*. One cannot change the names of the characters and a few other details and thereby escape the copyright. But Peter Mayle's copyright does not prevent others from publishing an original work about life in a quaint countryside.

Copyright prevents the literal duplication of a computer program's code. In addition, a computer program may infringe on the copyright of another program if it closely replicates the 'look and feel' of the program, which includes its display and the structure and arrangement of the commands that the user employs to interact with the program. For example, Lotus used its copyright protection to prevent the sale of a competing spreadsheet program that employed the same menu command and user interface.[5]

A second important area for the scope of copyright protection is the definition of a copy. Because copyright does not prevent the independent creation of a similar work, infringement cannot occur without first making a copy. Clearly, a book is copied when it is duplicated in a Xerox machine. However, merely reading a book and thereby making an image of the words on the retina does not constitute a copy. What about reading a computer program? In *Advanced Computer Services of Michigan, et al. v. MAI Systems Corp.*,[6] the court ruled that a software copyright is infringed when the code is copied into the random access memory of the computer. The ruling has significant competitive consequences. The case of *Advanced Computer Systems v. MAI* involved companies (affiliated with Advanced Computer Systems) that serviced MAI's computers. The customer (the owner of the MAI computer) had a licence to use MAI's diagnostic software. The independent service companies did not have a licence. MAI argued that the independent service-company infringed its copyright when it turned on the customer's computer and loaded the diagnostic software into the computer's memory. Without a licence to use MAI's software, the independent service-company was arguably disadvantaged in its ability to service the MAI systems.

The definition of copying will be increasingly important in the new digital age. It is currently a controversial issue for access to digital works on the Internet. The US government report on the *National Information Infrastructure* recommends changes in copyright law that would tighten intellectual property protection for electronic media. Among other proposals, the report recommends that the distribution of digital works should be considered equivalent to a performance of those works. Hence, without authorization by the copyright holder, the posting of a digital work on the Internet and inspection of the work ('browsing') could be a copyright violation.

Copyright protects only expression, not ideas or functions, but sometimes, particularly in computer software, it is difficult to distinguish the two. For example, Sega and Nintendo, both manufacturers of computer video game systems, employed a lockout mechanism to prevent the use of non-authorized video games in their systems. Authorized game cartridges contained a security code that had to be recognized by the game console for the game to work in the system. The security code itself is functional, yet its expression may be protectable under copyright. In *Sega Enterprises Ltd v. Accolade, Inc.*,[7] the court concluded that the copying of the code was a fair use of the copyright and did not infringe. However, in *Atari Games Corp. v. Nintendo of America, Inc.*,[8] faced with only somewhat different circumstances, another court concluded the opposite.

The question of the merger of function and expression in copyright cases has arisen in other contexts. The US Supreme Court recently failed to reach a decision about whether Borland violated Lotus's copyright by including the Lotus 1–2–3 commands in its Quattro spreadsheet macro feature. This enabled users of Borland's spreadsheet program to more easily translate macro routines that were written for Lotus' 1–2–3 spreadsheet program. The failure of the Supreme Court to reach consensus let stand a lower court decision which held that Borland's use of Lotus's command structure was not a copyright violation.[9] In that decision, the court held that Lotus's command menu was a method of operation, analogous to the buttons on a VCR, and thus not protectable by copyright. It is the utilitarian nature of the command menu in the macro translator that distinguishes this case from the earlier *Lotus v. Paperback* case, which held that Paperback had violated Lotus's copyright by copying its user interface.

Another example of a case that presents issues of merger of function and expression is the complaint brought by the Department of Justice and state Attorneys-General to prevent the proposed acquisition of West Publishing Company by the Thompson Corporation.[10] Thompson and West publish law books and legal research materials. These include compilations of legal opinions that are enhanced with annotations that facilitate search for relevant case citations. Publishers of legal opinions have no copyright on the legal decisions themselves, as these are public documents. However, publishers do have copyright protection on their particular expressions of these opinions, which includes the organization, keywords and other annotations, and the pagination. West, in particular, claims copyright protection for the 'star pagination' of its National Reporter System, which is widely used by courts and attorneys. Citations to legal opinions conventionally refer to the specific page numbers as they appear in West's National Reporter System.

An alternative compilation of legal decisions, with a different organization and presentation would not violate West's copyright. However, such a publication would be of limited utility in the legal community, because the page location of the opinions would not correspond to the page numbers in West's National Reporter System and would cause confusion unless the particular publication was included in each citation. In a sense, West's pagination system (which is literal expression protectable by copyright) has acquired an element of function (which is not protectable by copyright).

Thompson and West settled the complaint by divesting certain products and by agreeing to license the star pagination in West's National Reporter System. The settlement requires the merged company to license star pagination to any requesting party at mutually agreed upon terms that are not to exceed a specified fixed rate. This consent decree is an interesting use of merger policy to constrain the reach of intellectual property protection. The merger would not necessarily increase any market power that the West Publishing Company possessed as a consequence of its star pagination system; West claimed the unilateral right to prevent others, including Thompson, from using this system. However, the compulsory licence facilitates the entry of new competitors in markets for enhanced legal research publications. In this respect, the compulsory licence acts to limit whatever market power may be created by a merger of the two publishing companies.

Another important issue in the intersection of intellectual property and international competition policies is the protectability of software code that is necessary for an application program to access elements of an operating system. The application programs cannot run unless they can interact with the operating system. Hence, this aspect of the operating system has a functional component. None the less, US courts have held that the operating system is protectable by copyright and that this protection extends to code that is required for application programs to operate under the control of the operating system.[11] However, in *Sega v. Accolade* and other cases, courts have concluded that the copying of copyrighted works for the purpose of identifying unprotected program elements that must be utilized to create compatible products may be permissible as a 'fair use' exemption to the copyright. The EU is more explicit about this limitation to copyright protection. The 14 May 1991 directive of the Council of Ministers of the European Economic Community specifically states that authorization of the right-holder is not required where reproduction of the code and translation of its form are indispensable to obtain the information necessary to achieve the interoperability of an independently created computer program with other programs.[12]

Intellectual property and the antitrust laws

The intellectual property laws define the scope of intellectual property rights. The antitrust laws constrain the use of intellectual property. There are two general ways that the antitrust laws may limit the use of intellectual property. Owners of intellectual property are not permitted to engage in coordinated conduct that raises price or reduces output, such as cross-licensing arrangements that fix prices for potentially competing technologies, or in conduct that monopolizes a relevant market. Compulsory licensing is sometimes sought as a remedy for such behaviour. Another approach that may limit intellectual property rights is to invoke what is called the 'essential facilities doctrine'. The essential facilities doctrine does not require an intent to monopolize. Rather, it follows from a presumption that property cannot be duplicated and that access to the property is necessary for competition.

Under the US antitrust laws, conduct by a firm with market power may be illegal if the effect of that conduct is to tend to create or sustain a monopoly, and if that monopoly is not the consequence of superior skill, foresight or business acumen, or historical accident.[13] A firm with monopoly power does not violate the antitrust laws merely by charging a monopoly price.[14] However, a refusal to deal by a firm or a joint venture with monopoly power can be an antitrust offence. In other words, although antitrust law permits a firm to charge the price it pleases, the antitrust laws may, under some conditions, compel the firm to offer some price at which it will sell to others.

The 'refusal to deal' label has been applied to many cases with very different competitive circumstances.[15] This discussion focuses on a situation in which an integrated firm (or joint venture) controls a factor of production that is costly to reproduce and competes in another market against one or more firms that desire access to the factor of production. Examples include a local telephone network, exclusive contracts with distributors, intellectual property, and the control of proprietary interface standards.[16] Access is often of particular significance in network industries,[17] where the facility may be a common interface or proprietary interface standards that enable the supply of complementary network products and services.[18] The firms seeking access may be competitors in upstream, downstream, or otherwise complementary markets. This discussion will focus on refusals to license intellectual property, particularly software that is protected by copyright.

The legal precedent in the US for an essential facilities action dates back to 1912, with the case of *United States v. Terminal R.R. Ass'n.*[19] The Terminal Railroad Association was a joint venture of companies that controlled the major bridges, railroad terminals, and ferries along a 100 mile stretch of the Mississippi River leading to St Louis. The US Supreme Court did not find that the joint venture had engaged in monopolization; the Court concluded that the joint venture was pro-competitive. However, the Court also concluded that it was not feasible for others to duplicate the facilities of the joint venture and ordered the joint venture to deal with others under reasonable terms.[20]

A long time has passed since the *Terminal Railroad* case, and the US courts have issued conflicting opinions on the subject of a duty to deal. In 1983, in deciding MCI's case against AT&T, in which MCI alleged that AT&T had monopolized long distance telecommunications, the Court of Appeals for the Seventh Circuit set out four factors that describe the necessary elements of an essential facilities claim.[21] They are:

1 control of an essential facility by a monopolist;
2 a competitor's inability practically or reasonably to duplicate the essential facility;
3 the denial of the use of the facility to a competitor; and
4 the feasibility of providing the facility.

None of these elements is sufficiently well defined to provide operational guidance. The factors are circular, in that they assume an essential facility and do not provide a definition to determine when a facility is essential. A competitor's 'inability practically or reasonably to duplicate the essential facility' is not a workable definition because, among other things (such as assuming the existence of the essential facility), it does not specify what is reasonable or practical, and this is likely to depend on the price that the owner of the facility is charging for the services that the facility provides. A not unreasonable definition is that a facility is essential if it is a natural monopoly. A different, and also not unreasonable definition, is that a facility is essential if it cannot be profitably duplicated when the owner of the facility charges a monopoly price. But these are details that have been ignored by the courts.

The essential facility doctrine is not uniformly recognized as a valid concept in all US courts of law. Some courts still follow precedent, such as that in the Supreme Court's 1919 *Colgate* decision:

> In the absence of a purpose to create or maintain a monopoly, the [Sherman] act does not restrict the long-recognized right of a trader or manufacturer engaged in an entirely private business, freely to exercise his own independent discretion as to parties with whom he will deal.[22]

This is particularly true for patents.[23] There is, however, other legal dictum in support of a unilateral duty to deal. The Supreme Court recently opined in its decision in *Image Technical Services, Inc. v. Eastman Kodak Company* that: 'It is true as a general matter a firm can refuse to deal with its competitors. But such a right is not absolute: it exists only if there are legitimate competitive reasons for the refusal.'[24]

A refusal to deal by a vertically integrated firm appears on its face to adversely affect competition by denying rivals a product or service that is a necessary input for effective competition. This is hardly a complete analysis however, since it does not account for the incentives to create the essential input, nor the price at which that input can optimally be sold. The mere fact that a firm controls an input that is valuable to its competitors should not be sufficient to compel a duty to deal. A comprehensive duty to deal would dull competition both because competitors could employ a compulsory license to free-ride on investments made by others and because the expectation of free-riding would suppress incentives for innovation. Moreover, a firm can have many innocent reasons for refusing to supply a rival. In considering antitrust policy toward refusals to deal, a useful starting point is to evaluate the economic rationale for refusing to sell, rather than setting a high price.[25] We identify four basic arguments below. Although these arguments are presented in the context of a refusal to deal, such as denying access to a facility or refusing to sell a commodity, they also apply generally to the licensing of intellectual property.[26]

Assuring quality and avoiding free-riding on reputations

A manufacturer of a complex system may refuse to deal with parties that provide complementary products or services because the quality of these products or services may be inadequate or uncertain. The manufacturer may have a greater stake in providing high quality service. For example, poor maintenance service could result in fewer new system sales, which would cause more harm to the manufacturer (who would lose the profits on those system sales) than to an independent service organization. System profits give the manufacturer an incentive to invest in quality systems and service. Others may free-ride on this reputation for quality, thereby undermining its value to the manufacturer and reducing its incentive to invest in quality. Thus, for these reasons, a manufacture may refuse to license software that is necessary for independent service organizations to provide effective competition.

Preventing entry into a related product can increase barriers to entry

For example, entry into the manufacture and sale of cars is more difficult if new entrants have to invest in their own network of dealers and service organizations. Thus, established manufacturers may increase barriers to entry by refusing to permit their dealers to sell and service competing makes of cars. By requiring entry to occur in sales and service in addition to manufacturing, entry is made more difficult and established firms may be able to charge higher prices.

A refusal to deal may facilitate profit-maximizing price discrimination

There are several ways in which a firm may employ a refusal to deal, or related conduct, to achieve more effective price discrimination. For example, a manufacturer of a basic commodity may selectively vertically integrate into the manufacture of some products for which the commodity is an input. At the same time, the manufacturer may set a commodity price that is so high that only the vertically integrated firm can profitably manufacture the product. Although there is no formal refusal to deal, this 'vertical price squeeze' has a similar effect.[27] Another example is a package or 'tied' sale in which sale of a machine, such as a Xerox copier, is conditioned on purchase of a commodity, such as paper. The commodity product may be used to meter the intensity of demand, and thereby facilitate pricing to maximize profit. The 'refusal to deal' is a refusal to allow the buyer to purchase the machine and the commodity separately.

A refusal to deal may permit a firm with market power to prevent costly price competition

Under some circumstances, the owner of property that is necessary for the production of other goods can maximize profit solely by charging the monopoly price for the input. For example, this would be the case if the input is used in fixed proportions with other products or services, and if these other services are supplied in competitive markets. As Bowman described in the context of tied sales,[28] under these conditions there is a single monopoly rent that can be collected either by the supplier of the input or by a firm that is a vertically integrated producer of products or services that use the input. When these conditions apply, the owner would gain no financial advantage by refusing to sell or license its property, even if the buyer or the licensee is a competing supplier of a product or service for which the property is an input. Attempts to vertically integrate or otherwise leverage into other markets would not provide the owner of the property with additional returns and would not be pursued except for efficiency gains.

The conditions, however, under which 'one-monopoly-rent' theory applies are restrictive. Even if production occurs with fixed proportions, the users of the input may engage in inefficient 'double-marginalization' by marking-up the already marked-up price of the input. A vertically integrated producer would price more efficiently, and in the process may squeeze out competing suppliers that purchase the input. The 'one-monopoly-rent' theory also may not apply if demand substitution or regulation limits the ability of the owner of the input to earn profits at that stage. Whinston provides examples in which a monopoly owner of an input may profit by refusing to sell the input as a separate component.[29]

73

Under many pricing arrangements, entry is costly to a monopoly owner of an input when production occurs with variable proportions. An established firm may refuse to deal with a potential competitor to preserve its market power. Katz and Shapiro provide examples under which the owner of an input earns greater profits by selling a final product or service and refusing to license the input for use by others.[30] In these examples, the owner of the property cannot construct financial terms that fully compensate for the effects of increased competition.

Refusals to deal generally reflect an inability to write contracts that specify desired levels of performance. An intellectual property rights owner may be unable to write such contracts, for many reasons. It could be impossible to describe and enforce the level of quality that independent service organizations must provide. Without this ability, the owner of the property cannot specify a contract that assures the desired level of service. Similarly, the owner of intellectual property may be unable to specify a contract that assures that the owner will be compensated for any loss of profits caused by competition from the licensee. This could be for reasons such as the inability to measure and enforce a licensee's level of output, or because such contracts may violate the antitrust laws if they require agreements between actual or potential competitors to set prices or divide markets.

It has long been argued that compulsory licensing, the flip-side of a refusal to deal, has negative consequences for incentives to engage in research and product development over the long run. In a recent joint paper, we considered the effects of a compulsory licensing requirement for short run efficiency.[31] One might expect that compulsory licensing would be beneficial in the short run, because licensing contributes to the dissemination of technology at a low marginal cost. This is not always correct. The effect of compulsory licensing depends on the form of the licensing agreement, on the ways that firms compete, and on the technology that exists with and without the licence. Compulsory licensing can force a firm to license a competitor that it would not license voluntarily. Although the licence can result in lower prices for consumers, it can also result in higher production costs and higher prices. For example, the competitor may not be a very efficient producer using the licensed technology. The compulsory licence can cause total industry production costs to increase.

Compulsory licensing can have other, undesirable costs in the short run. If the licensor and the licensee employ technologies that are potential substitutes, a compulsory licence can encourage firms to divide markets and raise prices. Furthermore, a compulsory licence requirement can encourage costly strategic behaviour to negotiate for more favourable licence terms. And every obligation to deal carries with it the administrative burdens of determining the price and terms of access.

Against this overview of the costs and benefits of compulsory licensing, we would like to discuss two recent decisions, one by a US court and the other by the European Court of Appeals. The US case is *Data General Corp. v. Grumman Systems Support Corp.*[32] The case involved competition from Grumman in the maintenance and repair of Data General's computers. Grumman had been engaged in service of Data General machines, using Data General's diagnostic software. Data General subsequently refused to license its diagnostic software to Grumman. The question before the court was whether Data General's refusal to license caused 'unjustifiabl[e] harm to the competitive process by frustrating consumer preferences and erecting barriers to competition'. The court concluded that there was no material effect on 'the competitive process'.[33] Data General was the dominant supplier of repair services for its own machines, both when it chose to license its diagnostic software to independent service organizations and later, when it chose not to license independents.

The court's analysis in *Data General* failed to address the central question, which is whether a policy that required Data General to license its software to independent service organizations would enhance economic welfare. Instead, the court focused on the narrow question of how Data General's conduct impacted the overall level of competition in the service of Data General's machines. In addition to not dealing with the central issue of effects on consumer welfare, the court's focus on preserving the competitive process raises obvious difficulties. As one antitrust scholar noted, '. . . lawyers will advise their clients not to cooperate with a rival; once you start, the *Sherman Act* may be read as an anti-divorce statute'.[34]

My second example is from the European Community. This is *Radio Telefis Eirann v. Commission* and *Independent Television Publications Ltd v. Commission*,[35] more commonly known as the '*Magill* case', after the company that brought the complaint to the European Economic Commission. The *Magill* case was a copyright dispute over television programme listings. Both Radio Telefis Eirann (RTE) and Independent Television Publications (ITP) published their own, separate programme listings (as did the BBC). Magill combined their listings in a TV Guide-like format. RTE and ITP sued, alleging copyright infringement.

The European Court of Appeals stated that:

> The appellants' refusal to provide basic information by relying on national copyright provisions thus prevented the appearance of a new product, a comprehensive weekly guide to television programmes, which the appellants did not offer and for which there was a potential consumer demand. Such refusal constitutes an abuse . . . of Article 86. . . .[36]

Moreover, the court said there was no business justification for such refusal, and ordered licensing of the programmes at reasonable royalties.

The logic of this opinion seems to imply that compulsory licensing can be justified whenever it can be demonstrated that there is an unsatisfied demand for a product or service that can be met using the licensed technology. The costs of compulsory licensing, both in the short run and in the long run, suggest that this is not a policy that would necessarily promote the welfare of consumers. The decision is also odd because the European Court could have concluded that TV listings are not protected under copyright – there was a similar conclusion in a US court concerning telephone directories.[37] That would have eliminated the compulsory licence issue altogether.

Concluding remarks

Compulsory licensing generally reduces long-run incentives to engage in research, product development, and reputation-building. In the short run, compulsory licensing can lower economic efficiency by compelling licences that increase production costs or by facilitating licences that fix prices or divide markets.

In addition, compulsory licensing, and, more generally, obligations to deal, carry the administrative burdens of regulation. It is not enough to merely compel an intellectual property rights holder to license its technology. For such a requirement to be economically meaningful, the licence must be economically attractive to the licensee. It is often difficult to determine the boundaries of reasonable licensing terms. Surely, what is reasonable is likely to differ from the perspectives of the licensor and the licensee.[38]

Case law, both in the US and Europe, does not provide a coherent basis to determine when compulsory licensing (or an obligation to deal) is in the public interest from an economic perspective. This is not surprising, given the difficulties of drafting general rules for identifying conditions under which compulsory licensing will increase economic welfare. The complex consequences of licensing for short and long run economic performance, and the difficulty of administrating a licensing obligation, lead to a conclusion that compulsory licensing should be limited to extraordinary circumstances for which the public benefits of wider dissemination clearly justify the costs of price and access regulation.

NOTES

1 See E. Denison, *Accounting for United States Economic Growth, 1929–1969,* Brookings Institution, Washington DC, 1974. Denison estimates that 48 per cent of the increase in output per worker between 1929 and 1969 can be attributed to the advance of scientific and technological knowledge.
2 *Atari Games Corp. v. Nintendo of America, Inc.*, 897 F.2d 1572, 1576 (Fed. Cir. 1990).
3 *United States of America v. Pilkington plc and Pilkington Holdings Inc.*, 1994–2 (CCH) 70,842 (D.C. Ariz. 1994).

4 17 USC. § 102(b).

5 See *Lotus Development Corp. v. Paperback Software International*, 740 F. Supp. 37 USP.Q.2d 1577 (D. Mass. 1990).

6 845 F. Supp. 356 (E.D. Va. 1994).

7 785 F. Supp. 1392 (N.D. Cal).

8 897 F. 2d 1572 (Fed. Cir. 1990).

9 *Lotus v. Borland*, 1995 US App. LEXIS 4618 (1st Cir. 1995).

10 *United States of America et al. v. The Thompson Corporation and West Publishing Co.*, US District Court for the District of Columbia (1996).

11 See, for example, *Apple Computer v. Franklin Computer Corp.*, 714 F. 2d 1240 (3rd Cir. 1983).

12 Council Directive 91/250, 'On the legal protection of computer programs', Art. 6, 1991 O.J. (L 122/142), reprinted in 3 Common Mkt. Rep. (CCH) 5991 at 4881 (1991).

13 *United States v. Grinnell Corp.*, 384 US 563, 571 (1966).

14 See, for example, *United States v. Aluminum Co. of America*, 148 F. 2d 416, 430 (2nd Cir. 1945).

15 See K. L. Glazer and A. B. Lipsky, Jr., 'Unilateral refusals to deal under section 2 of the *Sherman Act*', *Antitrust Law Journal*, 1995, vol. 63, pp. 749–800. Glazer and Lipsky provide a comprehensive review of various types of competitive situations in which refusals to deal have been adjudicated.

16 Other examples include the control of quality or safety standards. See J. J. Anton and D. A. Yao, 'Standard-setting consortia, antitrust, and high-technology industries', *Antitrust Law Journal*, 1995, vol. 64, no. 1, pp. 247–65.

17 See D. I. Baker, 'Compulsory access to network joint ventures under the *Sherman Act*: Rules or roulette?', *Utah Law Review*, 1993, p. 999; D. W. Carlton and M. Klammer, 'The need for coordination among firms with special reference to network industries', *University of Chicago Law Review*, 1983, Spring, pp. 446–65; D. W. Carlton and S. C. Salop, 'You keep on knocking but you can't come in: Evaluating restrictions on access to input joint ventures', University of Chicago working paper, April 1995; and H. Hovenkamp, 'Exclusive joint ventures and antitrust policy', working paper, 1995. The authors discuss issues that bear on mandatory access for network joint ventures.

18 See J. Church and N. Gandal, 'Equilibrium foreclosure and complementary products', Tel Aviv University, working paper, 1993. Church and Gandal consider competition in a market in which firms offer complementary products, such as hardware and software, and have the choice of making their products compatible with the products of a rival. In this framework, intentional incompatibility has similar effects as a refusal to deal.

19 *United States v. Terminal R.R. Ass'n*, 224 US 383 (1912) and 236 US 194 (1915).

20 See D. Reiffen and A. Kleit, 'Terminal railroad revisited: Foreclosure of an essential facility or simple horizontal monopoly?', *Journal of Law & Economics*, 1990, vol. 33, pp. 419–38. Reiffen and Kleit argue that the antitrust issue in Terminal R.R. was not the denial of access, but rather the horizontal combination of competitors in the joint venture, and that the Supreme Court erred in its conclusion that the joint venture was pro-competitive.

21 *MCI Communications Corporation v. AT&T*, 708 F. 2d 1081 (7th Cir.), cert. denied, 464 US 955 (1983).

22 *United States v. Colgate Co.*, 250 US 300, 307 (1919).

23 See, for example, *United States v. Westinghouse Elec. Corp.*, 648 F. 2d 642 (9th Cir. 1981).

24 *Image Technical Services v. Eastman Kodak Company*, 504 US 541 (1992).

25 See G. Werden, 'The law and economics of the essential facilities doctrine', *St. Louis University Law Review*, 1988. Werden provides an economic perspective on legal cases involving refusals to deal.

26 J. Ordover, G. Saloner and S. C. Salop, 'Equilibrium vertical foreclosure', *American Economic Review*, 1992, vol. 80, pp. 127–42; M. H. Riordan and S. C. Salop, 'Evaluating vertical mergers: A post-Chicago approach', *Antitrust Law Journal*, 1995, vol. 63, pp. 513–68. See the authors for analysis of related competitive effects in the context of vertical mergers.

27 See M. K. Perry, 'Price discrimination and forward integration', *Bell Journal of Economics*, 1978, vol. 9, pp. 209–17. Perry describes how a refusal to deal, implemented by a price squeeze, can facilitate price discrimination.

28 See W. S. Bowman, *Patent and Antitrust Law*, University of Chicago Press, 1973.

29 M. Whinston, 'Tying, foreclosure, and exclusion', *American Economic Review*, 1987, vol. 80, no. 4, pp. 837–59.

30 M. L. Katz and C. Shapiro, 'On the licensing of innovations', *The Rand Journal of Economics*, 1985, vol. 16, pp. 504–20.

31 See R. Gilbert and C. Shapiro, 'An economic analysis of unilateral refusals to license intellectual property', *Proceedings of the National Academy of Sciences*, 1996, vol. 93, pp. 12749–55.

32 36 F. 3d 1147 (1st Cir. 1994).

33 *Ibid.*

34 See P. Areeda, 'Essential facilities: An epithet in need of limiting principles', *Antitrust Law Journal*, 1990, vol. 58, pp. 841–53. F. H. Easterbrook makes a similar argument in 'On identifying exclusionary conduct', *Notre Dame Law Review*, 1986, vol. 61, pp. 972–80.

35 Joint Cases C-241/91P & 242/91P, ECJ 6 April 1995.

36 *Ibid.*

37 See *Feist Publ. v. Rural Telephone Serv. Co.*, 111 S. Ct. 1282 (1991) (telephone listings lacked creativity and thus did not satisfy the originality requirement for copyright protection).

38 See Baker, *op. cit.*, p. 999. Baker notes that the Supreme Court had to revisit the terms and conditions of the duty to deal in the *Terminal Railroad* case.

Part II

NETWORK INDUSTRIES

7

ACCESS AND INTERCONNECTION IN NETWORK INDUSTRIES

Henry Ergas

'The most important innovation (in recent regulatory policy)' notes Sir Christopher Foster, an eminent British expert in the field, 'has been the realization that there is no compelling reason why a monopolist should have the exclusive right to use its distribution network'.[1] Removing this exclusive right – thereby allowing a range of firms to compete in delivering services over that distribution network – is, however, no easy matter. Rather, it has become one of the most central but also most complex and controversial tasks of regulatory authorities.

The essence of this task is the creation of rights of access by third parties to some part of the incumbent operator's facilitates. This paper examines the issues that arise in the definition and implementation of these rights. The main arguments can be readily summarized:

1 Asymmetries of power and of interest ensure that issues of third party access to 'essential facilities' will be a source of continuing conflict between the incumbent owners of these facilities and potential downstream competitors; leaving these issues to private negotiation may entail substantial welfare costs.

2 There are no simple but economically compelling rules which can be used to guide the resolution of these issues; rather, the appropriate outcomes – in terms of the scope of access and the conditions on which it is granted – vary from case to case, and hence must be determined on a basis which allows for the exercise of discretion.

3 Given the risks which creating an obligation to supply entails, it is important that this discretion be shielded from rent-seeking and the abuse of political influence; this tells against vesting it in ministerial decision-making or in industry-specific regulatory bodies.

The paper is structured in three parts. The first part reviews the context in which competitive access issues arise. The second analyses the possibility of developing clear rules for handling these issues. The third part examines the design of institutional mechanisms for resolving access disputes.

CREATING MARKETS FOR ACCESS: THE OBSTACLES

Public utilities have generally operated on a highly vertically integrated basis. Services have typically been sold solely to final consumers, with intermediaries playing little or no role in the supply chain. The refusal to sell to intermediaries has excluded or in other ways inhibited competitors from even those parts of these industries which are not inherently natural monopolies: e.g., long distance service in telecommunications, or generation in the electricity industry. Creating 'wholesale' markets at key steps in the supply chain would allow competition to develop in individual parts of the service, even though other parts might retain their monopoly character. Whether this happens will depend on the willingness of the incumbent firm (the former monopolist) to sell services at these wholesale layers, and – absent this willingness – on the ability of the regulatory authorities to intervene so as to induce the incumbent to do so.

Requirements

Creating a functioning wholesale market generally involves two key elements: the definition and allocation of property rights, which may be translatable into tradable entitlements; and in the event that they are tradable, the setting of rules under which trading may occur.

In conventional markets, property rights are defined and traded through implicit and explicit contracts. This process is driven by the self-interest of the parties involved, which derive mutual benefit from reallocating entitlements to those who place the greatest value upon them. Subject to the normal, economy-wide constraints of the law of contract and of competition law, the voluntary actions of the parties can usually be relied upon to shape an efficient vertical structure of transactions – that is to create wholesale markets, and the resulting room for intermediaries to operate, where these are likely to contribute to efficiency.

In the public utilities, however, it may be inappropriate to rely on the voluntary action of the parties to identify and exploit opportunities for the efficient unbundling of services. In effect, unbundling involves agreements between a former monopolist on the one hand, and actual or potential competitors on the other, for the use by those competitors of the former monopolist's facilities and/or services. The former monopolist, it can be argued, is likely to have little experience of these agreements and even less incentive to enter into them.

Complexities

Lack of experience

The lack of experience reflects these industries' traditional mode of operation.

1   Because wholesale markets have not existed, the relevant property rights may be poorly defined.[2] This is especially important because it can give rise to negative externalities – for example, when the overflow demand from one firm using a shared transmission system creates uncompensated congestion for other users. While properly specifying these rights is a complex task in any industry, it is likely to prove especially difficult in those industries where networks of interdependent users play a central role.[3]

2   The operation of these industries' retail segments provides little guidance in defining contractual rights of use. Retail supply has usually occurred not through contracts but under tariffs – that is, posted terms and conditions made available to all users with designated characteristics. These tariffs, which reflect an obligation to meet all reasonable demands, are usually short-term (that is, they bear primarily on spot prices) and they limit (where they do not entirely negate) the suppliers' liability – such limitations being to some extent inevitable if the supplier is not allowed to differentiate among customers on the basis of risk. The absence of contractual liability has made it less important for suppliers to precisely define the services being provided, and has limited the degree to which issues of property rights definition have been tested in the courts. There are consequently few precedents to draw on.

Lack of incentives to unbundle

While lack of experience might slow the emergence of a viable and robustly competitive wholesale market, it would hardly prevent it altogether – were this development in the interests of the former monopolist. In practice, however, the former monopolist usually faces strong incentives to either entirely prevent, or at least substantially distort, the unbundling process. This is because competing entry downstream may erode its monopoly rents – all the more so when prices poorly reflect costs. Even were some entry to occur, the former monopolist may seek to distort its outcomes through collusion. Each of these circumstances is reviewed below.

Effect on monopoly rents

First, downstream entry may reduce the monopoly rents available to the incumbent. This may seem self-evidently true but it is not; indeed, the denial of this proposition has been an important element in the 'Chicago' approach to industrial organization.[4]

Consider, for example, a vertically integrated firm controlling what in US antitrust law is referred to as an 'essential facility'. As is shown below, this term is difficult to define precisely. It is intended to describe facilities which are or could be made available to some firms but not to others, with the effect that the firms denied access to these facilities would be placed at so severe a competitive disadvantage as to be effectively excluded from a market other than that for the services directly provided by that facility, thereby causing substantial and socially undesirable harm to consumers.[5]

Assume (i) that the facility in question is indeed 'essential' to competition in a downstream market; and (ii) that this downstream market is fully competitive (i.e. characterized by the absence of welfare-reducing impediments to entry). Now assume further that to produce the service sold downstream, the services derived from the facility need to be combined with other inputs in essentially fixed proportions – an assumption which may seem strong, but could be justified in the context of many natural monopolies, and notably of reticulation networks.[6] Under these circumstances, the owner of the essential facility, so long as it can price as it wants,[7] does not have an interest in refusing to deal with, and thereby excluding competitors from, the downstream market. Rather, it can extract whatever monopoly rents are available in that market by raising the price of access to the facility to the profit-maximizing point.

Three factors may alter this situation.

First, regulation may prevent the firm from charging for access on a basis which allows it to fully secure the rents which its control of those facilities would otherwise give rise to. If it can 'recoup' some part of these forgone rents through its control of the downstream layer, it will have incentives to engage in an upstream refusal to deal so as to prevent competitive entry downstream.

Second, even in the absence of regulation, structural conditions may differ from those hypothesized in the simple 'Chicago School' model:

1   The multi-part access charges needed to fully recoup monopoly rents may not be sustainable in an unregulated market.[8] This is especially likely if some 'by-pass' is possible – that is, the upstream facility is not a pure natural monopoly.
2   These problems are accentuated when (i) there is some scope for by-pass, (ii) the owner of the facility is vertically integrated and (iii) the downstream market is not perfectly competitive:
    • Assume by-pass is possible (although costly) upstream and that the downstream market comes close to being a 'natural oligopoly' – a market characterized by sufficient entry and exit barriers to drive it in the long term towards a structure of supply in which suppliers each

face a downward sloping demand curve and engage in conscious strategic interaction.

- Even with fixed proportions and full pricing freedom, it may then be in the interest of the essential facility's owner to exclude rivals by refusing to deal with them.
- This is primarily because vertical integration will (i) change the firm's incentives to engage in price-cutting in the input market and (ii) increase its ability to prevent such price-cutting from occurring downstream as well.
- The effect of vertical integration in this case will generally be to increase prices to consumers – a result which may seem obvious to those engaged in business, but which has proved extremely difficult to demonstrate analytically.[9]

Most of the downstream markets associated with the reticulation networks of public utilities are indeed likely to be imperfectly competitive,[10] while there is some, however limited, scope for by-pass of the upstream layer. As a result, even in the absence of other regulatory distortions, the firms in control of these networks may face incentives to refuse to deal with rivals in circumstances where it would be socially desirable for them to do so.

Third and last, even if it were in the incumbent's interests to allow competing entry (because its owners' losses from increased competition in the downstream market would be outweighed by gains from access revenues and enhanced internal efficiency[11]), principal–agent problems may still lead the firm's managers into a refusal to deal. Particularly in enterprises with a history of public ownership, managers may be output or employment maximizers, more interested in retaining market share than in increasing shareholder value. Being risk-averse, the incumbent's managers may weigh the certain loss of a 'quiet life' far more heavily than the uncertain gains which they could secure from operating in a competitive environment.[12] At the same time, the natural reluctance of managers to assist competitors may be aggravated by the perception that the entrants are seeking to 'free-ride' on the incumbent's historic investments. As a result, the firm's managers may stall or obstruct access by the entrant, even when such access would have been granted by the facility's owners.

Impact of price distortions

Even assuming away the protection of monopoly rents, incentives to refuse to deal may arise from inherited price distortions. In almost all public utilities, retail prices bear little relation to the costs of providing service. Margins over attributable cost typically differ significantly both as between services and as between customer groups – a situation often described as cross-subsidization but which is best viewed as price discrimination.[13]

In considering the nature and effects of these pricing structures, it is useful to distinguish two sources of price discrimination.

A first lies in goals of public policy, and notably of income distribution. For example, service is often provided to rural areas at charges which do not fully compensate for the higher costs of supplying these areas – the classic case being the geographically uniform tariffs typically found in postal systems.[14] The higher costs incurred in these areas are then recovered from other areas, where margins are correspondingly high. There is a strong and familiar case against using public utility pricing in this way, especially as compared to relying on direct and targeted subsidies.[15] None the less, the pricing distortions, while they persist, create room for inefficient entry, so long as entrants do not bear the same obligation to serve as does the incumbent. If inefficient entry is to be avoided, policy changes are needed to 'level the playing field'.

Second, price discrimination may arise from the pre-competitive but commercial choices of the service provider:

1   Where the value of a network depends on the number of its users – a situation often referred to as involving demand-side scale economies – the service provider may seek to maximize usage by setting a relatively low access price to marginal consumers.

2   Where users are uncertain of the quality or value of a service they may obtain (say, placing telephone calls), but to be in a position to secure this service must incur fixed (and largely sunk) access costs, it may be worthwhile for the service provider to reduce the risk they face by converting some part of the fixed access fee into a usage charge. As a result, access may be provided at a lower margin over attributable costs than is usage.

3   In industries characterized by economies of scale or scope (arising, for example, from the sharing of common inputs or fixed overheads), prices equal to marginal cost will not yield sufficient revenues for the supplying firm to break-even. Assuming the firm is not subsidized, efficiently recovering total costs will generally require prices which secure greater margins (that is, contributions to the joint and common costs of supply) from some services and customers than from others.

Each of these motives for price discrimination is likely to enhance economic efficiency; but the resulting price structures may not be sustainable in a competitive environment. If entrants can 'pick and choose' among services and/or customers, and the downstream market is relatively competitive, it is likely that margins across services and customer groups will be equalized.[16] Where downstream markets are oligopolistic, this tendency to equalization may not occur, or may occur only weakly;[17] but the pricing structures established in these markets may depart in important respects from those which would be chosen under monopoly supply.

As a result, the incumbent firm may well view the emergence of down-stream competition as threatening pricing structures that on purely commercial grounds it either wishes to preserve or sees little scope to vary. By refusing to deal, and preventing the development of a wholesale market, it could perpetuate its current pricing arrangements, or at least control the pace at which they were modified.

Scope for collusion

While the desire to continue earning monopoly rents and to preserve existing pricing structures may lead to refusals to deal, it may also lead the former monopolist to other outcomes. In particular, if the incumbent views the emergence of a wholesale market as largely unavoidable, it may seek to collude with entrants. When entry is only viable through shared use of facilities, the opportunities for *de facto* collusion are likely to be especially great:

1   The putative competitors in the downstream market will be engaged in the extensive sharing of information and will be exceptionally well placed to observe each other's conduct.
2   The sharing of key facilities will limit the scope for rivalrous product differentiation and tend to equalize competitors' cost structures.
3   The incumbent may structure access arrangements so as to provide for *de facto* profit-sharing. For example, access charges may be specified in contingent terms (with what are in effect market share thresholds triggering increased rates) so as to control entrants' sales or growth of sales.
4   Regulatory requirements may facilitate or stabilize tacit coordination. For example, the former monopolist may be required to post its prices and not to provide discounts or rebates. While this may help prevent the abuse of market power, it may also exclude price chiselling – which is likely to be the main form of competition in markets where products are relatively homogeneous.[18] Other common restrictions on former monopolists which tend to reduce competition (even while preventing the incumbent from behaving anti-competitively) include limitations on quantity or cross-service discounts (bundling) from engaging in long-term contracts.

The risk, consequently, is not solely that a former monopolist may refuse to deal, but also that should it deal, it may – with the acquiescence of entrants – set terms which are not in the public interest.

REMEDIES: RULES VERSUS STANDARDS

Overall, significant 'market failure' may occur in the absence of public inter-vention. The incumbents may seek to preserve monopoly rents by refusing to deal or by setting access charges at levels which substantially hinder or prevent the development of a wholesale market and of workable downstream competition. At the same time, if retail prices are distorted and the incum-bent's revenue losses cannot be fully recovered by its access charges, some entry may occur which merely reflects the price distortions and which hence is socially wasteful.[19] Minimizing the scope for anti-competitive conduct, while ensuring that conflicts of interest are handled in a manner consistent with economic efficiency, is consequently a major challenge for public policy.

In practice, this task has two major component parts: (i) defining the facilities to which some form of access needs to be provided; and (ii) defin-ing parameters for the terms and conditions on which that access may occur. Given their strongly distributional nature (the incumbent's losses appear as the entrants' gain), each of these decisions is likely to prove highly contro-versial; can clear but economically compelling rules be found which would help frame negotiations between the parties and expeditiously resolve the disputes which are likely to arise?

Experience and analysis suggests that 'bright line' rules are of limited relevance to resolving access issues. Rather, the complexity of the fact situa-tions involved, the need to determine trade-offs between possibly conflicting objectives, and the problems involved in implementation all push towards reliance on the administration of broad standards involving substantial discretion.[20] Three factors are especially important.

The uncertain content and use of 'essentiality'

Dangers of over-inclusiveness

While there is a clear case for providing entrants with some relief from access refusals by incumbents, there are equally clear dangers involved in any doctrine which imposes an obligation to supply on firms with considerable market power:[21]

1   Such an obligation may undermine the development of genuine competition. Entrants will have incentives to invoke the compulsory access provisions, rather than bearing the difficulties and risks entailed in organizing to meet their own needs. Given the similarity in cost structures and in grade of service which is likely to arise when common facilities are used, consumers could be deprived of real diversity in the market-place.

2   Providing compulsory third-party access will alter the incumbent's incentives to expand and modernize its facilities. If competitors are guaranteed access to any under-utilized capacity, the former monopolist may well become reluctant to expand its facilities on a cost-minimizing basis, preferring small, suboptimal capacity increments to ones which are larger and ultimately more economic. A similar chilling impact on incentives will arise if the incumbent is required to share with downstream rivals unique know-how, intellectual property or the other fruits of investments in R&D.

3   The third-party access arrangements can also reduce the incumbent's incentive to compete vigorously with its new rivals. If the apparent retention of market power – as measured, say, by market share – ensures that compulsory access arrangements remain in place, the incumbent may have an interest in providing rivals with artificial room to grow. By the same token, entrants may seek to continue to appear weak, merely for the sake of ensuring that the access requirements remain in place.

Difficulties in defining 'limiting principles'

As a result, even putting aside the more 'constitutional' concerns that might be triggered by the curtailment of property rights, it would seem desirable on competition grounds to narrowly define the scope of any 'essential facilities' doctrine. However, the inherently judgemental nature of the processes involved in defining the scope of the facilities at issue, diagnosing the extent of the power they confer in any practical circumstance, and assessing the consequences which should flow from this diagnosis, limit the feasibility of unambiguously doing so.

1   To describe a facility as 'essential' is merely to say that the control of that facility confers a high degree of market power. Indeed, one scholar of the subject argues that the distinction between 'essentiality' on the one hand and 'market power' on the other involves 'labelling, not substance'.[22] Judgements of market power are themselves not amenable to mechanical rules (as the diminishing respectability of market share criteria shows); nor has it proved possible to unambiguously define the threshold level of power which distinguishes the control granted by an 'essential' facility from that accruing to other possessors of a substantial degree of pricing independence.[23]

2   The diagnosis of whether such a threshold, however, defined, is met, is then particularly complex in industries subject to some degree of price and output regulation. Professor William Landes and Judge Richard Posner have put the problem well:

> In view of the growing importance of antitrust enforcement in regulated industries, we shall note briefly the significant limitations

of formal analysis when applied to a market in which rates are regulated by a government agency. To the extent that regulation is effective, its effect is to sever market power from market share. . . . This is obviously so when the effect of regulation is to limit a monopolist's price to the competitive price level. A subtle effect should also be noted, however, regulation may increase a firm's market share in circumstances where only the appearance and not the reality of market power is created thereby. For example, in many regulated industries firms are compelled to charge uniform prices in different product or geographical markets despite the different costs of serving the markets. As a result, price may be above marginal cost in some markets and below marginal costs in others. In the latter group of markets, the regulated firm is apt to have a 100 per cent market share. The reason is not that it has market power but that the market is so unattractive to sellers that the only firm that will serve it is one that is induced to remain in it by the opportunity to recoup its losses in its other markets. . . . In these circumstances, a 100 per cent market share is a symptom of a lack, rather than the possession of market power.

Notice in this case that the causality between price and market share is reversed. Instead of a large market share leading to a high price, a low price leads to a large market share; and it would be improper to infer market power simply from observing the large market share.[24]

3   No lesser difficulties are likely to be encountered in assessing the reasonableness or otherwise of any refusal to deal by the owner of that facility and the related feasibility and desirability of allowing third-party use to occur.[25] The incumbent may, for example, point to the trans-actions costs which would need to be incurred so as to protect its quality of service from the effects of third-party use; it may equally point to for-gone economies of scope. The legitimacy of these business justifications needs to be examined, and set against any genuinely exclusionary effect.

As a result, substantial judgement, of the 'rule of reason' variety, must be involved in determining whether the facility to which access is being sought is, in fact, essential, and, if so, whether an access right should be provided. Principles which need to be considered in taking these decisions can be identified,[26] but they are far from constituting 'bright line' rules.

The setting of 'efficient' access prices

The difficulties involved in defining efficient rules are at least as great in the area of access pricing. At issue here are the bounds to be imposed on the charges which an incumbent may set to third parties for the use of any 'essential facilities' the incumbent controls.

It should not be taken for granted that private negotiations between an incumbent and potential users of its facilities will invariably fail. It may be that the strong tendency of negotiators to seek 'to split the difference' and the scope to develop 'win–win' solutions will lead to mutually acceptable outcomes (though there is a natural suspicion in these cases that the agreement reached does not provide for the greatest competition between the parties). None the less, the likelihood must be that the great asymmetry in bargaining position and the disparity in the parties' interests will preclude agreement through private negotiation and – left unchecked – lead to outcomes that are not in the interests of consumers. There may consequently be a role for access pricing rules, whose function would be to provide socially efficient 'threat points' in the negotiation process.

In examining such rules,[27] it is useful to consider a hypothetical situation in which there are no variable costs in the upstream ('monopolized') market but solely joint and common costs which need to be recovered (these may be the costs of a 'Community Service Obligation' or they may simply reflect economies of scale and scope to service provision); and ask whether the proposed rules, in addition to their performance in terms of the standard (and admittedly inadequate) metric of maximizing the sum of consumer and producer surplus:[28]

- allow competition to develop where it is efficient and to an extent which ensures that consumers reap the benefits which competition can provide;
- maintain the viability of the upstream ('monopoly') market and of any obligations which may bear on providers in that market; and
- do this in a manner which is practical, recognizes that taxation and on-budget subsidies are problematic, and is mindful of the limited ability of policy-makers to comprehend and police markets.

Two broad sets of approaches have been developed in this respect. In the first, bounds on access charges are defined by reference to resource costs (broadly, costs of production). In the second – most famously the Efficient Component (Baumol–Willig) Pricing Rule – the incumbent is allowed some scope to influence these charges by its own pricing behaviour in the retail market.

Cost-based approaches

Four approaches are representative of pricing rules based on resource costs.

Lump sum fees

A particularly simple way of ensuring that the joint and common costs of the network are recouped while at the same time allowing some degree of competition would be to levy a lump sum 'entry tax' intended to cover the joint and common costs incurred upstream. This would have the strong advantage of not affecting the marginal choices of any entrant in the downstream market; it would also be consistent with some axiomatic cost-sharing rules that have desirable welfare properties.[29]

Unfortunately, the simplicity of the approach is largely illusory. In practice, markets are shared, but rarely equally, and multiple entry can occur. Since new entrants can rarely claim more than a small fraction of the existing market, at least initially, such a fee would seem to exclude entry by all but those with the wealthiest backers. Even were this not undesirable, the possibility of multiple entry means that the 'correct' charge will vary with the expected number of entrants, requiring estimation of the equilibrium number of firms – a task which exceeds the current limits not only of practice but even of economic theory.

Per unit charges

An alternative to lump sum charges is to set a fixed per unit access fee (units being defined in terms of the relevant measure of the flow of output), with the fee being calculated so as to exactly allow recovery of the upstream joint and common costs.

Unlike lump sum charges, per unit fees readily deal with unequally split market shares and multiple entrants. However, this approach may entail considerable welfare losses. In effect, the use of per unit fees to recover non-variable costs will almost inevitably distort downstream pricing and output decisions. Moreover, if the downstream market is imperfectly competitive, the per unit fee will lead to double marginalization, so that a fee lower than that which actually recovers costs would be required to maximize social surplus. Finally, even were these welfare losses considered acceptable, implementing this approach requires knowledge of downstream market elasticities – since the fee chosen must exactly cover the joint and common costs *after* firms set their prices and demand is realized. This difficulty is even greater in practice, since access will be provided to multiple interrelated downstream markets, requiring interdependent estimation of the relevant demand schedules.

Incremental costs

Here the access fee is set to recover any additional costs the upstream monopolist must incur as a result of serving the downstream entrants. So long as these costs are determined as an approximation to short-run marginal cost[30] (so that they fluctuate with capacity utilization), fees set on this basis will maximize consumer welfare if the downstream market is contestable.[31] Additionally, since the incremental cost base will tend to be below those provided by other rules, this rule will usually encourage entry, thus yielding any efficiencies which increases in the number of market participants may give rise to.[32]

However, the use of incremental costs has a number of important drawbacks:

- Since incremental costs are not readily related to the upstream deficit, setting access charges on this basis will not usually guarantee that the incumbent covers its costs.
- Moreover, if the incumbent is forced to recover any upstream deficits through its pricing in downstream markets, the use of an incremental cost access fee can seriously distort outcomes when competition in the downstream market is imperfect.
- Finally, this approach is informationally demanding, and may be vulnerable to strategic manipulation. Incremental costs, which should be forward looking, are notoriously difficult to estimate and can only rarely be derived from standard accounting systems. Further, where 'access' involves multiple services, such costs must be estimated for every possible access service, as well as all combinations thereof, and in some cases may be only poorly defined.

Fully distributed cost (FDC) allocations

Fully distributed cost, or FDC, is a cost allocation approach which provides for an exhaustive allocation of joint and common costs. This approach involves dividing the costs of serving customers into attributable and joint costs and then distributing the joint costs, for example 'on the basis of some common physical measure of utilization, such as minutes, circuit-miles, message-minute-miles, gross ton-miles, MK., or kwh'.[33] Other common FDC rules distribute costs on the basis of relative service revenues (so that services which account for a high share of revenues are allocated a high share of joint costs) and relative attributable costs. Given an FDC allocation, the access fee is allocated to output components (lines, minutes, kilometres of haulage) so as to recover the sum of the costs the allocation rule imputes to the downstream market.

Economists (and increasingly, accountants) view FDC approaches with great suspicion.[34]

- FDC allocations are inherently arbitrary since the costs which the FDC approach distributes to a particular service bear no relation to the actual consequences of either providing or not providing that service.
- Access prices set on the basis of FDC allocations can therefore be highly misleading as a guide to action, since they may cause a firm not to enter the downstream market even though the prices it could set in that market would more than recover the costs its actions actually caused.

- FDC prices may not be demand consistent, so they may not even recover costs.
- Precisely because of their arbitrary nature, access charges based on FDC costs may be unsustainable in an environment where some by-pass of the monopoly facility can occur.
- Finally, the ability to recover FDC costs from competitors may reduce the pressures within the incumbent firm to monitor and control joint and common costs, leading to long-term losses in technical efficiency.

Despite seemingly unanimous condemnation, FDC remains the most commonly used approach to cost determination. This is partly because of its acceptability by regulatory, audit and tax authorities, which ensures that the data on which it is based are almost always directly available from standard accounting systems and are readily subject to independent audit. It is also because top managers perceive FDC as helping ensure that their business will recover the totality of its costs,[35] even though this belief is rarely accurate in a competitive environment. Finally, FDC may well appeal to perceptions of 'fairness' since it allocates the 'burden' of the joint costs according to keys (such as output or usage) which have the appearance of objectivity.

Revenue-based approaches

In contrast to cost-based approaches are rules that base access charges on the incumbent's prices. These too are vulnerable to strategic manipulation: just as a rate-of-return regulated firm can alter its asset base to maximize its profits, so a firm subject to a condition which relates the charges it imposes on incumbents to its prices in the downstream market will take that condition into account in its price-setting. None the less, it can be claimed that these rules can be designed to provide the incumbent with stronger incentives to accommodate entry when it is efficient. Two variants of these rules are considered below.

The efficient component pricing (ECPR) rule

Although often referred to as the Baumol–Willig Rule,[36] the rule's origins lie in the vertical price squeeze standard set down by Judge Learned Hand in the *Alcoa* case.[37] In that case, Judge Hand proposed what has become known as the 'transfer price test', designed to determine whether a vertically integrated firm with market power had set prices in the upstream market in such a way as to unreasonably exclude downstream competitors. Under this test, simply put, unreasonable exclusion would be found if the integrated firm could not have sold its downstream products profitably, had it had to pay a 'transfer price' equal to the market price it had set for the input over which it had market power. It follows that the lawful price at which such a firm may set the upstream ('access') price cannot exceed its own downstream price minus the incremental cost it incurs in the downstream processing stage. This test, which has played an important role in US and EU[38] case law, constitutes the essence of the ECPR.

The ECPR ensures that the incumbent firm will never be forced to operate at a loss. When retail prices are regulated (for example, so as to provide for a Community Service Obligation), the rule protects (rather than undermines) the price structure which the regulators have set. It can none the less allow for entry when the entrant is more efficient than the incumbent, and indeed is consistent in this respect with the standard antitrust test for unreasonable exclusion. And even though the ECPR is criticized for leading to access prices which are too high, there are a range of circumstances in which prices set according to this rule will be below those which maximize social surplus.[39] Finally, the ECPR appears to be minimally invasive of the incumbent's property rights.

These are very considerable advantages; but the ECPR also suffers from a number of significant weaknesses:

- When downstream competition is intense, and the entrant's costs are lower than those of the incumbent, the incumbent's downstream prices are poorly defined (its market share should tend towards zero), voiding the ECPR of an empirical anchor.
- Conversely, if there are economies of scope between the upstream and downstream markets, the ECPR, rather than providing welfare improvements, can serve to maintain monopoly prices. It may be that this outcome can be averted by price regulation – for example, by ensuring that prices are no lower than incremental costs and no higher than stand-alone costs. However, were price regulation in fact able to achieve such unambiguous welfare-enhancing outcomes, downstream competition would be superfluous; the fact that policy is seeking to allow competition suggests that price regulation cannot really do the job.
- Finally, when the downstream market is not contestable, the ECPR may actually reduce welfare. For example, if product differentiation is endogenous (the service being supplied is not perfectly homogeneous and producers can outlay costs which will subsequently be sunk so as to affect demand), the ECPR (which treats differently reductions in retail market prices on the one hand and increases in retail market quality on the other) creates incentives for the incumbent to invest in excess product differentiation.

In addition to these analytical weaknesses, the ECPR is more difficult to implement than it may seem to be. Thus, if the incumbent's retail (downstream) prices are non-linear, the ECPR generally requires the calculation of a linear approximation to downstream consumers' outlay schedules. Equally, implementation of the ECPR involves knowledge of the incremental costs incurred by the incumbent in the provision of the downstream service; these costs are not likely to be available in satisfactory form from the incumbent's system of accounts. Given these information imperfections, the incumbent will face strong incentives to 'allocate' costs to the monopoly level, thereby positioning itself to recoup them from rivals.

An upstream revenue cap

In this rule, proposed by Ralph,[40] with a more general variant (in the form of a global price cap) being advanced by Laffont and Tirole,[41] the incumbent is free to set the access charge subject to the constraints that the charge it sets is (i) less than its downstream price; and (ii) consistent with a simple revenue cap: such that the revenues derived from sales in the upstream market (to consumers, downstream competitors, and – on an imputed basis – to the incumbent itself) do not exceed upstream costs (including the costs of any social obligations bearing on the upstream operator). Only total upstream costs and *ex post* revenues need to be known to implement this mechanism, so that – compared to alternatives – it is informationally efficient.

In the upstream market, the revenue cap is very similar to a price cap. It always allows for non-zero profits, and hence ensures the funding of any cost 'burdens'. In the downstream market, the least-cost competitor can achieve profits up to the difference between its costs and those of its closest competitor. Firms therefore face the same incentives to innovate and reduce costs as in any competitive market.

These results ensure that welfare is improved over the unregulated case – indeed, by more than in any other mechanism surveyed here (excepting lump sum charges that outperform the revenue cap when they allow entry *and* there is downstream market power). None the less, welfare is not brought to first-best levels: profits are not reduced to zero and price relativities (the ratio of upstream to downstream prices) are not necessarily optimal.

Overall outcomes

In short, none of the mechanisms – or 'pricing rules' – reviewed here can be excluded outright: rather, they each have strengths and weaknesses that need to be taken into account. Much as with the scope of the 'essential facilities' doctrine, balancing these strengths and weaknesses – summarized in Table 7.1 at the end of this paper – involves complex and inevitably controversial policy trade-offs. The choice of rule will depend on circumstances: on the extent of regulatory distortions in retail prices (generally, the greater these distortions are, the stronger the case for the ECPR); on the extent of downstream entry barriers (the closer the downstream market is to being potentially contestable, the stronger the case for a fee set on the basis of incremental costs); on the lumpiness of upstream investment (which makes for short-run marginal cost rather than long-run incremental cost); and on the extent and quality of the information available (the poorer that information, the stronger the case for mechanisms which encourage substantial self-revelation of information, such as the local price cap).

The administration of the access process

The difficulties involved in attempting to constrain access processes through mechanical rules are even more apparent at the implementation stage. Three points can be made in this regard:

1   Given the incentives for anti-competitive conduct, the lack of experience with a wholesale market, and the problems of coordination characteristic of network industries, access entitlements will prove difficult to define and to price, at least initially. This can be expected to give rise to frequent disputes between the parties. In a 'normal' market, the effective management of these disputes would probably involve vertical integration – that is, the internalization of activities within an enterprise, allowing disputes to be more expeditiously handled through administrative processes.[42] It is, however, a goal of policy in these industries to promote the emergence of trading relations between distinct entities located at differing points in the vertical chains. There is consequently a transactions cost issue which needs to be faced.

2   Relatedly, experience with access and interconnection issues in a broad range of industries confirms that it is simply not possible to cover in an initial agreement the full set of contingencies which will ultimately arise. This is in no small part because network interconnection involves a large number of non-price issues (such as the location of interfaces, the provisioning of links and the management of end-to-end service quality), each of which creates scope for opportunistic conduct at the implementation stage by the parties to the agreement. Moreover, the sharp asymmetry of interests between the parties, and the fact that neither is actually in a situation where it stands to gain much by building goodwill, means that contracts are not self-enforcing and that incentives for strict compliance may be weak.

3   Resolving these disputes almost invariably involves functions of arbitration, in which expert judgement is used to assess the reasonableness (rather than the rule-conformity) of conflicting claims. It may be possible for the parties themselves to determine a mechanism (such as commercial arbitration) which meets these needs. None the less, in the absence of such mechanisms or in the event of their break down, there will be strong pressures for policy to provide a low-cost mechanism for

dispute-resolution. The costs which acceding to these pressures entails – including in terms of reducing the incentives for the parties to address and resolve disputes in good faith – then need to be balanced against the benefits of speedier and possibly cheaper conflict resolution.

INSTITUTIONAL DESIGN

Addressing these complexities seems to call for a highly discretionary model of public policy, capable of making trade-offs in the light of particular fact situations, using incrementalism to adapt to new information and to evolving circumstances, and providing for the arbitration of disputes according to standards of reasonableness. So high a level of discretion must none the less give some cause for concern; after all, the issues being determined can have a major impact on property rights and income distribution, as well as on efficiency both in the markets directly concerned and in the economy more broadly. To the extent to which the exercise of discretion cannot be hemmed in by conduct-related rules, it would seem desirable to do so through 'jurisdictional rules'[43] which, by locating responsibility for rule-setting in institutions with given characteristics, provide (to use Kelsen's famous description of constrained discretion) the process of mediating access disputes with 'a frame if not a picture'.[44]

In analysing these issues of choice of jurisdiction, the natural starting point is the fact that those making and implementing policy operate with highly imperfect information, have objectives which may not be identical with those of the public most broadly defined, and hence cannot be expected to guide an industry, activity or market to full efficiency. As a result, policy-driven outcomes (including those of the putatively low-cost mechanism for dispute resolution) are likely to be inferior to those of a workably competitive market, in some cases drastically so. In deciding the extent and form of intervention in the granting of third party access, the risks of 'government failure' must therefore be weighed relative to those of their 'market' counterpart. Two recommendations flow from this starting point:

1   Intervention to grant third party access should be confined to areas where markets are least likely to work satisfactorily – that is, to areas that are far from being workably competitive.
2   In structuring intervention in those areas, the choice of policy instrument should be mindful of the costs and benefits of institutional alternatives – that is, the vulnerability of each policy instrument to the various pathologies of public policy which underpin 'government failure'.[45] Presumably, intervention to promote interconnection should only occur if policies and instruments can be designed whose net costs fall short of those of simply leaving outcomes to commercial negotiation.

The second of these points is arguably the most difficult. Primarily at issue are the incentives and constraints bearing on each of the means by which policy can be made and implemented – means which (in Australia, at least) include Parliament, ministerial departments, industry-specific regulatory agencies, regulatory agencies whose mandate is defined in terms of an issue area (rather than an industry), and the system of courts and tribunals. In practice, several of these are typically involved in any issue area, and would be in the implementation of policies for access and interconnection; but to what extent are the costs of the 'government failures' they entail likely to be less than the costs of the 'market failures' for which remedies are being sought?

This issue can be explored by considering first, a conceptual framework for analysing the question of choice of institutions and then some of this framework's insights to the Australian experience with regulating interconnection in telecommunications.

Analysing institutional choice

The classical theory of public administration addresses questions of institutional design primarily in terms of institutional capability. Institutions are seen as differing mainly in terms of (i) their capacity to initiate action; (ii) their access to resources (including of expertise); and (iii) the nature of their accountability (which is essentially an aspect of access to resources). Broadly, ministerial processes tend to be the least constrained in each of these respects, with the system of courts and tribunals falling at the other extreme. Institutional choice then depends on matching each function of government with capabilities it requires.

More recent work, informed by the debates surrounding the 'interest group theory of politics', emphasizes a rather different set of institutional features.[46] In particular, stress is placed on what might be described as the 'permeability' of the various institutional alternatives – the degree to which, and the manner in which, they are open to external influence or (less pejoratively) participation. Here too, ministerial processes tend to be the least constrained, with the system of courts and tribunal again falling at the other extreme. This is readily illustrated, albeit at the cost of considerable simplification.

Consider, for example, the process by which parties express a position on an issue. Interested parties face relatively low costs in putting their views to ministerial departments and to regulatory agencies; moreover, they can do so without disclosing those views to public scrutiny. Far greater constraints are involved in participating in the more formal adjudicative processes of the system of courts and tribunals, and only in narrowly defined circumstances can one do so without accepting public disclosure.

Consider equally the outcomes of the respective processes. The decisions taken by ministerial departments may affect many parties – e.g., a whole industry, or an entire class of participant within that industry. As a result, it is not unusual for complex coalitions of interested parties to participate in the making of policy. Moreover, ministerial decisions are only loosely bound by what has been done to date: past outcomes do not bind current processes. Participation by interested parties is therefore a fairly ongoing process, especially as there is always the prospect and/or risk that decisions previously taken will be reversed. In contrast, the outcomes of court adjudication, although they may have substantial impacts on third parties, typically centre on the parties directly before the Court, and only limited room is left for coalitions of interested parties. At the same time, adjudication is generally a time-limited process, so that it is only in exceptional cases (generally associated with broad social issues) that any coalitions that may have been formed persist.

Finally, consider the processes' ultimate transparency. Despite the conventions of parliamentary accountability, it seems fair to say that Ministers face relatively little burden in having to give reasons for their decisions, other than to the extent needed to retain Parliamentary support. This inevitably reduces the information available to the broader public and its agents (such as the press). At the other extreme, the courts are subject to relatively stringent requirements to give reasons and to do so in a manner capable of meeting the needs of the system of appeals.[47]

Three broad implications are generally drawn from these differences.

1   Ministerial decision-making is especially vulnerable to rent seeking:
    • Putting aside the exploitation of disenfranchised minorities (the problem of the 'tyranny of the majority'), this type of decision-making is most likely to fail when the gains associated with a policy are concentrated while the costs it imposes are diffuse. The potential gainers can then organize to exert the maximum influence on the taking and implementing of decisions – through threats and inducements, by distorting the information they provide, and (in coalition with the Minister) by making it difficult for those who are losing out to realize the costs which are being imposed on them.
    • However, ministerial decision-making is also relatively unstable. This has some obvious advantages in allowing scope for iterating towards better public policy – for example, by incorporating new information and/or accommodating changing community values. From the point of view of interested parties, however, the threat of future changes must reduce the value of any gains currently secured.
2   The system of courts and tribunals is substantially less vulnerable to these forms of manipulation, although it does not escape them altogether. Some scholars, most prominently Judge Posner, have claimed that this system, at least in countries of the common law, tends to

produce economically efficient outcomes – because it is the parties with the most to gain which have the strongest incentive to seek redress; while the procedural and substantive safeguards under which the system works limit the scope for rent-seeking, especially in countries in which costs can be recovered.[48] In the strongest version of this claim, court-made law is seen as more conducive to efficiency than the setting of rules or standards by statute.[49] However, even those writing within this literature admit that a number of factors constrain the effectiveness of courts and tribunals.

- Courts typically deal with a fairly narrowly defined range of issues. The doctrine of justiciability restricts the judiciary in its ability to issue advisory opinions, and prevents it from examining issues that are moot or where the parties have no standing to maintain the action. At the same time, there is a general requirement that the controversy in a case be immediately present and involve a real, and not merely speculative, injury to a party.[50]
- Even within this class of issues, only a few are resolved through litigation. The high costs and complexities involved in taking or participating in legal action mean that cases are most likely to arise when highly concentrated interests are involved, and when it is those interests which capture the greatest part of the value of outcomes. When the outcomes are of substantial value to third parties, directly or through precedent, the difficulties involved in securing from these parties a contribution to costs may lead to under-investment in litigation.
- Moreover, the courts face severe constraints in terms of how they resolve even those issues which they do address. Courts have limited access to resources: they do not, and even in countries of civil law cannot, resemble Weberian bureaucracies.[51] As a result, the expertise on which they can draw is necessarily of a different, more generalist, kind than that found in ministerial departments and regulatory agencies. Nor are courts well equipped to administer remedies which entail continuing oversight and the taking of a range of ancillary decisions, as is typically the case in the provision of access to 'essential facilities'.[52]
- More controversial is the standard Benthamite critique of the cognoscibility of the common law. According to this view, court decisions, because they are cast in terms of the issues immediately facing the court, may not be sufficient to establish clear guidelines for future conduct. However, this view would seem to under-estimate the value of precedent and the ability of courts to create what are, in fact, if not in name, rules.[53]

3   Regulatory agencies are in an intermediate position between Ministers and courts.[54] More explicitly set out functions and more formalized

procedures for determining standing, assessing the admissibility of evidence and justifying the decisions taken, reduce vulnerability to rent-seeking, as do rules limiting *ex parte* consultation. The agencies are also generally able to call on in-house expertise, enhancing the scope for pro-active rule making and enforcement. At the same time, the agencies typically retain the powers of initiative needed to address issues on an *ex ante* basis and to resort to policy incrementalism as a response to uncertainty.

But there are also substantial pathologies, whose effects may be heightened by the complex technical nature of many regulatory decisions and the result-ing community ignorance of what regulators do – ignorance reflecting the relatively low stakes (and hence limited incentive to invest in information) which most individuals have in the outcomes of the regulatory process. Four aspects of these pathologies are especially striking in industry-specific regulatory agencies:

- An industry-specific agency typically escapes scrutiny not only by the general public but also by firms in other industries, since (i) the industry being regulated will generally account for a very small part of other industries' total costs; and (ii) the agency's limited scope shields firms in other industries from the precedent value of its decisions. The stakes mobilized by the agency are consequently almost inherently more fragmented, reducing *de facto* accountability.
- As a result, Ministers can use such an agency as a means of enhancing the value of decisions they have taken. In particular, the agency can provide a means of creating specially enfranchised constituents with privileged access to the decision-making process. Because the agency is less vulnerable to policy shifts (being constrained, for example, by sub-stantive and procedural legislation), these constituents – the 'winners' in the prior 'rent-seeking' game – can thereby be given a greater degree of commitment about the durability of the bargains they have struck. The arcane nature of many regulatory decisions, and the complex and opaque rhetoric in which they are cast, may allow the regulatory agency to get away with implementing policies which are even more directly re-distributable and responsive to special interests than those announced by the Minister to Parliament – suggesting that from a rent-seeking point of view, industry-specific regulation may well be a fairly natural complement to, rather than substitute for, ministerial involvement.
- At the same time, the agency, to fulfil its functions, is likely to need a substantial degree of autonomy. This enhances the scope for goal displacement (the conflict between the agency's ostensible goals and the actual goals of its members), as well as introducing a degree of uncer-tainty into the agency's decisions. To perpetuate their organizational

culture and protect their access to resources, agency administrators will have incentives to make the gains they provide to agency stakeholders dependent on the agency's survival. They may therefore actively seek out new 'winners', thereby expanding their clientele, while reminding prior clients of the need to invest in retaining agency loyalty. The result may be even more complex redistributions than those originally intended.

Implications in the context of access and interconnection

What do these institutional characteristics imply for the design of access regimes? These implications can be illustrated by considering the regulation of interconnection in Australian telecommunications. Especially striking is the interaction of extensive ministerial involvement with industry-specific regulation. Three points are worth making.

1   The decision to open the market to competition, though undoubtedly a step to full liberalization, was tied up with a significant ministerial 'bargain' with interested parties. In particular, the need to successfully complete the sale of the AUSSAT satellite and of the licence to operate as a second general carrier, had a major influence on government policy. Above and beyond a genuine interest in promoting competition, the government was anxious to ensure the credibility of its commitments to the consortium that purchased the second licence. Three instruments proved especially important in this respect:
    - Direct commitments negotiated 'off the public record' (and in some cases, apparently inconsistently with the public record) by the Minister.[55]
    - The use of ministerial direction to establish principles for inter-connection charging, thereby curtailing the risk that other parties (most notably Telstra, the communications unions and consumer groups) might amend the bargain at the implementation stage.
    - Reliance on AUSTEL, rather than on agencies exposed to broader scrutiny, as the primary instrument for policy implementation, with the Telecommunications Act 1991 clearly vesting special rights of consultation in the general carriers.
2   The continued public ownership of Telstra, the incumbent carrier, sub-stantially increased the Government's ability to engineer a redistributive bargain. In effect, the Minister was able to curtail Telstra's appeal against incursions on property rights – most notably by making it clear that the Government expected Telstra to accept the process underway. Given the rights of appeal which had to be provided for in the Act, is questionable whether a privately owned firm would have acquiesced to anywhere near the same extent.

3   Since that time, the successful implementation of the first stage of full competition (duopoly) and changes in broader public goals (most notably the importance attached to developing a national competition policy) have undermined the legitimacy and stability of the original bargain (which in any case involved a sunset clause). Paralleling these changes in circumstances, AUSTEL has used its autonomy to seek to alter its client base, notably by creating a constituency of 'service providers' (essentially resellers) dependent on it for privileged access to Telstra's network.[56] While politically astute, this strategy seems likely to create substantial economic costs as AUSTEL seeks to impose on the market outcomes quite different from those which would prevail in a less regulated environment.

CONCLUSIONS

Interconnection will remain a formidable policy problem so long as incumbents control 'essential facilities' in markets subject to severe retail price distortions. Economic theory does not provide simple means of resolving the disputes these circumstances give rise to; moreover, even putting the pricing issues aside, there may be a need for more permanent structures to help govern the non-price aspects of third party access. These governance problems do not seem resolvable without substantial scope for discretionary judgement. The question then is whether institutions can be designed which can address these tasks without themselves giving rise to formidable costs.

The institutions through which policies are made and implemented can be analysed in terms of their institutional capability on the one hand and of their vulnerability to rent-seeking on the other. Ministerial decision-making tends to be the most vulnerable to manipulation by concentrated interests. Industry-specific regulators have a greater degree of autonomy, but frequently serve to add credibility to the special bargains made by Ministers. Moreover, Australian experience suggests that industry-specific bodies are liable to substantial goal-displacement, seeking to perpetuate intervention even where it is not needed. Though courts tend to be less vulnerable to rent-seeking than the other institutions of public governance, there are severe limits on their capabilities.

This suggests reliance on institutions that are subject to effective surveillance by broad interest coalitions, as is typically the case with national competition policy authorities. At the same time, it is important to ensure that these bodies themselves remain subject to judicial review. While this may somewhat slow the process of dispute resolution, it is likely to yield substantial benefits over the longer run in terms of the predictability and consistency of the rules which can guide private behaviour in this area.

Table 7.1 A comparison of access pricing approaches

	Always covers costs?	Encourages competition?	Downstream price distortion	Welfare rank		Requires knowledge of:						Degree of difficulty
				Model	Judgement	Local costs	LongD costs	Total costs	Local dem.	Long dist. dem.	Other info.	
	Yes	Discourages	Little (1a)	5th	2nd–3rd	Yes	Yes	Yes	Yes	Yes		V. hard
	Yes	Yes	Distorts	5th	5th	Yes	Yes	Yes	Yes	Yes		V.v. hard
	No (3a)	Depends	Distorts		Depends	Yes	Yes	Yes	Depends	Depends	(3b)	Easy–v. hard (3c)
1 cost (4)	No (4a)	Strongly	Little (4b)	1st	1st–2nd	(4c)						V. hard
	Yes	V. weakly	Distorts	6th	6th (5a)		(5b)					V.v. hard
(5)	Yes	Weakly	Distorts	4th	2nd–4th	(6)	(6)	(6)				Extremely hard
bal cap	Yes	Yes	Opt dist (7a)	3rd	3rd	Yes		Yes	Yes	Yes	(7b)	V.v. hard
+ ECPR	Yes	Yes	Opt dist (7a)	3rd	3rd	Yes	(5b)	Yes	Yes	Yes	(8)	Extremely hard
ocal cap (9)	Yes	Yes	Distorts	5th	5th	Yes					(9a)	'Easiest'
bal cap (9)	Yes	Yes	Distorts	4th	4th			Yes			(10)	Hard

Notes
(1) a Distortion only occurs if per call or per subscriber incremental costs are significant. To avoid this these could be additionally charged, but such information is difficult to obtain.

Table 7.1 cont.

(3) **a** FDC allocation rules can lead to demand incompatible prices. **b** Cost allocation keys require additional information such as attributable costs, traffic carried, etc. **c** Easy if the firm already uses FDC and its procedures are acceptable to the regulator. In general FDC rules will need to be specified and policed, and these will be subject to much regulatory dispute.

(4) Assumes incremental costs are not averaged across calls, call minute, etc. **a** Entry is unlikely to create losses in the short run, and need not do so in the long run. **b** Distortion only arises with downstream market power. **c** Requires the incremental cost to the incumbent of the competitor's downstream services.

(5) ECPR not defined if the incumbent sets non-linear downstream prices. **a** Welfare improves over the unregulated case only if (1) the entrant is the least cost supplier (its start-up costs are less than the incumbent's incremental costs) and it is profitable for the incumbent to exclude entry, or (2) there is only one potential entrant and the incumbent does not have a first mover advantage. **b** Requires the incremental cost *savings* to the incumbent due to entry.

(6) As 5b, and additionally requires marginal costs, and the stand alone and incremental costs of all service agglomerations.

(7) **a** Archives Ramsey prices, that is optimal prices given no subsidy/taxation and uniform pricing. **b** Requires estimation of optimal local and long distance call volumes by carrier, and standard price cap estimations of total factor productivity and cost movements for the incumbent's entire operations.

(8) As for 5, and 7b but only total long distance call volumes (not market shares) are required.

(9) For welfare comparisons it is assumed local prices are not lowered. **a** Requires standard price cap estimations for the local market only, and *ex post* local, interconnect, and long distance call volumes and revenues.

(10) Requires standard price cap estimations for the incumbent's entire operations.

NOTES

1 C. D. Foster, *Privatization, Public Ownership and the Regulation of Natural Monopoly*, Blackwell, 1992, p. 167.

2 See, for example, R. T. Smith, A. S. De Vany and R. J. Michaels, 'Defining a right of access to interstate natural gas pipelines', *Contemporary Policy Issues*, 1990, vol. 8, p. 142; and W. W. Hogan, *Coordination for Competition in an Electricity Market*, 1995.

3 On the railways, for example, 'capacity' is a relatively poorly defined concept, since the volume of traffic which can be handled upon a given network depends not only on the number and origin/destination of trains but also on the speed at which they are operated. Hence, a fully exchangeable 'transport entitlement', governing access to tracks by competing users, would have to be a complex set of rights. Moreover the value of this entitlement might be significantly affected by the behaviour of third parties. For example, a breakdown on a track will delay all the scheduled traffic on that path and on the paths used to provide redundancy, imposing external costs on network users (that is, costs which are internal to the network but external to the party causing them). If moral hazard is to be avoided, these costs would need to be internalized (that is, imposed upon the party causing them, thus reducing the incentive to create delays by (for example) using poor quality rolling stock). Properly specified contracts for access to track by competing users must consequently provide for penalties in the event that the user imposes delays on third parties. Correctly setting these penalties requires knowledge of the value of delays. This can be calculated in principle, for example, if the right to use tracks at a particular time, on a particular path and at a particular speed is auctioned to competing users, the bids made will reflect the value of delayed or lost load. However, this requires mechanisms that go well beyond the experience of current operators, and is therefore likely to prove controversial.

   In these industries, diminished vertical coordination, as well as creating third party effects in the quality of service, may also undermine least cost capacity expansion, unless complex cost-sharing mechanisms can be put in place. Simulations suggest that the excess costs arising from this reduction in coordination may be substantial; see, for example, R. Baldick and E. Kahn, 'Network costs and the regulation of wholesale competition in electric power', *Journal of Regulatory Economics*, 1993, vol. 5, p. 367.

4 Note, however, that the primary emphasis in the Chicago tradition has not been placed on denying that a firm controlling an essential facility may secure monopoly rents by refusing to deal. Rather, it has been on arguing that when the firm chooses to do so, the impact on social welfare (the sum of consumer and producer surplus) is generally positive. A good presentation of the Chicago argument is in D. J. Gerber, 'Rethinking the monopolist's duty to deal: A legal and economic critique of the doctrine of "essential facilities"', *Virginia Law Review*, 1988, vol. 74, p. 1069.

5 Although the term 'essential facility' only appears in a reported judicial decision in 1977, receiving its first authoritative statement *in haec verba* in Hecht v. Pro-Football, Inc., 570 F. 2d 982, 992 (D.C. Cir. 1977) cert. denied, 436 US 956 (1978), the doctrine can be traced back to the Supreme Court's 1912 ruling in *United States v. Terminal Railroad Association*, 224 US 383 (1912). The main

features of the doctrine were concisely summarized by the US Seventh Circuit in 1983 as requiring that a plaintiff seeking access to a facility establish the following elements to show liability: '(1) control of the essential facility by a monopolist; (2) a competitor's inability practically or reasonably to duplicate the facility; (3) the denial of the use of the essential facility to a competitor; and (4) the feasibility of providing the facility'. See *MCI Comm. Corp. v. American Tel. & Tel. Co.*, 708 F. 2d 1081, 1132–33 (7th Cir.) cert. denied, 464 US 891 (1983).

6 For example, transmitting a unit of electricity from point A to point B requires the use of the high voltage transmission grid in essentially fixed proportions. Equally, fixed amounts of transmission are required to transport a given volume of natural gas from one point to another. Finally, while some substitution opportunities do exist, providing a telephone connection on demand in a network with many users is difficult to do without using a local loop at each end.

7 Including terms of costlessly designing and implementing a menu of two-part tariffs, so that it could derive the full benefits of price discrimination.

8 See D. M. Mandy, 'Non uniform Bertrand competition', *Econometrica*, 1992, vol. 60, p. 1293.

9 See O. Hart and J. Tirole, 'Vertical integration and market foreclosure', *Brookings Papers on Economic Activity*, 1990, p. 205; J. A. Ordover, S. C. Salop and G. Saloner, 'Equilibrium market foreclosure', *American Economic Review*, 1990, vol. 80, p. 127; and J. A. Ordover, S. C. Salop and G. Saloner 'Equilibrium market foreclosure: Reply', *American Economic Review*, 1992, p. 698.

10 In telecommunications, for example, margins in the US market for long distance service to residential consumers appear to have remained high since the divestiture of AT&T, at least partly because of price leadership exercised by the dominant firm. This has been largely facilitated by regulation, which has forced AT&T to disclose its charges and imposed lags on price changes, making price coordination easier. One view of the evidence can be found in the United States District Court for the District of Colombia *Motion of Bell Atlantic Corporation, BellSouth Corporation, NYNEX Corporation and Southwestern Bell Corporation to Vacate the Decree* in *United States of America v. Western Electric Co. Inc., and American Telephone and Telegraph company*, Civil Action No. 82–0192 (HHG); but see also, dissenting, affidavit of B. Douglas Bernheim and Robert D. Willig United States District Court for the District of Colombia in *United States of America v. Western Electric Co. Inc., and American Telephone and Telegraph Company*, Civil Action No. 82–0192 (HHG) *ATT's Opposition to the Four RBOC's Motion to Vacate the Decree* 1, Appendix A.

11 Entry may provide benefits to the owners of the incumbent firm by allowing some measure of 'yardstick competition'. This refers to the impact of product market conditions on agency costs, that is, on the costs involved in ensuring that owners and managers have adequate incentives to act efficiently. The underlying notion is that in a more competitive market (and assuming that the firms in the market can be prevented from colluding), owners can more readily compare performance across firms. This allows them to discriminate between, say, low profits due to industry-wide demand shocks and low profits due to managerial slack or to rent-sharing between managers and workers. As a result, owners can better structure the incentives that managers face, securing a closer alignment between managerial actions and public objectives.

12 This is merely a manifestation of the endowment effects analysed by D. Kahneman, J. Knetsch and R. Thaler, 'The endowment effect, loss aversion and status quo bias', *The Journal of Economic Perspectives*, 1991, vol. 5, p. 193.

13 In economic analysis, cross-subsidies only occur when charges are below attributable cost for some consumers (and/or services) and/or above stand-alone cost to others. In other words, price discrimination does not necessarily involve cross-subsidization. See, for a thorough discussion, D. F. Spulber, *Regulation and Markets*, 1989, p. 113.

14 On which see notably R. Coase, 'The economics of uniform pricing systems', *The Manchester School*, 1947, vol. 15, pp. 139–56.

15 An especially interesting recent restatement of this case is in M. Fuss and L. Waverman, 'Efficiency principles for telecommunications pricing', paper presented to the National Conference on the Future of Telecommunications in Canada, Toronto, 1–2 April 1993. Fuss and Waverman's argument that basic access in telephony is not a Feldstein good is consistent with the findings on subsidy incidence reported in H. Ergas, E. Ralph and S. Sivakumar, *Reforming Australian Telecommunications*, 1991.

16 Note that many of the problems associated with price de-averaging (and notably the unsustainability of efficient – that is, welfare-increasing – cross-subsidies between services) could be avoided were each customer required to obtain *all* of the services provided by the utility from a single supplier. In this case, the competing suppliers could continue to set prices for individual services in a way which came close to maximizing the sum of consumer and producer surplus (which requires revenue transfers between *services*) while ensuring that there were no revenue transfers between *consumers*. The resulting set of prices would fall in the 'second best core' – that is, the set of prices which would allow a supplier of the service in question to recover the totality of its costs without creating incentives for any group of consumers to 'break away from the grand coalition to produce the vector of goods on its own'. The concept of the second-best core, which is central to the analysis of efficient pricing in markets characterized (i) by cost sub-additivity (economies of scale and scope) and (ii) competitive entry, was initially developed in R. Guesnerie and C. Oddou, 'Second best taxation as a game', *Journal of Economic Theory*, 1981, vol. 25, pp. 67–91. A full treatment can be found in D. Spulber, *Regulation and Markets*, 1989, pp. 180–98.

17 Recent analysis suggests that there can be more price discrimination in a differentiated products oligopoly than in the corresponding monopoly: see S. Borenstein, 'Price discrimination in a free entry market', *Rand Journal of Economics*, 1985, vol. 16, p. 380; and T. J. Holmes, 'The effects of third-degree price discrimination in oligopoly', *American Economic Review*, 1989, vol. 79, p. 244. The passenger airline market can be cited as a case where deregulation and competitive entry have resulted in increased price dispersion; see S. Borenstein and N. Rose, 'Competition and price dispersion in the US airline industry', NBER Working Paper, 1991, p. 3785.

18 Some evidence to this effect is provided in J. T. Hong and C. Plott, 'Rate filing policies for inland water transportation', *Bell Journal of Economics*, 1982, vol. 13, p. 1; D. M. Grether and C. Plott, 'The effects of market practices in oligopolistic markets', *Economic Inquiry*, 1984, vol. 22, p. 479; and (with more mixed results) in F. J. Ruppel, S. Fuller and M. McKnight, 'Grain shipper/railroad

contract disclosure', *Journal of Agricultural Economics Research*, 1990, vol. 42, p. 8. A comprehensive survey of the evidence on the competition-chilling effect of posted prices in concentrated markets can be found in D. Davis and C. Holt, *Experimental Economics*, 1993.

19 Note that even this 'uneconomic entry' may be economically desirable if (i) the costs associated with the price distortions exceed those arising from the transfer of output from the (lower cost) incumbent to the (higher cost) entrant; and/or (ii) if it accelerates the process of price adjustment by the incumbent. Even in the unlikely circumstance in which a regulator could accurately measure the relative costs and competitiveness of the entrant and any given incumbent (so that 'agency cost' considerations are not relevant), it would consequently be wrong to seek to prevent all 'uneconomic entry'. Rather, the 'first best' option in these circumstances is to act on the price distortions so as to minimize the likelihood that uneconomic entry will occur. However, where the price distortions are actually a desired outcome of policy, then there is a case for ensuring that the burden of providing uneconomic services does not unduly disadvantage the incumbent (taking account, in this equation, of any special advantages the incumbent secure from statute or merely from inherited dominance).

20 *Rules* can be defined as decision norms entailing an advance determination of what conduct is permissible, leaving only factual issues for the adjudicator. In contrast, a *standard*, while specifying some goals and criteria, may leave both the detailed specification of the scope of permissible conduct and the determination of factual issues to the adjudicator. Thus, 'driving in excess of 90 kilometres per hour is prohibited' is a rule; 'driving unsafely is prohibited' is a standard. Rules allow those likely to be influenced by a norm to ascertain the permissibility of conduct prior to engaging in that conduct, but they generally also involve higher initial costs of production (at least, if one is trying to 'get them right') than standards. See F. Schauer, *Playing By the Rules: A Philosophical Examination of Rule-Based Decision-Making in Law and in Life*, 1991; and L. Kaplow, 'Rules versus standards: An economic analysis', *Duke Law Journal*, 1992, vol. 42, p. 557.

21 W. Blumenthal, 'Three vexing issues under the essential facilities doctrine', *Antitrust Law Journal*, 1990, vol. 58, p. 868; and generally, P. Areedan and H. Hovenkamp, *Antitrust Law*, §736.2 (Supp. 1993).

22 J. G. Sidak, private communication.

23 According to the *Hecht* court, for example, the facility involved does not need to be 'indispensable; it is sufficient if duplication would be economically infeasible and if denial of its use inflicts a severe handicap on potential market entrants'; *Hecht v. Pro-Football, Inc.*, 570 F. 2d 982, 992 (D.C. Cir. 1977) cert. denied, 436 US 956 (1978). Since then, the standard has become more stringent: for example, '[a]s the word 'essential' indicates, a plaintiff must show more than inconvenience, or even some economic loss; he must show that an alternative to the facility is not feasible'; *Twin Laboratories Inc. v. Weider Health & Fitness.*, 900 F. 2d 556, 569–70 (2nd Cir. 1990); and similarly *Alaska Airlines Inc. v. United Airlines Inc.*, 948 F. 2d 536, 544 (9th Cir. 1991) cert. denied, 112 S. Ct. 1603 (1992) (asserting that an essential facility must confer a power not merely to harm competitors, but to eliminate competition in the downstream market). It can be argued, however, that even this trend has not been sufficient to set clear

bounds on the threshold of essentiality; see P. Areeda, 'Essential facilities: An epithet in search of limiting principles', *Antitrust Law Journal*, 1989, vol. 58, p. 841.

24 W. M. Landes and R. A. Posner, 'Market power in antitrust cases', *Harvard Law Review*, 1981, vol. 94, pp. 937, 975–6.

25 See, for example, P. J. Ahern, 'Refusals to deal after *Aspen*', *Antitrust Law Journal*, 1994, vol. 63, p. 153.

26 See, for example, Areeda and Hovenkamp, *op. cit.*, § 736.2a, Supp. 1993; and D. I. Baker, 'Compulsory access to network joint ventures under the *Sherman Act*: Rules or roulette?', *Utah Law Review*, 1993, vol. 56, p. 999.

27 More comprehensive reviews can be found in *WIK–EAC Network Interconnection in the Domain of ONP: Study for DG XIII of the European Commission – Final Report*, 1994; and H. Ergas and E. Ralph, 'The interconnection problem with a focus on telecommunications', *Communications & Strategies*, 1994, vol. 16, p. 9, on which this discussion draws.

28 This metric relies on strong assumptions about compensation and income distribution. A fuller treatment would take account of the concerns reviewed in M. Trebilcock *The Limits of Freedom of Contract*, 1993; and H. Peyton Young, *Equity in Theory and Practice*, 1994.

29 See, for example, the 'Minimum Cost Steiner Network' algorithms reviewed in W. W. Sharkey, 'Network models in economics', in *The Handbook of Operations Research and Management Science*, 1995; and the serial cost allocation techniques set out in H. Moulin, 'Serial cost sharing', *Econometrica*, vol. 60, p. 1009.

30 The importance of using short-term marginal costs, rather than long-run incremental costs, emerges clearly from the simulations reported in R. E. Park, *Incremental Costs and Efficient Prices With Lumpy Capacity: The Two Product Case*, RAND, Santa Monica, California, 1994. The relevant theory is set out in D. Starrett, *Foundations of Public Economics*, 1988, pp. 283–91. Useful examples of practical application are in F.C. Schweppe *et al.*, *Spot Pricing of Electricity*, 1988.

31 The resulting charges will obviously fluctuate more than the smoothed approximations provided by long-run incremental costs. However, market participants should be able to offset these fluctuations through hedge contracts; see W. W. Hogan, 'Contract networks for electric power transmission', *Journal of Regulatory Economics*, 1992, vol. 4, p. 211.

32 By reducing price-cost margins, greater competition will yield improvements in allocative efficiency; but it may also increase technical efficiency, that is, the productivity with which resources are used. Recent, largely theoretical, work identifies three mechanisms through which productive efficiency may be affected by changing product market conditions.

First are the 'yardstick competition effects' discussed above at note 11.

Second, though yardstick efficiency depends on the basic environmental (i.e. non-managerial) factors determining profits within an industry being highly correlated across firms (since this is what allows managerial performance to be compared), product market competition may also yield efficiencies when the firms within an industry differ in important respects. In particular, if firms are viewed as taking bets on particular ways of doing things, having a greater number of firms in a market will, all other things being equal, accelerate the rate at which the most efficient approaches are discovered by managers, owners and regulators. to the extent to which there are spill-over effects (that is, the firms in an industry can learn from each other, for example through the yardstick effects of benchmarking), learning will increase efficiency not only in the innovating firm but also across the firm population as a whole. This mechanism, which is similar to the notion that one should 'let a thousand flowers bloom', can be referred to as increasing 'sampling efficiency'.

Third and last, increased product market competition will alter the process by which inefficient firms are 'weeded out' and efficient firms rewarded. The presumption here is that firms are indeed asymmetric, and that superior performance cannot be costlessly imitated. Stronger product market competition is then presumed to result in the more rapid and complete sorting of firms into distinct performance classes, with the less productive firms being forced to exit the market. The most natural route through which this Darwinian process occurs is the reduction in price-cost margins brought by increased competition, since this will make it more difficult for inefficient firms to survive. At the same time, regulators, now better able to compare performance, are not likely to continue protecting inefficient firms, while potential investors and employees, mindful of the costs of poor performance, will be less willing to supply capital and labour to the firms least likely to survive. As a result, inefficient firms will face tighter price and cost constraints, making their continued existence less likely.

Given these sources of greater efficiency, competition may increase welfare, even in industries where there are substantial economies of scale (bearing in mind that in these industries, free entry would – in the absence of the mechanisms described above – usually lead to wasteful duplication of investment). See J. Vicker, *Concepts of Competition*, 1994.

33 Alfred Kahn, *The Economics of Regulation: Principles and Institutions*, 1970, vol I, p. 150.

34 Economists' critiques of FDC include A. Kahn, *ibid.*; R. Braeutigam, 'An analysis of fully distributed cost pricing in regulated industries', *Bell Journal of Economics*, 1980, vol. 11, p. 182; J. C. Bonbright *et al.*, *Principles of Public Utility Rates* (2nd edn), 1988; and B. Mitchell and I. Vogelsang, *Telecommunications Pricing: Theory and Practice*, 1991. Criticisms by accountants include K. B. Monroe, *Pricing: Making Profitable Decisions*, 1979; and R. Cooper and R. Kaplan, 'Measure costs right: Make the right decisions', *Harvard Business Review*, 1988.

35 See, for example, the survey results presented in S. Ramadan 'The rationale for cost allocation: A study of UK divisionalized companies', *Accounting and Business Research*, 1989, vol. 20, p. 31.

36 The term reflects the formal setting out of the rule in R. D. Willig, 'The theory of network access pricing', in H. Trebing (ed.), *Issues in Public Utility Regulation*, 1979, p. 109; and W. J. Baumol and G. Sidak, *Towards Competition in Local Telephony*, 1974.

37 *United States v. Aluminium Company of America et al.*, 1945 *Trade Regulation Reports* (57,342), 57,689–91, F. 2d. 416, 436–8.

38 For example, in *Napier Brown v. British Sugar*, OJ (1988) L 284/41, (1990) 4 CMLR 196, the ECJ found that 'a dominant firm has an obligation to fix its prices at such a level that a reasonably efficient competitor on the derivatives (downstream) market is able to survive'. UK and EC precedents are discussed in R. Whish, *Competition Law*, (3rd edn), 1993, p. 532.

8

REGULATION, COMPETITION POLICY AND MARKET ACCESS NEGOTIATIONS

Lessons from the telecommunications sector

Bernard Hoekman, Patrick Low and Petros C. Mavroidis

Introduction

The current debate on the merits of seeking international agreement on competition policies has revealed a wide spectrum of views. They range from those who would design a blueprint for comprehensive multilateral rules on competition to those who doubt the utility of doing very much in this sphere at the international level, at least until traditional trade and investment barriers imposed by governments have yielded to a more fully integrated world economy. This paper examines the case for multilateral rules on competition in the light of recent initiatives to incorporate certain regulatory principles into multilateral commitments undertaken in the context of the negotiations on basic telecommunications under the auspices of the World Trade Organization (WTO).

Telecommunications is of interest in this connection because it is an industry where there is great scope for the application of pro-competitive policies. Telecommunications markets are frequently characterized by dominant suppliers that control bottleneck or essential facilities. Negotiators therefore sought agreement on principles covering such matters as interconnection obligations and competition safeguards. These principles were negotiated in recognition of the fact that private dominant players in the telecoms market, left free to make decisions about how to treat other suppliers, would be capable of frustrating the market access and national treatment commitments made by governments in the negotiations. Some thirty governments are likely to adopt the principles when the results of the telecom negotiations enter into force.

In principle, there are two approaches that can be taken: one based on anti-trust or competition law, the other on sector-specific regulation. Competition policy refers to general laws, applicable on an economy-wide basis, which aim to maintain competitive conditions in markets. Regulation, on the other hand, is more sector-specific, comprising measures whose primary focus is to constrain anti-competitive behaviour arising from the presence of dominant suppliers in the market. While competition or antitrust laws may be brought to bear in any sector where a firm seeks to abuse a market position, or where mergers or acquisitions threaten to give rise to excessive market concentration, an industry-specific regulatory framework is tailor-made through *ex ante* restraints and requirements to promote competition in the face of market dominance arising from control over bottleneck facilities. Industries that are subject to regulation are assumed at the outset to lack the necessary structure to ensure competition. In contrast to competition policy, there is nothing contingent in the application of the regulatory framework.

Negotiators in the WTO telecom talks decided to agree to regulatory principles, not a competition policy framework. This reflects the sector-specificity of the negotiations as well as the fact that government influence over telecom operators is often prevalent. The same preference for regulation is likely to occur in other sectors where competition is often limited, such as air and maritime transport or medical and distribution services. Many of the industries where competition may remain effectively restricted even if the government withdraws exclusive rights are service industries, and the General Agreement on Trade in Services (GATS) is therefore likely to become an important forum for discussion of antitrust-type issues. The basic telecom talks suggest that governments may have a preference for regulation and regulatory commitments instead of the pursuit of more generic antitrust disciplines at the multilateral level. The wider the sectoral ambit of such regulatory commitments, the less pressing the perceived 'need' for multi-lateral antitrust rules may be.

The plan of the paper is as follows. It first briefly revisits the continuing debate about the merits of developing international competition rules, and argues in cases where anti-competitive outcomes are attributable to government policies, the justification for applying antitrust rules is weak, as market distortions should be addressed at source. It then examines telecoms policy in the European Union, as the EU represents the foremost attempt involving sovereign states to liberalize access to markets for goods and services with network characteristics. The EU has shown a preference for sector-specific regulation in telecoms, notwithstanding the existence of general antitrust laws. The paper goes on to discuss some of the potential problems that may arise as a result of a regulatory approach, before examining the implications of internationalizing regulatory commitments. The paper then explores some of the lessons that can be drawn from the WTO negotiations to date, before concluding.

Trade and competition

The case for negotiating multilateral disciplines on competition (antitrust) rules, and the scope of any such rules, have become the subject of some debate.[1] A number of prominent commentators have called for such efforts, reflecting a perception that active enforcement of multilateral antitrust rules is necessary to ensure that foreign firms are able to contest markets.[2] This advocacy has influenced policy-makers, some of whom now take a position in favour of a world-wide negotiation on trade and competition. The EU has recently published a report (prepared by a Group of Experts) supportive of an initiative of this nature.[3] This report to a large extent reproduces opinions already expressed in the literature. The basic grounds advanced for mandating multilateral action essentially deal with negative international spillovers, unfair advantages for firms that benefit from lax enforcement of domestic antitrust laws, problems created by extraterritorial application of laws, and the need to protect developing countries, which because of their limited bargaining power can be particularly harmed by anti-competitive practices.

It is generally recognized that there is a great deal of diversity across countries with respect to competition legislation and enforcement. This greatly complicates any effort to establish unified rules on competition at the multilateral level.[4] So too do the clear differences of opinion that exist regarding the relative importance of different policies in promoting competitive market conditions. The relationship between international competition policy and international trade and investment policy is particularly relevant here.

Most of the discussion on trade and competition has been rather general and conceptual, and proponents of common competition rules at the multilateral level have been confronted with a number of arguments advanced by sceptics. Some of the doubts raised can be summarized as follows:

1   Common competition rules should not be a priority because there is little empirical evidence that negotiating such rules is important. Finger and Fung examined US 'Section 301' investigations initiated upon complaints by private companies,[5] and found only one out of the dozens of cases that had been filed over the years in which a positive '301' determination was based on the existence of anti-competitive practices.[6]

2   Governments have not fully exploited the existing multilateral trade regime. Hoekman and Mavroidis argue that many anti-competitive practices can be attacked through violation complaints (to the extent that they can be attributed to government policies that violate GATT rules) or non-violation 'nullification' complaints (insofar as GATT-legal policies nullify reasonable expectations).[7] Some of the concerns of the EU Group of Experts could be met by enforcing the existing regime.

3   Certain important market access restricting policies are not yet covered by the WTO. Low and Subramanian,[8] for example, have discussed the role of investment liberalization in rendering non-tradable sectors more competitive. Clearly, if establishment by foreign firms is prohibited, competition rules will do little.

4   Much can be achieved by means of bilateral cooperation in the antitrust field among competent national authorities.[9]

5   Problems arising from the extraterritorial application of antitrust laws are best subjected to the International Court of Justice to determine the legitimate reach of domestic jurisdictions.

Proponents of multilateral competition rules may agree with some or all of these points, but nevertheless argue that a properly designed set of multilateral rules would contribute to the continuing development of open markets. To a degree, the differences in the debate may be a matter of emphasis, rather than fundamental disagreement. In any event, the discussion can only be advanced by focusing on the specifics of the issues, and the basic telecoms negotiations offer one such opportunity.

The potential relevance of antitrust disciplines in basic telecommunications is clear; these tend to be industries where competition is often limited. Once basic telecommunications was on the negotiating table at the WTO, negotiators had to decide how, if at all, to deal multilaterally with those determinants of market access attributable to firm behaviour which normal GATT/WTO market access and national treatment commitments were unable to reach.[10] Broadly, three options suggest themselves. First, the 'harmonization' approach would involve agreement on uniform substantive rules at the multilateral level. These may be of two types: generic antitrust-type rules, and sector-specific regulation. Second, the 'procedural obligations' approach would require governments to accept a multilateral obligation to enforce their own rules (both antitrust and regulatory), without any requirement to make changes in substantive or procedural requirements at the national level. Third, the 'do nothing' approach would require that negotiators restrict themselves to market access and national treatment commitments, thus relying (implicitly or explicitly) on independent national regulatory interventions and/or on market forces to ensure that markets are contestable.

The harmonization approach has the advantage of guaranteeing legal security, but agreement may be difficult to obtain. The procedural obligations approach presupposes provisional acceptance by WTO members of each country's national regulatory or competition framework. The 'do nothing' approach assumes either that national regulatory or competition frameworks are acceptable and will be appropriately enforced, or that the degree to which the relevant market can be contested is sufficient for aspiring entrants. In the event, the harmonization approach was selected by WTO negotiators. It was constrained harmonization, in that not all the WTO membership intends to subscribe to the negotiated disciplines, and certain modifications will be made by some parties to the common text on regulatory principles that has been negotiated. Moreover, the disciplines that were negotiated are regulatory in nature; they do not entail commitments on enforcement of antitrust disciplines.

To a large extent, the same choices confronting negotiators in the GATS setting were faced by the European Community in its attempts to open EU telecoms markets. The EU differs from the GATS negotiations in that there is a framework of common competition rules that applies to undertakings operating in the internal EU market. The EU experience may therefore shed some light on the issue of whether the GATS approach – regulatory commitments – is second best. That is, did negotiators agree to regulatory commitments because common antitrust disciplines do not exist and clearly could not be developed in the context of a sector-specific negotiation? The EU experience suggests this is not the case. In part this is simply because telecom operators may be exempt from antitrust. More interestingly, recent decisions by the Community institutions suggest that even in a situation where exclusive rights are steadily being eroded through competition, governments prefer to continue to rely on regulation.

The EU experience

A number of phases can be distinguished in EC telecom policy.

1957–87 Telecoms were essentially outside the reach of the EC. After 1984 some EC action programmes were launched, focusing on R&D and regional development.

1987–92 The Commission launched its Green Paper setting out a common framework for the future development and liberalization of the EC telecom market. Directives on the implementation of open network provisions and value added services were among the most important legislative acts. In 1991 the Commission issued its 'Guidelines on the Application of the EEC Competition Rules in the Telecommunications Sector', setting out its opinion on the reach of competition law in telecoms. Telecom services began to be progressively liberalized, together with terminal equipment trade (in part through the adoption of mutual recognition of equipment testing). In April 1988, the European Telecommunications Standards Institute (ETSI) was established to create common standards for telecoms networks to enable pan-European interconnection.

1992–8 Following a Commission review of telecom services, a political agreement was reached to fully liberalize all services and infrastructure, including voice telephony (which had remained an exclusive monopoly right

119

in most member states), by 1 January 1998. The Commission assumed the responsibility to prepare proposals necessary for the development of the regulatory framework. As of 1996 most mobile voice telephony standards were already liberalized at EC level (Directive 96/2 EC).[11]

1998 Full liberalization of the EC telecoms market is to be attained by the end of 1997. Some EC member states have already liberalized voice telephony (e.g., UK, Sweden) or plan to do so before 1998 (e.g., Netherlands in 1997).

The reach of EU competition policy

The competition disciplines of the EU are contained in Articles 85–94 of the European Community Treaty (ECT). Of particular relevance to telecommunications is the relationship between disciplines pertaining to private firms and those that are publicly owned or granted special or exclusive rights. In principle, the latter are subject to EU competition rules, unless this would obstruct the performance of the services supplied by companies holding special or exclusive rights, which have to be of 'general economic interest'.[12] In practice, most telecom suppliers in the EU have historically been public sector monopolies. For a long time, it was perceived that the EC legal system was neutral with respect to property ownership in EC member states. Article 222 ECT explicitly states that: 'This Treaty shall in no way prejudice the rules of the Member States governing the system of property ownership.'[13] By the same token, although Article 37 ECT calls for adjustment of state monopolies so as to eliminate possible discrimination between nationals of member states, it does not require elimination of such monopolies, thus implicitly recognizing their legitimacy. On the other hand, Article 5 ECT requires member states not to take any action that might frustrate the attainment of the objectives assigned to the ECT, including those espoused in Articles 85 and 86 ECT (the EC competition rules). Hence, the tension between regulated service monopolies that can, in principle, operate beyond the reach of EC competition laws (Article 90 ECT) and the obligation of member states not to frustrate the objectives of the ECT (including those on competition).

Over time, there has been some encroachment on the freedom of member states regarding public ownership. The Treaty on Economic Union (TEU) states:

> the activities of the Members States and the Community shall include . . . the adoption of an economic policy which is based on the close coordination of Member States' economic policies, on the internal market and on the definition of common objectives, and conducted in accordance with the principle of an open market economy with free competition.[14]

Article 3 TEU is part of the 'principles' of the Treaty so that the obligations imposed in the main body of the TEU have to be interpreted against this background. Gardner[15] concludes that 'the neutrality towards public and privileged enterprises in the text of the Treaty of Rome as signed in 1957 has now been supplanted by a presumption of illegality'.[16]

Recent ECJ case law on Article 90 ECT illustrates the rising challenge to state ownership.[17] In the early case law in this field, the ECJ essentially attacked the 'abusive' exercise of special or exclusive rights. More recent case law suggests that even the mere existence of a monopoly can constitute abuse of dominant position and thus violate the ECT.[18] Indeed, the ECJ appears to have set limits regarding the permissible extent of regulated monopolies. This is crucial, because it automatically defines the extent to which such undertakings are subject to the EC competition laws (Articles 85–6). In *Corbeau*, the ECJ was presented with the case of Paul Corbeau, who provided delivery services in the city of Liege, Belgium. He specialized in rapid delivery (within one day). It was alleged that this interfered with the monopoly of the Belgian Régie des Postes and proceedings against Mr Corbeau were instituted in the competent Belgian court. The ECJ, to which the case was submitted by the Belgian court, concluded that:

> It is contrary to Article 90 of the EEC Treaty for a legislation of a Member State which confers on a body such as the Régie des Postes the exclusive right to collect, carry and distribute mail, to prohibit, under threat of criminal penalties, an economic operator established in that State from offering certain specific services dissociable from the service operated of general interest which meet the special needs of economic operators and call for certain additional services not offered by the traditional postal service, in so far as those services do not compromise the economic stability of the service of general economic interest performed by the holder of the exclusive right. It is for the national court to consider whether the services in question in the main proceedings meet those criteria.[19]

An overall appraisal of the ECJ case law in this field suggests that (i) 'immunization' against EC competition laws must be *necessary* to ensure performance of the tasks entrusted to the exclusive service provider (which must serve the general economic interest); and (ii) the entity must satisfy market demand. Thus, it appears as if the recent ECJ case law acknowledges the primacy of competition law. It is against this background that the non-economic reasons advanced in support of entry restrictions in the telecoms market, such as the need to ensure universal service, should be evaluated.

Turning to private (privatized) telecom markets, the most often cited arguments against the adequacy of EC competition laws to address problems that might occur relate to access to 'bottleneck' infrastructure. In principle,

Article 86 ECT and the well-established case law on refusal to deal applies. Of particular relevance to the telecoms market is the doctrine of essential facilities.[20] According to the ECJ case law, four conditions have to be met for the doctrine to apply: (i) a refusal to supply a downstream competitor; (ii) the 'bottleneck' does not require all capacity for own use; (iii) no other justification for refusal to deal has been offered; (iv) a handicap is created as a result of the refusal. US case law on the doctrine of essential facilities follows a similar path. In a recent case, the competent US court, reproducing previous case law, stated the elements of the essential facilities doctrine, namely (i) control of the essential facility by the monopolist, (ii) a competitor's inability practically or reasonably to duplicate the essential facility, (iii) the denial of the use of the facility to a competitor and (iv) the feasibility of providing the facility to competitors. The court noted that denial of access should not simply cause inconvenience, but rather should impose a severe handicap that threatens to eliminate competition in the downstream market.[21] This doctrine seems particularly appropriate to deal with anti-competitive practices by privatized state 'giants', as refusal to grant access to networks by such entities (interconnection) can be addressed. This includes abusive clauses concerning the bundle of services on offer, dialling parity, etc.[22]

Thus, the reach of EU competition enforcement in disciplining dominant telecom suppliers is significant. However, although the ECJ has been becoming more pro-active, it has not gone very far in seeking to 'de-monopolize' markets. There is no comparison with what the Department of Justice in the US undertook in the telecom sector in the early 1980s. Any action in this direction on the part of the ECJ has been limited to niche markets at the periphery of monopolies. This suggests that reliance on antitrust disciplines in the multilateral WTO context would be even less of an option. Notwithstanding the fact that common competition laws could in principle address anti-competitive practices by telecom operators, EC member states decided to go for industry-specific regulation as well. For example, the directive on open network provisions requires national regulators of member states to ensure that operators of public telecoms networks which have exclusive or special rights do not restrict access to the network, except for reasons based on essential requirements (that is, security of network operations, maintenance of network integrity, inter-operability of services where justified, and data protection).

The belief that sector-specific regulation in telecoms, enforced by national regulatory authorities, must complement mainstream antitrust rules to safeguard competition in newly liberalized markets is not limited to the EU. A similar view underlies the US approach to regulation in this sector, and for that matter, the approach of many other governments. A few countries such as New Zealand have emphasized recourse to general statutes dealing with competition and consumer protection.[23] Some authors have criticized

New Zealand's approach on the grounds that these broad-based laws are inadequate to the task.[24]

It is difficult to say how much sector-specific regulation is required, or for how long. Part of the reason why a regulatory approach is favoured in so many countries is that telecoms is still regarded as a sector in which governments have public policy obligations, most notably in respect of universal service, even where the state no longer retains direct economic interests or a direct responsibility to deliver telecommunication services. Additionally, the history of government involvement in telecoms, entailing the maintenance of monopoly service providers owned by the state, has rendered governments at least in part responsible for the predominance of single suppliers in so many telecommunication markets world-wide. These arguments apply in similar fashion to other deregulated (and privatized) utilities, such as gas, postal services, electricity and water supply.

What, precisely, does the regulatory approach offer that is unavailable through reliance on mainstream competition principles? Four elements suggest themselves. First, sector-specific regulations can address complex details in a manner that general competition rules cannot. The complexity of the telecommunications sector is undeniable and is reflected, for example, in the myriad ways in which market incumbents can frustrate new entrants. In the EU context, courts, whether national or the ECJ, were considered ill-suited to address complex issues such as effective interconnection without a clear point of reference. Second, a regulatory approach can accommodate multiple objectives that could not otherwise be combined. For example, governments can aim through regulation simultaneously to lower prices to consumers by forcing suppliers to be more efficient, promote competition through facilitating market entry, and aim for universal service. The pursuit of these different objectives may in practice create a number of contradictions calling for trade-offs, but the main point is that the pursuit of multiple objectives in this manner is not an option under mainstream competition policy.

Third, the establishment of specific regulations defines detailed *ex ante* rights and obligations in a manner that more general pro-competitive principles may not. A regulation that imposes an interconnection obligation upon a dominant supplier, for example, may also define the terms and conditions under which interconnection should be offered. By contrast, a broad-based competition law may not go much further than establishing a general prohibition against a 'refusal to deal' and market foreclosure. In the event of a dispute between an incumbent and a new entrant over inter-connection, a detailed regulatory framework is obviously advantageous to the new entrant, and to some extent involves a shift in the burden of proof in favour of the latter. In the case of regulatory disciplines, plaintiffs only need to demonstrate violations (such as a refusal to deal by incumbents) without having to show why this contravenes competition rules.

Fourth, there is the temporal dimension. The administration of commercial relationships through regulation is likely to entail far shorter time-lags than due legal process through the courts. Suppliers and potential suppliers will be able to make more rapid use of policy-created opportunities for market access. In sum, compared to mainstream antitrust law, sector-specific regulation accommodates a multiplicity of policy objectives, reduces complexity, makes the policy environment more predictable, and offers a relatively rapid resolution of any conflicts arising between suppliers.

Regulation: potential problems

The risks associated with sector-specific regulation can be significant. First, even in the best of circumstances, the efforts of a regulator to perform the function of markets is a hazardous business, given imperfect information. Second, public choice analysis has shown how readily regulatory capture can occur. The closer and more specific the interaction between regulators and the regulated, the greater the degree to which the overarching regulatory objectives of promoting efficiency and protecting consumer welfare may be in jeopardy. On the other hand, manipulation of the regulator may not only be the prerogative of market incumbents – potential market entrants in whose favour a regulatory structure is often skewed can also play the regulatory game to their own advantage. The problem of how and how much to regulate is in essence no different from any other judgement forced upon governments when they intervene in markets.

The dangers of regulatory subversion make the institutional setting in which regulation is carried out of considerable importance.[25] Various institutional approaches aimed at underwriting regulatory independence can be identified in telecommunications.[26] The Federal Communications Commission in the US is set up as an independent agency with defined powers through which it endeavours to balance the interests of suppliers in relation to consumers, and among suppliers. In other countries, regulatory authority has been shared with the executive branch of government, and executed via political directives. A more recently established regulatory approach adopted, for example, in the case of OFTEL in the UK and AUSTEL in Australia, involves the regulatory authorities in a continuing relationship with the mainstream competition authorities.

Assuming that the case is accepted for a pro-competitive regulatory approach after a government has withdrawn monopoly or exclusive privileges from telecom operators and permitted free entry by new suppliers, a fundamental question remains about the degree of permanence of regulation. Is regulation to be seen as a transitory phenomenon aimed at facilitating the advent of market forces, or as an essential ongoing requirement for ensuring a competitive outcome in the market? The answer to this question comes in two parts, one relating to the degree of intrinsic contestability of telecoms markets, and the other to regulatory objectives that are additional to the promotion of competition. Technological advances have ensured that natural monopoly arguments no longer provide a rational basis for restricting entry,[27] and by the same token entry should promote market-based competition. While network externalities continue to exist, a restrictive policy towards market entry has ceased to be necessary for their realization. All that is required is interconnection on commercial terms between networks.

At the same time, alternative investments in telecommunications infrastructure can enhance competition. Once governments allow basic telecoms services to be supplied by whatever alternative means are available – such as radio-based as opposed to wire-based services, cable for television, and the infrastructural facilities of utilities (e.g. electricity companies and railways) – interconnection with existing networks ceases to be the only means of market access. Indeed, the possibility of market entry via alternative infrastructure is important if governments intend to allow regulation to be gradually substituted by mainstream antitrust authority. If interconnection with existing facilities remains the only vehicle for market entry, regulation will tend to persist, as the number of suppliers able to offer interconnection possibilities will be fewer. In practice, many countries are encouraging market entry through alternative networks, especially in satellite and terrestrial radio-based services. Local telephone network competition is also beginning to emerge.[28]

Even where a regulator is genuinely committed to creating the conditions under which it will be possible to cede authority to the market, this objective can be frustrated. This problem refers to the dual role of a regulator, and illustrates the inherent inferiority of regulation compared to a market-based solution. On the one hand, the regulator seeks to impose operating efficiency upon incumbents in order to protect consumer interests. While this used to be done through cost-plus approaches or rates of return calculations, the use of price caps has increasingly been the preferred approach. Whatever the approach, if these restraints on the operating environment of an incumbent are sufficiently rigid, they can lead to a situation where the operator becomes so efficient that entry is not profitable. It has been argued that this tendency has emerged in the UK, where price-cap regulation has made it difficult for prospective entrants to compete on price with British Telecom, the dominant supplier.[29] If this situation occurs, it becomes difficult for the regulator to pursue his other role, that of promoting competition through diversification of the sources of supply. In the absence of new entrants, the regulator remains the only bulwark against the monopolistic abuse of market power by a dominant supplier. In these circumstances, regulation can become a permanent feature in a sector where scope for making the market contestable clearly exists, and where the regulatory approach should ideally play a transitory role in establishing a competitive environment driven by the market.

Is this an inescapable paradox, such that overzealous regulation that maximizes consumer welfare also sets the scene for a sub-optimal outcome in the longer-term, involving the permanence of regulatory oversight? It would indeed be awkward to argue that in order to prepare the ground for regulatory withdrawal, the regulator should show indulgence towards incumbents, allowing them to generate economic rents that will in turn induce new suppliers to enter the market. An alternative is to emphasize the statutory break-up of former monopolies into separate operating entities at the time that de-monopolization or market opening occurs. This is what happened in the case of AT&T in the US,[30] but was not the chosen course of action with respect to British Telecom in the UK. Another approach, currently being attempted by Chile, is to limit the permissible market share of dominant suppliers on a transitionary basis, with the objective of establishing more than one supplier of significant size in the market.

The rationale for attempting to influence the structure of the market through direct means may reasonably be seen as an implicit expression of doubt as to the ability of a regulator simultaneously to both change the structure of the market and promote the welfare of consumers. By the same token, it may also be argued by those favouring direct intervention to influence market structure that following withdrawal from the market by the regulator, mainstream competition policy remedies prove inadequate to address anti-competitive behaviour by a dominant supplier. Perhaps the way this issue has been addressed in different jurisdictions reflects underlying policy predilections in the field of competition. It is well known, for example, that historically, the US has shown a greater willingness to break up monopolies or oppose mergers via antitrust actions than European countries. By the same token, the Europeans would seem to have placed more confidence in the ability of regulators to redress market failure, especially if the failure can be characterized as a transient phenomenon. As noted in the previous section, antitrust interventions by the ECJ impinging on questions of market structure have generally not gone further than somewhat peripheral challenges to market dominance where this can clearly be shown to be disadvantageous to consumers.

Whatever position is taken on whether to emphasize market structure by attacking it directly at the outset, rather than allowing new market structures to evolve through judicious regulation, in the final analysis the difference may only be of a temporal nature. Alternative means of contesting markets in which dominant suppliers maintain advantageous positions will become increasingly viable as new technologies come on stream. At the same time, governments are increasingly allowing suppliers from other sectors (cable television, railways, etc.) who already possess significant infrastructure to enter the market. The need for regulation may well persist longer if potential competitors of comparable size grow gradually, rather than being forced into existence via mandated structural reform at the time of de-monopolization. But the outcome should eventually be the same.

It should always be remembered, however, that telecoms is an unusual industry. In the absence of parallel infrastructure and multiple interconnection options offered by firms capable of competing among themselves, the role of the regulator in facilitating new entry is, in a sense, to prevail upon dominant suppliers to cooperate, if not in their own demise, then at least in lowering their profits. It is this element of forced cooperation via the granting by dominant incumbent suppliers of competitively priced interconnection rights that confers such a vital and challenging role upon regulatory authorities. And it is the very nature of this regulatory intervention that makes changes in market structure so important in ensuring a competitive outcome in the absence of regulatory intervention.

Independently of the degree of success that regulation may achieve in creating competitive market conditions, some objectives of regulation may dictate that the regulatory approach will have certain permanence. The most obvious case where this might occur in telecoms is if a government subscribes to a universal service objective. In these circumstances, it is not so much the longevity of regulation that is a matter for concern, but rather the efficiency of the chosen intervention. Standard economic theory suggests that market failures, such as the non-provision of distant subscribers if full costs are charged, is best addressed through targeted subsidies financed through general taxation. It is unnecessary to oblige suppliers to cross-subsidize between groups of consumers – suppliers can be compensated directly for the cost of providing universal service at reasonable rates. This approach does not distort markets, nor support arguments for restricting market entry in the name of universal service.

Possible implications of internationalizing the regulatory approach

Three important implications of internationalizing a regulatory regime deserve mention. First, if governments agree to create mutual obligations to enforce a given set of regulatory principles, they tie themselves into an established pattern of regulation and a common right to challenge one another through multilateral dispute settlement on grounds of non-compliance. While this approach may be appealing for governments as they open up market access to one another on a broadly reciprocal basis, it also has the potential drawback of locking in a uniform approach in circumstances that might be quite different among countries.

To some extent, this problem can be accommodated through the design of the regulatory principles, such that they cease to apply when a certain threshold of diversification has occurred in relation to the sources of supply available in the market.[31] An example is the decision taken in the US by the Federal Communications Commission to the effect that AT&T was no longer a dominant supplier in the US domestic long-distance market. This decision was predicated on the finding that sufficient competition existed in that market to permit the regulator to withdraw, leaving mainstream antitrust remedies as the instrument for dealing with any anti-competitive behaviour that might occur.[32] Even if the applicability of regulatory principles can be conditioned by the definition of covered entities, such that regulation recedes as markets begin to assert their own influence, multilateral uniformity may still in some circumstances impose a policy straightjacket that produces a sub-optimal degree of regulatory intervention. In other words, the regulatory authorities, or the governments to whom they are ultimately responsible, could find that multilateral commitments make regulatory forbearance harder in circumstances where it might seem desirable.

A second implication of multilateralizing sector-specific regulation is that the life span of desirable regulation may be pre-judged. Unless governments consider that competitive market conditions can never be created in basic telecoms – which is not a view that would seem to be widely shared – regulatory authorities will increasingly find themselves in a situation where they wish to forebear in matters of regulation, or eliminate aspects of regulation altogether. Will uniform and open-ended regulatory commitments adopted at the multilateral level frustrate this objective? The potential for such a conflict to arise is obviated to some degree by built-in definitions limiting the coverage of regulations to particular market situations. And awareness that these difficulties may arise should ensure the appropriate design of multilateral commitments.

The third and by far most noteworthy aspect of multilateralized regulatory principles deserving mention is the risk that regulatory interventions putatively designed to promote competition instead become a vehicle primarily for securing market access advantages, and only in a secondary sense concerned with protecting competition. The basic objective of trade policy officials in putting competition policy enforcement on the negotiating agenda has to do with the realization of 'legitimate expectations' associated with negotiated trade barrier reductions (i.e. with private practices that may 'nullify or impair' market access commitments undertaken by governments). The actual state of competition in a particular market may not be of concern in this connection.[33] After all, negotiated liberalization commitments will not necessarily lead to greater sales by foreign firms. For example, if a market is extremely competitive, entry will be difficult no matter what the public policy stance vis-à-vis foreign firms. It has been argued that many Japanese markets are so competitive that long-run profit margins are simply too low to attract foreign competition.[34] If there are high fixed costs of entry, or significant exit costs, entry also may not be profitable. Whatever the case may be for a particular market, the state of domestic competition and technological factors such as economies of scale are important in determining whether market access is restricted.

The domestic welfare concern that there may be natural monopolies or very large sunk costs involved in contesting a market, providing the rationale for the government to regulate the industry, will be irrelevant to foreign firms (potential suppliers), as the market is simply not contestable. Of course, technological change will gradually allow previously 'natural monopoly' markets to become contestable – telecommunications is a prime example. Regardless of how quickly this happens, however, the policy issue for foreign firms is to induce the relevant government to allow entry.

In sum, it is important to recognize that mainstream antitrust and regulatory approaches may differ in their fundamental objectives at the international level. Regulatory commitments certainly may lead to greater competition, but in the multilateral setting they are more likely to be oriented toward 'guaranteeing' negotiated market access concessions; antitrust enforcement is instead focused on competition *per se* and is nationality blind. Of course, it must also be recognized that antitrust laws and their enforcement may reflect multiple objectives, including industrial policy considerations. Indeed, differences in the approach to antitrust policy across countries is one of the reasons why agreeing on substantive multilateral antitrust rules may be difficult. It is also true that antitrust authorities may be subject to the similar problems of capture and political influence as other types of regulators.[35]

Two key points underlie the discussion of these last two sections. First, regulation in the telecoms sector is best seen as a fundamentally transient phenomenon. The argument is that new suppliers entering the market via interconnection with existing networks or via the creation of new infrastructure will ensure after an initial period that the market is competitive. The regulator will be able to withdraw. Second, an international agreement involving the liberalization of telecoms markets needs to be supplemented by regulatory undertakings, otherwise the market access and national treatment commitments made by governments may be nullified by anti-competitive behaviour on the part of dominant suppliers. An important question remains. If regulation is a transient phenomenon and is to involve international commitments, does this mean that when mainstream competition policy takes over from regulation, there will also be a need for international competition policy? In other words, where does the case for multilateral agreement on a transitional set of regulatory disciplines leave the case against multilateral competition policy?

This paper argues that multilateral competition rules only make sense in circumstances where anti-competitive behaviour is to be found in private sector action made possible by a concentrated market structure, as opposed to being rooted in or sustained by government policy. Other considerations that would weigh in the determination of whether to seek to establish common antitrust rules among countries as a matter of priority include: (i) the empirical question of how pervasive anti-competitive practices frustrating market entry are at the international level; and (ii) how far it is possible to deal with international spill-overs involving the control of anti-competitive private sector behaviour through comity-based cooperative arrangements among national competition authorities. Thus, if a regulatory regime in telecoms is successful in ensuring competitive market conditions once the transition from monopolistic supply is complete, the arguments for and against common multilateral antitrust rules are no different from those applying to most other sectors.

What matters from a narrowly pragmatic perspective is that regulatory commitments are likely to be necessary for quite some time to come, implying that as far as telecoms are concerned, common antitrust rules are not a priority for governments. Indeed, by putting the main burden on regulation the need for discussing antitrust automatically is reduced. In so far as the same pattern is likely to emerge in other sectors where competition is restricted and where negotiating attention is likely to focus in the years to come – such as air and maritime transport – the regulatory approach may to a large extent 'crowd out' more general attempts to pursue an antitrust agenda.

The WTO negotiations on telecommunications

The negotiations on basic telecommunications were not completed by the time the Uruguay Round drew to a close in December 1993, and rather than leave the issue aside, governments agreed to continue negotiating. It became increasingly apparent to those engaged in the negotiations that if they limited themselves to the traditional approach of scheduling commitments on market access and national treatment, they would not be able to guarantee much multilaterally by way of liberalization commitments that would translate into effective access to market.[36] The removal of government-inspired entry barriers is clearly a necessary condition of access, but such action would have little impact in the face of non-governmental barriers based on the ability of incumbents to frustrate market entry. Thus, a significant component of the extended negotiations involved a search for a set of multilaterally acceptable regulatory principles that would be enforceable through WTO dispute settlement procedures.

Competition policy-related issues arising in the basic telecommunications negotiations concerned interconnection, market conduct safeguards, and transparency. To a degree, these issues had already been touched upon in the Annex on Basic Telecommunications negotiated in the Uruguay Round and in the GATS itself.[37] It had become apparent as the Uruguay Round negotiations on services proceeded that governments saw telecommunications as special because of their importance in the supply of many other services. Without access to telecom services, many other services cannot be delivered, making specific commitments in relation to the latter of dubious value. Thus, paragraph 5(a) of the Annex states that:

130

each Member shall ensure that any service supplier of any other
Member is accorded access to and use of public telecommunications
transport networks and services on reasonable and non-discriminatory
terms and conditions for the supply of a service included in its
Schedule.[38]

Suppliers of such services are entitled to access to and use of any public
telecommunications transport network or service offered within or across the
border, including private leased circuits, the right to purchase or lease and
attach terminal or other equipment to the network, and to interconnect
private leased or owned circuits with public telecommunications transport
networks and services, or with circuits leased or owned by another service
supplier. These rights are qualified by the right of the entity owning and/or
controlling the network to impose conditions on access and use in order to
safeguard public service responsibilities, protect the technical integrity of the
networks or services, and to restrict network use where this is not required
pursuant to a scheduled commitment. The obligations of the Annex extend
not only to service suppliers in other sectors, but also to those in the telecommunications sector who would compete with incumbent network
operators.[39]

Some negotiators felt that the Annex commitments were too general to
guarantee new entrants adequate opportunity to compete. Proposals were
made to define interconnection rights more specifically, including in terms
of timeliness, cost-based pricing and 'unbundling',[40] and these were among
the issues taken up in the subsequent discussions on regulatory principles.
Market conduct safeguards were also sought to ensure that suppliers with
market power (dominant suppliers or those controlling essential bottleneck
facilities) refrain from a range of anti-competitive practices, including
cross-subsidization from more to less profitable segments of the market and
misuse of commercially valuable information. Finally, transparency requirements were sought in order to ensure the availability of all information
necessary for prompt and trouble-free interconnection.

The discussion of regulatory principles in the WTO negotiations revealed
a preference among governments for a sector-specific approach over a more
horizontal approach based on general rules. In part, this choice was undoubtedly made on pragmatic grounds, as the general disciplines in GATS relating
to competition are not well developed.[41] Moreover, the competition policy
option is by its nature general, not sector-specific. General competition
disciplines applying to all sectors would entail the kinds of problems referred
to above in the more general discussion of the case for internationalizing
competition policy. Agreement on such provisions would not come easily,
and certainly not soon enough to accommodate the specific interests of
governments in liberalizing trade in basic telecommunication services. Some
thirty governments made preliminary commitments to apply the regulatory

131

principles, pending confirmation and completion of the negotiations in February 1997. There are six main principles: competitive safeguards to prevent anti-competitive practices in telecommunications; interconnection; the right to require universal service; public availability of licensing criteria; establishment of independent regulatory bodies; and the use of objective, transparent and non-discriminatory allocation procedures for scarce resources such as frequency, numbers, and rights of way.[42]

During most of the extended negotiations, regulatory principles were discussed exclusively in terms of protecting the interests of new market entrants against possible abuse of dominant position by incumbents. Later on, however, the problem of 'one-way by-pass' in international telecom services was raised, and a case was made that the interests of incumbents needed to be protected against potential predation by foreign entrants with dominant positions in their home markets.[43] Thus, a proposal was made for a licensing criterion designed to protect the conditions of competition in the domestic ('importing') market. Agreement on the terms of this licensing commitment was not reached before the extension of the negotiating period for basic telecoms to mid-February 1997. Among the reasons why agreement was not reached were questions regarding the MFN status of such measures, whether licenses should be subject to particular conditions or simply denied *ex ante*, and whether restrictive licensing of this nature should be applicable only in respect of monopolists and exclusive service suppliers or also in respect of major suppliers.[44]

The concern that a foreign supplier could engage in disruptive behaviour arises in circumstances where such a supplier commands a monopolistic position in its home market. Consider two different circumstances in which this problem might arise. First, the alleged disruptive behaviour against which the 'importing' country wishes to take preventive or remedial action results from a government policy (protection of a monopoly), and not from a problem of market structure *per se*. The case for defensive action of this kind disappears if new suppliers are permitted to enter the market, making one-way by-pass impossible. Within the framework of WTO negotiations leading to liberalized market access backed up by competition-enhancing regulation, a restrictive licensing policy could only be justified in circumstances where another government refrains from making the necessary WTO-based commitments, which are enforceable if necessary through multilateral dispute settlement.

In the second case, suppose that instead of enjoying a government-supported monopoly position in its home market, a dominant supplier could abuse its dominance and distort competition in a foreign market without any support from a government. This situation should be of limited concern if commitments to liberalization are in place and the regulatory principles are adhered to, since the domestic market should become contestable, again making one-way by-pass impossible. But assuming that some 'residual' difficulty remains, or that there is a time lag between market opening and new entry, then two possible remedies are available in these circumstances. Either the 'importing' country whose market is being distorted could act unilaterally through its licensing regime to avoid the problem, much in the same terms that were being discussed in the WTO telecom negotiations, or governments could agree multilaterally to prevent their dominant domestic suppliers from distorting foreign markets. In the first case, market access restrictions are brought to bear to correct a market distortion, and in the second, the distortion is attacked at source.

In the tradition of optimal intervention theory, there can be little doubt that the latter alternative is superior, but of course it requires a degree of international cooperation that might prove elusive to obtain. In the context of the WTO telecom negotiations, it would have implied supplementing the regulatory principles to control the abuse of dominant market positions by incumbents with policy disciplines that would protect the conditions of competition in *foreign* markets. Such a commitment would be innovative indeed, considering the usual exemptions that national competition law provides for export cartels in most countries. For present purposes, however, perhaps the most significant point is that if the second-best option of market access restrictions is employed to address the problem, then there will always be a risk that such restrictions may be more burdensome than necessary for the task at hand, and subject to undue protectionist influence. It is for this reason that the precise conditions under which restrictive licensing arrangements would be permitted, as well as the question of the kind of supplier that would be liable to them, becomes so important.

Conclusions

The telecom sector, in common with other industries based on networks of one sort or another, and perhaps with other sectors in which governments have historically consolidated strong monopoly positions, provides an example of an industry where market structure and firm behaviour may, at least for a time, cause market distortions. Corrective regulation designed to prevent the abuse of market dominance may well be called for in these circumstances. The WTO negotiations on basic telecommunications led to the development of a set of common (harmonized) multilateral regulatory principles designed to ensure that liberalization commitments are not undermined by anti-competitive behaviour on the part of dominant basic telecom suppliers that have recently lost, or are about to lose, their historical monopoly privileges. These regulatory principles cannot be equated with mainstream competition policy; they comprise sector-specific regulatory commitments.

It is noteworthy that in the design of policy for the basic telecoms sector, the EU has also shown a clear preference for a regulatory approach, even though there exists a strong antitrust tradition at the Community-wide level.

Regulation handles detail and complexity more readily than broad-based competition policy rules, engenders greater certainty for actual and potential suppliers in the market by establishing *ex ante* rules of conduct, ensures quicker resolution of any conflicts arising among suppliers, and permits pursuit of multiple policy objectives. But it also gives rise to a greater risk of capture, and to all the difficulties associated with market intervention in the face of imperfect information. For these reasons, the design of regulations and the institutional setting in which they are administered deserve close attention.

In the international context there is also a risk that a multilateralized regulatory regime may impose an unwarranted degree of uniformity upon diverse domestic market conditions, and that regulators may extend the reach of their interventions, or delay forbearance or withdrawal from regulatory activities because of their multilateral commitments. An adequate degree of flexibility in the design and coverage of the principles, which balances variations in national needs with the attractions of multilateral accountability, should avoid these difficulties. A more serious risk relates to the shift in emphasis intrinsic to multilateral regulatory commitments forged in the context of a market access negotiation. Sectoral regulation of the kind discussed here focuses primarily upon market access for foreign suppliers. At best, this does nothing to change the pro-competitive outcome that is the putative objective of market-opening efforts. At worst, the narrow focus of a market access negotiation could lead to market outcomes not entirely supportive of nationality-blind competition and fully open markets.

The telecom negotiations suggest that the political need for multilateral antitrust rules may be reduced, as regulatory commitments may make such rules redundant in the eyes of policy-makers. To the extent that the regulatory approach to cooperation will be emulated in the GATS context once discussions begin to centre on other sectors where competition is limited (such as transport), the ambit of possible multilateral rules on antitrust may be further reduced. Indeed, it is noteworthy that much of the current interest in developing multilateral rules on antitrust is motivated by market structure and conduct in service industries (transport cartels, distribution, telecoms). The GATS is therefore likely to be an important forum for future deliberations on antitrust disciplines. The same can be said with respect to the issue of investment, which is one of the modes of supply that is covered by the GATS (for services only, of course), but is not covered by GATT. National treatment and market access commitments on investment (establishment) under the GATS are sector-specific. The more governments pursue sector-specific regulatory commitments, the less there will be left for antitrust talks to focus on. While the telecoms example suggests a pragmatic reason why antitrust issues may not figure very prominently on the negotiating agenda in the medium term, if governments go down the sector-specific path the rationale for common antitrust principles may perversely increase. There is after all a clear danger that a sector-specific regulatory approach will result in a hotchpotch of rules and excessive reliance on bureaucratic surveillance and control.

ACKNOWLEDGEMENTS

The authors are grateful to Marco Bronckers, Jacqueline Coumans, Eleanor Fox, Robert Howse, Masamichi Kono, Mark Koulen, Sebastián Saez, and Lee Tuthill for helpful discussions and comments on previous drafts of this paper. The views expressed are personal and should not be attributed to the institutions with which the authors are associated.

NOTES

1 Competition policy in this paper is used in the conventional antitrust sense – disciplines on anti-competitive practices such as collusion between enterprises, the abuse of dominant market positions, or their creation through mergers and acquisitions.

2 See, for example, L. Brittan, 'A framework for international competition', Address to the Davos Symposium, 1992; A. Jacquemin, 'The international dimension of European competition policy', *Journal of Common Market Studies*, 1993, vol. 31, pp. 91–101; F. M. Scherer, *Competition Policies for an Integrated World Economy*, The Brookings Institution, Washington DC, 1994.

3 See European Commission, *Competition Policy in The New Trade Order: Strengthening International Cooperation and Rules*, Report of the Group of Experts, 1995.

4 Even determining the impact of particular disciplines (or absence of policies) may be difficult. For example, A. Dick argues that exemptions may alter the form of competition (e.g., induce a shift from price to non-price), which can be both pro-competitive and/or welfare enhancing. See A. Dick, 'Japanese antitrust: Reconciling theory and evidence', *Contemporary Policy Issues*, 1993, vol. 9, pp. 50–60.

5 J. M. Finger and K. C. Fung, 'Can Competition Policy Control "301"?', *Aussenwirtschaft*, 1994, vol. 49, pp. 379–416.

6 It may be noted that the 'anti-competitive clause' only entered into the law in 1988. Nevertheless, some cases had been brought on grounds of anti-competitive behaviour in foreign markets prior to 1988, the lack of the clause notwithstanding. Other legislative attempts to attack anti-competitive practices in foreign markets have been exclusively inter-governmental in nature (e.g. Super 301), and may not therefore be predicated on narrowly defined market access concerns. See D. N. Palmeter, 'Competition policy and "unfair" trade: First do no harm', *Aussenwirtschaft*, 1994, vol. 49, pp. 417–22.

7 B. Hoekman and P. C. Mavroidis, 'Competition, competition policy and the GATT', *The World Economy*, 1994, vol. 17, pp. 121–50.

8 P. Low and A. Subramanian, 'TRIMS in the Uruguay Round: An unfinished business?' in W. Martin and L. A. Winters (eds), *The Uruguay Round and the developing economies*, Discussion Paper No. 307, The World Bank, Washington DC, 1995.

9 D. Wood, 'Options for the future', *De Paul Law Review*, 1995, vol. 44, p. 1289.

10 Typical firm-based access barriers in telecoms include a denial of network interconnection, a refusal to provide interconnection on commercial terms, and misuse of commercial information.

11 New licensing arrangements announced recently permit member states to issue individual licences under four conditions: for radio frequency or numbers, to grant particular access to land, to impose universal service obligations, or to ensure that suppliers with a significant market share uphold competition rules. Licences may only be refused where there is a scarcity of radio frequency or a temporary shortage of numbers. In the absence of agreement on a centralized regulatory policing function at the Community level, it remains unclear what the precise nature of recourse will be in the face of an allegation that a member state is not implementing the directive appropriately. See *Financial Times*, 'EU in accord on rules for telecom licensing', p. 2, 30 September 1996.

12 Article 90 reads as follows:

    1. In the case of public undertakings and undertakings to which Members States grant special or exclusive rights, Member States shall neither enact nor maintain in force any measure contrary to the rules contained in this Treaty, in particular those rules provided for in Article 6 and Articles 85–94.

    2. Undertakings entrusted with the operation of services of general economic interest or having the character of a revenue producing monopoly shall be subject to the rules contained in this Treaty, in particular the rules on competition, insofar as the application of such rules does not obstruct the performance in law or in fact of the particular tasks assigned to them. The development of trade must not be affected to such an extent as would be contrary to the interests of the Community.

    3. The Commission shall ensure the application of the provisions of this Article and shall where necessary address the appropriate directives or decisions to Member States.

13 European Community Treaty, Art. 222.

14 Treaty on Economic Union, Art. 3.

15 A. Gardner, 'The velvet revolution: Article 90 and the triumph of the free market in Europe's regulated sectors', *European Community Law Review*, 1995, vol. 2, pp. 78–86.

16 This has led some observers to conclude that competition policy is of higher hierarchical value than either trade or industrial policies. See J. Bourgeois and P. Demaret, 'The EC trade, competition and industrial policies', in A. Jacquemin, P. Buigues and A. Sapir (eds), *The EC Policies on Competition, Trade and Industry: Complementarities and Conflicts*, Elgar, United Kingdom, 1995.

17 See, e.g., D. Edward and M. Hoskins, 'Article 89: Deregulation and EC law: Reflections arising from the XVI FIDE conference', *Common Market Law Review*, 1995, vol. 32, pp. 157–86.

18 In *Port of Genoa* (Case C-19/93), the ECJ found that an undertaking was abusing its dominant position by pricing excessively. In the *ERT* case (C-260/89, *ERT v. Dimotiki*, 1991, ECR I-2925), the ECJ found that the likelihood that the existence of the special or exclusive right might lead to abuse was enough to take action. In *Höfner* (C-41/90, *Höfner and Elser v. Macrotron*, 1991, ECR I-1979), the ECJ concluded that Members States will violate Article 90 ECT if the undertaking enjoying special or exclusive rights cannot avoid abusive behaviour when exercising such rights. In this case, the German Government had granted the Federal Employment Office an exclusive right to conduct job placement. No other private or public undertaking was permitted under German law to perform similar functions. The Federal Employment Office was unable to satisfy demand, leading the ECJ to find against it. The Court decided that this was: 'incompatible avec les régles du traité toute mesure d'un Etat member qui maintiendrait en vigueur une disposition légale créant une situation dans laquelle un office public pour l'emploi serait nécessairement amené a contrevenir aux termes de l'Article 86'. See Edward and Hoskins, *ibid*. It is the 'inevitability' captured in the word 'nécessairement' that probably led the ECJ to formulate its position.

19 C-320/91, *Criminal Proceedings against Paul Corbeau*, (1993) ECR I-2533.

20 For an excellent review of the ECJ case law in this field, see J. Temple-Lang, 'Defining legitimate competition: Companies duties to supply competitors and access to essential facilities', in B. Hawk (ed.), *1994 Fordham Corporate Law Institute Proceedings*, 1995, pp. 245–313.

21 See *Advanced Health Care Services Inc. v. Giles Memorial Hospital*, 846 F. Supp. 488 (W.D. Va. 1994). In the US, compulsory access is an exception as antitrust laws, in principle, go against cooperation among competitors. This is not necessarily the case in the EC legal order. See J. Temple-Lang, *ibid.*, pp. 245–313.

22 Minor problems could arise. J. Pelkmanns and D. Young question, for example, to what extent the impossibility of number portability could provide a deterrent against moving to a competitor supplier. Such issues are unrelated to the basic proposal that competition laws can, in principle, address most anti-competitive practices by privatized 'giants'. See J. Pelkmans and D. Young, 'European telecommunications: How to regulate a liberalized market', *CEPS Working Party Report*, 1995, vol. 13.

23 H. Donaldson, 'Telecommunications liberalization and privatization: The New Zealand experience', in B. Wellenius and P. Stern (eds), *Implementing Reforms in the Telecommunications Sector*, The World Bank, Washington DC, 1994.

24 See R. Schultz, 'Regulation and telecommunications reform: Exploring the alternatives', in B. Wellenius and P. Stern (eds), *op. cit.*; and P. Smith and G. Staple, *Telecommunications sector reform in Asia: Towards a new pragmatism*, Discussion Paper 232, The World Bank, Washington DC, 1994.

25 See, e.g., N. Miller, 'Regulation: Reconciling policy objectives', B. Wellenius and P. Stern (eds), *op. cit.*

26 See R. Schultz, *op. cit.*

27 P. Smith and G. Staple, *op. cit.*

28 P. Smith, 'End of the line for the local loop monopoly? Technology, competition,

and investment in telecom networks', *Viewpoint*, No. 63, The World Bank, Washington DC, 1995.

29 *The Economist*, 'The great telephone paradox', 23 March 1996, p. 74.

30 It is true that in the original break-up of AT&T, the constituent parts were in some cases (in particular, local service) granted monopoly market positions. But as liberalization has proceeded, these large suppliers are increasingly being forced to compete against one another.

31 As previously discussed, the speed with which alternative sources of supply of basic telecom services become available depends on the relative degree of emphasis placed on antitrust-motivated actions to modify market structure on the one hand, and gradualism via sector-specific regulatory oversight on the other.

32 R. W. Crandall and L.Waverman, *Talk is Cheap: The Promise of Regulatory Reform in North American Telecommunications*, The Brookings Institution, Washington DC, 1996.

33 B. Hoekman, 'Focal points and multilateral negotiations on the contestability of markets', in K. Maskus, P. Hooper, E. Leamer and J. D. Richardson (eds), *Quiet Pioneering: Robert M. Stern and His International Economic Legacy*, Ann Arbor, University of Michigan Press, 1996.

34 See, for example, I. Nakatani, 'The economic role of financial corporate grouping', in M. Aoki (ed.), *The Economic Analysis of the Japanese Firm*, Amsterdam, North Holland, 1984.

35 See, for example, contributions in F. McChesney and W. Shughart (eds), *Causes and Consequences of Antitrust: The Public Choice Perspective*, University of Chicago Press, 1995.

36 P. Low, 'Multilateral rules on competition: What can we learn from the telecommunications sector?', presented November 1995 at an OECD workshop on 'Trade Policy for a Globalizing Economy', Santiago, Chile.

37 For a description and analysis of the GATS, see B. Hoekman, 'Tentative first steps: An assessment of the Uruguay Round *Agreement on Services*', in W. Martin and L. A. Winters (eds), *The Uruguay Round and the Developing Economies*, Discussion Paper 307, The World Bank, Washington DC, 1995.

38 Annex on Basic Telecommunications, para. 5(a). Non-discrimination in this context comprises both MFN and national treatment.

39 It should be noted that Annex commitments only apply in those sectors where governments have accepted specific market access and national treatment commitments. Under the GATS, governments have negotiated these commitments on a sector-by-sector basis, and in sectors that are not covered in this manner, the only obligations that apply relate to most-favoured-nation treatment and transparency.

40 Unbundling means allowing a new entrant to choose exactly which services to buy from the network operator, rather than being obliged to purchase a package that may raise costs and undermine competitiveness.

41 B. Hoekman, *op. cit.*

42 See B. Petrazzini, *Global Telecom Talks: A Trillion Dollar Deal*, The Institute for International Economics, Washington DC, 1996, pp. 86–8.

43 In essence, one-way by-pass occurs because a monopoly supplier in one market can appropriate outgoing traffic to another (liberalized) market by establishing

a subsidiary or leasing capacity in the latter market, thus closing out competition on the route. At the same time, all return traffic to the home territory of the monopolist has to be routed through the monopoly supplier. The fact that outgoing traffic from the monopolist's home base may be priced at whatever level the monopolist chooses, while all return traffic will be priced at the prevailing (and supposedly much higher) accounting rate is also perceived as a problem because of its implications for the settlement of the bilateral financial balance on telephone traffic between the two countries concerned. But the main point for present purposes is that unimpeded access to an open market for a foreign supplier with monopoly power in its home market can lead to anti-competitive behaviour and a market distortion in the liberalized market.

44 See B. Petrazzini, *op. cit.* A major supplier is defined in the negotiated regulatory principles as 'a supplier which has the ability to materially affect the terms of participation (having regard to price and supply) in the market for basic telecommunications as a result of: a) control over essential facilities; or b) use of its position in the market'. Monopoly suppliers are defined in Art. XXVIII(h) of GATS as 'any person, public or private, which in the relevant market of the territory of a Member is authorized or established formally or in effect by that Member as the sole supplier of that service'. Exclusive service suppliers are similarly defined where 'a Member, formally or in effect, (a) authorises or establishes a small number of service suppliers and (b) substantially prevents competition among those suppliers in its territory' (Art. VIII: 5).

Part III

DEVELOPMENT ASPECTS

9

A BRIEF NOTE ON THE ROLE OF COMPETITION POLICY IN ECONOMIC DEVELOPMENT

R. Shyam Khemani

Towards the end of the last century, the first set of competition (antitrust) laws were enacted among the western industrialized countries, namely by Canada (1889) and the US (1890). It is interesting to observe that 100 years later, several developing and transition market economies are now embracing competition laws. Since 1990 alone, more than thirty-five such countries have adopted new (or have substantially revised their existing) competition laws including virtually all of the former communist centrally planned economies in Central and Eastern Europe, and the former Soviet Union. Several other countries are in the process of following suit. However, the underlying basis for the renewed interest in competition law differs from that a hundred years ago. The concerns during the end of the last century centred around preventing increased levels of industry and aggregate concentration which could give rise to the exercise of 'market power' and undue economic-political influence. The competition laws were passed during a period of unprecedented corporate merger and acquisition activity, consolidations and formation of 'trusts'. In contrast, competition laws in developing and transition market countries are being adopted in an environment where economic activity is already highly concentrated, mainly due to past government policies and interventions. These laws are now seen as instruments to accelerate the transformation process where economic activity is primarily determined by private ownership and market forces instead of state ownership and controls. Although, during the past 100 years, the role and importance of competition law has varied across countries and over time, it has evolved as not only being an instrument to prevent anti-competitive business practices, but also to pro-actively strengthen market forces.

Do countries need a specific competition law to complete their national economic policy framework? Are other policies that promote competition, such as liberalization of international trade, privatization and deregulation, not sufficient? Is enacting of competition law not a low priority, worth considering only after other more urgent policy measures have been introduced?

This article puts forward the view that a well-designed competition law should be accorded a central place in economic framework policies. Policy makers in various countries – not exclusively developing and transition market economies – have too often relied on regulatory controls, state enterprises, promotional instruments, and trade restrictions to spur industrial development. Measures such as entry and capacity licensing, subsidies, targeted investments, central planning, and trade barriers, have led to concentration of industry, sheltered domestic markets, distorted price and profit signals, dampened pursuit of static and dynamic efficiencies and failed in allocating and mobilizing resources from lower to higher valued uses. An effective competition law prevents artificial barriers to entry and facilitates market access. It complements and buttresses other policies, particularly trade liberalization, in promoting competition, and domestic and international market integration. The absence or ineffective application of competition law can itself pose a barrier to entry.

The 'trade liberalization alone' approach

In many economies where high levels of industry concentration prevail, it is suggested that anti-competitive business practices are less feasible if domestic markets are exposed to international competition. In the absence of barriers to trade, domestic monopolists or oligopolists lose their ability to exercise market power, irrespective of actual imports' share of the domestic market, in view of the threat of potential competition.

The view that imports limit market power gains support from studies that find differing degrees of convergence between domestic and international prices in face of trade liberalization and a negative relationship between price and cost or profit margins and imports. But some recent empirical studies suggest that effects of trade liberalization may be less significant than previously thought, raising questions about the true effect of trade liberalization on competition.

The insufficiency of trade liberalization as a guarantor of competition

The pro-competitive effects of tariff reductions may be diluted if the import supply is not very elastic. This occurs when increased demand for imports can be met only at significantly higher prices, or when imports are comparatively insensitive to changes in domestic prices. It is possible to construct various economic models where imports meet only a small part of domestic demand and are provided by a fringe of firms which domestic oligopolists have already taken into account in their pricing strategies. In addition, in an environment of floating exchange rates, if domestic firms fail to rationalize high-cost operations and improve productivity, the domestic currency is likely to depreciate, offering new protection from import competition. In Mexico for example, recent currency devaluations have more than offset the tariff reductions negotiated under the North American Free Trade Agreement (NAFTA).

Furthermore, trade policy consists of more than tariff policy. Quotas, voluntary export restraints (VERs), anti-dumping and countervailing duties are among the instruments that governments can wield to limit import competition. While a true free trade policy would require that all such measures are removed, in reality this never happens. Indeed, as import tariffs are liberalized, the pressure to invoke other measures only increase. Over the past few years, as more countries have liberalized trade policies, a simultaneous movement has occurred to put in place systems of protection against dumping and subsidies. By the end of the 1980s, more than thirty countries had become new signatories or observers of the GATT anti-dumping code, and in 1980–92 more than 2,000 anti-dumping and countervailing duty actions were taken. It is often suggested that enacting an anti-dumping law does not generally serve the best interests of a country. Such a law can thwart the benefits of trade liberalization; it tends to be used to protect (inefficient) competitors rather than competition. Consumers end up paying higher prices while having reduced product choice and quality. Provisions in competition law dealing with perdation and price discrimination offer a reasonable substitute to remedy dumping practices by firms.

Even if trade barriers such as anti-dumping duties are eliminated, other factors can impede the pro-competitive effect of trade liberalization. First an increasing share of economic activity in developing as well as industrial countries relates to non-tradable goods and services. These include high weight-to-value products with high transport costs (such as cement and steel), perishables (such as food), and legal, financial, and other services. Second, in the absence of effective competition, domestic firms can raise prices up to the international price, plus transport costs, and still keep out imports. Third, interfirm contractual arrangements and vertical integration may prevent the development of new sources of inputs or new distribution channels. This problem has been cited by many American firms as limiting their ability to gain access to markets in Japan and forms part of the 'framework' and 'structural impediments initiatives' discussions between the US and Japanese governments. Fourth, international cartels may divide up markets through price-fixing or geographic market-sharing agreements. Importers and foreign firms may find it more profitable to become parties to domestic anti-competitive arrangements than to compete. Indeed, foreign firms have often been charged with just this offence in several jurisdictions. In concentrated industries such as pharmaceuticals, petrochemicals, and telecommunications equipment where the total number of firms world-wide is small, such arrangements are particularly common. Fifth, differences in income, tastes, culture, product safety, consumer protection and technical standards may also separate markets.

Some empirical examples serve to illustrate these points. In Colombia, the leading brewer allegedly has geographic market-sharing agreements with existing and potential competitors in neighbouring countries, particularly Venezuela. It also owns and controls the sole bottle-manufacturing plant and has exclusive dealing clauses with the great majority of distributors. Recently, the same dominant Colombian brewer acquired all the breweries in Ecuador, precluding potential competition or entry from firms in close geographic proximity.

A leading US biscuit manufacturer found it difficult to enter the Colombian market due to exclusive distribution clauses between the dominant domestic manufacturer and major retailers. It has instead entered into licensing and joint marketing arrangements with the dominant firm because of the barriers these restrictive distribution agreements posed to both importation and local manufacture.

In many product areas such as fertilizers, pharmaceuticals and plate glass, domestic and international price differentials persist despite trade liberalization, due to manufacturing and marketing linkages between domestic and foreign firms. In Ecuador, government enterprises and private sector counterparts are alleged to engage in tacit price and market-sharing agreements in cement and steel. In the case of many other industrial products, the government continues to regulate the market through price controls. The industry associations for domestic oil and pharmaceuticals have successfully obtained government mandate to limit entry, coordinate and increase prices. While importation of cars has been liberalized, distribution remains the exclusive area of government-owned or appointed dealers.

In Indonesia, importation, production and/or domestic marketing of products as diverse as cars, oil and gas, rattan, steel, citrus fruit and wheat remain with state-designated monopolies.

For these and other reasons, liberalized trade cannot effectively substitute for competition law. The two policy areas should be viewed as complementary. Both can help a country to elicit the maximum benefits obtainable from specialization and scale economies. Competition law can lower barriers to trade and investment and thereby enlarge markets by improving access to profitable business opportunities. Chapter 15 of the NAFTA Treaty between Canada, Mexico and the US explicitly recognized this view, and to enhance business and investor confidence, Mexico decided to modernize its competition law.

Mexico's decision highlights an important final point. In a world where multinational companies have grown accustomed to operating under competition laws, the absence of competition law, or a poorly designed one, can act as a barrier to trade and foreign investment in a country. A pending matter in Brazil is of interest in this context. Colgate Palmolive recently acquired a dominant Brazilian healthcare products manufacturer, Kolynos, which through exclusive dealing and vertical arrangements is reputed to control 80 per cent of the toothpaste market. Another US multinational enterprise, Proctor & Gamble (P&G), has argued that market penetration is difficult due to anti-competitive business practices which include the various inter-firm contractual arrangements and weak competition law enforcement. It is reportedly reconsidering its medium- to long-term investments, including its subsidiary operations in Brazil. In this and many other cases referred to, a more complete assessment needs to be conducted before it can be established that competition has been significantly limited and that there are no off-setting efficiencies. However, it should be clear that various business practices could impede competition even in face of free trade.

Large firm size and economic performance

In recent years, a number of dynamic and high-performing economies in East Asia have had higher growth rates than other developing and transition market economies and western industrialized countries. Yet many of these countries have no specific competition law. What is interesting is that the countries that have been successful have had what is in effect a competition policy. A World Bank study – *The East Asian Miracle* (1993) – indicates that there are distinctive differences in the economic strategies followed in the twenty-three Asian countries which were the subject of the study. A strategy that is successful for one country is not necessarily transferable to another. The one common denominator is, however, the high degree to which firms were exposed to domestic and/or international sources of competition. In the case of Japan, the intense domestic and international rivalry between firms manufacturing its most successful products – cars, cameras, consumer electronics, computers, etc. – is noticeable even to the casual observer. In other economies (e.g., Malaysia, Singapore, and Taiwan) where domestic markets tend to be small, this rivalry is unavoidable, given their need to adopt export market-led growth strategies for economic development.

It has also become clear that while national governments can control their domestic markets, they cannot – if they are exporting nations – control the environment in which their firms operate. Since, in the case of export industries, the government is unable to control market conditions, protecting national industry may simply encourage inefficient practices which would be reflected in those firms' performance on the international level. An appropriate competition law that tempers domestic market conditions can help to ensure that firms will be able to withstand competition at the international level. The above-mentioned World Bank study appears to confirm that firms which have faced domestic competition are those which have been most successful internationally.

This means that even countries without a competition law – so long as they have a policy to expose their firms to competition in the domestic market – will find that this will foster growth. What would assist in ensuring that such growth is sustainable is a vigorous competition policy, including a competition law.

Major provisions of competition law

What is an appropriate competition law? Competition law generally consists of substantive conduct and structural provisions relating to business activity, together with additional procedural provisions on administration and enforcement. An advocacy role for the competition agency to promote competition in government policy-making is a very useful addition. This role is particularly important in developing and transition market economies where an appropriate understanding or appreciation of the merits of competitive market economic systems is often lacking. Moreover, a competition advocacy is an important vehicle for creating a popular base of support for competition policy.

Laws which deal with the effects of horizontal collusion – restraints agreed by enterprises operating in the same market – are a key feature of most competition laws. Although it is accepted that such practices, which include price-fixing, market-sharing and bid-rigging, are serious violations, they are often very difficult to prove and it may be important that the law includes provisions which give incentives to participants or injured parties to provide evidence to authorities of these activities and impose tough penalties as deterrent. Many countries do in fact exempt certain types of cartels from prosecution where it is likely that they have little impact on competition or, as is the case with R&D agreements, where they have a positive impact. There is currently an active debate going on as to whether export cartels should be permitted as an effective means of penetrating foreign markets, or prohibited as likely to lead to unhealthy collusion on domestic markets.

Vertical restraints between suppliers and purchasers in separate upstream and downstream markets may also, in certain circumstances, prove to be anticompetitive. There remains considerable controversy over whether particular types of agreements, while prima facie being restrictive of competition, may in fact be beneficial to economic efficiency by overcoming certain market failures. Whether distribution networks in newly developing countries pose any particular problems is not clear. Given the speed of evolution of the market structures in those countries it may be prudent to disallow long-term exclusionary provisions in contracts between manufacturers and distributors, but generally to examine vertical restraints on a case-by-case basis to judge whether the overall impact is likely to be positive or negative.

Of particular concern to competition authorities is the phenomenon whereby firms which are dominant in a market adopt anti-competitive business practices in order to maintain and entrench their market position. In spite of the fact that most competition laws contain provisions aimed at preventing the abuse of a dominant position, there is no clear determinant of what constitutes dominance. Moreover, the size of a firm is not itself a determining factor, since large firm size, particularly in market economies, may simply be an indicator of economic efficiency. The analysis therefore should focus on the behaviour of the firm and its ability to strategically deter other entrants to the market. In what previously were centrally planned economies, dominant firms often are the result of government policy. This raises the question of whether an active policy of deconcentration should be pursued in order to create the structural basis for future competition.

Mergers and acquisitions are another form of business agreement where scrutiny may be required. It is not always easy to balance the trade-offs between the possible reduction in competition that occurs as a result of certain mergers, particularly in horizontal merger cases, and the economic efficiency gains that may come as a result. However, the timely assessment of such arrangements may be very useful in preventing the creation or entrenchment of concentrated market structures which impede future competition. In certain developing countries, concentration of wealth among a small number of families or groups may require attention to be given to conglomerate mergers. These tend to be of less concern to competition authorities in industrialized countries, where the trend at present is more towards divestment of unrelated activities.

It should be borne in mind, however, that competition policy instruments are blunt, not sharp surgical instruments, and they have to be handled with care. For countries without experience in this field, a rule-based approach to competition would be appropriate and that there should be the fullest interplay for market force; and the mobility of resources, deregulation and lowering of barriers to entry as instruments for promoting competition rather than law itself. The priorities and application of different provisions will of course differ across countries and their stages of economic development. For example, structural de-concentration (de-monopolization) measures may be more appropriate in transition market economies where many large enterprises were formed through 'administrative fiats' than in other countries.

Administration and enforcement

The experience to date with countries which have had long-standing competition regimes points to a few basic guidelines with respect to the administration and enforcement of competition law. These are that:

- the competition agency should be independent, insulated from political and budgetary interference and capture by interest groups;

- the agency should nevertheless be accountable, for example through an annual report to Parliament or appropriate legislative committee;
- competition law should separate the activities of investigation, prosecution and adjudication;
- the process should build in checks and balances with rights of appeal, reviews of decisions, confidential treatment accorded to sensitive business information, transparent administrative procedures and regulations;
- proceedings and case resolutions should be expeditious to avoid unnecessary transaction costs;
- to have a deterrent effect, the enforcement of the law should permit the imposition of significant penalties and various remedial remedies;
- there should be increased access to the application of competition law through appropriately designed provisions for class and private actions.

International convergence and harmonization of competition laws

As local enterprises begin to operate more in international markets, a national law that is in harmony with competitors' laws makes it easier for them to adapt. It also spares foreign firms any additional hurdles in their business activities. In this connection, a number of bilateral and multilateral approaches to the enforcement of competition law have been forged by different countries. Canada and the US have signed a memorandum of understanding (MOU) and a mutual legal assistance treaty. MOUs have been drafted though not yet finalized between Canada and the EU and the US and the EU. Twenty-four member nations are signatories to the OECD Council Recommendations Concerning Cooperation on Restrictive Business Practices (1986). The UNCTAD Set of Multilaterally Agreed Equitable Principles and Rules for the Control of Restrictive Business Practices (1980) is another multilateral agreement. These arrangements are designated to facilitate cooperation and information-sharing. While these measures do not involve complete harmonizing or developing common principles for administering and enforcing competition law, they contribute towards reducing business transaction costs that may arise from frictions between different legal economic systems. This is becoming increasingly recognized among the developing countries.

Conclusion

What does all this imply for the role of government and for the role of competition policy? Competition policy should not only be designed to prevent artificial constraints or private restraints on the market by business, but also to foster the mobility of business from lower to higher value uses. This is not a question of ideology but of efficiency. Why should consumers, including business firms purchasing inputs, pay higher prices than is necessary? Why should market mechanisms that can organize production and allocate resources more efficiently than government not be given unfettered role to play?

Competition law, by preventing the erection of artificial barriers to entry and facilitating market access to competitors, complements and buttresses the benefits of other government policies that promote competition. The absence of, or a badly designed and implemented competition law, can itself be a barrier to entry. To be 'appropriate' a competition law requires more than just effective enforcement. It further requires the conditioning of the business environment in which firms operate so that the process of competition itself operates to limit the discretionary exercise of market power.

What is being advocated is therefore not simply a reactive approach to specific anti-competitive situations, but also a pro-active approach. Competition authorities need to play an advocacy role to ensure that the competitive process is properly taken into consideration in broader economic policy-making. This implies the upgrading of the competition enforcement authority to an active economic policy-oriented agency, well placed to argue for reduced barriers to entry and enhanced mobility of resources. This role is vital since many of the restraints on competition lie not only in the hands of private enterprise, but also within the competence of government institutions and regulations. Competition law policy should be viewed as the fourth cornerstone of government economic framework policies, the other three being monetary, fiscal and trade.

10

COMPETITION AT THE CROSSROADS

Philippe Brusick[1]

I From Havana to Singapore

The first attempt to adopt multilateral competition rules was made at the Havana Conference in 1946. The proposed Havana Charter contained principles and rules to control restrictive business practices. It envisaged procedures for consultation, investigations and cooperative remedial arrangements, and the stillborn International Trade Organization would have been empowered to undertake studies related to restrictive business practices. The proposal would have included services in addition to goods, and would have concerned practices by both private and public commercial enterprises.

Mainly, the system rested on the investigation procedure envisaged for the ITO and the obligation made on each member 'to take all possible measures by legislation or otherwise', to ensure compliance within its jurisdiction.

In 1980, after practically ten years of work at UNCTAD, the Set of Multilaterally Agreed Equitable Principles and Rules for the Control of Restrictive Business Practices (the RBP Set) was unanimously adopted by the United Nations General Assembly in its Resolution 35/61 of 5 December 1980 (see Annex I)[2], in the form of a recommendation addressed to states and enterprises. Notwithstanding its voluntary nature, the Set gave birth to the Intergovernmental Group of Experts on RBPs when the General Assembly, in line with Section G of the Set, instructed UNCTAD's Trade and Development Board to establish the RBP Group to monitor the application and implementation of the Set. A closer look at the RBP Set is provided later in this note. In acceptance of one of the recommendations contained in Section G of the Set, the General Assembly decided to convene five years after the adoption of the Set, a first UN Conference to review all aspects of the Set (the First Review Conference). This took place in 1985 and was followed by a Second, then a Third Review Conference at five-year intervals. The latest Conference, which took place on 13–21 November 1995, adopted a resolution in which it confirmed a wide-ranging research and technical cooperation mandate for UNCTAD in the area of competition law and policy. By the same token, it recommended to the General Assembly to change the name of the IGE on RBPs to that of IGE on Competition Law and Policy, and to convene a Fourth Review Conference in the year 2000, thus clarifying UNCTAD's long-term mandate in this field.

Meanwhile, the GATT concluded its widest-ranging round of negotiations, the Uruguay Round. Although the Round did not include a specific item devoted to competition policy or restrictive business practices, as had been requested by developing countries at the opening meeting of Punta del Este, most of the resulting Uruguay Round Agreements finally concern competition issues, either directly or indirectly. Broadly speaking, of course, all trade-liberalizing arrangements, even if limited in their scope, are a step towards increased global competition. However, a closer look at individual Agreements (see below) shows that many of these Agreements, such as those on Safeguards, Anti-dumping, Subsidies, but also TRIMs, TRIPs, Services and Government Procurement, have important implications in the area of competition. In particular, the TRIMs agreement calls for the Council for Trade in Goods to consider, no later than five years after entry into force of the Agreement, whether the Agreement should be complemented with provisions on investment policy and competition policy.

The adoption of the Uruguay Round at Marrakesh was the occasion for countries to make proposals for opening negotiations on so-called 'new or emerging' issues. Among these, competition policy, export-credit guarantees and corrupt practices, as well as environmental and labour standards were proposed. Part IV of this note devotes some thought to these issues, as far as they are related to competition in a broad sense, and leads to the concluding Part V, which attempts at providing an outlook into the future multilateral action in the field of competition policy and control of restrictive business practices. Should the world community continue addressing competition issues in a piecemeal approach, by reaching agreements on international trade which do indeed increase world-wide competition as they open new markets, but address the competition issue in a patchwork manner? Or should the world community consider competition issues in a methodologic approach, aimed at creating a comprehensive multilateral competition framework which would strengthen the international trading system with a set of basic competition principles? Dropping a strictly legalistic approach to antitrust would, in the author's view, accelerate the achievement of the logical convergence and ultimately merger of competition policy with trade policy. This would at least ensure full compatibility of multilateral trade agreements such as WTO Agreements with basic or intrinsic competition principles as they presently evolve from a rapidly growing number of national and regional jurisdictions.

II The United Nations Restrictive Business
Practices Set

A short description of the Set of Multilaterally Agreed Equitable Principles and Rules for the Control of Restrictive Business Practices (see Annex I, pp. 166–80) is given below.

Objectives

The Set's first objective is to ensure that RBPs do not impede or negate the realization of benefits that should arise from the liberalization of tariff and non-tariff barriers affecting world trade, particularly those affecting the trade and development of developing countries. It also seeks to attain greater efficiency in international trade and development through, *inter alia*, promoting competition, control of concentration of economic power and encouragement of innovation. Moreover, it aims at protecting and promoting social welfare in general and, in particular, the interests of consumers.

Voluntary nature of the Set

The Set, as adopted by the General Assembly in its Resolution 35/63 of 5 December 1980, is in the form of a recommendation. In other words, its application and implementation depends upon the willingness of states which have accepted the Set to meet their commitment to it. Moreover, it is stipulated in the Set that, in the performance of its functions, neither the Intergovernmental Group of Experts on Restrictive Business Practices, established in UNCTAD to provide the institutional machinery for the Set, nor its subsidiary organs 'shall act like a tribunal or otherwise pass judgement on the activities or conduct of individual Governments or of individual enterprises in connection with a specific business transaction'. It is also stipulated in section B (ii) of the Set, 'Scope of application', that the Set 'shall not apply to intergovernmental agreements, nor to RBPs directly caused by such agreements'.

The scope of the Set

The Set applies to all enterprises, including transnational corporations, whether private or state-owned, and it is universally applicable to all countries and to all transactions in goods and services. It also applies to regional groupings of states, such as the EU and the European Economic Area, to the extent that they have competence in the area of competition law and policy.

Preferential or differential treatment for developing countries

Under section C of the Set, which lists multilaterally agreed principles for the control of RBPs, the specific needs of developing countries, and in particular the least developed, are taken into account, as it was agreed that:

> in order to ensure the equitable application of the Set of Principles and Rules, States, particularly developed countries, should take into account in their control of restrictive business practices the development, financial and trade needs of developing countries, in particular of the least developed countries, for the purposes especially of developing countries in:

> (a) Promoting the establishment or development of domestic industries and the economic development of other sectors in the economy; and
> (b) Encouraging their economic development through regional or global arrangements among developing countries.

The Set and enterprise behaviour, including transnational or multinational corporations: prohibited horizontal and vertical practices

Section D of the Set states that:

> enterprises should conform to the restrictive business practices laws and the provisions concerning restrictive business practices in the laws of the countries in which they operate and, in the event of proceedings under these laws, should be subject to the competence of the courts and relevant administrative bodies therein.

Paragraphs 3 and 4 of section D deal with the main types of RBPs that enterprises should refrain from. Concerning intrafirm transactions between different entities of a transnational corporation, while paragraph 3 excludes enterprises 'when dealing with each other in the context of an economic entity wherein they are under common control, including through ownership, or otherwise not able to act independently of each other', paragraph 4 covers all enterprises which 'limit access to markets or otherwise unduly restrain competition . . . through an abuse or acquisition and abuse of a dominant position of market power'. This same paragraph goes on to list practices in this respect, which include predatory behaviour towards competitors and

> discriminatory (i.e. unjustifiably differentiated) pricing or terms or conditions in the supply or purchase of goods or services, including by means of the use of pricing policies in transactions between

affiliated enterprises which overcharge or undercharge for goods or services purchased or supplied as compared with prices for similar or comparable transactions outside the affiliated enterprises.

Action by states at national, regional and sub-regional levels: competition legislation and cooperation between national competition authorities

In order for states to be able to take effective action against RBPs, the Set calls for the adoption, improvement and effective enforcement of appropriate legislation and the implementation of judicial and administrative procedures. In this respect, continued work is also prescribed within UNCTAD on the elaboration of a model law or laws on RBPs in order to assist developing countries in devising appropriate legislation. UNCTAD and other relevant organizations of the United Nations system working in conjunction with UNCTAD are also to provide technical assistance, and advisory and training programmes for this purpose.

In order to facilitate the control of RBPs by states, the Set calls for the institution of improved procedures for obtaining information from enterprises, including transnational corporations, and the establishment of appropriate mechanisms at the regional and sub-regional levels to promote exchange of information on RBPs and to assist each other in this area.

Action at the international level

This includes in particular the establishment of consultation procedures whereby a state may request a consultation with other states in regard to issues concerning the control of RBPs. In this connection, the states involved may request the Secretary General of UNCTAD to provide mutually agreed conference facilities for such consultations. Action at the international level at UNCTAD also includes work by the Intergovernmental Group of Experts on Restrictive Business Practices and the United Nations Conferences to Review All Aspects of the Set (the Review Conferences).

III The Uruguay Round and competition

As noted in the introduction, any action that leads to the opening of markets and reducing of entry barriers, such as trade barriers, is pro-competitive by definition. Competition policy, as a means to ensure that markets always remain open to direct or potential competition – or 'free competition' as it is sometimes called – is indeed close by definition to 'free trade policy', which seeks to eliminate all governmental barriers to trade and combat all forms of protectionism. One important difference, however, is that while 'free competition' seeks to eliminate all barriers to market entry, it deals mainly with enterprise barriers to entry, whereas trade policy is primarily addressed at governmental barriers, and only incidentally at enterprise barriers to market entry by competitors.

This is probably why trade policy experts rejected the Havana Charter's restrictive business practices chapter, which led to the GATT being primarily and quasi-exclusively a trade policy forum.

It is only in the nineties, in the advent of globalization and liberalization, that trade barriers at the frontier have started to rapidly disappear, that external trade and domestic trade have become increasingly blurred, and that the traditional distinction between trade policy's exclusive external or international field and competition policy's mainly domestic or internal domain are getting increasingly blurred.

The creation of the EU, and later of the European Economic Area, has shown that when governmental trade barriers are eliminated, one has to deal with enterprise barriers to trade or restrictive business practices: the traditional field of competition policy.

As the successive GATT trade-liberalization rounds gradually reduced protectionist trade barriers, enterprise level competition policy issues started to creep into the negotiations. This is clearly witnessed by the negotiations that led to the successful conclusion of the Uruguay Round, and the proposed 'new issues' thereafter.

At Punta del Este in 1986, when the Round was launched, developed countries flatly rejected calls from some developing countries for the new round to examine the issue of 'restrictive business practices' or competition policy. Nevertheless, most of the resulting Uruguay Round Agreements are closely related to competition policy issues and some, like the services, TRIPs and TRIMs Agreements, directly address the issue. The TRIMs Agreement concedes that five years after entry into force of the Agreement, the Council for Trade in Goods will consider whether negotiations on an investment code and a competition code are to be launched.

After briefly reviewing the competition aspects of some of the Uruguay Round Agreements, an attempt is made to clarify some of the important links that exist between foreign direct investment (FDI) and competition policy issues.

Safeguards

The Safeguard Agreement outlaws voluntary export restraints and orderly marketing arrangements (VERs and OMAs), both of which are market-sharing and sometimes price-fixing agreements. Hence, to the extent that the Agreement manages to limit resort to such enterprise-level trade-distorting cartels, it will be favourable to competition. Proper safeguard action, if taken in accordance with the Agreement should be of a temporary nature, and applied in a non-discriminatory fashion, hence having a limited impact on competition.

Subsidies

State subsidies obviously distort competition. The Agreement does not prohibit subsidies; it only allows states to take countervailing action in the way of a duty that should not be greater than the subsidy itself. While countervailing action allows states to redress anti-competitive subsidies in international trade transactions, subsidies can also distort competition in domestic trade. Besides, 'subsidies' can originate from parent corporations or firms having deeper pockets, and applying subsidies in the way of transfer pricing by under-invoicing intermediate inputs in order to favour their subsidiary firm. This sort of predatory pricing behaviour, which is a common restrictive business practice, is banned under most competition laws. Another indirect form of subsidy results from state facilities designed to attract foreign investors. In certain cases foreign investors are afforded tax holidays and permission to import inputs without customs duty, while local firms are not. This might seriously distort domestic competition, to the disadvantage of local producers.

Finally, another form of export subsidy should be discussed as was proposed at the Marrakesh final conference adopting the Uruguay Round in 1993: export-credit guarantees. It is clear that through export credit, countries with deep pockets can easily win markets to the detriment of their financially weaker competitors.

Anti-dumping

The Anti-dumping Agreement also increases competition in that it bans anti-competitive distortions such as VERs and OMAs and sets down better defined conditions for imposing anti-dumping duties. The new Agreement contains an improved market-sharing definition, more strict conditions for causality and proof of injury. However, it remains that the only rationale for adopting anti-dumping countervail is to avoid predatory pricing by foreign firms which unduly apply price differentials to penetrate the import market and predate by injuring domestic competitors with the intent of drawing them out of the market, in order to monopolize once that aim is achieved. Nevertheless, anti-dumping action would gain by being considered a competition issue, and being treated according to competition criteria, due regard being given to the relevant market, market share of a significant size, and anti-dumping redress should be afforded to anti-competitive cases only. This would eliminate the important element of protectionism which is inherent otherwise to the system.

Agriculture

If, as we believe, competition policy makes sense in all sectors, agriculture is no exception to the rule. Administrative prices have resulted in excessive supplies in some countries, while competitive exports of developing and other food-exporting countries are being hampered. The results obtained under the Agreement – however minimal – are a step in the right direction. It is better to have import competition in 5 per cent of the domestic market than no import competition at all.

Textiles

The same can be said for the gradual extinction of the MFA. One criticism is that while concessions in other Agreements that are part of the Uruguay Round 'package' are to be implemented outright, some 50 per cent of the MFA restrictions will only be scrapped after the year 2000.

GATS

The General Agreement on Trade in Services provides, *inter alia*, that members will ensure that monopoly suppliers of services in their domestic market will not act in a manner inconsistent with their MFN treatment obligations. In particular, where a monopoly supplier of a service competes, either directly or through an affiliated company, in the supply of a service outside the scope of its monopoly rights, the member will ensure that the supplier does not abuse its monopoly position. The GATS Agreement entitles the Council for Trade in Services to take remedial action with regard to a complaint by a member against a monopoly supplier of a service. The Agreement also recognizes that certain business practices may restrain competition and thereby trade in services, and provides for consultations among members in order to remedy such practices.

TRIPs

The Agreement on Trade-Related Aspects of Intellectual Property Rights (TRIPs) provides, with respect to licensing agreements, that members are free to specify in their national legislation restrictive practices that constitute an abuse of intellectual property rights that have an adverse effect on competition. It is also established, for the purpose of dispute settlement, that nothing in the Agreement may be used to address the issue of the exhaustion of rights. Nevertheless, apart from seriously strengthening intellectual property rights, the Agreement falls short from defining the borderline between competition rules and IPRs. Views on this question are far from being harmonized and much remains to be done.

159

TRIMs: foreign direct investment and competition rules

Restrictive investment measures were seen by developing countries unable to avoid restrictive business practices for lack of legislation and effective controls, as a means to avoid certain restrictive business practices. As a long list of countries have liberalized their FDI rules to attract foreign investment, the TRIMs Agreement concedes that 'no later than 5 years after entry into force of the WTO, the Trade Committee will consider the necessity of launching negotiations on codes on investment and competition'. While negotiations are already taking place under the auspices of OECD, nothing so far has been decided on the competition front. National competition policy can no doubt be used to counter possible anti-competitive practices of foreign investors. In particular, monopoly or dominant position-creating mergers or take-overs by foreign firms can be challenged by the national competition authority, on the condition that the competition law of the host country includes merger provisions. On the other hand, FDI may be attracted if a host country applies similar competition rules as those applied in the parent firm's country. This would ensure the investor that the domestic market will not be blocked from entry by restrictive arrangements among local competitors. Of course, competition legislation will also ensure that foreign firms – in the same way as domestic ones – do not apply RBPs or dominate the relevant market.

The Plurilateral Agreement on Government Procurement

Subsequent to the Uruguay Round, but also directly linked to the competition issue, the government procurement code (signed by twenty-one countries, mostly developed) contains a number of provisions aimed at ensuring correct use of tendering procedures and opening competition to foreign bidders, thus opening markets and increasing the competitive process in international trade. It also provides for procedures enabling suppliers and service providers to challenge alleged misconduct in the award of contracts.

IV Competition and some 'new issues' for the trade agenda

Along with restrictive business practices, a number of other issues such as export credit guarantees, labour standards, etc. were proposed at Marrakesh as new issues for inclusion in the future trade agenda. In this connection, it is important to note that the WTO ministerial conference was due to meet in December 1996 to assess implementation of the 1994 GATT world trade treaty, at which meeting it might well decide to initiate work in some of the 'new issues'. The Minister for Trade and Industry of Singapore, speaking at a conference on 'Future Directions for the Multilateral Trading System'

160

in Brisbane, Australia, on 22 February 1996, said that 'the Ministerial Conference must first consolidate the achievements of the Uruguay Round'. 'Secondly, its agenda must reflect a balance between the interests and concerns of all WTO members, both developing and developed. And thirdly, the agenda must provide further impetus to the ongoing evolution of the global trading system'. He then proposed a five-point agenda: (i) stock-taking; (ii) unfinished business (financial services interim agreement; telecoms and maritime transport); (iii) trade and environment; (iv) the new issues; and (v) further trade liberalization: in particular the 'built-in' agenda of the Uruguay Round of negotiations in agriculture and services, a review by no later than 2001 of the TRIMs Agreement, TRIPs, etc.

Concerning the choice of new issues, he proposed three questions as criteria of decision:

1   Is the issue trade-related?
2   Is the WTO the best forum to address the issue?
3   Is the issue mature for negotiations within the WTO?

We might qualify the first question: Is the issue trade-related and *does it substantially affect markets*? And pose a fourth question:

4   Which international organization is best qualified to tackle the issue effectively, given its background, its objectives and experience?

Apart from competition and trade, several other new issues proposed are considered trade-distorting issues and have therefore been proposed for inclusion in the new trade agenda.

Environment and trade

This issue is clearly on the trade agenda because countries with strict environmental standards feel at a competitive disadvantage when competing with exports of countries where such costly regulations are not in place or not enforced. Hence, the issue is already receiving due attention both at UNCTAD and at WTO.

Labour standards

Also considered to distort competition, everybody agrees that child labour and prisoner labour are to be banned. However, the extent to which low labour standards distort trade flows is unclear, and in competition terms the market share involved in such products is likely to be irrelevant, making it an unlikely subject for the new trade agenda. It would seem that the best way to deal with this issue is to bring it to the International Labour

Organization, which is specialized in dealing with labour issues. Moreover, the WTO does not seem suited to enforce labour standards, as it should not be made to diverge from its goal of trade liberalization, providing a pretext for legitimizing protectionist measures.

Corruption and bribery

Another trade (and competition) distorting practice, bribing can undoubtedly interfere with proper tendering procedures and contract awards. A proposed Draft International Agreement on Illicit Payments has been prepared by the United Nations and is pending since 1991. Provided further negotiations, the UN Code on Corrupt Practices might be used as a basis for agreement in this area. Beneficiaries would, *inter alia*, be taxpayers all over the world. Nevertheless, this issue is mainly a government procurement and penal law problem. While it is easy to see how the government as a purchaser might wish to redress collusive tendering (bid-rigging), it is more difficult to foresee how states would act if they were in a position to bribe foreign officials in order to get an important order through.

Export credit guarantees

Competing conditions including grants and long-term preferential credit for exports end up favouring the countries whose export credit guarantee systems are the strongest and the most efficient; hence resulting in a sort of trade-distorting subsidy. It is obvious that developing countries which are weaker financial partners might be unable to compete in such circumstances, even if the goods they sell are competitive on grounds of price and quality. However, for heavy-investment purchases where developing countries are not competitors, export facilities might be considered very favourably, as they facilitate acquisition by these countries. The problem is that in many other sectors, where developing countries and countries in transition are potential exporters, competition among export credit schemes might result in distorting trade to the detriment of financially less powerful countries.

V An outlook: competition beyond Singapore

The main questions to be answered in this area are the following:

1   Is the issue of competition trade-related, and does it affect trade in such a substantial manner that it deserves consideration at the multilateral level?
2   Is a comprehensive multilateral framework necessary, or is it sufficient to let competition and trade issues evolve 'naturally', so to speak, under specific WTO agreements, and in bilateral and regional competition cooperation agreements?

162

3   Is the WTO the best forum to address the issue of competition and trade? Should the issue first be matured in other, more appropriate fora, such as OECD and UNCTAD?

To answer the first question, it is evident that competition and trade are closely related, and that any trade distortion is, in essence, a distortion to competition. Moreover, if the basic gains to be derived from competition (namely, increased efficiency in resource allocation, lower prices and better quality and choice for the consumer, as a result of increased innovation brought about by the incentives of competition) are recognized to exist at the domestic level, as demonstrated by the rapidly increasing number of countries – developed, developing, as well as in transition adopting competition policy – then the same advantages should also exist at the global level. Moreover, anti-competitive practices, or RBPs, obviously affect international trade substantially and deserve attention at the multilateral level. Experience of the EU is also relevant in this respect.

As to question two, we have seen that, in the absence of a comprehensive multilateral framework other than the United Nations' Set on RBPs, a growing number of countries have, or are in the process of adopting national competition legislation and establishing national competition authorities. Some countries, mainly the big trading partners, have established bilateral cooperation agreements involving notification, consultations and sometimes conciliation procedures. The OECD has adopted a recommendation in this respect, and consultation procedures are provided in the United Nations' Set, and the UNCTAD Expert Group, at its annual meeting, provides the facilities for consultations among its participants.

Moreover, as described earlier in this paper, the Uruguay Round Agreements are related, directly or indirectly, to competition considerations, in a somewhat piecemeal approach.

The time might well be ripe for competition to be addressed in a comprehensive multilateral framework, rather than under the present patchwork of evolving trade agreements. There are many reasons for this. First, bilateral agreements are only between a few important trading partners. Most other countries, and especially developing countries, are not covered in that framework. Besides, even if such bilateral agreements could flourish, they would inevitably involve overlaps, gaps and might even include conflicting requirements. They would also bring together unequal partners where the agreement might favour the largest trading partner either in its rules, or in practice.

On the other hand, momentum exists at the multilateral level, as a result of the Uruguay Round and in the light of pressures of globalization and liberalization. A multilateral framework would eliminate inconsistencies and gaps, create a level playing field, where all partners, whether large or small, developed or developing would benefit from equal protection in a more predictable, transparent and politically coherent system.

163

As to question three, is the WTO the best forum to address this issue?

- At present some twenty-nine countries, including the Russian Federation and China, have applied to join the WTO but are still not members.
- Many countries still need to adopt national competition law and develop expertise in implementation. They need technical assistance urgently.
- Developing countries and many countries in transition need to train their own negotiators in this relatively new and complex area before being ready to enter into multilateral negotiations on competition policy.
- Other than the piecemeal approach in its Uruguay Round Agreements, the WTO has presently no experience in this field.

Other international organizations, such as the OECD, the World Bank and in particular UNCTAD, have long-term experience in the area of restrictive business practices and competition in developing countries. UNCTAD IX reconfirmed UNCTAD's role as the principal development arm of the General Assembly of the United Nations.

Therefore, it would seem essential, irrespective of whether a formal or informal working group on competition and trade is established in WTO in December, that close cooperation between WTO and other organizations active in this field, such as UNCTAD, be ensured, in line with the cooperation agreement reached earlier last year between the Secretary General of UNCTAD and the Director General of WTO.

This brings me to the subsidiary question: what would the multilateral competition framework look like?

In the final analysis, a comprehensive multilateral competition framework should be placed under the chapeau of the WTO dispute settlement mechanism, to form an integral part of the international trading system. As envisaged, such a multilateral competition framework within the international trading system should not in the foreseeable future result in the creation of a supranational world competition authority entrusted with the mammoth task of investigating infringements and of fining enterprises and their managers. This task would continue to be that of domestic or regional competition authorities. Rather, the multilateral framework would:

- promote increased harmonization of domestic competition systems, while recognizing national particularities (domestic laws would still be tailor-made and implemented nationally);
- ensure that national competition regimes adhere to the same basic principles, such as national treatment and non-discrimination in application of competition legislation; and
- place international competition policy under the aegis of the multilateral dispute settlement mechanism established in the WTO.

To this end, a first stage of work would involve an effort to 'clear the ground' before a final set of principles and rules can be adopted. This would, in particular, include:

- creating awareness in developing countries;
- training negotiators from developing countries;
- analysis and study of the main issues of 'common ground';
- narrowing the gaps in issues where the 'common ground' is presently absent; and
- gathering the relevant material, data and empirical evidence.

This work could be done in pursuance of the broad mandate given to UNCTAD by the Third United Nations Conference to Review All Aspects of the Set, as well as the Midrand UNCTAD IX Conference, in close cooperation with the other international organizations active in this area.

NOTES

1 The author is Chief of UNCTAD's Restrictive Business Practices Unit. The views expressed in this note, however, are those of the author, and do not necessarily reflect those of UNCTAD.
2 For all references to the Set of Multilaterally Agreed Equitable Principles and Rules for the Control of Restrictive Business Practices, Resolution adopted by the United Nations conference on restricitive business practices on 22 April 1980, see Annex I.

ANNEX I

II. Resolution adopted by the United Nations Conference on Restrictive Business Practices on 22 April 1980

The Set of Multilaterally Agreed Equitable Principles and Rules for the Control of Restrictive Business Practices

The United Nations Conference on Restrictive Business Practices,

Recalling General Assembly resolution 33/153 of 20 December 1978, which required the Conference to negotiate, on the basis of the work of the Third *Ad hoc* Group of Experts on Restrictive Business Practices, and to take all decisions necessary for the adoption of, a set of multilaterally agreed equitable principles and rules for the control of restrictive business practices having adverse effects on international trade, particularly that of developing countries, and on the economic development of those countries, including a decision on the legal character of the principles and rules,

Having held its first session from 19 November to 8 December 1979 and its second session from 8 to 22 April 1980,

1 *Approves* the Set of Multilaterally Agreed Equitable Principles and Rules for the Control of Restrictive Business Practices annexed hereto;[1]
2 *Transmits* to the General Assembly at its thirty-fifth session this Set of Principles and Rules, having taken all decisions necessary for its adoption as a resolution;
3 *Recommends also* that the General Assembly, 5 years after the adoption of the Set of Principles and Rules, convene a United Nations Conference under the auspices of UNCTAD for the purpose of reviewing all the aspects of the Set of Principles and Rules.

7th plenary meeting
22 April 1980

III. Resolution 35/63 adopted by the General Assembly at its Thirty-Fifth Session, on 5 December 1980

Restrictive business practices

The General Assembly

Recalling its resolution 3201 (S–VI) and 3202 (S–VI) of 1 May 1974, containing the Declaration and the Programme of Action on the Establishment of a New International Economic Order, 3281 (XXIX) of 12 December 1974, containing the Charter of Economic Rights and Duties of States, and 3362 (S–VII) of 16 September 1975 on development and international economic co-operation,

Recalling that the United Nations Conference on Restrictive Business Practices, convened by the General Assembly in its resolution 33/153 of 20 December 1978, held its first session from 19 November to 8 December 1979 and, in accordance with Assembly decision 34/447 of 19 December 1979, held a second session from 8 to 22 April 1989,

Noting with satisfaction that the Conference approved the Set of Multilaterally Agreed Equitable Principles and Rules for the Control of Restrictive Business Practices[2] and transmitted it to the General Assembly at its thirty-fifth session, having taken all the necessary decisions for its adoption as a resolution,

Noting that the United Nations Conference on Trade and Development, by its resolution 103 (V) of 30 May 1979,[3] requested the United Nations Conference on Restrictive Business Practices to make recommendations through the General Assembly to the Trade and Development Board with regard to the institutional aspects of future work on restrictive business practices within the framework of the United Nations Conference on Trade and Development, bearing in mind the work done in this field elsewhere in the United Nations,

1 *Adopts* the Set of Multilaterally Agreed Equitable Principles and Rules for the Control of Restrictive Business Practices, approved by the United Nations Conference on Restrictive Business Practices;

2 *Decides* to convene, in 1985, under the auspices of the United Nations Conference on Trade and Development, a United Nations conference to review all aspects of the Set of Multilaterally Agreed Equitable Principles and Rules for the Control of Restrictive Business Practices;

3 *Takes note* of the recommendation of the United Nations Conference on Restrictive Business Practices regarding international institutional machinery, contained in section G of the Set of Principles and Rules, and requests the Trade and Development Board, at its twenty-second session, to establish an intergovernmental group of experts on restrictive business practices, operating within the framework of a committee of the United Nations Conference on Trade and Development, to perform the functions designated in that section;

4 *Decides also* that the necessary resources should be made available to the United Nations Conference on Trade and Development to carry out the tasks embodied in the Set of Principles and Rules.

83rd plenary meeting
5 December 1980

IV. The Set of Multilaterally Agreed Equitable Principles and Rules for the Control of Restrictive Business Practices[4]

The United Nations Conference on Restrictive Business Practices

Recognising that restrictive business practices can adversely affect international trade, particularly that of developing countries, and the economic development of these countries,

Affirming that a set of multilaterally agreed equitable principles and rules for the control of restrictive business practices can contribute to attaining the objective in the establishment of a new international economic order to eliminate restrictive business practices adversely affecting international trade and thereby contribute to development and improvement of international economic relations on a just and equitable basis,

Recognising also the need to ensure that restrictive business practices do not impede or negate the realisation of benefits that should arise from the liberalisation of tariff and non-tariff barriers affecting international trade, particularly those affecting the trade and development of developing countries,

Considering the possible adverse impact of restrictive business practices, including among others those resulting from the increased

168

activities of transnational corporations, on the trade and development of developing countries,

Convinced of the need for action to be taken by countries in a mutually reinforcing manner at the national, regional and international levels to eliminate or effectively deal with restrictive business practices, including those of transnational corporations, adversely affecting international trade, particularly that of developing countries, and the economic development of these countries,

Convinced also of the benefits to be derived from a universally applicable set of multilaterally agreed equitable principles and rules for the control of restrictive business practices and that all countries should encourage their enterprises to follow in all respects the provisions of such a set of multilaterally agreed equitable principles and rules,

Convinced further that the adoption of such a set of multilaterally agreed equitable principles and rules for the control of restrictive business practices will thereby facilitate the adoption and strengthening of laws and policies in the area of restrictive business practices at the national and regional levels and thus lead to improved conditions and attain greater efficiency and participation in international trade and development, particularly that of developing countries, and to protect and promote social welfare in general, and in particular the interests of consumers in both developed and developing countries,

Affirming also the need to eliminate the disadvantages to trade and development which may result from the restrictive business practices of transnational corporations or other enterprises, and thus help to maximise benefits to international trade and particularly the trade and development of developing countries,

Affirming further the need that measures adopted by States for the control of restrictive business practices should be applied fairly, equitably, on the same basis to all enterprises and in accordance with established procedures of law; and for States to take into account the principles and objectives of the Set of Multilaterally Agreed Equitable Principles and Rules,

Hereby agrees on the following Set of Principles and Rules for the control of restrictive business practice, which take the form of recommendation:

A. *Objectives*

Taking into account the interests of all countries, particularly those of developing countries, the Set of Multilaterally Agreed Equitable

Principles and Rules are framed in order to achieve the following objectives:

1 To ensure that restrictive business practices do not impede or negate the realisation of benefits that should arise from the liberalisation of tariff and non-tariff barriers affecting world trade, particularly those affecting the trade and development of countries;

2 To attain greater efficiency in international trade and development particularly that of developing countries, in accordance with national aims of economic and social development and existing economic structures, such as through:

(a) The creation, encouragement and protection of competition
(b) Control of the concentration of capital and/or economic power
(c) Encouragement of innovation

3 To protect and promote social welfare in general and, in particular, the interests of consumers in both developed and developing countries;

4 To eliminate the disadvantages to trade and development which may result from the restrictive business practices of transnational corporations or other enterprises, and thus help to maximise benefits to international trade and particularly the trade and development of developing countries;

5 To provide a Set of Multilaterally Agreed Equitable Principles and Rules for the control of restrictive business practices for adoption at the international level and thereby to facilitate the adoption and strengthening of laws and policies in this area at the national and regional levels.

B. Definitions and scope of application

For the purpose of this Set of Multilaterally Agreed Equitable Principles and Rules:

(i) Definitions

1 'Restrictive business practices' means acts of behaviour of enterprises which, through an abuse or acquisition and abuse of a dominant position of market power, limit access to markets or otherwise unduly restrain competition, having or being likely to have adverse effects on international trade, particularly that of developing

170

countries, and on the economic development of these countries, or which though formal, informal, written or unwritten agreements or arrangements among enterprises, have the same impact.

2 'Dominant position of market power' refers to a situation where an enterprise, either by itself or acting together with a few other enterprises, is in a position to control the relevant market for a particular good service or group of goods or services.

3 'Enterprises' means firms, partnerships, corporations, companies, other associations, natural of juridical persons, or any combination thereof, irrespective of the mode of creation or control or ownership, private or State, which are engaged in commercial activities, and included their branches, subsidiaries, affiliates, or other entities directly or indirectly controlled by them.

(ii) Scope of application

4 The Set of Principles and Rules applies to restrictive business practices, including those of transnational corporations, adversely affecting international trade, particularly that of developing countries and the economic development of these countries. It applies irrespective of whether such practices involve enterprises in one or more countries.

5 The 'principles and rules for enterprises, including transnational corporations' apply to all transactions in goods and services.

6 The 'principles and rules for enterprises, including transnational corporations' are addressed to all enterprises.

7 The provisions of the Set of Principles and Rules shall be universally applicable to all countries and enterprises regardless of the parties involved in the transactions, acts or behaviour.

Any reference to 'States' or 'Governments' shall be construed as including any regional grouping of States, to the extent that they have competence in the area of restrictive business practices.

9 The Set of Principles and Rules shall not apply to intergovernmental agreements, not to restrictive business practices directly caused by such agreements.

C. Multilaterally agreed equitable principles for the control of restrictive business practices

In line with the objectives set forth, the following principles are to apply:

(i) General principles

1 Appropriate action should be taken in a mutually reinforcing manner at national, regional and international levels to eliminate, or effectively deal with, restrictive business practices, including those of transnational corporations, adversely affecting international trade, particularly that of developing countries and the economic development of these countries.

2 Collaboration between Governments at bilateral and multilateral levels should be established and, where such collaboration has been established, it should be improved to facilitate the control of restrictive business practices.

3 Appropriate mechanisms should be devised at the international level and/or the use of existing international machinery improved to facilitate exchange and dissemination of information among Governments with respect to restrictive business practices.

4 Appropriate means should be devised to facilitate the holding of multilateral consultations with regard to policy issues relating to the control of restrictive business practices.

5 The provisions of the Set of Principles and Rules should not be construed as justifying conduct by enterprises which is unlawful under applicable national or regional legislation.

(ii) Relevant factors in the application of the Set of Principles and Rules

6 In order to ensure the fair and equitable application of the Set of Principles and Rules, States, while bearing in mind the need to ensure the comprehensive application of the Set of Principles and Rules, should take due account of the extent to which the conduct of enterprises, whether or not created or controlled by States, is accepted under applicable legislation or regulations, bearing in mind that such laws and regulations should be clearly defined and publicly and readily available, as is required by States.

(iii) Preferential or differential treatment for developing countries

7 In order to ensure the equitable application of the Set of Principles and Rules, States, particularly developed countries, should take into account in their control of restrictive business practices the development, financial and trade needs of developing countries, in

particular of the least developed countries, for the purposes especially of developing countries in:

(a) Promoting the establishment or development of domestic industries and the economic development of other sectors of the economy; and

(b) Encouraging their economic development through regional or global arrangements among developing countries.

D. Principles and rules for enterprises, including transnational corporations

1 Enterprises should conform to the restrictive business practices laws, and the provisions concerning restrictive business practices in other laws, of the countries in which they operate, and, in the event of proceedings under these laws, should be subject to the competence of the courts and relevant administrative bodies therein.

2 Enterprises should consult and co-operate with competent authorities of countries directly affected in controlling restrictive business practices adversely affecting the interests of those countries. In this regard, enterprises should also provide information, in particular details of restrictive arrangements, required for this purpose, including that which may be located in foreign countries, to the extent that in the latter event such production or disclosure is not prevented by applicable law or established public policy. Whenever the provision of information is on a voluntary basis, its provision should be in accordance with safeguards normally applicable in this field.

3 Enterprises, except when dealing with each other in the context of an economic entity wherein they are under common control, including through ownership, or otherwise not able to act independently of each other, engaged on the market in rival, or potentially rival activities, should refrain from practices such as the following when, through formal, informal, written or unwritten agreements or arrangements, they limit access to markets or otherwise unduly restrain competition, having or being likely to have adverse effects on international trade, particularly that of developing countries, and on the economic development of these countries:

(a) Agreements fixing prices, including as to exports and imports;

(b) Collusive tendering;

(c) Market or customer allocation arrangements;

(d) Allocation by quota as to sales and production;

(e) Collective action to enforce arrangements, e.g. by concerted refusals to deal;

(f) Concerted refusal of supplies to potential importers;

(g) Collective denial of access to an arrangement, or association, which is crucial to competition.

4 Enterprises should refrain from the following acts or behaviour in a relevant market when, through an abuse[5] or acquisition and abuse of a dominant position of market power, they limit access to markets or otherwise unduly restrain competition, having or being likely to have adverse effects on international trade, particularly that of developing countries, and on the economic development of these countries:

(a) Predatory behaviour towards competitors, such as using below-cost pricing to eliminate competitors;

(b) Discriminatory (i.e. unjustifiably differentiated) pricing or terms or conditions in the supply or purchase of goods or services, including by means of the use of pricing policies in transactions between affiliated enterprises which overcharge or undercharge for goods or services purchased or supplied as compared with prices for similar or comparable transactions outside the affiliated enterprises;

(c) Mergers, take-overs, joint ventures or other acquisitions of control, whether of a horizontal, vertical or a conglomerate nature;

(d) Fixing the prices at which good exported can be resold in importing countries;

(e) Restrictions on the importation of goods which have been legitimately marked abroad with a trademark identical with or similar to the trademark protected as to identical or similar goods in the importing country where the trademarks in question are of the same origin, i.e. belong to the same owner or are used by enterprises between which there is economic, organizational, managerial or legal interdependence and where the purpose of such restrictions is to maintain artificially high prices;

(f) When not for ensuring the achievement of legitimate business purposes, such as quality, safety, adequate distribution or service:

(i) Partial or complete refusals to deal on the enterprise's customary commerical terms;

(ii) Making the supply of particular goods or services dependent upon the acceptance of restrictions on the distribution or manufacture of competing or other goods;

(iii) Imposing restrictions concerning where, or to whom, or in what form or quantities, goods supplied or other goods may be resold or exported;

(iv) Making the supply of particular goods or services dependent upon the purchase of other goods or services from the supplier or his designee.

E. Principles and rules for state at national, regional and subregional levels

1 States should, at the national level or through regional groupings, adopt, improve and effectively enforce appropriate legislation and implementing judicial and administrative procedures for the control of restrictive business practices, including those of transnational corporations.

2 States should base their legislation primarily on the principle of eliminating or effectively dealing with acts or behaviour of enterprises which, through an abuse or acquisition and abuse of a dominant position of market power, limit access to markets or otherwise unduly restrain competition, having or being likely to have adverse effects on their trade or economic development, or which through formal, informal, written or unwritten agreements or arrangements among enterprises have the same impact.

3 States, in their control of restrictive business practices, should ensure treatment of enterprises which is fair, equitable, on the same basis to all enterprises, and in accordance with established procedures of law. The laws and regulations should be publicly and readily available.

4 States should seek appropriate remedial or preventive measures to prevent and/or control the use of restrictive business practices within their competence when it comes to the attention of States that such practices adversely affect international trade, and particularly the trade and development of the developing countries.

5 Where, for the purposes of the control of restrictive business practices, a State obtains information from enterprises containing legitimate business secrets, it should accord such information reasonable safeguards normally applicable in this field, particularly to protect its confidentiality.

6 States should institute or improve procedures for obtaining

information from enterprises, including transnational corporations, necessary for their effective control of restrictive business practices, including in this respect details of restrictive agreements, under-standings and other arrangements.

7 States should establish appropriate mechanisms at the regional and subregional levels to promote exchange of information on restrictive business practices and on the application of national laws and poli-cies in this area, and to assist each other to their mutual advantage regarding control of restrictive business practices at the regional and subregional levels.

8 States with greater expertise in the operation of systems for the control of restrictive business practices should, on request, share their experience with, or otherwise provide technical assistance to, other States wishing to develop or improve such systems.

9 States should, on request, or at their own initiate when the need comes to their attention, supply to other States, particularly devel-oping countries, publicly available information, and, to the extent consistent with their laws and established public policy, other infor-mation necessary to the receiving interested State for its effective control of restrictive business practices.

F. International measures

Collaboration at the international level should aim at eliminating or effectively dealing with restrictive business practices, including those of transnational corporations, through strengthening and improving controls over restrictive business practices adversely affecting inter-national trade, particularly that of developing countries, and the economic development of these countries. In this regard, action should include:

1 Work aimed at achieving common approaches in national policies relating to restrictive business practices compatible with the Set of Principles and Rules.

2 Communication annually to the Secretary-General of UNCTAD of appropriate information on steps taken by States and regional group-ings to meet their commitment to the Set of Principles and Rules, and information on the adoption, development and application of legislation, regulations and policies concerning restrictive business practices.

3 Continued publication annually by UNCTAD of a report on

developments in restrictive business practices legislation and on restrictive business practices adversely affecting international trade, particularly the trade and development of developing countries, based upon publicly available information and as far as possible other information, particularly on the basis of requests addressed to all member States or provided at their own initiative and, where appropriate, to the United Nations Centre on Transnational Corporations and other competent international organizations.

4 Consultations:

(a) Where a State, particularly of a developing country, believes that a consultation with another State or States is appropriate in regard to an issue concerning control of restrictive business practices, it may request a consultation with those States with a view to finding a mutually acceptable solution. When a consultation is to be held, the State involved may request the secretary-general of UNCTAD to provide mutually agreed conference facilities for such a consultation;

(b) States should accord full consideration to requests for consultations and, upon agreement as to the subject of and the procedures for such a consultation, the consultation should take place at an appropriate time;

(c) If the States involved so agree, a joint report on the consultations and their results should be prepared by the States involved and, if they so wish, with the assistance of the UNCTAD secretariat, and be made available to the secretary-general of UNCTAD for inclusion in the annual report on restrictive business practices.

5 Continued work within UNCTAD on the elaboration of a model law or laws on restrictive business practices in order to assist developing countries in devising appropriate legislation. States should provide necessary information and experience to UNCTAD in this connection.

6 Implementation within or facilitation by UNCTAD, and other relevant organisations of the United Nations system in conjunction with UNCTAD, of technical assistance, advisory and training programmes on restrictive business practices, particularly for developing countries:

(a) Experts should be provided to assist developing countries, at their request, in formulating or improving restrictive business practices legislation and procedures;

(b) Seminars, training programmes or courses should be held, primarily in developing countries, to train officials involved or likely to be involved in administering restrictive business practices legislation and, in this connection, advantages should be taken, *inter alia*, of the experience and knowledge of administrative authorities, especially in developed countries, in detecting the use of restrictive business practises;

(c) A handbook on restrictive business practices legislation should be compiled;

(d) Relevant books, documents, manuals and any other information on matters related to restrictive business practices should be collected and made available, particularly to developing countries;

(e) Exchange of personnel between restrictive business practices authorities should be arranged and facilitated;

(f) International conferences on restrictive business practices legislation and policy should be arranged;

(g) Seminars for an exchange of views on restrictive business practices among persons in the public and private sectors should be arranged.

7 International organisations and financing programmes, in particular the United Nations Development Programme, should be called upon to provide resources through appropriate channels and modalities for the financing of activities set out in Paragraph 6 above. Furthermore, all countries are invited, in particular the developed countries, to make voluntary financial and other contributions for the above-mentioned activities.

G. *International institutional machinery*

(i) *Institutional arrangements*

1 An Intergovernmental Group of Experts on Restrictive Business Practices operating within the framework of a Committee of UNCTAD will provide the institutional machinery.

2 States which have accepted the Set of Principles and Rules should take appropriate steps at the national or regional levels to meet their commitment to the Set of Principles and Rules.

(ii)   Functions of the Intergovernmental Group

3   The Intergovernmental Group shall have the following functions:

(a)   To provide a forum and modalities for multilateral consultations, discussion and exchange of view between States on matters related to the Set of Principles and rules, in particular its operation and the experience arising therefrom;

(b)   To undertake and disseminate periodically studies and research on restrictive business practices related to the provisions of the Set of Principles and Rules, with a view to increasing exchange of experience and giving greater effect to the Set of Principles and Rules;

(c)   To invite and consider relevant studies, documentation and reports from relevant organisations of the United Nations system;

(d)   To study matters relating to the Set of Principles and Rules and which might be characterised by data covering business transactions and other relevant information obtained upon request addressed to all States;

(e)   To collect and disseminate information on matters relating to the Set of Principles and Rules to the over-all attainment of its goals and to appropriate steps States have taken at the national or regional levels to promote an effective Set of Principles and Rules, including its objectives and principles;

(f)   To make appropriate reports and recommendations to States on matters within its competence, including the application and implementation of the Set of Multilaterally Agreed Equitable Principles and Rules;

(g)   To submit reports at least once a year on its work.

4   In the performance of its functions, neither the Intergovernmental Group nor its subsidiary organs shall act like a tribunal or otherwise pass judgement on the activities or conduct of individual Governments or of individual enterprises in connection with a specific business transaction. The Intergovernmental Group or its subsidiary organs should avoid becoming involved when enterprises to a specific business transaction are in dispute.

5   The Intergovernmental Group shall establish such procedures as may be necessary to deal with issues related to confidentiality.

(iii)   Review procedure

6 Subject to the approval of the General Assembly, five years after the adoption of the Set of Principles and Rules, a United Nations Conference shall be convened by the Secretary-General of the United Nations under the auspices of UNCTAD for the purpose of reviewing all the aspects of the Set of Principles and Rules. Towards this end, the Intergovernmental Group shall make proposals to the Conference for the improvement and further development of the Set of Principles and Rules.

Notes to the annex

1 See section IV below.

2 See section IV below.

3 See *Proceedings of the United Nations Conference on Trade and Development, Fifth Session, vol. I, Report and Annexes* (United Nations publication, Sales No. E.79.II.D.14), part one, sect. A.

4 The Set of Principles and Rules was adopted by the United Nations Conference on Restrictive Business Practices and an annex to its resolution of 22 April 1989 (see section II above).

5 Whether acts or behaviour are abusive or not should be examined in terms of their purpose and effects in the actual situation, in particular with reference to whether they limit access to markers or otherwise unduly restrain competition, having or being likely to have adverse affects on international trade, particularly that of developing countries, and on the economic development of these countries, and to whether they are:

(a) appropriate in the light of the organizational, managerial and legal relationship among the enterprises concerned, such as in the context of relations within an economic entity and not having restrictive effects outside the related enterprises;

(b) appropriate in light of special conditions or economic circumstances in the relevant market such as exceptional conditions of supply and demand or the size of the market;

(c) of types which are usually treated as acceptable under pertinent national or regional laws and regulations for the control of restrictive business practices;

(d) consistent with the purpose and objectives of these principles and rules.

Part IV

EUROPEAN ECONOMIC
AREA POLICIES

11

EU COMPETITION POLICY IN THE NEW TRADE ORDER

Karel van Miert

Why do we need more cooperation in the field of competition policy?

I would like to begin by commenting briefly on those factors which lead us in Europe, especially those of us at the European Commission, to the belief that increased international cooperation is essential – even inevitable – in the coming years. I will then take a look at the state of international cooperation in competition policy and enforcement, before putting forward some ideas on how cooperation might develop in the future.

To begin, two main factors have nurtured the belief that increased international cooperation is essential in the new trade order. The first is increased globalization. The second – stemming directly from this increased globalization – is the inevitability of increasing overlap, and thus contact, between the activities of national competition authorities.

Globalization

Globalization is no longer a trend, but a reality which is changing our lives. The eight GATT negotiating rounds and the resulting reduction in tariffs have led to a boom in world trade – from about US$2,000 billion in the early 1960s to over US$5,000 billion in 1994. An increasing part of this is represented by 'vertical trade' in which different stages in the production chain are completed by companies (and sometimes by the same company) in different countries.

With the increasing influence of new technologies this process will continue to accelerate in the coming years. In particular the 'telecommunications revolution', which has only just got under way, is certain to have a dramatic impact.

Another consequence of globalization is that regulatory measures adopted in one country may have a positive or negative impact in other countries. This is clearly true for the environment, but the same can be said about fiscal and monetary policies, securities regulation, standards, certification procedures and many other fields of government activity.

Similarly the way competition policies are (or are not) enforced has an inevitable impact on a country's trading partners.

More specifically two different problems may be identified.

First, in a world where state-imposed trade barriers are disappearing, especially in the wake of the (GATT) Uruguay Round, anti-competitive practices are becoming more prominent in determining the development of cross-border trade. There is a risk that public trade barriers may be replaced by restrictive business practices, undermining years of effort to liberalize world trade.

We have some experience of this phenomenon within the EU. As we completed our Single Market programme, businesses were sometimes tempted to take steps to protect their traditional 'national markets', for example, through horizontal cartels designed to divide the European market. We have enforced our competition law vigorously against such practices and have imposed fines at high, deterrent levels. We have also acted against vertical distribution arrangements which partition markets within the EU.

We face a comparable challenge at a world-wide level, with a comparable need to provide, at least among the world's main trading partners, for consistency in the enforcement of competition rules against anti-competitive conduct which impedes international trade.

Inevitability

Secondly, even if competition law were enforced with equal determination by all the world's main trading partners, closer cooperation among competition agencies would still be necessary because more and more competition problems transcend national boundaries. International cartels, mergers or abuses of market power are rarely limited to just one country.

It is not surprising that national authorities face increasing difficulties in dealing with such cross-border practises. Crucial evidence may be located outside their jurisdiction. Other agencies, looking at the same case, might adopt a different approach or different remedies. Consultation and some exchange of information and/or coordination of enforcement action may be the only way to apply the competition rules effectively.

Impediments to closer cooperation

Given the fact of globalization, the increasing interconnection and inter-reliance of national economies, and the increasingly international nature of commerce which has resulted from these trends, why has there been so little cooperation between competition authorities until recently?

One reason may be that countries do not always agree on the purposes of competition policy. For example, even if the details of tax law differ from one country to another, most countries would agree that tax fraud is an offence. More generally, democratic countries share basically the same approach on the scope of criminal law, although rules differ from jurisdiction to jurisdiction. This sort of broad consensus has not yet been achieved in some areas of competition policy.

Moreover, within the same country, policy emphasis may vary over time. Competition policy is influenced by political change and a developing understanding of economics. Above all, policy must adapt to the rapid evolution of the industries and markets that are its focus of attention. Competition policies focus on domestic markets. A good illustration of this is the fact that export cartels, which have harmful effects on foreign markets, in most instances are not subject to competition rules.

A second obstacle to cooperation among competition authorities stems from the very nature of competition policy. This can be better understood if we compare competition policy with trade policy.

Trade policy deals with measures adopted by countries that, in most cases, are publicly known and easily identifiable. It has therefore been possible under the GATT (and now under the WTO) to set up dispute settlement mechanisms in order to ensure that measures adopted by national authorities are consistent with internationally agreed principles and rules. Assuming that comparable sets of common rules could be negotiated among competition authorities, we would still have difficulty with fact-finding, which is, after all, an essential part of competition policy. Anti-competitive practises are often concealed and are certainly not readily identifiable. Even if all the contracting parties to an international agreement on competition rules undertook to put an end to certain anti-competitive practices, it would be far from easy to make sure that these commitments were fully complied with.

Existing models of cooperation

Bilateral agreements

Let me now turn to the efforts that have been made in the attempt to adapt to the realities of the new trade order. Of all efforts employed to date, bilateral agreements have been the most frequently utilized.

In spite of the difficulties outlined above, competition agencies in many parts of the world have tried to find ways of exchanging views on general or specific issues and to develop cooperation schemes.

Several bilateral agreements have been concluded. Some contain far-reaching provisions. For instance, the Mutual Legal Assistance Treaty between the US and Canada has made it possible for both sides to carry out joint investigations in both territories in the premises of companies allegedly involved in cartel practices (a criminal offence under both US and Canadian laws). Even more far-reaching is the agreement between Australia and New Zealand, which allows the respective authorities, in certain circumstances, to extend their jurisdiction to the territory of the other. The provisions of the Australia–New Zealand agreement which grant access to confidential files (except where confidentiality conditions apply), are among the most advanced of any existing bilateral agreement.

Relations between the European Commission and the EFTA Surveillance Authority in administering the competition provisions of the European Economic Area Agreement are also very close.

Our agreement with the US is more limited in scope. In substance, the agreement provides for:

- extensive exchanges of information about enforcement activities which might affect the interest of the other party;
- the procedure known as 'negative' or 'traditional' comity, whereby each party within the limits of its legal obligations refrains from measures which could affect the interests of the other party;
- the more innovative procedure of 'positive comity' whereby a party may invite the other party to act under the latter's own laws against practices which have a harmful effect on the former's interests. Some degree of coordination of enforcement activities is also provided for.

In practice, this agreement has resulted in a much closer relationship between the competition authorities of the two parties. Cooperation has developed even further in the last few months, as a result of experience with cases of major importance dealt with by both authorities.

So, in spite of different legislation, constant contact between authorities, often confronted with similar problems, offers great opportunities to bring their approaches closer together.

However, our experience also suggests that there are limits to how far such cooperation can go. In particular, there are three factors that tend to hinder the cooperation process:

- Differences in procedural rules make coordination difficult; for example, time limits and other procedural rules are different from one system to another.
- As noted earlier, each system of competition rules deals with practices that harm its own markets. In Europe, for example, we have no legal power to investigate practices that have no effect on our own market and we can therefore not assist our American colleagues in circumstances in which US interests are allegedly harmed by practices that have no impact in Europe, even if they are partly or wholly organized on our side of the Atlantic.
- Finally, the content of the information we exchange is limited by

186

confidentiality rules. Although we are free to exchange information about procedural aspects of a case, we can share substantive analysis that reveals confidential data only with the consent of the party or parties involved.

In spite of these limitations, the experience we have gained so far under the agreement is highly valuable and it is expected that the agreement will undergo further development in the future.

Multilateral and regional cooperation

Two international organizations (UNCTAD and the OECD) have also made efforts to develop principles for cooperation.

The UNCTAD 'set of rules' provides an interesting model for possible future common basic rules on competition.

The OECD recommendation on cooperation among authorities, although no more legally binding than the UNCTAD set of rules, has been used as a reference for the negotiation of several bilateral agreements. It is a useful instrument for providing some cooperation between authorities, which are not party to more far-reaching bilateral agreements.

Many regional organizations provide for some degree of cooperation among their members. This is the case for NAFTA (Canada, the US and Mexico), although these provisions, if they are to be effective, remain to be developed and clarified at a further stage, as provided for by the agreement.

Agreements concluded with six Central and Eastern European countries (the CEEDs) also provide for competition rules based on the EU model. Implementing rules contain detailed provisions to ensure the effective implementation of competition policy and cooperation between the European Commission and the CEEDs' new competition agencies.

The European Union

Turning to Europe, it may be fairly stated that the world's most sophisticated mechanism for regional cooperation is that developed by the EU. It is built on the secure foundations of Community law, which is directly enforceable by the courts of the EU member states and which prevails over national law in the event of a conflict. An independent authority, the European Commission, has been granted extensive fact-finding and enforcement powers.

The audacious model, whereby member states have shared part of their national sovereignty, has been very effective in establishing a respected competition policy system within the Union.

Along with other provisions for the elimination of restrictions to trade, the implementation of an effective and uniform competition policy in Europe has made it possible to dismantle trade instruments such as anti-dumping and countervailing duties within the Union. Moreover, these principles have been extended to the European Economic Area (the EU and EFTA countries with the exception of Switzerland).

Agreements concluded with six Central and Eastern European countries also provide for competition rules based on the EU model. Implementing rules contain detailed provisions to ensure the effective implementation of competition policy and cooperation between the European Commission and the CEEDs new competition agencies.

Agreements are also being negotiated or have been concluded with other European countries (the Baltic states, Slovenia), Turkey and other Mediterranean countries.

As a result of these initiatives, a wide area is being created in Europe and in the Mediterranean Basin in which similar competition rules are or will be applied and where close cooperation among competition authorities will be the order of the day.

Future developments

What has been achieved so far in a short period of time is impressive. However, in today's globalized world, regional cooperation, even extended to very large areas, may not be enough. We think the time has come to take new steps forward.

The world 'competition community' is under increasing pressure from the 'trade community'. Our trade colleagues, who are not necessarily aware of all the practical difficulties in establishing cooperation among competition authorities, find it difficult to admit that their tremendous efforts in achieving a new trade order could be undermined by the inability of competition authorities to effectively tackle private restrictive behaviour which results in the partitioning of world trade.

Bilateral cooperation

Countries involved in bilateral cooperation have gained experience from the 'first generation' agreements concluded in the last few years. It is now time to think about new steps, building on this experience.

It is difficult at this stage to say exactly what will happen next in this fast-moving field. It may be helpful to look at developments that are taking place in certain countries and regions of the world.

For instance in 1994 the US Congress adopted an important law which enables the Federal antitrust agencies to negotiate 'second generation' agreements with agencies of third countries. Such new agreements would provide, under certain conditions, for the exchange of confidential information. US antitrust authorities could, under conditions of reciprocity, collect information and evidence from companies located in the US on behalf of foreign competition authorities in order to facilitate the enforcement of the latter's competition rules, even if the practices at issue would not violate US competition laws.

In Canada, where a review of competition law is under way, consideration is being given to relaxing rules on the protection of confidentiality for the purpose of international cooperation.

As I said at the outset, last year I invited a small group of independent experts to consider the issue of international cooperation in the competition field and to make recommendations to the EU on how it might develop this area. In its report, the group suggested that the EU should negotiate a 'second generation bilateral agreement', including provisions for the exchange of confidential information and more far-reaching positive comity instruments. Positive comity could progressively lead to some burden-sharing among partner agencies. A requesting agency would refrain from acting (or at least would delay action) in respect of behaviour which has its 'centre of gravity' in the market and is mainly organized and implemented within the jurisdiction of the other agency. The latter would then 'go first'. If successful, such a development should replace efforts to enforce competition law extra-territorially.

Of course this might appear a distant goal. Well-balanced bilateral cooperation between authorities equally involved in the enforcement of effective competition policies might be the most fruitful approach in the short term.

Multilateral cooperation

The other major recommendation of the group of experts is the development of a plurilateral framework which might include elements already incorporated in the bilateral agreements. Through a binding positive comity instrument and an effective dispute settlement mechanism, a progressive solution might be found to the problem of trade distortions arising from the unequal effectiveness of the enforcement of competition policies throughout the world.

The report's recommendation does not bind the Commission but they have played a positive role in generating wide-ranging and international discussion. Now we must decide where we go from here.

Trade-related aspects of competition policy will inevitably figure more prominently in the years to come and it is appropriate therefore that they should be included in the WTO's work programme. The WTO is a prime candidate for developing a competition framework, because:

- it has near universal membership and can take into account the different interests of both developed and developing countries;
- it is also the recognized institution for trade-related international economic rules;

- the institutional infrastructure of the WTO could ensure an appropriate system of transparency and surveillance through notification and monitoring provisions. The WTO could also provide a forum for continuous negotiation and consultation where members could bring their trade-related competition concerns. In addition the WTO's dispute settlement mechanism could back-up agreed rules, and provide a means for the resolution of conflicts between governments; and finally
- should it be considered appropriate, Annex IV of the WTO Agreement allows the development of agreements relating to specific disciplines between a limited number of countries.

This is not to diminish in any way the role of the OECD in the trade and competition debate. The OECD has accomplished the most significant work done in this area to date, and it combines the countries with the most developed competition policies. Its continuing contribution will remain a key element in determining the direction taken by the debate.

None the less, the Singapore ministerial meeting offers an ideal opportunity to launch a working group to consider the complex issue of trade and competition. The working group could consider the elements of an international competition framework with the objective of strengthening cooperation through a gradual, 'building-block' approach.

A starting point would be the need for all countries to have adequate domestic competition laws (including laws to address restrictive agreements, abuse of dominance and mergers) coupled with adequate enforcement instruments. This implies that domestic structures should be transparent and non-discriminatory, allow injured parties access to enforcement authorities, including the courts, and provide for dissuasive sanctions.

Secondly, the working group might seek to identify core principles and work toward their adoption at international level. Initially this might mean looking at the horizontal restrains although, given the problems they present for trade, vertical restrains could not be ignored.

Thirdly, the group might wish to consider how to develop instruments to facilitate cooperation between competition authorities, including notification, information exchange, cooperation procedures and positive and negative comity.

Finally, the working group could consider how the WTO's dispute settlement mechanism could be used to resolve conflicts between governments relating to non-respect of those international obligations created by the new framework.

The Community should, in parallel, prepare and discuss the issues for examination by a WTO working group and develop a common position as regards possible future negotiations at the multilateral level in light of what seems practicable and feasible for the Community and its member states.

The Commission is currently developing a position that it will shortly submit to the Council, with a view to defining a Community position which can be taken forward to the WTO ministerial meeting at the end of the year.

Conclusion

The issues raised by multilateral cooperation will have to be dealt with in a gradual, measured way and we must be realistic in our expectations as regards the speed of progress in such an endeavour. Therefore, it seems that an approach aimed at enhancing and developing both bilateral and multilateral cooperation in parallel presents us with the most promising means of addressing the challenges of the new trade order, and will be an endeavour that is to the benefit of us all.

12

THE COMPETITION POLICY IN THE EUROPEAN ECONOMIC AREA

A unique system of international cooperation

Knut Almestad

Introduction

The Agreement on the European Economic Area (EEA Agreement) entered into force on 1 January 1994. The entry into force of the Agreement marked the completion of the undertaking made by Ministers of the EC member states and the EFTA states, at the first Joint EC–EFTA Ministerial Meeting in Luxembourg on 9 April 1984, to establish 'a dynamic European Economic Space'.

The contracting parties to the Agreement were originally the European Economic Community, the European Coal and Steel Community and the then twelve EC member states, on the one hand, and five EFTA states – Austria, Finland, Iceland, Norway and Sweden – on the other. On 1 January 1995 Austria, Finland and Sweden acceded to the EU, thus moving to the EC pillar of the EEA and leaving Iceland and Norway as the only remaining EFTA states. The number of EFTA states was subsequently brought to three when, on 1 May 1995, the Agreement entered into force for the Principality of Liechtenstein.

Legal framework

The pronounced objective of the Agreement is to establish a dynamic and homogeneous EEA, based on common rules and equal conditions of competition. To this end, the fundamental four freedoms of the internal market of the Community, as well as a wide range of accompanying Community rules and policies, are extended to the participating EFTA states.

Accordingly, the Agreement contains basic provisions, which are drafted as closely as possible to the corresponding provisions of the EC Treaty, on the free movement of goods, persons, services and capital, on competition and other common rules, such as state aid and public procurement, and on a number of Community policies relevant to the four freedoms, such as social policy, consumer protection and environment. The Agreement further provides for close cooperation in certain fields, not related to the four freedoms.

Secondary Community legislation in areas covered by the Agreement is brought into the EEA by means of direct references in the Agreement to the relevant Community acts. Accordingly, in twenty-two Annexes and some of the Protocols to the Agreement, references are made to presently some 2,000 directives, regulations, decisions and other acts, which are by virtue of the Agreement applicable throughout the EEA, subject only to the necessary technical adaptations.

The Agreement thus implies that two separate legal systems are applied in parallel within the EEA, the EEA Agreement to relations between the EFTA and EC sides as well as between the EFTA states themselves, and Community law to the relations between the EU member states. This being the case, for the EEA to be homogeneous the two legal systems will have to develop in parallel and be applied and enforced in a uniform manner. To this end, the Agreement provides for decision-making procedures for the integration into the EEA of new secondary Community legislation and for a surveillance mechanism to ensure the fulfilment of obligations under the Agreement and a uniform interpretation and application of its provisions.

The task of ensuring that new Community legislation is timely extended to the EEA rests in the first place with the EEA Joint Committee, a committee composed of representatives of the contracting parties. By decisions of the EEA Joint Committee, more than 600 new Community acts have been integrated into the EEA Agreement since its entry into force on 1 January 1994.

While the introduction of new rules within the EEA is thus entrusted to a joint body composed of representatives of the contracting parties, the surveillance mechanism is arranged in the form of a two-pillar structure of independent bodies of the two sides. The implementation and application of the Agreement within the Community is monitored by the European Commission using its existing competences and procedures, whereas the Surveillance Authority is to carry out the same task within the EFTA pillar in a similar manner. In order to ensure a uniform surveillance throughout the EEA, the two bodies are to cooperate, exchange information and consult each other on surveillance policy issues and individual cases.

The two-pillar structure also applies to the judicial control mechanism, with the EFTA Court exercising competences similar to those of the EC Court of Justice and the Court of First Instance with regard to, *inter alia*, the surveillance procedure regarding the EFTA states and appeals concerning decisions taken by the EFTA Surveillance Authority.

Competition rules

The competition rules applicable to undertakings contained in the EEA Agreement are a new piece of European legislation, which has been applied for only slightly less than two and a half years. Still, the provisions of this legislation would be familiar to anyone who is acquainted with the EC competition regime. The reason is, of course, that these EEA rules have been modelled as a mirror image of the competition provisions laid down in the Rome Treaty, as well as in the Paris Treaty on the European Coal and Steel Community. There is, thus, no need to give this distinguished audience any detailed description of the EEA version of Articles 85 and 86, of Regulation 4064/89, of the block exemptions or of the EFTA correspondence to Regulation 17. Suffice here to say that the basic competition provisions of the European Community Treaties, as well as the comprehensive secondary legislation in this field in so far as it has been deemed relevant in this new context, are to be found also in the EEA. Also the soft law adopted by the European Commission in the form of notices and guidelines was replicated for the EFTA side by the Surveillance Authority and since developed in parallel.

Why, then, was this almost identical set-up of competition rules in the EEA Agreement, as compared to the Community Treaties, considered to be of such importance? One answer could be found in the first Article of the EEA Agreement, which lays down the aim of the Agreement. It is stated, there, that the aim of the Agreement is to promote a continuous and balanced strengthening of trade and economic relations between the contracting parties, with equal conditions of competition, and in accordance with the same rules, with a view to creating a homogeneous EEA. In order to attain these objectives, the association shall entail, in addition to the so-called 'four freedoms' of the Single Market, the setting up of a system ensuring that competition is not distorted and that the rules thereon are equally respected.

Homogeneity is thus a central concept in the EEA. Economic operators should be entitled to meet the same rules and equal conditions of competition in all parts of this European market, covering seventeen countries and some 370 million citizens. This is the famous concept of 'a level playing field', which, when it comes to market behaviour, should mean that undertakings meet the same competition rules in the territory of the three participating EFTA countries, as they do inside the Community.

Now, having the same competition rules is not in itself a novelty when it comes to international agreements. Corresponding provisions have existed for a long time in other international agreements. You will find them in the Stockholm Convention, from 1959, establishing the European Free Trade Association. You will also find basic prohibition rules in the bilateral Free Trade Agreements from 1973–4, between the European Communities and a number of EFTA states which then did not join the Communities. Recently, corresponding competition rules have been included in the Europe Agreements between the EU and certain states in Central and Eastern Europe.

However, in spite of the rules being there, you would rarely hear about infringement proceedings related to competition rules under such agreements. The reason for that is of course that it is not sufficient to have rules of substance. In order to create a competition regime you must also have institutions, procedures and competences. And that is exactly what is special with the EEA Agreement: a structure has been created for the efficient application of the rules modelled on the supranational system of the EU.

How the system works

I will not attempt in this brief intervention to explain the intricacies of legal architecture required to build a bridge between a supranational system and individual national legal systems which in the end should ensure uniform application and enforcement. Instead I will try to set out how the system works in practice.

The starting point is Articles 108 and 109 EEA establishing the two-pillar system for surveillance and judicial control. For the field of competition rules applicable to undertakings, the system is specifically set forth in Protocol 21 to the Agreement. Here it is stated that the EFTA Surveillance Authority, for the application of the competition rules of the Agreement, shall be entrusted with equivalent powers and similar functions as the European Commission has for the application of the competition rules of the EEC and ECSC Treaties. It is further stated that the Community shall ensure that these existing competences of the European Commission, in the field of competition, also apply to the handling of competition rules under the EEA Agreement.

On the EFTA side, the institutional set-up and the creation of necessary procedures and competences have been achieved through a separate agreement between the EFTA states – the so-called 'Surveillance and Court Agreement'. Through this Agreement, which establishes the Surveillance Authority and the EFTA Court, this Authority has, *inter alia*, been given powers to ensure the application of the competition rules of the EEA Agreement. To this end, Protocol 4 to the Surveillance and Court Agreement reproduces all relevant procedural rules for the application of competition rules to undertakings, starting with the famous Regulation 17/62, which in its EFTA version is called Chapter II to Protocol 4.

In practice this means that from 1 January 1994 we find two international competition authorities in Brussels. One is the Commission and the other one is the EFTA Surveillance Authority. I will not here give any closer description of the EU 'pillar' of the EEA competition regime, assuming that this is fairly common knowledge. Let me just point to the fact that today the Commission is not only applying Articles 85 and 86 of the Rome Treaty and

Regulation 4064/89 on the control of concentrations. It is also applying Articles 53, 54 and 57 of the EEA Agreement.

The EFTA Surveillance Authority is a quite small organization, total staff amounting to less than fifty. It is organized in five directorates, and headed by the so-called College composed by the three Members of the Authority. These Members have been appointed by common accord of the governments of the EFTA states. Like the Members of the Commission, they do not represent their home states in the fulfilment of their duties. On the contrary, they – and the Authority as a whole – may neither seek nor take instructions from any government or any other body external to the Authority. The formal decisions of the Authority are taken by majority of its Members.

Whereas the division of competences between the Commission and the Surveillance Authority, when it comes to the obligations of states, follows a strict and straightforward territorial criterion, the attribution of competences in the competition field follows from Article 56 of the EEA Agreement. I could not, honestly, say that the clarity of this Article is impressive. However, the short version of its interpretation in relation to cartels is as follows: when there is an effect upon trade only between EFTA states it is evident that the Surveillance Authority is competent. When there is only an effect upon trade within the Community, the EEA Agreement does not apply at all. Here the Commission would apply only the EC rules. When there is an effect upon trade between EC member states plus one or more EFTA states, then the Commission is competent. However, when in such 'mixed' cases there is no appreciable effect upon trade between EC member states, the Surveillance Authority decides upon the case.

This may seem complicated, but for the individual company it does not matter much. Regardless of which Authority is competent, the rules and their application are the same. Further, in the event of an undertaking giving an application/notification to the 'wrong' authority, the case would be transferred to the competent authority without the undertaking losing any of its legal rights.

With regard to abuse of a dominant position, the starting point is in which territory a dominant position is found to exist. If it is in the EU territory the case goes to the Commission, and when there is a dominance in the EFTA territory we handle the case. If there is a dominance in both territories you will have to go back to the rules for 'mixed' cases I just referred to.

Concentrations are handled according to rules in Article 57. The main rule is that the Commission handles all concentrations where they had a competence before the EEA Agreement, neither more nor less.

Homogeneity is the keyword to the EEA. The basic prerequisite is the equality of rules, both on substance and on procedures.

Article 6 of the EEA Agreement deals with the interpretation of the rules. It states that, in so far as EEA rules are identical in substance to corresponding

EEC or ECSC rules, they shall in their implementation and application be interpreted in conformity with the relevant rulings of the European Court of Justice before the signature of the EEA Agreement, i.e. before 2 May 1992. In order to support a homogeneous interpretation of EEA rules in the future, the EFTA Surveillance and Court Agreement obliges the Surveillance Authority and the EFTA Court to pay due account to the principles laid down by relevant ECJ rulings also after the date of signature.

However, homogeneity is not achieved by uniform sources of law alone. Uniformity of legal and administrative practices are equally important. Thus Protocol 23 of the EEA Agreement provides for exchange of information, consultation on general policy issues and cooperation in the handling of individual cases between the EFTA Surveillance Authority and the European Commission in respect of the so-called 'mixed' cases. Corresponding rules on cooperation in the handling of concentrations are laid down in Protocol 24.

The cooperation follows in practice the following pattern: as a first step, a copy of applications and notifications is sent to the other authority, inviting it to present its comments. This receiving authority, in its turn, forwards copies to the national competition authorities in its own territory.

Consultation with the other authority takes place before certain formal steps in the proceedings are taken. The other authority, together with competition experts from the member states, is entitled to participate in hearings and Advisory Committee meetings. A written opinion on a case of an Advisory Committee, which is formulated by the national representatives relating to the competent authority, will be supplemented by a view of the national representatives related to the other authority.

Generally, the EFTA Surveillance Authority will, in the field of competition, follow mainly the same procedures as the Commission. That follows from the fact the procedural rules of Protocol 4 to the Surveillance and Court Agreement are more or less a blueprint of the different EC Regulations laying down rules of procedure for the handling of competition cases.

This pertains notably to the rules on fact-finding. Thus the Authority may collect information through Article 11 letters or inspections – including 'dawn raids' – in exactly the same way as the Commission. There is, however, one limitation: we may only make inspection visits in the EFTA states. If we need an inspection to be performed in any of the Community member states, we will have to require the Commission to do the job. In the same way, we have an obligation to assist the Commission making inspections on their behalf in the EFTA states. This system, which makes it possible to carry out comprehensive investigations throughout the entire EEA, has been tested in practice. It is significant that it has proved to work well.

Agreements which are found to be incompatible with the EEA Agreement are, as an immediate consequence, null and void. In addition, both prohibited agreements and the abuse of a dominant position may be grounds for a private action for damages in national courts.

Moreover, the EFTA Surveillance Authority has, like the European Commission, the power to impose fines or periodic penalties. In cases of intentional or negligent infringement of Articles 53 or 54, fines may be set to an amount of up to 10 per cent of the company's yearly turnover. Decisions on periodic penalties may aim at putting an end to an infringement of the competition rules. They may also be imposed in order to obtain complete and correct information from an enterprise. According to Article 110 EEA pecuniary obligations following decisions of the Surveillance Authorities and the courts are enforceable throughout the EEA.

Decision by the EFTA Surveillance Authority in the field of competition may be appealed to the EFTA Court by the person to whom the decision is directed. Also other persons may challenge a decision if it is of direct and individual concern to them.

Decisions in competition cases handled by the European Commission may be challenged in accordance with Community procedures. Appeals against such decisions are made to the Court of First Instance.

The formal rules on the involvement of the national competition authorities on the EFTA side are, like others rules on procedures, the same as those laid down in Regulation 17/62. Our experience, so far, supports the idea of maintaining quite informal and intensive contacts with the national level.

The national authorities' market knowledge and research resources have already been a most valuable asset, and through the close cooperation we also feel that we are moving towards converging views on competition policy matters. One proof of this convergence, which was under way already before the entry into force of the EEA Agreement, is the tendency to let the principles of EU and EEA competition law inspire national legislation.

Concluding remarks

Before concluding my presentation I would like briefly to emphasize what is indicated in its title: the uniqueness of the system of international co-operation which I have endeavoured to describe. Its uniqueness lies not only in the fact that the EEA establishes an area of economic cooperation and integration which in many respects has the characteristics of a home market, extending the most essential aspects of the substance and disciplines of the EU Internal Market. Perhaps even more remarkable is the fact that one has found a formula which makes it possible through the medium of an agreement under international law to extend enforceable rights and obligations in respect of enterprises in a way that indeed creates a level playing field. Moreover, it has been demonstrated that it works in practice.

V

VERTICAL RESTRAINTS

13

REFLECTIONS ON VERTICAL RESTRAINTS OF TRADE AND NATIONAL COMPETITION LAWS IN AN INTEGRATED WORLD ECONOMY

Stephen Calkins

I will initially describe the United States' laws regarding vertical restraints, and review some recent governmental enforcement actions. I will then discuss the connection between vertical restraint antitrust policy and international market access, and finally consider whether, and in what ways, various national laws regarding vertical restraints might be harmonized.

US vertical restraint law

As in other countries, legislatures and competition policy authorities in the US have been charged with the difficult task of determining when vertical arrangements promote efficiency and when they inhibit competition. Often, of course, vertical restraints do both, and distinguishing between helpful and harmful effects can be a daunting task. Starting in the late 1970s, antitrust authorities and US courts tended to focus on horizontal collusion and to hesitate to challenge vertical arrangements, absent the clearest proof of harm to competition. Carried further, such an approach could, in the words of Jon Baker, the current Director of the Federal Trade Commission's Bureau of Economics, be 'reduce[d] to a deceptively simple maxim: "Vertical good, horizontal bad".'[1] As will be seen, however, the pendulum has been swinging back.

Description of US law

What follows is a description of the US antitrust rules applicable to four different kinds of vertical restraints. To summarize, resale price maintenance is viewed the most harshly. As a restraint on price, it is, and has been for eight decades, *per se* illegal, but courts require fairly clear evidence of an agreement regarding price or price levels before finding illegality. Tying is also *per se* illegal, but this rule is a special multifactor *per se* rule that requires proof of coercive power. Customer and territorial restraints used to be *per se* unlawful. Such restraints are now evaluated under a rule of reason, however, and typically are held lawful in the absence of market power or associated horizontal collusion. Exclusive dealing, has, for the past thirty-five years, been judged under the rule of reason, with particular emphasis on the extent of market foreclosure.

Resale price maintenance

As early as 1911, in *Dr Miles Medical Co. v. John D. Park & Sons Co.*,[2] the Supreme Court declared resale price maintenance to be illegal *per se*. This means that courts may find the conduct illegal as a matter of law without a showing of competitive injury because, in the view of the *Dr Miles* court, resale price maintenance usually causes competitive injury and seldom, if ever, has redeeming value.[3]

Some observers have challenged this reasoning, especially in circumstances where newly entered suppliers need to offer dealers a significant, protected profit margin as an inducement to carry a product, or where dealers need protection from discounters to be able to cover the costs of providing customers with important product education or other services.[4] Others reply that efficient dealers should not be prevented from offering customers the best prices possible, and that resale price maintenance may prevent potential entrants from undercutting the prices of the established firms in order to gain market access.[5] Despite the ongoing controversy as to whether resale price maintenance is as unequivocally harmful as the *Dr Miles* court believed, the *per se* condemnation of resale price maintenance remains today.[6]

Notwithstanding the facial strictness of the *Dr Miles* rule, three related factors have materially limited its scope and application.[7] The first factor is the generous reading that courts have given to what is known as the *Colgate* doctrine, a rule that is almost as venerable as *Dr Miles*. This doctrine holds that firms, acting independently and without monopoly power, generally have the right to decide with whom they will or will not do business.[8] Thus, in *United States v. Colgate & Co.*, the Supreme Court held that a manufacturer may establish a policy regarding resale prices and refuse to deal with firms, such as discounters, that do not comply. Absent evidence of an agreement between the parties, courts now generally uphold vertical refusals to deal except where both an anti-competitive purpose and an adverse effect on competition are evident.[9]

The second limiting factor is the Supreme Court's strict evidentiary requirements for proving an agreement. In 1960, the Court somewhat weakened Colgate by holding that, although a manufacturer may suggest resale prices, the firm's actions may not 'go beyond mere announcement of [its] policy and the simple refusal to deal', such as by employing 'other means which effect adherence to [its] resale prices'.[10] In its 1984 *Monsanto* decision, the Court tightened the evidentiary requirements for demonstrating the existence of an agreement by holding that there must be 'direct or circumstantial evidence that reasonably tends to prove that the manufacturer and others had a conscious commitment to a common scheme designed to achieve an unlawful objective'.[11] In *Monsanto*, the Supreme Court held that complaints by distributors about a rival, discounting distributor followed by the manufacturer's termination of that distributor did not sufficiently foreclose the possibility that the manufacturer, even though it may have considered the complaints, acted independently rather than pursuant to some mutual understanding with the complaining parties.[12]

The third factor, presented most strongly in *Business Electronics Corp. v. Sharp Electronics Corp.*,[13] tightened the evidentiary requirements regarding the content of any alleged resale price maintenance agreement. In this case, the Supreme Court held that 'a vertical restraint is not illegal *per se* unless it includes some agreement on price or price levels'.[14] Thus, the Supreme Court found no violation of the rule against resale price maintenance notwithstanding that the agreement between the manufacturer and a distributor required the manufacturer to terminate a discounting distributor. Although the termination of the rival dealer made it possible for the new retailer to charge the manufacturer's 'suggested retail price' without facing intrabrand price competition, the agreement did not contain any specific understanding regarding the prices that the new distributor would charge; accordingly, the Court held that there was no illegal agreement.

In essence, the *Dr Miles per se* rule against vertical price-fixing and the *Colgate* doctrine permitting unilateral (non-collusive) refusals to deal have lived in tension since before 1920. Although the *per se* proscription remains, the impact of *Monsanto* and *Business Electronics* has been greatly to narrow the number of agreements to which it may be applied.

Tying

Under US law, tying is *per se* illegal, and has been so since 1947.[15] As with the *per se* rule against resale price maintenance, however, a plaintiff's evidentiary burdens are greater, and thus a business manager's options are broader, than might initially appear. The Supreme Court has defined tying as 'an agreement by a party to sell one product (the tying product) but only on the condition that the buyer also purchase a different (or tied) product, or at least agree that he will not purchase that product from any other supplier'.[16] The subject of the tying arrangement may be either a commodity or a service, as in *United States v. Loew's Inc.*,[17] and the transaction may be either a sale or a lease, as in *United Shoe Mach. Corp. v. United States*.[18]

Tying has been challenged on the ground that it not only can distort consumer choices regarding the tying product, but also can foreclose access to, and otherwise limit competition in, the market for the tied product. Justice White summarized these effects as follows:

> The tying seller may be working toward a monopoly position in the tied product and, even if he is not, the practice of tying forecloses other sellers of the tied product and makes it more difficult for new firms to enter that market. They must be prepared not only to match existing sellers of the tied product in price and quality, but to offset the attraction of the tying product itself. Even if this is possible through simultaneous entry into production of the tying product, entry into both markets is significantly more expensive than simple entry into the tied market, and shifting buying habits in the tied product is considerable more cumbersome and less responsive to variations in competitive offers. In addition to these anti-competitive effects in the tied product, tying arrangements may be used to evade price control in the tying product through clandestine transfer of the profit to the tied product; they may be used as a counting device to effect price discrimination; and they may be used to force a full line of products on the customer so as to extract more easily from him a monopoly return on one unique product in the line.[19]

As with the *per se* rule against vertical price-fixing, in the last two decades many economists and others have been asserting that tying can serve pro-competitive as well as anti-competitive purposes, and that *per se* condemnation is inappropriate. For example, some manufacturers might experience distributional or marketing efficiencies when selling two products together. Firms also might find tying to be an effective means to protect a reputation for quality. Other commentators are less sanguine about tying, and worry that tying can inhibit competition and efficient allocation of consumer resources for complementary goods by preventing each consumer from deciding for itself how best to achieve its most desirable balance of quality and price.[20]

In 1984, the same year in which the Supreme Court issued its opinion in *Monsanto*, the controversy regarding *per se* condemnation of tying came to a head in *Jefferson Parish Hospital Dist. No. 2 v. Hyde*.[21] In this case, the Court unanimously rejected a contention by a group of anaesthesiologists that a hospital's exclusive contract with another anaesthesiology group illegally tied the provision of surgical services at the hospital to the purchase of services from this latter group. Four Justices opined that the *per se* rule against tying should be abandoned. The majority voted to retain it, however, but to apply it only if four elements are satisfied:

1   The tying and tied products must constitute separate products.[22]
2   The seller of the tying product must condition the sale of the tying product either on (a) the buyer's purchase of a second product or service that the buyer would otherwise have purchased elsewhere, on different terms, or, perhaps, not at all, or (b) the buyer's agreement not to purchase the tied product from any other supplier.[23]
3   The seller of the tying product must possess 'appreciable economic power in the tying market', i.e., sufficient power 'to force a purchaser to do something that he would not do in a competitive market'.[24]
4   The tying arrangement must 'affect a substantial volume of commerce in the tied market'.[25] In addition, the majority wrote that 'as a threshold matter there must be a substantial potential for impact on competition in order to justify *per se* condemnation'.[26] Some courts have relied on this to find an additional 'competitive effect' requirement; others have disagreed.

Since it is necessary to conduct a rather detailed analysis in order to determine whether or not each of these elements is present, many view *Jefferson Parish* as having reduced the *per se* rule against tying to being *per se* in name only, or, at least, a special kind of *per se* rule. Although *Kodak* initially set forth only three elements for a tying violation (a linking of two products, economic power, and sufficient volume of commerce affected),[27] the Court concluded by observing that a trial might ultimately prove 'that any anti-competitive effects of Kodak's behaviour are outweighed by its pro-competitive effects',[28] which was a fairly clear nod toward the rule of reason. Moreover, the US Department of Justice and the Federal Trade Commission have jointly announced that, as a matter of prosecutorial discretion, in situations involving the licensing of intellectual property (e.g. patents, copy-rights, trade secrets, know-how), they 'will be likely to challenge a tying arrangement if: (1) the seller has market power in the tying product, (2) the arrangement has an adverse effect on competition in the relevant market for the tied product, and (3) efficiency justifications for the arrangement do not outweigh the anti-competitive arrangements'.[29] This approach essentially involves a rule of reason assessment in all instances involving intellectual property licensing. Perhaps the rule of reason ultimately will sweep the field of tying analysis, or perhaps the quite special tying *per se* rule will continue to be applied. Either way, defendants will be able to make most of the arguments they consider important.

Territorial and customer restrictions

Territorial and customer restraints may take many forms. Exclusive distribu-torships necessarily involve territorial or customer restraints that prevent sales by all other distributors who might otherwise try to sell the manufacturer's products within the geographic area, or to the specified customers, that are the designated province of the exclusive distributor. Or, the supplier may assign each distributor a primary area of responsibility, possibly requiring the distributors to meet a sales quota within its territory before selling beyond its boundaries. Sometimes such restraints may be bolstered by profit pass-over arrangements under which a distributor making a sale in another distributor's territory will pay a specified compensation to that dealer. Other limitations might specify the particular location or locations from which the distributor may sell the supplier's product, or designate a particular class of customers to which, and only to which, the distributor may make sales.

Ever since the watershed 1977 case, *Continental T.V., Inc. v. GTE Sylvania*,[30] the Supreme Court has applied the 'rule of reason' to vertical non-price restraints.[31] In *GTE Sylvania*, the Court valued the interests of consumers over those of competitors, and evinced greater concern for horizontal effects than vertical ones. The Court recognized that a competitive limitation imposed by a supplier on a distributor might enhance competition and efficiency in the overall market, notwithstanding that it limits intrabrand competition in the process.

US courts now recognize that territorial and customer restrictions have the potential for both ill and good. On the negative side of the ledger, customer and territorial limitations may serve to eliminate intrabrand competition; facilitate bid-rigging, resale price maintenance, or other collusive arrangements; reinforce oligopolistic behaviour, especially if suppliers of competing products also impose territorial restrictions on their distributors; and raise barriers to market entry by locking established sellers and distributors into exclusive relationships. On the positive side of the ledger, however, territorial and customer restraints can increase a distributor's loyalty to the supplier by freeing that distributor from intrabrand competition. In addition, such restraints can serve to expand a distributor's financial ability and incentives to engage in vigorous interbrand competition, increase investment in product promotion, and accept new or unestablished products for sale.

In trying to predict, assess, and balance all of these potential effects, courts have considered a myriad of factors. These include the market power (if any) of each party to the arrangement; the purpose, geographic scope, and duration of the restraint; and the degree to which the market at issue is susceptible to successful horizontal collusion. The focus in evaluating all of these factors is to ensure that, on balance, antitrust law serves to encourage rather than interfere with the market's meeting consumer demands for price and quality.

Exclusive dealing

Exclusive dealing relationships, or requirements contracts, are the opposite of exclusive distributorships. In the former, a distributor agrees to use only one supplier to meet its requirements for the given product, whereas in the latter a supplier agrees to use only a specified distributor for all of its product sales within the given territory. One is a limitation on the distributor, the other on the supplier. Although customer and territorial restraints are not treated harshly under US law, requirements contracts have enjoyed a longer-standing recognition for usually being benign or beneficial. In 1949, the Supreme Court summarized the benefits of such arrangements, as follows:

> Requirements contracts . . . may well be of economic advantage to buyers as well as to sellers, and thus indirectly of advantage to the consuming public. In the case of the buyer, they may assure supply, afford protection against rises in price, enable long-term planning on the basis of known costs, and obviate the expense and risk of storage in the quantity necessary for a commodity having a fluctuating demand. From the seller's point of view, requirements contracts may make possible the substantial reduction of selling expenses, give protection against price fluctuations, and – of particular advantage to a newcomer to the field to whom it is important to know what capital expenditures are justified – offer the possibility of a predictable market. They may be useful, moreover, to a seller trying to establish a foothold against the counterattacks of entrenched competitors.[32]

The leading Supreme Court exclusive dealing case, *Tampa Electric Co. v. Nashville Coal Co.*,[33] set forth what was known as a 'qualitative substantiality' test. This inquiry involves a traditional, multifactor rule of reason assessment; as such, it requires enforcers and courts to identify the relevant product and geographic markets, and then to evaluate whether or not the exclusive dealing relationship forecloses a substantial share of competition within the relevant market.[34] As described by Justice O'Connor:

> In determining whether an exclusive-dealing contract is unreasonable, the proper focus is on the structure of the market for the products or services in question – the number of sellers and buyers in the market, the volume of their business, and the ease with which buyers and sellers can redirect their purchases or sales to others. Exclusive dealing is an unreasonable restraint on trade only when a significant fraction of buyers or sellers are frozen out of a market by the exclusive deal. When the sellers of services are numerous and mobile, and the number of buyers is large, exclusive-dealing arrangements of narrow scope pose no threat of adverse economic consequences. To the contrary, they may be substantially pro-competitive by ensuring stable markets and encouraging long-term mutually advantageous business relationships.[35]

US government enforcement

For several years now, US government enforcement agencies have taken a more sceptical view of vertical restraints than may have been true during the 1980s. Commentators point to the Commission's complaint against Toys 'R' Us as a leading example of this scepticism.[36] In that proceeding, which is currently in litigation, the Commission 'alleged that Toys 'R' Us extracted agreements from toy manufacturers to stop selling certain toys to warehouse clubs, or to put the toys into more expensive combination packages, so consumers could not obtain lower-priced toys from the clubs, or compare prices easily'.[37] More generally, for most of the vertical restraints discussed above, there is demonstrated government interest in bringing well-founded cases. Examples of this activity are examined below.

Resale price maintenance

Resale price maintenance has been enforced with some vigour in the 1990s. The FTC, often joined by the state attorneys general, has filed a series of well-publicized resale price maintenance cases, including the following:

New Balance Athletic Shoes, Inc.[38]   The FTC has filed a complaint against New Balance alleging that it engaged in resale price maintenance by surveilling retailer prices and threatening to terminate discounters. New Balance allegedly assured dealers that it would secure resale price maintenance co-operation from its other dealers. The complaint also alleges that New Balance practised structured terminations by giving discounters 'one-time warnings', and used this policy as a means of entering agreements with non-complying dealers. The proposed consent agreement, if accepted by the Commission, would prohibit New Balance from maintaining the prices at which New Balance products are sold or advertised for sale, or coercing or pressuring dealers to cooperate with such a policy. The consent would also prohibit New Balance for ten years from notifying dealers in advance that they will be subject to a structured termination policy.

Reebok International Ltd[39]   The consent order prevents Reebok and its sub-sidiary Rockport from fixing the prices at which shoes are sold or advertised, or using coercion or pressure to gain adherence to Reebok's resale pricing policy. It also prevents the use of structured terminations for ten years ('three violations of the RPM policy and you're terminated'). Although less harsh than a simple unilateral termination for a failure to follow the manufacturer's pricing policy, structured terminations are seen by some as objectionable (a 'grey area' in the law[40]), since they can achieve much the same result as a more explicit agreement.

New England Juvenile Retailers Ass'n and *Baby Furniture Plus Ass'n*[41] In each case, a group of horizontal rivals allegedly colluded to threaten a boycott of various manufacturers unless the manufacturers refused to deal with a discount catalogue sales company. The order prohibits this conduct and required the New England Juvenile Retailers Association, a putative trade association, to disband.

Ked's Corp.[42] The consent order prohibits Keds from fixing the prices that are charged or advertised for Ked's casual or athletic shoes; from coercing, or securing commitments from, dealers regarding the prices that they charge or advertise for these products; and from suggesting that dealers report discounting dealers.

Nintendo[43] The consent order prevents Nintendo from engaging in vertical price-fixing on video game hardware. The consent order prohibits Nintendo from: (a) fixing the prices at which dealers sell or advertise to sell; (b) coercing, or securing commitments from, dealers to comply with Nintendo's pricing policies; (c) suggesting that dealers report discounting dealers; (d) taking any punitive actions against discounters, such as reducing their product supply or denying them favourable credit terms; and (e) terminating dealers for discounting (a five-year limitation of Nintendo's *Colgate* rights).[44]

Kreepy Krauly, USA, Inc.[45] The order requires Kreepy Krauly to refrain from setting the prices of its swimming pool cleaning devices. The case is unusual because the RPM Agreement was set forth in the written distributorship agreement.

Tying

As with resale price maintenance, federal antitrust agencies have recently evidenced more concern about tying violations than they once did. Three examples stand out:

United States v. City of Stillwell[46] The Department of Justice filed the federal government's first challenge to a municipality's refusal to sell water and sewer services to new business and residential customers in annexed areas unless those customers also agreed to purchase electricity from the city. In response to the complaint, the city halted the practice.

Sandoz Pharmaceuticals Corp.[47] Although the consent order permits Sandoz to require that purchasers of clozapine, a schizophrenia drug, provide patient monitoring services (including pharmacy, distribution and delivery, blood drawing, patient tracking, and clinical laboratory services), the order prohibits Sandoz from requiring that purchasers of clozapine also purchase these services from Sandoz.

Gerald S. Friedman, M.D.[48] A doctor with market power in the provision of outpatient dialysis services tied the provision of those services to the purchase of his in-patient services, for which he did not have market power. Since the amount that the doctor could charge for his outpatient services was limited by Medicare, the doctor could use the tying device not only to expand his in-hospital business but also to charge excessively for those services, thereby evading the governmental price regulations.

Exclusive dealing

Exclusive dealing, too, has been the subject of renewed activity at the agencies. Here the Antitrust Division has had the leading role, in terms of publicly announced developments. The Division's jousting with Microsoft is the best known of these cases, but in other complaints, as well, the Division has shown new concern about exclusive dealing.[49]

Why the change?

This renewed concern about vertical restraints has more than one cause. Part of the change flows from personnel. FTC Chairman Pitofsky has long been a leading proponent of antitrust challenges to resale price maintenance. In 1993, Chairman Pitofsky, while still a professor at Georgetown Law School, offered predictions regarding antitrust enforcement under the Clinton administration. Regarding vertical restraints, he wrote as follows:

> The rule outlawing vertical price-fixing, established in 1911 in
> *Dr Miles*, would be enforced and the opportunity for discounters
> to offer low prices to consumers protected. The Supreme Court's
> *Sharp* decision would be overruled, and *Monsanto* clarified legisla-
> tively. It has always struck me that the nullification of enforcement
> against resale price maintenance, despite support for the *per se* rule
> in the Supreme court and in Congress, was the most indefensible
> prosecutorial decision in the last twelve years.[50]

Pitofsky's predecessor, Chairman (now Commissioner) Janet Steiger, started the movement toward greater FTC concern about vertical restraints. At the Antitrust Division, too, first James Rill and then Anne Bingaman evinced more concern about vertical restraints than their predecessors. The change reflects more than people, however. New scholarship has also made its mark, by moving to what conventionally is referred to as 'beyond the Chicago School'.[51] I do not mean to suggest that the Chicago School's focus on efficiencies, market power, and injury to competition has been abandoned. These concerns are undeniably important, and Chicago School analysts have contributed enormously to our understanding of how markets operate. But

210

subsequent scholarship is adding its own contributions. Substantively, the new work is exciting, adding to the traditional Chicago School concerns an attempt to understand the strategic implications of one firm's market timing, vertical integration and other decisions on its rivals' costs, market access, and responsive business decisions. This perspective offers richness to our under-standing of market power, efficiency, and foreclosure that was not previously available. The scholarly base of much of the new concern with vertical restraints suggests that newly appointed Commissioners and Assistant Attorney Generals will continue to treat vertical restraints seriously.

Vertical restraint law and international market access

At first blush, vertical restraints policy might appear central to issues of access to foreign markets.[52] 'Vertical restraints' connotes geographic restrictions; government attacks on such restrictions would seem conducive to free-flowing international commerce. The EU has made vertical restraints enforcement a centrepiece of its efforts to achieve economic integration. Some observers have asked, moreover, whether it is appropriate for a nation to worry about vertical restraints as external trade barriers when it would be untroubled by vertical restraints at home.

Upon reflection, however, it seems clear that international coordination of vertical restraint standards is unlikely to play an important role in facilitating transnational market access. There are several reasons for this.

Importance of other factors

First and foremost, government competition policy plays a comparatively tiny role in influencing international access to markets. Perhaps the critical factor in this regard is, of course, trade policy and practice. Government regulations, including tax, labour, environmental, and other regulations by national and sub-national governmental units, also play a key role. Simple national preferences are important, as well. In this array of factors, competition policy is simply dwarfed.

Even within the world of competition policy, vertical restraints do not loom especially large. Horizontal restraints may well be more important. Group boycotts, for example, can disadvantage national and foreign competitors. Standard-setting abuses can make competition more difficult. Customer or market division can cabin in competitors. Few arrangements are as destructive of international access-creation than an old-fashioned inter-national cartel that parcels out the four corners of the globe.

Merger policy also is important to access. Consumers may be denied access to the products of a foreign producer if that producer is purchased by a dominant national firm. Entrance by a foreign competitor could also be slowed were a dominant domestic producer to forestall competition by buying a disruptive purchaser that had been encouraging foreign firms to begin supplying a market.

Although challenges to such mergers can thus promote access, enforcement, if misdirected, can also retard access; acquisitions are, after all, a key avenue of international expansion. For example, a merger policy that unnecessarily prevents the achievement of important efficiencies can prevent foreign or domestic firms from gaining competitive advantages needed to compete in other markets.[53] Additionally, a merger policy of encouraging the emergence of 'national champions', at the expense of competition, may forestall entry and harm consumers, at least in the short run, even if such a policy may be unlikely permanently to prevent entry by a more efficient foreign firm.

Finally, issues of monopolization or abuse of a dominant position intersect with questions of access. If a dominant firm is permitted to punish attempted entry by wrongfully imposing costs on potential market entrants (for instance, by the bad faith invocation of government process), access is made more challenging, or even impossible. As with mergers, however, overly aggressive as well as unduly lax enforcement can impede entry. For example, consumers would be hurt and access made problematic were vigorous new competition on the merits to be wrongly condemned as predatory pricing.

Enforcement already exists, and increasing enforcement might be counterproductive

When observers link market access and coordination of vertical restraints enforcement, they appear to assume (a) that government enforcers are turning a blind eye to violations, (b) that an internationally coordinated policy will reinvigorate enforcement, and (c) that such strengthened enforcement will improve access. At least in the context of the prevailing US competition policy enforcement, these presuppositions are either problematic or wrong.

First, in the US, vertical restraints are being challenged. State attorneys general have joined in several of these cases and also brought others of their own. The singular feature of the US system of competition enforcement, moreover, is that enforcement is not entirely entrusted to elected officials and their appointees. Foreign firms denied access to US markets because of vertical restraints may (and do) seize their day in court to address the perceived misdeeds and to reap trebled damages in the process.

Second, it is hard to predict in advance whether an internationally coordinated policy would relax or bolster enforcement. Enforcement efforts regarding conduct as varied as vertical restraints, and with such potential both to injure and aid competition, must be well-measured and economically sensitive.

Third, as noted above, not only is substantial enforcement against anti-competitive vertical restraints occurring in the US, but, also, greater enforcement efforts may be counterproductive with respect to market access. Many of the well-known pro-competitive benefits of vertical restrictions, e.g., reduction of free-riding, encouragement of investment in a new product, quality control, etc., may be particularly important for new entrants and especially foreign entrants. If a distributor might hesitate to invest in a new domestic brand without some reassurance that others won't reap what it has sown, how much more might the distributor hesitate to promote a foreign brand? If consumers need assurance as to the quality even of a domestic firm's products, how much greater assurance might be necessary for the products of unknown, newly entered, foreign firms? In many respects, therefore, the beneficial aspects of vertical restraints may be of special importance to foreign competitors, and overly aggressive challenges may interfere with access, rather than help it.

Harmonization of vertical restraint law

We turn finally to the question of international harmonization of vertical restraint law and policy. My personal view is that vertical restraints are an unlikely candidate for leading the way toward formal harmonization. It is important, in this context, to distinguish between formal harmonizing of standards through an international code or agreement, and a more gradual convergence of standards over time. The latter is happening already.[54] This conference has demonstrated the existence of substantial commonalities in the approach to vertical restraints among the countries represented. Time and again, the discussants have found ourselves echoing each other as we described our nation's view of vertical restraints.

There are several reasons why formal steps toward harmonization appear unpromising. One reason, which was illustrated at this conference, is that the EU has special concerns about the impact of vertical restraints on internal economic integration – concerns that the EU is unlikely to abandon.[55] More generalized reasons include the following.

Difficulty of evaluating enforcement decisions

Real harmonization is possible only with sufficient transparency. That is, the parties to any harmonization agreement must be able to understand and evaluate each other's enforcement decisions. This is perhaps even truer with respect to enforcement inaction than action. Harmonizing verbal formulas means little unless there are enforcement consequences.

Connecting standards and consequences, however, is exceptionally difficult when the subject is vertical restraints. Almost without exception, vertical restraint enforcement seeks to balance pro-competitive and anti-competitive results. When an enforcement authority fails to challenge any mergers, or any horizontal restraints, observers can be reasonably confident that the agency has adopted an extremely permissive approach. This is less true for vertical restraints. Even an agency committed to vertical restraint enforcement can investigate a series of restraints but conclude that each one, on balance, is pro-competitive or benign. To be sure, a complete failure to bring vertical cases eventually proves a lack of commitment, but the linkage between inaction and proof of actual views is much more attenuated than for mergers and horizontal restraints. This attenuation reduces transparency. Evaluation of agency performance lags, making it difficult to determine whether harmonization is verbal or real.

Markets differ

The same restraint can have markedly different consequences, depending on the economic, legal, and historical context in which it is used.[56] The US has quite open, fluid markets. This makes harm from most vertical restraints relatively unlikely. An impartial enforcer might find a restraint unobjectionable in the US but troublesome elsewhere.

Harmonizing standards is not the same as harmonizing operative rules

Achieving harmonization requires more than mere agreement on standards. One standard may appear rigorous or even draconian but go largely un-enforced. For instance, there was a time when US antitrust enforcers were widely assumed to have both written merger guidelines and what were known as more permissive 'shadow guidelines'. Another standard may appear permissive but dramatically affect performance because it is aggressively pursued. Similarly, firms seeking to adjust their conduct to respond to enforcement risks must consider not just standards, and not just enforcement policies, but also penalties. Firms may skate much closer to a line enforced with a wrist-slap than with the corporate equivalent of the death penalty. Harmonizing standards but not penalties would not achieve consistency.

Application of standards matters

Standards with common verbal formulas can mean very different things if the words incorporated therein are treated differently. Most notably, standards for vertical conduct may refer to 'agreements', or to defined markets, or to ease of entry, or to efficiencies. Yet agreement can be found frequently or rarely; markets can be defined broadly or narrowly; entry can be measured in widely differing ways; and claimed efficiencies can be simply assumed or subjected to searching, sceptical scrutiny. Standards incorporating such elastic terms and concepts are challenging to harmonize in any real sense.

Vertical restraints law is still evolving within legal systems

Harmonization is more difficult when targets move, and vertical restraints law is unsettled. At the time of writing, the EU's long-awaited Green Paper was yet to emerge.[57] That document, and the delay in producing it, are symptomatic of rethinking. In the US, vertical restraints law swung from a position of hostility to almost unqualified acceptance of such practices, and now has swung back a little.[58] This kind of movement is conducive to possible gradual convergence of views, but makes formal harmonization more difficult.

For all of the above reasons, and likely other ones as well, vertical restraints seem an unlikely candidate for leading the way to international harmonization. Better candidates would include core subjects such as cartels, or transparency, or perhaps positive comity, deregulation, or non-discriminatory enforcement. While I doubt that formal international harmonization of vertical restraints laws would be a successful venture at this time, the exchange of views and the mutual education that occurs at conferences such as this one are invaluable. Each of us learns where and why other systems differ from our own. The resulting understanding and respect for such differences promotes cooperation and mutual assistance, and ultimately may sow the seeds of substantive convergence as well.

In concluding this review of US antitrust law regarding vertical restraints, and international implications thereof, it is important to note that the engine that carried the US into the period of *Sylvania, Monsanto, Jefferson Parish,* and *Business Electronics* – academic scholarship and the development of our understanding of competition issues – is the same engine that continues to transport us forward. I cannot predict where this engine will go. Not all theories of competitive harm, even if valid, will be suitable for use as antitrust standards, and, of course, not all proposed standards will be adopted by the courts or the FTC.

ACKNOWLEDGEMENTS

These remarks benefited from discussions with too many people to mention and from the special assistance of J. D. Hurwitz of the Federal Trade Commission's Office of the General Counsel, which I am pleased to acknowledge. The views I present are my own, however, and do not represent the views of the US Federal Trade Commission or of any individual Commissioner.

NOTES

1 J. B. Baker, 'Vertical restraints with horizontal consequences: Competitive effects of "most-favored-customer" clauses', prepared remarks before Business Development Associates, Inc. 2–3, 28 September 1995.
2 220 US 373 (1911).
3 See also *California Retail Liquor Dealers Ass'n v. Midcal Aluminum, Inc.*, 445 US 97 (103) (1980); and *Caribe BMW, Inc. v. Bayerische Motoren Werke AG*, 19 F. 3d 745, 752 (1st Cir. 1994) (Breyer, J.).
4 See, for example, F. H. Easterbrook, 'The limits of antitrust', *Texas Law Review*, 1984, vol. 63, p. 1; H. Marvel, 'The resale price maintenance controversy: Beyond the conventional wisdom, *Antitrust Law Journal*, 1994, vol. 63, p. 59; R. Posner, 'The next step in the antitrust treatment of restricted distribution: *Per se* legality', *University of Chicago Law Review*, 1981, vol. 48, p. 6.
5 See, for example, W. S. Grimes, 'Spiff, polish, and consumer demand quality: Vertical price restraints revisited', *California Law Review*, 1992, vol. 80, p. 817; R. Pitofsky, 'In defense of discounters: The no frills case for a *per se* rule against vertical price-fixing', *Georgetown U. Law Journal*, 1983, vol. 71, p.1487.
6 *Cf. Khan v. State Oil Co.*, No. 96–1309 (7th Cir. Aug. 29, 1996) (Posner, J.) (reviewing potential benefits especially of maximum resale price maintenance, but deferring to Supreme Court teaching) *cert. granted*, Dkt. No. 96-871, 117 S. Ct. 941 (1997); brief for the United States and the Federal Trade Commission as Amici Curiae Supporting Reversal, *Khan*.
7 For a recent, comprehensive discussion of these factors, see M. A. Fajer, 'Taming the wayward children of Monsanto and Sylvania: Some thoughts on developmental disorders in vertical restraints doctrine', *Temple Law Review*, 1995, vol. 68, p.1. The law's reaction to the perceived strictness of the *per se* rule, especially in light of the existence of treble damages remedies, is discussed in S. Calkins, 'Summary judgement, motions to dismiss, and other examples of equilibrating tendencies in the antitrust system', *Georgetown U. Law Journal*, 1986, vol. 74, pp. 1065–94.
8 *United States v. Colgate & Co.*, 250 US 300 (1919).
9 See, for example, *Monsanto Co. v. Spray-Rite Service Corp.*, 465 US 752, 762 (1984); and *Continental T.V., Inc. v. GTE Sylvania Inc.*, 433 US 36, 51 (1977).
10 *United States v. Parke, Davis & Co.*, 362 US 29, 44 (1960).
11 *Monsanto Co. v. Spray-Rite Service Corp.*, 465 US at 768 (1984).
12 *Ibid.*
13 485 US 717 (1988).
14 *Ibid*, at 735–6.
15 See *International Salt Co. v. United States*, 332 US 392, 396 (1947).
16 See *Eastman Kodak Co. v. Image Technical Services, Inc.*, 504 US 451, 461 (1992) (quoting *Northern Pacific Ry. v. United States*, 356 US 1, 5–6 (1958)).
17 371 US 38 (1962).
18 258 US 451 (1922).
19 *Fortner Enterprises v. United States Steel Corp.*, 394 US 495, 512–14 (*Fortner I*) (White, J., dissenting), quoted in *Jefferson Parish Hospital District No. 2 v. Hyde*, 466 US 2, 13 n.19 (1984) (Stevens, J.).
20 Many of these issues were freshly aired in the debates following the Supreme

Court's much analysed recent tying opinion, *Eastman Kodak Co. v. Image Technical Serv., Inc.*, 504 US 451 (1992). See, for example, 'Comments on Kodak', *Antitrust Law Journal*, 1993, vol. 62, p. 177; 'Comment and reply', *Antitrust Law Journal*, 1994, vol. 63, p. 239.

21 466 US 2 (1984).

22 *Ibid.*, at 21.

23 *Jefferson Parish* states the test as follows:

> Our cases have concluded that the essential characteristic of an invalid tying arrangement lies in the seller's exploitation of its control over the tying product to force the buyer into the purchase of a tied product that the buyer either did not want at all, or might have preferred to purchase elsewhere on different terms. When such 'forcing' is present, competition on the merits in the market for the tied item is restrained and the Sherman Act is violated.
>
> 466 US at 12.

Some courts and observers have found in that language an additional requirement that 'forcing' or 'coercion' be proven; others have disagreed.

24 See *Eastman Kodak Co. v. Image Technical Services, Inc.*, 504 US 451, 464 (1992) (quoting *Jefferson Parish*, 466 US at 14).

25 *Kodak*, 504 US at 462, *Jefferson Parish*, 466 US at 16.

26 *Ibid.*

27 504 US at 461–2.

28 *Ibid*, at 486.

29 US Department of Justice and the Federal Trade Commission, Antitrust Guidelines for the Licensing of Intellectual Property §5.3, 6 April 1995.

30 433 US 36 (1977).

31 *GTE Sylvania* reflected a reversal of the *per se* approach espoused by *US v. Arnold, Schwinn & Co.*, 388 US 365 (1967). The Court retained the *per se* approach, however, when the customer or territorial restriction is used as an integral part of a resale price maintenance scheme.

32 *Standard Oil Co. v. United States*, 337 US 293, 306–7 (1949). Accord *Jefferson Parish Hosp. Dist. no. 2 v. Hyde*, 466 US 2, 45 (1984) (O'Connor, J., concurring). The Court in *Standard Oil* continued by distinguishing its views of tying and exclusive dealing:

> Since the advantages of requirements contracts may be sufficient to account for their use, the coverage by such contracts of a substantial amount of business affords a weaker basis for the inference that competition may be lessened than would similar coverage by tying clauses, especially where use of the latter is combined with market control of the tying device.
>
> *Standard Oil*, 337 US at 307.

33 365 US 320 (1961).

34 365 US at 327–9. Thus (at p. 329) the Court directed courts to evaluate the 'relative strength of the parties, the proportionate volume of commerce involved in relation to the total volume of commerce in the relevant market area, and the

probable immediate and future effects which pre-exemption of that share of the market might have on effective competition therein'.

35 *Jefferson Parish Hosp. No. 2 v. Hyde*, 466 US 2, 45 (1984) (O'Connor, J., concurring).

36 See, for example, M. L. Weiner, 'Enforcement activity heats up (again)', *Antitrust*, Summer 1996, p. 4. The FTC has not issued an opinion in a litigated vertical restraints case since its decision in *Beltone Electronics Corp.*, 100 FTC. 68,176 (1982), in which the Commission overturned an initial decision in which the ALJ found that Beltone had imposed unreasonable, anti-competitive territorial and customer restrictions on its dealers, and pressured them to carry only Beltone products. In its opinion, the Commission found that there was little likelihood of injury to competition in light of Beltone's falling market share, the rapidly increasing share of foreign rivals, and the generally low barriers to market entry.

37 *FTC News*, 22 May 1996, at 1. Administrative Law Judge Timothy has entered an initial decision finding a violation of the FTC Act. FTC Dkt 9273 (25 September 1997).

38 FTC File No. 9210050 (proposed consent order announced 12 June 1996) (Commissioner Azcuenaga concurring; Commissioner Starek dissenting), noted at 5 Trade Reg. (CCH) 24,048.

39 FTC Dkt. C-3592 (consent order 18 July 1995) (Commissioner Starek dissenting), noted at 5 Trade Reg. Rep. (CCH) 23,813.

40 This issue has been subject to some discussion by commentators. See, for example, R. M. Steuer, 'The distribution superhighway', *Antitrust*, 1994, vol. 8, pp. 4–6; J. L. MacDavid, 'Pricing issues in dealer and franchise relationships', *Antitrust Law Journal*, 1992, vol. 60, pp. 497, 504–5.

41 *New England Juvenile Retailers Ass'n*, FTC Dkt. C-3552 (consent order 18 January 1995), and *Baby Furniture Plus Ass'n*, FTC Dkt. C-3553 (consent order 18 January 1995), both noted at 5 Trade Reg. Rep. (CCH) 23,689.

42 FTC Dkt. C-3490 (1 April 1994), noted at 5 Trade Reg. Rep. (CCH) 23,463.

43 111 FTC 702 (1991) (consent order).

44 By contrast, the Commission has modified consent orders to restore *Colgate* rights in *US Pioneer Electronics Corp.*, 115 FTC. 590 (1992) (order reopening and modifying order issued 24 October 1975), and *Magnavox Co.*, 13 FTC 255 (1990) (order granting in part and denying in part request to reopen and modify order).

45 114 FTC 777 (1991).

46 No. 96–196–B (E. D. Okla complaint filed 25 April 1996).

47 115 FTC 625 (1992) (consent order).

48 113 FTC 625 (1990) (consent order).

49 For a review of these developments, see M. L. Steptoe and D. L. Wilson, 'Developments in Exclusive Dealing', *Antitrust*, Summer 1996, p. 25.

50 R. Pitofsky, 'Antitrust policy in a Clinton administration', *Antitrust Law Journal*, 1993, vol. 62, pp. 217–19 (citations omitted); see also Commissioner Christine A. Varney, 'Vertical restraints enforcement at the FTC, ALI-ABA'. Eleventh annual advanced course on product distribution and marketing, 15 January 1996 ('the bottom line in our enforcement agenda today is that resale price maintenance agreements are unlawful *per se* and the Commission will enforce the law in this area').

51 For a review of this scholarship, see 'Symposium on post-Chicago economics', *Antitrust Law Journal*, 1995, vol. 63:2; for its application to vertical restraints see J. B. Baker, *op. cit.*, note 2, and W. K. Tom, 'Distribution and marketing', Address Before the Practising Law Institute, New York, 17 January 1996.

52 See generally OECD, *Interim Report on Convergence of Competition Policies*, June 1994; American Bar Association Section of International Law and Practice, Report to the House of Delegates, 'Using antitrust laws to enhance access of US firms to foreign markets', *International Law*, 1995, vol. 29, p. 945.

53 See *Anticipating the 21st Century: Competition Policy in the New High-Tech, Global Marketplace*, FTC Staff Report 1996.

54 Informal convergence also is facilitated by increased information-sharing. See generally *International Antitrust Enforcement Assistance Act of 1994*, Pub. L. No. 103–438, 108 Stat. 4,597 (1994).

55 B. E. Hawk, 'System failure: Vertical restraints and EC competition law', *Common Market Law Review*, 1995, vol. 32, p. 973.

56 B. E. Hawk, *Antitrust and Market Access: The Scope of Coverage of Competition Laws and Implications for Trade*, 1996.

57 See European Commission, *Report on Competition Policy*, 1995, vol. XXV, pp. 28–9; D. Deacon, 'Vertical restraints under EU competition law: New directions', B. E. Hawk (ed.), Fordham Corporate Law Institute, 1995.

58 See M. A. Fajer, *op. cit.*

14

VERTICAL RESTRAINTS

A United Kingdom perspective

Martin Howe[1]

Introduction

Vertical restraints are the means by which an upstream firm (the supplier) seeks to control the conduct of a downstream firm (the distributor). They come in a myriad of forms. The main categories are resale price maintenance, selective distribution, and exclusive distribution where a distributor has the exclusive right to distribute a product within a territory or to a category of customer. By restraining the selling conduct of distributors, these practices restrict intrabrand competition. A further category of vertical restraint is exclusive dealing or purchasing, which prevents distributors from handling other suppliers' products. As the restraint here bites on distributors' conduct as buyers, it mainly affects interbrand competition through market fore-closure.

It is the restrictions in the contractual relationships between supplier and distributor that can attract the attention of the competition authorities. On the other hand there can be benefits in the arrangements, and it is this which has made the treatment of vertical restraints so difficult an issue to handle for competition policy.

The treatment of vertical restraints has also become important from a trade policy perspective. With the reduction in tariffs, culminating in the completion of the Uruguay Round, and in other governmental barriers to trade, attention has switched to ways in which practices of domestic firms, for example exclusive dealing, might inhibit market access and therefore restrain international trade.

After a summary of some of the analytical issues raised by vertical restraints, this paper considers their treatment under competition law, with particular reference to the law of the UK.

Analysis

It is customary in the analysis of vertical restraints to distinguish, and as necessary to trade off, restrictions on intrabrand competition and the possible promotion of interbrand competition. The view that vertical restraints are invariably beneficial is identified with the Chicago School. The contribution of Robert Bork[2] and his followers was to focus attention on economic efficiency as the objective of antitrust policy and to elevate the role of economic analysis in antitrust enforcement in the US. Policy should be directed at the promotion of the competitive process and not at the protection of competitors. From this standpoint, the Chicago School argued that vertical restraints will invariably be pro-competitive in the sense that they will lead to an increase in output and so to an increase in economic efficiency. Suppliers will not seek to restrict their distributors in the way they do business unless suppliers consider that a better policy for expanding their own sales and market share than unrestricted distribution. Vertical restraints can have a number of attractions in this respect. They can help to align the incentives of otherwise independent firms and strengthen their commitment to their commercial relationship. The restrictions in the vertical relationship ensure that complementary functions are performed efficiently from a joint perspective. As with full vertical integration, there can be savings in marketing and transaction costs.

A further attraction is that vertical restraints can eliminate the inefficiencies that arise if consumers are able to free-ride on the services provided by distributors for the supplier's brand. These may be pre-sales service (advice, demonstrations, trial runs etc.) or an in-store ambience and service aimed to enhance the quality image of the brand. Such requirements raise distributors', here usually retailers', costs, and hence the prices they will need to charge. Without a restriction on the retailers who will be granted supplies, free-riding will mean that welfare enhancing retail services will not be provided and economic efficiency thereby will be reduced.

Experience is, however, that the free-rider argument for vertical restraints is overdone. Clearly free-riding will be impossible where the service and the purchase of the product can be separated. Consumers will then buy the level of service they want. Separate information markets have grown up for many products. Where consumers link pre- and post-sales service, the free-rider argument is weakened. As a matter of fact, high- and low-service outlets coexist in many markets. Not only does this suggest that the free-rider problem is less serious than the Chicago School assumes (if only because of market imperfections), it meets the point that different consumers – or groups of consumers – can have different preferences as between those retailers offering a relatively high level of service and price and those charging less but with a lower level of service, preferences which cannot be expressed if the vertical restraint dictates that a specified level of service shall be provided.

The classic objection to vertical restraints such as exclusive dealing is market foreclosure. The seriousness of the effects upon interbrand competition depends heavily upon the proportion of the market that is foreclosed and upon entry conditions. The effects are likely to be particularly significant where the restraint is widely practised by established firms, as in the markets for beer and petrol in the UK. Otherwise the market share of the forecloser will be relevant. Exclusionary practices can be used strategically by established firms to inhibit entry and to raise rivals' costs, particularly in oligopolistic markets. The strategic potential of vertical restraints undermines the Chicago School view that entrants, faced by exclusive dealing arrangements, will always be able to tempt distributors away by the offer of higher margins or, at worst, to establish their own equally efficient distribution system. Experience suggests that this is too optimistic a view of the capacity of market forces to resolve any competition problem.

The Chicago School analysis of vertical restraints assumes perfect competition at the distributor (retail) level so that restrictions on intrabrand competition aimed to enhance the efficiency of the distribution process are of no consequence and the focus can be upon the effects, if any, on interbrand competition. A less benign view of such vertical restraints as exclusive distribution that restrict intrabrand competition can emerge when market imperfections at this level are taken into account. If competition in the downstream (retail) market is imperfect, as is often and perhaps increasingly the case, a vertical restraint limiting intrabrand competition can add to the market power of the retailer, allowing him to widen his margins and charge higher prices than would merely cover the cost of any extra services he provides. Where this occurs (when the supplier faces a less elastic demand for his output) there is likely to be a dampening effect on competition in the upstream market. This will be compounded by any oligopolistic tendencies. While these effects are likely to be difficult to identify in practice, the dampening of upstream competition can be a most significant consequence of any vertical restraint.

While it is now generally accepted that there are circumstances in which a vertical restraint can enhance the efficiency of the distribution process, it is also recognized that they can lead to structural rigidities and cosy relationships between a supplier and distributor and hence hold back efficiency improvements and innovation in a downstream market. This risk will be particularly acute where a restraint is practised widely in a market. The possibility that vertical restraints may damage dynamic efficiency is a major reason why competition authorities should continue to regard them with suspicion.

It seems that in the abstract, almost any vertical restraint can be argued to have anti- and pro-competitive effects. This suggests that the law should provide for a rule of reason approach, with each restraint analysed and assessed in its product and market context. The assessment needs to be fact-intensive and to cover both the upstream and the downstream markets. Structural rules are likely to be useful only as a very preliminary screening device.

Legal treatment of vertical restraints

There is considerable variation in the treatment of vertical restraints under competition laws. There are *per se* prohibitions, such as the prohibition in the laws of many countries of resale price maintenance. There are laws that prohibit vertical agreements which restrict competition, but then allow for the exemption from the prohibition of those agreements that can be shown to have beneficial effects. The obvious example of a law involving such a two-step procedure is Article 85 of the Treaty of Rome. Then there are laws under which vertical agreements can be prohibited only if the adverse effects on competition can be shown in some way to outweigh any benefits of the agreements. In most laws following this approach, agreements may only fall for consideration if one or other party can be found to be in a market-dominating position or otherwise to be able to exercise market power.

The position under UK competition law is rather complex. Resale price maintenance has been, to all intents and purposes, unlawful in the UK since 1964. Only books and certain pharmaceuticals are exempt from the prohibition of resale price maintenance under the present law, the Resale Prices Act, and the case for continuing these exemptions is currently under review.[3]

For various technical reasons, relatively few vertical agreements other than franchise agreements are caught by the UK law on restrictive agreements, the Restrictive Trade Practices Act, the domestic equivalent to Article 85 of the Treaty of Rome. Most that are caught are dealt with administratively without reference to the Restrictive Practices Court. There is therefore little case law.

Vertical restraints such as selective distribution, exclusive distribution and exclusive dealing will usually fall to be dealt with under the monopoly provisions of the Fair Trading Act or the anti-competitive practice provisions of the Competition Act. These statutes allow for a case-by-case investigation of a variety of business practices which may have anti-competitive effects, and they give powers for these practices to be prohibited or modified if they are found to operate, or to be likely to operate, against the public interest. The procedures are administrative with a high degree of discretion for the authorities. Investigations are initiated by the Director General of Fair Trading (DGFT), head of the Office of Fair Trading (OFT), and are conducted by the Monopolies and Mergers Commission (MMC), an independent administrative tribunal. The MMC reports, with recommendations, to the Secretary of State for Trade and Industry. Where the MMC have identified effects of the matters referred to them adverse to the public interest, it is for the Secretary of State to decide the action, if any, to be taken.

While the market share thresholds for activating an investigation by the MMC are quite low (25 per cent), policy is to invoke these statutes only where a firm, or group of firms acting in a similar fashion, has market power and appears to use it to damage the competitive process or to exploit consumers. There is no notification system under these statutes (in contrast to Article 85) and most cases originate in complaints from frustrated distributors or competing suppliers.

Legislative reform

Reform of UK competition law has been on the political agenda for a number of years. In March this year (1996) the Department of Trade and Industry published a Consultation Document seeking views on how the Government's proposals for reform might be implemented.[4] These could affect the treatment of vertical restraints. The main proposal is to replace the Restrictive Trade Practices Act with a law which would prohibit agreements having the object or effect of preventing, restricting or distorting competition, but with a provision for exemption of agreements which are nevertheless beneficial. The proposal was first made in 1989, and at that time it was envisaged that the new law would be closely aligned on Article 85 of the Treaty of Rome.

The Government continues to see advantage in a law similar to the law of the EU, partly because this law has proved an effective means for dealing with cartels, where the Restrictive Trade Practices Act is singularly weak – no financial penalties even if a cartel is not notified and is declared against the public interest and very limited investigatory powers for the DGFT – partly because of the advantages to business when domestic law is similar to European law. Business strongly supported this view in 1989, but more recently doubts have emerged in various quarters about the Article 85 model, particularly about the wide scope of Article 85 (1) when, as interpreted by the European Commission, agreements that limit parties' freedom of action can be caught whatever their impact on competition in a relevant market.[5] This criticism is one of the reasons, along with the imminent expiry of a number of the block exemptions which have been the main device by which agreements, particularly vertical agreements, caught by Article 85 (1) nevertheless benefit from an exemption under Article 85 (3), why the Commission is conducting its own review of its policy towards vertical restraints. A Green Paper setting out various options for possible reform is expected to be published by the European Commission later in the year.

The Department of Trade and Industry's Consultation Document recognizes the criticism of the way Article 85 has operated. It says: 'In framing United Kingdom legislation it would be possible to narrow the scope of the prohibition and reduce the need for scrutiny of essentially benign agreements for exemption'.[6] Among the possibilities on which views are invited are a one-step procedure with agreements prohibited if any anti-competitive effects were held to outweigh any beneficial and pro-competitive effects, a rule of reason approach. Another possibility would be to exclude vertical agreements from the new law altogether leaving them to be dealt with, as is largely the present situation, under the Competition Act or Fair Trading Act (which will remain basically unchanged under the Government's proposals). Since the effects of any vertical restraint can never be known with any certainty until after it has been thoroughly investigated, there is merit in this approach, whatever the need to strengthen the UK law on cartels.

The Government has made clear, however, that any exclusion of vertical agreements from a new law (should that option be eventually chosen) would not extend to agreements imposing minimum resale prices: either vertical price-fixing would explicitly be included within the scope of the new law, or the Resale Prices Act would be retained. Either way, the more hostile view taken of vertical price restraints than of non-price restraints would continue. A justification for this position is that restrictions on price competition are particularly likely to hold back efficiency improvements and innovation in a market.

Some UK cases

Over the years several investigations under the Competition Act and Fair Trading Act have been concerned with vertical restraints. While not case law in the sense of decisions of the European Commission or judgments of the Court of First Instance or European Court of Justice, the reports on these investigations provide insight into UK policy on vertical restraints.

The Fair Trading Act has been used for the investigation of a number of markets characterized by networks of vertical restraints and with oligopolistic structures at the supplier level.[7] Prominent among these are beer, where brewers' ownership of outlets (public houses) was reinforced by exclusive purchasing and loan ties; petrol, where again the oil companies' ownership of outlets was reinforced by exclusive dealing with independent petrol stations; motor cars, selective and exclusive distribution through franchised dealers with the dealer usually undertaking not to sell competing brands from the same site; and newspaper distribution with exclusive distribution to wholesalers by publishers and selective distribution by wholesalers to retailers.

The reports on these investigations make varied reading.[8] In its report on petrol, the MMC concluded that the wholesale market was competitive with little brand loyalty, and that neither the oil companies' ownership of retail outlets nor exclusive dealing (the solus tie system where the length of the tie was restricted to a maximum of five years following an earlier report) had effects adverse to the public interest. In its report on motor cars, the MMC recognized that for a complex and expensive product like a motor car there were efficiency benefits from a system of selective and exclusive distribution. They concluded that interbrand competition was active, within the limits set by the then ruling voluntary export restraints, and encouraged by the suppliers' distribution system, notwithstanding the restrictions on the dealers' independence and freedom of action. In view of the importance of a purchase of a car and the willingness of consumers to shop around, the restriction of most dealers to one make of car was not a serious detriment. However, although the MMC did not make any fundamental criticisms of the distribution system, they did recommend a number of modifications designed to allow more competition between dealers, both interbrand and intrabrand. In the 1993 report on newspapers, the MMC noted that the publishers' system of exclusive distribution removed a stimulus to wholesalers to maintain efficiency, and inhibited new entry. Publishers argued, however, that the allocation of exclusive areas provided a rapid and effective distribution system for their titles and enabled them to maintain wide availability and to require the wholesaler to maintain supply throughout its designated area. The MMC accepted that the benefits of the system overrode its anti-competitive features. As far as selective distribution to retailers was concerned, the MMC recognized the efficiency argument for declining to grant supplies to additional retailers when an area was considered to be already adequately served, but were concerned that the system afforded too much protection to inefficient retailers and was too slow in adapting to consumers' changing demands. The MMC concluded that on balance the system operated against the public interest and recommended some modifications to the distribution system.[9] The Secretary of State went further and has required wholesalers not to refuse supplies on the grounds that an area is already adequately covered.

Of all the MMC's reports, that on beer has been the most dramatic. Seventy-five per cent of approximately 60,000 public houses were owned by the brewers, most of them tenanted. All these outlets were tied to the brewer for the supply of beer and other drinks, and in the 'free trade' about half the public houses were tied to brewers by the terms of favourable loans. Six national brewers with a combined market share of about 75 per cent dominated the market. The brewers emphasized the benefits of the exclusivity arrangements in encouraging investment in their public houses and improving amenities, but the MMC found that competition was restricted by the tied house system at all levels, brewing, wholesaling and retailing, to the detriment of consumers, with the main effect being the protection of brewers by the foreclosure of competitors from their managed and tenanted estate and from the free trade by tied loans. At retail, the restrictions were compounded by the restrictions on entry of the licensing system. The Government's response to the report was to require a substantial reduction in the number of tied houses of the national brewers and to require brewers to allow tenants both to buy non-beer drinks from where they chose and to sell at least one beer of another brewer. These requirements have forced the brewers to rethink their policies with regard to vertical integration. Through withdrawals and merger, concentration in brewing has increased since the report, while a number of significant pub chains have established themselves. Competition for the business of these chains, including from overseas brewers, has been intense, but so far there is little suggestion of the downward pressure on retail prices hoped for by the MMC. Consumer choice within pubs has widened, however, and many publicans are offering new services to their customers.

Aside from the cases already mentioned, there have been relatively few investigations of selective distribution. In an early case under the Competition Act 1980 (which facilitates investigations focused on specific practices of individual firms), the selective distribution system for bicycles of T. I. Raleigh Ltd was held first by the OFT and then by the MMC significantly to reduce intrabrand competition in view of the importance of the Raleigh brand and, because of elements of exclusivity in the system, also to inhibit the entry of newcomers. The MMC concluded that the policy led to higher retail prices than otherwise and denied consumers the opportunity to buy at outlets offering a lower level of service than specialist retailers, and that it operated against the public interest.[10] Yet the MMC conceded that Raleigh were entitled to restrict the availability of bicycles with the Raleigh brand and recommended only that other brands of bicycle manufactured by Raleigh should be supplied to non-specialist outlets. Raleigh's market share was steadily eroding at the time and the MMC's recommendation has had little impact on the market.

Raleigh argued that the need to protect specialist bicycle retailers from free-riding justified the restrictions in its distribution arrangements. Whatever a supplier's rationale for selective distribution, however, the OFT has always been concerned that it should not be used to cloak explicit resale price maintenance or to prevent the entry of retailers solely on the ground that they would be more willing than established outlets to charge less than the recommended price. This concern prompted a later investigation of the selective distribution of fine fragrances (notwithstanding that the two leading perfume houses had obtained an Article 85 (3) exemption for their distribution agreements), and an ongoing investigation into the distribution of no less than eight different types of electrical goods.[11]

In their report on fine fragrances the MMC accepted that suppliers of a luxury product such as fine fragrances should be able to control their distribution in order to protect the brand image and to prevent free-riding. They concluded that there was a reasonable degree of interbrand competition, despite the importance of product differentiation in this market, and noted significant differences between the distribution policies of the leading fragrance houses. While retail price competition was muted, the MMC found no clear evidence of unlawful resale price maintenance. The MMC concluded that selective distribution by the fine fragrance houses did not operate against the public interest.[12]

An interesting case more closely related to resale price maintenance concerned the policy of Black and Decker of withholding supplies from any retailer who sold at a price giving him less than a specified margin. This was not a violation of the Resale Prices Act. However, on reference to them, the MMC found the practice to be restrictive of intrabrand competition and to be against the public interest, in threatening the maintenance of innovative and competitive retail markets. The MMC did not accept the company's argument that its policy was pro-competitive in maintaining a wide range of outlets and servicing centres.[13]

Two other significant recent investigations of vertical restraints dealt with (*inter alia*) restrictions on the distribution of carbonated drinks and exclusive dealing in ice cream secured by the provision to retailers free of charge of freezer cabinets on condition that a cabinet is not used to stock competitors' brands (freezer exclusivity).

The exclusive dealing agreements of the leading suppliers of carbonated drinks with customers in the 'leisure trade' (public houses, clubs, fast food restaurants and the like) were held by the MMC to foreclose competitors from a significant part of the market and to be likely to restrict consumer choice and to lead to higher prices. The policy of the market leader, Coca-Cola and Schweppes Beverages, of also restricting the range of products that distributors could carry and the customers with whom they could deal was also found by the MMC to be against the public interest.[14] After a period of consultation by the Department of Trade and Industry following publication of the report, including with the European Commission, the suppliers undertook to modify their arrangements to meet most of the objections raised by the MMC.

In some contrast were the MMC's conclusions in its investigation of freezer exclusivity in ice cream as practised by Bird's Eye Walls (a subsidiary of Unilever) with around two-thirds of the market, and its main competitors Nestlé and, to a lesser extent, Mars. In view of the options open to a retailer, freezer exclusivity was held to limit interbrand competition only in a narrow sense and not to have been a serious deterrent to market entry (indeed some smaller suppliers had established themselves through providing exclusive freezers). Nor did the practice seriously limit consumer choice in the MMC's view. Consequently (and controversially), the MMC concluded that freezer exclusivity in the ice cream market did not operate against the public interest.[15]

The investigations of vertical restraints by the UK authorities confirm the analytical view that these practices may be anti-competitive or beneficial according to the circumstances of the case, and that *a priori* rules are unlikely to be helpful in distinguishing between them. Bearing in mind the relatively small number of investigations, and the conclusions reached, it has to be said that the UK authorities' policy towards vertical restraints, other than resale price maintenance, has been fairly relaxed. It is in oligopolistic markets where vertical restraints of a similar kind are widespread that harmful effects seem more likely to be found.

Towards convergence

Firms will often adopt similar distribution arrangements in a number of countries. Within Europe this will be encouraged by the completion of the Single Market. Familiar examples are the motor industry's system of franchised dealers, exclusive dealing in petrol, and the perfume houses' selective distribution systems. There is then the possibility that the competition authorities in the countries concerned may reach different decisions on the acceptability of the arrangements. For the member states of the EU this raises the familiar question of whether the primacy that has to be afforded to the law of the EU debars a national authority from taking action against a vertical restraint which has been granted an Article 85 (3) exemption by the European Commission or has satisfied the criteria of one or other of the several block exemptions relating to vertical agreements. There have been a number of investigations under UK law of arrangements that have been so approved under European law. However, although the MMC have made recommendations in the case of motor car distribution and brewers' loan ties that would prohibit terms in agreements that were permissable under the relevant European block exemptions, the Government decided, in the end, not to enforce these particular recommendations. While the double barrier theory was therefore not put to the test, these cases illustrate the risk of conflict between the two systems.

It might be suggested that the possibility of conflict between the law of the EU and of an important member state prove the need for convergence in those laws. Convergence in the treatment of vertical restraints will no doubt be particularly difficult to achieve. However, as already mentioned, the European Commission is reviewing its own policy towards vertical restraints. It may conclude that more emphasis should be put on the effects of a restraint on the competitive process – upon an economic assessment of the restraint – than on the restrictions that are placed on the parties' freedom of action. Within the Commission the treatment of vertical restraints has been much influenced by the overriding policy objective of integration of the common market leading the Commission to challenge any restraint which has the object or effect of frustrating parallel trading. The Single Market may not yet be fully achieved, but arguably less weight might now need to be given to the integration objective by the Commission. It remains to be seen what policy proposals will be put forward by the Commission, but there is a considerable body of support for the view that the present approach to the application of Article 85 to vertical agreements is inefficient and needs to be reformed, either by reducing the scope of Article 85 (1) or, more radically, by moving towards a rule of reason approach.

It also remains to be seen what reforms of UK competition law the UK Government will finally adopt. While these are likely to be radical as far as the treatment of horizontal agreements is concerned, vertical agreements seem likely to continue to be treated administratively with case-by-case investigation by the MMC on a broad rule of reason approach. There are some disadvantages in such an approach, not least in the lesser degree of legal certainty that can be given to business, but it does enable the authorities to concentrate upon the economic effects of the restraints, rather than upon their legal form. If any changes in the approach to Article 85 that are finally introduced by the Commission are a move in this direction, then there will be some convergence in how vertical restraints are to be assessed, even if differences in the respective laws continue. That would be a useful step.

Postscript

Since this paper was written and presented, the UK Government has published proposals to reform various parts of the competition law. A draft Bill published in August 1996[16] would prohibit agreements and concerted practices that have the object or effect of preventing, restricting or distorting competition in the UK. Any provision in an agreement that infringed the prohibition would be void. But agreements would be capable of exemption from the prohibition where they provided countervailing benefits on criteria in effect the same as Article 85 (3) of the Treaty of Rome. The prohibition would be narrower than Article 85 (1), however. In particular, the majority of vertical agreements would be excluded. But vertical agreements could still be examined under other provisions of UK law if a party to the agreement had a market share of 25 per cent or more, or a group of firms engaging in vertical restrictive agreements had a collective market share of 25 per cent or more.

In the event, the Bill was not included in the Government's legislative programme for the final session of Parliament. The Labour Government that came to power at the General Election of 1 May 1997 published its own proposals and draft Bill in August 1997.[17] As with its predecessor's proposals, the Bill would prohibit anti-competitive agreements and concerted practices with a provision for the exemption of agreements the benefits of which more than offset their anti-competitive effects. It is proposed that agreements should be excluded from this part of the law if it would be more efficient to consider them under other parts of the competition law. It is suggested that vertical agreements which do not involve any element of price-fixing should be dealt with this way (though it is recognised that it will be 'a significant challenge' to devise a definition of a vertical agreement suitable for the purpose).

In contrast to the August 1996 proposals, the draft Bill would also prohibit conduct amounting to an abuse of a dominant market position along the lines of Article 86 of the Treaty of Rome. The Competition Act

1980 (dealing with anti-competitive practices including those of a vertical nature) would be repealed but not the monopoly provisions of the Fair Trading Act 1973. This would enable wider ranging investigations by the Monopolies and Mergers Commission to be initiated than might be feasible under the proposed new prohibition, and it would also allow the possibility, following an investigation, of structural remedies.

The Government envisages that by making vertical agreements subject to the new prohibition of abuse of a dominant position and the monopoly provisions of the Fair Trading Act, especially the complex monopoly provisions, the authorities' attention will be targeted on those vertical agreements, or networks of such agreements, where, through the market power in the hands of at least one of the parties, an agreement is most likely to operate anti-competitively, to the ultimate detriment of consumers.

After a consultation on its proposals, which include significant changes to the respective functions and powers of the Director General of Fair Trading and the Monopolies and Mergers Commission (which will be renamed the Competition Commission), a Bill is likely to be introduced into Parliament in Autumn 1997.

NOTES

1 Any views expressed are those of the writer and are not necessarily shared by the Director General of Fair Trading or the United Kingdom Government.
2 R. Bork, *The Anti-Trust Paradox: A Policy at War with Itself*, Basic Books, New York, 1978.
3 Indeed resale price maintenance on books has effectively collapsed with the abandonment of the Net Book Agreement under which members of the Publishers' Association agreed that they would each enforce minimum resale prices on titles they designated 'net' books.
4 'Tackling Cartels and the Abuse of Market Power: Implementing the Government's policy for Competition Law Reform', Department of Trade and Industry, March 1996.
5 See, for example, 'Loosening the Straightjacket: CBI Proposals for Reform of the Scope and Administration of Article 85', Confederation of British Industry, 1995.
6 Department of Trade and Industry, Consultation Document, para. 2.8.
7 The 'complex monopoly' provisions of the Act allow the investigation of practices of a group of firms which together account for 25 per cent or more of a market.
8 *The Supply of Beer*, Cm. 651, March 1989; *The Supply of Petrol*, Cm. 972, February 1990; *New Motor Cars*, Cm. 1808, February 1992; *The Supply of National Newspapers*, Cm. 2622, December 1993, Monopolies and Mergers Commission. In the cases of beer, petrol and newspaper distribution there had been earlier MMC investigations.
9 In a previous investigation, reported upon in 1979, the MMC had concluded

that the wholesalers' distribution system did not operate against the public interest.

10 *T. I. Raleigh Ltd*, report by the Director General of Fair Trading on an Investigation under the Competition Act 1980, February 1981, and *Bicycles*, HC 67, Monopolies and Mergers Commission, December 1981. Competition Act investigations required a report first by the DGFT and then, by the MMC until a 1994 amendment. This amendment empowers the DGFT to refer a practice directly to the MMC.

11 The eight electrical goods included in the current MMC investigation are: televisions, video cassette recorders, hi-fi systems, camcorders, washing machines, tumble-driers and dishwashers.

12 *Fine Fragrances*, Cm. 2380, Monopolies and Mergers Commission, November 1993.

13 *Black and Decker*, report by the Director General of Fair Trading on an Investigation under the Competition Act 1980, March 1989; and *Black and Decker*, Cm. 805, Monopolies and Mergers Commission, October 1989.

14 *Carbonated Drinks*, Cm. 1625, Monopolies and Mergers Commission, August 1992.

15 *Ice Cream*, Cm. 2524, Monopolies and Mergers Commission, March 1994.

16 Department of Trade and Industry, *Tackling Cartels and the Abuse of Market Power: a Draft Bill*, August 1996.

17 Department of Trade and Industry, *A Prohibition Approach to Anti-Competitive Agreements and Abuse of Dominant Position: a Draft Bill*, August 1997.

15

EU COMPETITION POLICY ON VERTICAL RESTRAINTS

Christopher Jones

Introduction

The basic approach of Community competition policy to vertical restraints has not modified significantly since 1966,[1] and may be summarized as follows.

- Absolute territorial protection, where a distributor or licensee is prohibited from selling within its allotted territory to a customer if it is aware that the purchaser intends to export, is viewed as a serious infringement of Article 85 (1), will not be exempted,[2] and will usually attract high fines.
- Other territorial restraints – restrictions on passive sales, active sales or exclusivity – are usually viewed as falling under Article 85 (1). Exclusivity and active sales prohibitions usually are exempted, restrictions on passive sales may exceptionally be exempted for limited periods, depending on the agreement, although this is rare and is limited to cases where the agreement results in innovation necessitating significant sunk investment on the part of the distributor/licensee.
- Most non-territorial restraints are in practice viewed as falling within Article 85 (1), but are usually exempted, unless the companies concerned enjoy significant market power. Certain clauses, however, are unlikely to be exempted, irrespective of the market power of the companies concerned: price-fixing provisions, resale price maintenance.
- In practice, therefore, the ambit of Article 85 (1) is drawn widely with respect to vertical arrangements. No demonstration of the existence of market power has generally been considered to be necessary by the Commission to bring an agreement within Article 85 (1). Detailed economic analysis on a case-by-case basis has not, therefore, been a feature of the Community, or at least the Commission's, treatment of vertical restraints. Thus, large numbers of agreements have, at least potentially, required notification, the vast majority of which would have merited exemption. To deal with this, the Commission has adopted block exemption regulations in this area, the earliest in 1967.

The present block exemptions will expire at the end of 1999[3] and the purpose of the Green Paper recently issued by the Commission[4] is to determine whether the approach taken to date remains valid. It is not difficult to see why the Commission has chosen to undertake this exercise:

- Many product and service markets in the EU have evolved considerably since the Community's approach to vertical restraints was set in the early 1960s. Whilst it may have been true to say that in the 1960s most markets were national in scope, and oligopolistic in nature, this is not true, or is at least less true, today. The Single Market programme and the more general globalization of markets has changed the level of competition throughout the EU in almost every sector. Take 'gramo-phones' for example, the subject of the Grundig–Consten case. In 1964, one might choose between one, two, perhaps three brands, which would differ from member state to member state. The market for the equivalent products today could not be more different, with a wide variety of models offered by a large number of companies from different countries.

- A comparison with the approach taken to vertical restraints in other jurisdictions illustrates that the Community's policy – of viewing most agreements as potentially harmful, thus requiring notification and subse-quent approval (either individually or via block exemption regulations) – is largely isolated. The executive summary of the Green Paper describes the approach taken in other jurisdictions as follows.

    (i) Examination shows the diversity of arrangements for handling vertical arrangements. However, certain major aspects in which these systems are consistent, and consistent in differing from the Community system, can be identified.

    (ii) First they hold that economic analysis should be employed in the first instance to determine whether a violation is present. This is true of at least some of the member states with systems based on the Community system (most notably France and Italy), some of the member states with systems which differ from the Community system (most notably Germany and the UK) and third countries (both the US and Canada).

    (iii) Secondly neither the large member states nor the US, nor Canada, employ a notification system with respect to restrictive agree-ments. This is because they believe enforcement resources can be put to better use in other ways such as investigating complaints that involve vertical restraints. The absence of a notification system is also consistent with the premise that vertical agreements are *a priori* lawful.[5]

As the Green Paper explains in some detail, the structure of wholesale and retail distribution has been evolving rapidly in recent years, notably regarding concentration levels and inter-market penetration levels, the introduction of new management techniques and technology. Regarding distribution, for example, the Green Paper identifies the following trends:

- concentration, expressed in terms of a reduced number of larger operators, and closer vertical links between manufacturers, wholesalers and retailers;
- development of networks of independent traders, primarily in reaction to trends towards concentration and the growth of large integrated groups. In general terms, retailers without dedicated distribution facilities and the capacity to by-pass the wholesaler are unable to compete with the major retail groups in terms of price and service;
- a general reduction in the number of independent national distributors/ traditional wholesalers, bearing in mind the fact that the concept of wholesaling seems to have different meanings within different member states;
- a series of transformations in the retail sector, with significant differences between member states. Overall a slower increase than before in hyper-markets, a rise in franchising and a proliferation of forms of distance selling are prominent features;
- a tendency towards diversification of activities into other service areas. In addition some specific moves towards internationalization, although from a low base, such that retailing is still essentially national.[6]

Some introductory economic considerations

As mentioned above, the Community's, and in particular the Commission's approach to vertical restraints, has been to view them as potentially harmful (thus requiring notification), but has almost without exception subsequently approved them, usually via individual or block exemption, or comfort letter. Thus, they are viewed as *a priori* unlawful. The two main questions one must pose when considering this in the context of the Green Paper are whether this makes sense; first in economic terms, and second in regulatory terms.[7]

In economic terms, the executive summary sets out clearly the essential issues that must be borne in mind:

> The heated debate among economists concerning vertical restraints has calmed somewhat and a consensus is emerging. Vertical restraints are no longer regarded as *per se* suspicious or *per se* pro-competitive. Economists are less willing to make sweeping statements. Rather, they rely more on the analysis of the facts of a case in question. However, one element stands out: the importance of market structure in determining the impact of vertical restraints. The fiercer is inter-brand competition, the more likely are the pro-competitive and efficiency effects to outweigh any anti-competitive effects of vertical

restraints. Anti-competitive effects are only likely where interbrand competition is weak and there are barriers to entry at either producer or distributor level. In addition it is recognized that contracts in the distribution chain reduce transaction costs, and can allow the potential efficiencies in distribution to be realized. In contrast, there are cases where vertical restraints raise barriers to entry or further dampen horizontal competition in oligopolistic markets.

The questions posed by vertical restraints are still highly significant in terms of potential economic gains. Figures showing price differences between Member States demonstrate that, although there has been some price convergence, the potential economic gains from further integration are by no means exhausted.

Other conclusions that can be drawn from recent economic analysis are that:

- Individual clauses in an agreement or different types of vertical restraints cannot be considered *per se* as having a negative or positive effect on competition or integration.
- The combination of several vertical restraints does not necessarily increase the probability of any anti-competitive outcome but in some circumstances may make the outcome more favourable.
- Analysis should concentrate on the impact on the market rather than the form of the agreement. For example, whether entry is foreclosed by a network of agreements or whether theoretical agreement coupled with market power permits producers or distributors to practice price discrimination between different Member States.
- Given the risk associated with either entry into new markets or significant market expansion (i.e. creation of new trade flows that integrate the market), consideration should be given of a more favourable treatment of vertical restraints where this is accompanied by significant material or immaterial investment. This more favourable treatment should be limited in time.
- The nature of the products, the need for services and for investment to undertake efficient distribution and the needs and knowledge of consumers may all be important elements in determining both the objective efficiencies in distribution and to help guide policy.

It is clear that economic theory cannot be the only factor in the design of policy. Firstly it is only one source of policy. Secondly a full evaluation of every individual case would be too costly in resource terms and may lead to legal insecurity. Its use is therefore primarily to help develop basic policy and rules.[8]

Methodology

This paper sets out to review the Green Paper and to discuss the fundamental options presented therein. This discussion will be divided into four parts, which reflect the approach of the Commission on vertical restraints to date:

- *per se* infringements: absolute territorial protection and resale price maintenance;
- exclusivity;
- other territorial restrictions: active and passive restrictions; and
- other clauses limiting the commercial freedom of action of companies.

Absolute territorial protection

Price levels in the EU are far from uniform – see, e.g., the six-monthly survey on car prices in the EU published by the Commission, which highlights non-tax related price differences within the Community, typically of up to 25 per cent for an identical car, depending on the country of purchase. Many of these differences will no doubt be caused by cost differences in the various countries, particularly at distribution and retail level. Other differences may result, however, from the differing level of margins traditionally enjoyed on different EU markets. One of the principal objectives of the Single Market programme is, through inter-market penetration, to reduce or eliminate these monopoly profits, and, through increased competition and scale economies, to reduce prices throughout the EU. Manufacturers and distributors, however, have an interest in retaining these monopoly prices wherever possible. To do so, they must limit exports from low- to high-price member states.

An agreement will provide for absolute territorial protection where the distributor is obliged or agrees, explicitly in writing or through agreement backed up by action, to refuse to sell goods within its territory, to persons whom it believes intend to export. Such agreements are among the most effective mechanisms used by manufacturers wishing to limit trade, to maintain price differences between Member States.

In 1964, the Commission adopted its first decision, which subsequently became the fourth Court judgment: Grundig–Consten.[9] In this case, the Commission's policy towards export bans was fixed, and has not changed since. The Court fixed the *per se* applicability of Article 85 (1) to such agreements, against the advice of its Advocate General Roemer, who argued that when considering a territorial restriction, even an absolute one, it is necessary to consider the economic effects of the clause on the market, and in particular the prevailing level of interbrand competition.

Since this judgment, the Commission has prohibited and has fined heavily agreements containing absolute territorial protection:

- *Tretorn*   Ecu 640,000;[10]
- *Viho-Parker*   Ecu 750,000; [11]
- *Newitt-Dunlop*   Ecu 1,000,000;[12]
- *Viho–Toshiba*   Ecu 2,000,000 .[13]

For many agreements it is easy to see the logic behind this policy. Such arrangements are sometimes, or perhaps often, concluded simply with the objective of frustrating the EU's Single Market objectives, and reaping monopoly profits: an example of this can be seen in *Zera-Montedison*.[14] This concerned an exclusive distribution agreement for herbicides. Through the use of product differentiation on different national markets with the express intention of preventing parallel trade, combined with an active policy of preventing sales to exporters who succeeded in obtaining, or endeavoured to obtain, import authorization, Montedison succeeded in maintaining a price differentiation of up to 400 per cent between France and Germany. This price differentiation was possible in large part due to the highly oligopolistic market structure: the level of interbrand competition was not sufficiently intense to drive prices down towards marginal cost. The Commission's action, making parallel imports possible, clearly makes sense in antitrust terms, and in the light of the Community's Single Market objectives.

However, another example can demonstrate that in certain other cases, the logic of a *per se* approach is highly questionable. Absolute territorial restrictions can, depending on the nature of the market, be both pro-competitive, and can contribute to the achievement of the EU's Single Market objectives. Indeed the *per se* applicability of Article 85 (1) to such agreements can and will lead to the failure to conclude 'pro-integration' agreements, thus frustrating the EU's objectives. For example, assume that a small French company invents a revolutionary new pen. It enters a market dominated by a well-known manufacturer of cheap but effective pens – such as Bic. Many other brands are available from a number of manufacturers, including many from the Far East. Interbrand competition is fierce. The pen is launched, and is successful. Much of the investment, at least during the launch period, is concentrated on marketing and sales. The launch in France is a success, and the manufacturer, a small company, would like to expand into neighbouring countries, by licensing. However, given the homogeneous and easily transported nature of the product, the manufacturer is acutely concerned regarding parallel trade. If the distributor, in Belgium for example, should choose to limit its marketing efforts and sell at a lower price than neighbouring licensees, this would undermine the willingness of the other licensees to invest in marketing, for fear of 'free-riding'. The EC rules, however, prohibit any form of absolute territorial protection, and is unlikely to permit passive restraints on parallel trade. The manufacturer may therefore decide to delay plans to sell in these neighbouring markets until it can expand through the setting up of subsidiary companies.

In these circumstances, the EU's *per se* policy produces a perverse result: it frustrates its Single Market goal, as it deters the penetration into new EU markets of a new and innovative product. Furthermore, the price level will be fixed by interbrand competition. Intrabrand will play no role: it will provide no spur to competition as the manufacturer has no market power. Thus, in this example, the *per se* approach is a zero sum game, it is prohibiting a form of restraint which, given the market structure, could not possibly have any restrictive effects, whilst eliminating potential efficiency gains and depriving consumers of the opportunity to purchase a new product.

All defences raised by companies in the course of infringement proceedings regarding parallel trade restraints have been rejected:

Defence 1 Intense interbrand competition exists on the market, and the agreement cannot therefore be considered to be restrictive of competition in the narrow sense, nor prejudice the Single Market objective, because interbrand competition will ensure that prices are competitive. On the contrary, absolute territorial protection will permit the distributors/licensees to better promote the product, and thus competition will be intensified on the market, not diminished, by the existence of territorial restrictions.

This argument was rejected in *Grundig-Consten* by the Court, and is now rarely raised. The *Nungesser v. Commission* case provides a good example of the Court's *per se* approach. Regarding an 'open' licence (providing for exclusivity, but no additional territorial protection), the Court stated:

> In fact, in the case of a licence of breeder's right over hybrid maize seeds newly developed in one Member State, an undertaking established in another Member State which was not certain that it would not encounter competition from other licensees for the territory granted to it, or from the owner of the right itself, might be deterred from accepting the risk of cultivating and marketing that product; such a result would be damaging to the dissemination of a new technology and would prejudice competition in the Community between the new products and existing products.[15]

Having regard to the particular nature of the products in question, the Court concluded:

> . . . that in a case such as the present, the grant of an open exclusive license, that is to say a license which does not affect the position of third parties such as parallel importers and licensees for other territories, is not in itself incompatible with Article 85 (1) of the Treaty.[16]

However, regarding the argument that *absolute* territorial protection could be justified on similar ground, the Court stated:

As it is a question of seeds intended to be used by a large number of farmers for the production of maize, which is an important production for human and animal foodstuffs, absolute territorial protection manifestly goes beyond what is indispensable for the improvement of production and distribution or the promotion of technical progress, as is demonstrated in particular in the present case by the prohibition, agreed by both parties to the agreement, of any parallel imports of INRA maize seeds into Germany even if those seeds were bred by INRA itself and marketed in France.[17]

Clearly, the Court refuses to consider carefully this argument.

Defence 2 Market shares of the companies concerned are unimportant, thus no appreciable restriction of competition results from the agreement.

Unless market shares are truly negligible (1–5 per cent, see *de minimis* notice),[18] this defence is always rejected. In *Miller*, for example, where the company had a market share of 5 per cent, the Court said:

By its very nature, a clause prohibiting exports constitutes a restriction on competition, whether it is adopted at the instigation of the supplier or of the customer since the agreed purpose of the contracting parties is to endeavour to isolate a part of the market. Thus the fact that the supplier is not strict in enforcing such prohibitions cannot establish that they had no effect since their very existence may create a 'visual and psychological' background which satisfies customers and contributes to a more or less rigorous division of the markets.[19]

Defence 3 The argument can be raised that, because of the nature of the products (e.g. standard microchips), territorial protection only has any sense if it is absolute. Due to low unit transport costs, and the homogeneity of the products concerned, any lesser form of territorial protection, active/passive restrictions, for example, would be completely ineffective. Thus, as the Commission has recognized the importance of providing some protection for the licensee to encourage it to invest, in such situations, absolute territorial protection should be accepted. This defence has never been accepted, nor discussed in detail by the Court.

The question might therefore be raised why the Commission and the Court pursued and maintained this approach. There are two basic arguments that can be identified in this respect, one political, and one concerning regulatory enforcement. In political terms, the European Commission considers that the creation of the Single Market is a matter of fundamental political importance: it is viewed as vital that consumers have the right to purchase goods in whichever EU country they choose. The *per se* rule on parallel trade restraints is an important part in guaranteeing this 'right'. In regulatory terms, if one accepts the need to adopt a very strict enforcement line against a given category of agreements, a *per se* approach is entirely logical. This is why a *per se* approach is almost universally taken against clandestine price-fixing/market-sharing cartels. If each agreement is examined and judged in the light of the prevailing market conditions, a high fining policy (which is the essence of a 'strong' enforcement policy, as it is this, in the EU, which deters the conclusion of such agreements) become more difficult. Companies can legitimately argue that they acted in good faith, on the basis of a different, but none the less plausible market definition. Thus, on the assumption that a strict enforcement policy is necessary in this area – i.e. that most markets are not characterized by intense interbrand competition, and thus it is logical to sacrifice the (relatively low) efficiency/Single Market integration enhancing agreements in favour of the deterence of the vast majority of anti-competitive ones – this policy makes perfect sense. But this is a big 'if'.

It is difficult to argue the pros and cons of the Commission's approach. It is not based on empirical evidence or, apparently, studies on the relative efficiency gains and losses resulting from the *per se* approach. This is unsurprising – it is difficult to see from where such figures might be collated. However, it is clear that the benefits resulting from a *per se* approach will be larger if one can conclude that markets in the EU are generally oligopolistic. It is equally clear, on the one hand, that the benefits from a more permissive approach to absolute territorial protection will be larger, if markets in the EU are generally competitive, such that it is possible for intrabrand competition to play a determinative important role in setting the market price. The greater the number of markets that are competitive, the greater the number of agreements where intrabrand competition will play no role in determining market conditions.

Equally, it is clear that the number of product and service markets in the EU in which competition is intense has been increasing in recent years, and continues to do so. Thus, the balance that exists between the efficiency enhancing and reducing effects of the *per se* approach has been, and continues to be, gradually and continually tilting towards the relaxation of the *per se* rule.

At present, however, the Commission appears to be hostile to any change in the present approach. The Court has recently restated its support of the *per se* rule in unequivocal terms. Commissioner Van Miert stated the following in 1996:

> In addition, we in Brussels also regard absolute territorial protection as such an affront to the Single Market that it too is nearly always treated as illegal. By absolute territorial protection, I mean attempts to prevent parallel traders or individuals from reacting to price

differences between Member States and importing the product from a high price Member State to a low price one. To deny this right to consumers would be to deny the very nature of a single market and our Union – there must be no discrimination on basis of residence. . . . Of course having clear rules does not guarantee compliance. We still regularly get cases of distribution agreements in which firms have been trying to apply absolute territorial protection. . . . You should be in no doubt that such infringements are punished by heavy fines.[20]

Furthermore, in the Green Paper, the Commission notes that 'absolute territorial protection . . . which may affect trade between Member States will not only continue to fall *per se* within Article 85 (1), but [is] unlikely to be exempted'.[21]

Thus, at least for the foreseeable future, no change can be expected. None the less, it is clear that at some stage, this rule will necessarily be relaxed – for example by adopting a rebuttable presumption of illegality with respect to absolute territorial restraints, which could be rebutted by providing evidence that the agreement operates on a highly competitive market. No other regulatory system in the world adopts a *per se* approach to such provisions, rather than examining them on their own merits, in the light of the prevailing market structure The question for the EU is not therefore whether, but when.

Resale price maintenance (RPM) is the second area in which the Commission and the Court maintains a *per se* prohibition rule. This can be seen from a number of cases: *Deutsche Phillips*,[22] *Gerofabrik*,[23] and *Amp v. Biron*.[24] The limitation on this is that trade between member states must be appreciably affected. Thus, where a RPM system is purely national in scope, and is not likely to close a national market from foreign suppliers, the system will not be challenged by the Commission. This can be seen, for example, in the Net Book Agreement[25] case, where the Commission challenged the system of collective RPM for books, but limited the decision to cross-border traffic. The reasoning behind the strict approach is that RPM not only prevents any real competition at the retail and distribution levels, which in the EU probably represents a significant part of the final sales price, but furthermore it permits or facilitates parallel pricing patterns in oligopolistic markets, by increasing transparency. Finally, it can be used by manufacturers as a facilitating device to artificially maintain price differences between different member states. The reasons why the Commission and the Court maintains a *per se* approach to RPM are, unlike absolute territorial protection, not based on internal market considerations. They are purely limited to considerations of really effective control on a category of agreements that are viewed as particularly pernicious, and where, therefore, a *per se* policy is necessary: as mentioned above, it is equally for this reason why cartels are viewed as *per se* infringements of Article 85 (1). Furthermore, the arguments set out above concerning the countervailing efficiencies that can be produced by agreements providing for absolute territorial protection are far less evident regarding RPM. Whilst it can be argued that in markets where competition is intense, RPM will have little effect (at least RPM systems agreed between manufacturers/distributors/retailers, rather than collectively agreed systems such as the Net Book Agreement), it is more difficult to argue that the adoption of a *per se* approach in this area will prevent the conclusion of a number of pro-competitive agreements.

Again, therefore, it seems likely that no change will result from the Green Paper in this respect. Commissioner Van Miert confirmed this in a recent speech: 'I do not want to describe the detail of our block exemptions, but there is one common feature that needs stressing. Like most antitrust authorities, we regard resale price maintenance as illegal'.[26] This is confirmed in the Green Paper in unequivocal terms (paragraph 39).

Exclusivity

Where a distributor or licensee is granted exclusivity over a given area, it alone may operate as an established company manufacturing or distributing in the territory in question.

The Court's approach

As early as 1964 the Court established the rule that a distribution or licensing agreement that grants exclusivity to a distributor/licensee in a given area, but contains no other territorial limitation, may fall entirely outside the scope of Article 85 (1) depending on the nature of the market, and more particularly the intensity of interbrand competition that is prevalent. In *Consten–Grundig*, for example, the Court annulled part of the Commission's decision which found that an exclusive distribution agreement fell within Article 85 (1). The Court considered that the Commission had failed to give sufficient reasons why an open exclusive license was restrictive of competition, given the nature of the market in question. Equally, in *Technique Minière*, the Court found that an exclusive distribution agreement that does not provide for absolute territorial protection does not necessarily fall under Article 85 (1), particularly where the exclusivity is necessary to enable the penetration of new markets. In that case, the Court stated that in carrying out this analysis, it is necessary to consider:

> the nature and quantity, limited or not, of the products covered by the agreement, the position and importance of the grantor and the concessionaire on the market for the products concerned, the isolated nature of the disputed agreement or, alternatively, its position in a

series of agreements, the severity of the clauses intended to protect the exclusive dealership or, alternatively, the opportunities allowed for other commercial competitors in the same products by way of parallel re-exportation and importation.[27]

Confirmation of this can be seen from the *Maize Seeds* judgment, quoted above.

More recently, in the *Danish Fur Breeders* case,[28] the Court of First Instance stated that exclusive obligations do not in themselves fall within Article 85 (1), and must be considered in the light of the characteristics of the market in question. In that case, which concerned exclusive purchasing obligations, the Court observed that agreements containing such obligations may have the effect of intensifying rather than restricting competition, as the producer has a guaranteed outlet for its products and the distributor can invest in their distribution as it has a secure source of supply. These arguments are little different from the 'free-rider' arguments that the Court referred to in the *Nungesser* judgment.[29]

The Commission's approach

The Commission has taken a rather conservative approach in applying this case law. In the vast majority of cases in which it has considered vertical agreements providing for exclusivity, the text of the decisions only taken limited account of the factors identified by the Court in *Technique Minière*, and has readily found that an exclusive agreement falls within Article 85 (1).

In the early years of Community competition policy the Commission took a very open attitude towards vertical agreements. In 1962, for example, however, it issued a Notice, the 'Christmas message', declaring a very permissive attitude towards simple patent licenses.[30] This notice states that such licences 'are not covered by the prohibition laid down in Article 85 (1)', even if they contain the following clauses:

- the limitation of exploitation by reference to the field of use, time, territory, quantity, assignment or sub-licences;
- marking of the licensed product;
- quality standards;
- reciprocal non-exclusive grantbacks of improvements; and
- exclusivity.

In the early 1970s, however, the Commission began to adopt a number of individual decisions far more restrictive than the Christmas message. The following decision typifies this development.

In *Kabelmetal-Luchaire*,[31] Kabelmetal granted Luchaire an exclusive licence for the manufacture in France of certain products using specified patents, with the exclusive licence to sell the products in Spain and Portugal, and the non-exclusive licence to sell elsewhere in the EC. Other clauses included the obligation on Luchaire to license improvements. Other clauses were deleted at the insistence of the Commission: the obligations on Kabelmetal to assign improvements, not to sell outside Spain and Portugal and not to contest patents.

Kabelmetal's French market share was estimated at 20 per cent; its competitors were considered to be large and powerful. Prior to the grant of the licence, Kabelmetal had sold only in France and so the effect of the licence was to spread the penetration of the technology in the EC, therefore enhancing competition.

The fact that the licence was exclusive was found to fall under Article 85 (1), but was exempted.

In the exclusive distribution licensing regulation the Commission continued to pursue the line that the grant of an exclusive licence infringes Article 85 (1).[32] Exclusivity is exempted by Article 1 of the regulation. However, in the preamble no mention is made that exclusivity may, according to the circumstances of the particular case in question, fall outside Article 85 (1). Even more notable is the fact that an explanatory notice accompanying the regulation also fails to discuss this question.[33]

A similar line is pursued in the 1996 IP Licensing Block Exemption Regulation. Article 1 (1) of the regulation exempts 'an obligation on the licensor not to license other undertakings to exploit the licensed technology in the licensed territory'.[34] Article 1 (2) exempts the corresponding obligation on the licensor not to exploit the licensed invention in the granted territory. This position covers all agreements that are not able to benefit from the *de minimis* notice.

However, in the preamble to the regulation, the Commission acknowledges that in certain circumstances an exclusive licence can fall outside Article 85 (1):

> Exclusive licensing agreements, i.e. agreements in which the licensor undertakes not to exploit the licensed technology in the licensed territory himself or to grant further licenses there, may not in themselves be incompatible with Article 85 (1) where they are concerned with the introduction and protection of a new technology in the licensed territory, by reason of the scale of the research which has been undertaken, of the increase in the level of competition, in particular interbrand competition, and of the competitiveness of the undertakings concerned resulting from the dissemination of innovation within the Community. In so far as agreements of this kind fall, in other circumstances, within the scope of Article 85 (1), it is appropriate to include them in Article 1 in order that they may also been fit from the exemption.[35]

The willingness of the Commission to view such agreements in the context of prevailing market conditions is also stressed in the Green Paper:

> If a vertical agreement is neither *de minimis* nor constitutes one of the two restraints automatically triggering the application of Article 85 (1), a case by case analysis is necessary to see if Article 85 (1) applies. This analysis takes account of the real economic context of the case to see if competition is appreciably restricted. Even if the individual agreement does not fall within the scope of Article 85 (1), the cumulative impact of several similar agreements may appreciably restrict competition. This is particularly the case for networks of exclusive purchasing agreements where a large share of retail outlets are tied exclusively to existing producers. This can foreclose the market to new producers or prevent producers in other member states from entering the market.[36]

Thus, the Commission has clearly a willingness to consider the argument that an exclusive distribution agreement or licence will fall outside the scope of Article 85 (1) where interbrand competition is strong, but the very fact of the existence of the block exemption means that the issue is not dealt with in individual cases.

The Block Exemption Regulation is designed to exempt agreements that go further than containing simple exclusivity provisions; for example, they may include non-competition clauses. However, to fall within the regulation, companies must exclude provisions or clauses not explicitly exempted. Thus, whilst two companies may have an interest in including in their agreement a provision which would lead them to fall outside the regulation (and one that would improve the distribution of the product in question), in practice they will omit the clauses and choose to benefit from the regulation rather than to notify individually with all the cost and uncertainty that results. Thus, almost no notifications are received, so the willingness of the Commission to apply this 'more economic' approach is not seen in practice. It is again instructive to examine why the Commission went down the path of casting the Article 85 (1) net so wide, which is still applied today, due to the Block Exemption Regulation system.

The reasoning behind this early approach must presumably result from the view, taken when this policy was formulated, and then developed and applied to a range of cases principally in the late 1970s, that as a general rule the EC's markets were not characterized by fierce competition. In such circumstances the limitation of interbrand competition resulting from the grant of exclusivity, together with the possible reduction of interbrand competition resulting from the exclusive appointment of a distributor/licensee attractive to other potential manufactures, was viewed as appreciably restricting competition within the meaning of Article 85 (1). This may well explain the restrictive approach in individual cases and the block exemptions. Commissioner Van Miert in fact confirmed this logic in a recent speech:

> In order to develop a competition culture throughout the Community and avoid taking risks with the integration process, the Commission has adopted a wide interpretation of Article 85 (1) in respect of vertical restraints. However, when the Basic Implementing Regulation (BIR) came into effect in the early 1960s, it had the effect of creating a 'mass' problem of notification of vertical agreements – nearly 30,000 agreements came to the Commission. To give legal certainty to these agreements the system of block exemptions was devised.[37]

This is also reflected in the Green Paper:

> Because of concerns over threats to market integration and the ambiguous nature of their impact on competition, Commission policy has been to apply Article 85 (1) relatively widely to vertical restraints. It considers that both interbrand and intrabrand competition are important.[38]

As already mentioned, however, the markets in the EC for many products and services are now characterized by the existence of far more competitors compared to thirty or even twenty years ago, and this trend continues apace. The Single Market programme, whilst far from complete, is well advanced. It is logical, therefore that this development is one reason why the Commission has now chosen to re-examine its approach to vertical agreements.

The options available in this respect are examined below (pp. 251–254) as they concern not only exclusivity but also, active trade restraints, and other limitations of commercial freedom.

Active and passive restrictions on trade

Definitions

Active sales Licensees may not actively solicit customers outside their own territory, nor set up a sales agency. They may, however, sell outside their territory in response to unsolicited orders.

Passive sales A licensee/distributor may not sell outside its territory. It may, however, sell in its territory for export if the orders are unsolicited – usually sales to parallel traders.

The existing approach

Both the Court and the Commission have consistently taken the view that such clauses fall within Article 85 (1), but are in certain circumstances exemptable. This can be seen from the Green Paper:

> Although exclusive distributors may be forbidden from actively promoting the product outside their allocated exclusive territory, they must be free to respond to orders coming from outside that territory (passive sales). Customers must be free to purchase from any distributor they wish in the EU, even outside their territory of residence, and make or arrange for personal imports. Intermediaries and other traders must be able to buy from any distributor and sell in any other market, particular in response to significant price differences between Member States (parallel trade).[39]

As a general rule, therefore, active restrictions are exempted unless exceptional circumstances are found, such as the existence of a market structure in which interbrand competition is particularly weak, or prices between different member states vary enormously where a prohibition may result. This can be illustrated by the fact that such active restrictions are exempted in the exclusive distribution[40] and patent licensing[41] regulations.

Passive restraints, on the other hand, are only rarely exempted. An exemption may be given if the agreement in question concerns the introduction of new technology or a new manufacturing process, and, due to the level of investment and risk involved, a greater degree of territorial protection is necessary from free-riding. In such circumstances the Commission may exempt passive restrictions, but for a limited period only. In the Patent Licensing Regulation, for example, Article 1 (b) exempts 'such an obligation for a period not exceeding five years from the date when the product is first put on the market within the common market by one of his licensees'.[42] In the exclusive distribution, exclusive purchasing and franchising regulations, however, it is made clear that agreements providing for restrictions on passive sales fall outside in the regulation, as the 'innovation element' justifying such restrictions in the IP regulation cannot be presumed to exist in simple distribution arrangements.

The future?

The comments made above regarding absolute territorial protection equally apply to these clauses. Where interbrand competition is intense, it is not, at least in theory, necessary to insist that intrabrand competition exist in order to prevent price discrimination between national markets on grounds unrelated to cost. In such circumstances intrabrand competition may not be necessary to attain market integration. Again, therefore, where interbrand competition is fierce, such clauses might not, at least in theory, be seen as restrictive of competition.

Where, however, interbrand competition is less than fierce, the position is less clear. There is no clear line that can be drawn, or all-encompassing test that can be applied, to delineate between those markets where interbrand competition is sufficiently intense to ensure non-price discrimination between member states and those where it is not. There will always be a grey area where the question remains open. This area is the proper preserve of Article 85 (3).

However, it should be noted that restrictions on passive sales are, in reality, close to absolute territorial protection. Where used intelligently by manufacturers, they can effectively seal off a national territory. To give wholesale approval to such agreements would be likely to frustrate the results of a strict line on absolute territorial protection. In line with the analysis above, one can therefore expect the Commission to continue to take a strict line against such clauses, for Single Market objectives. Thus, the analysis below, which indicates a more 'economic' or market-based analysis to vertical restricts, is unlikely to extend to passive restrictions. Notwithstanding this, it does appear that the Green Paper does not exclude a softening of the Commission's approach in this area, unlike with respect to absolute territorial protection. This is further discussed below.

Regarding active sales, however, such clauses are more akin to the territorial restriction inevitably resulting from the grant of exclusivity and thus are also discussed below.

Other provisions commonly found in vertical agreements

A number of non-territorial clauses are also often included in vertical agreements, most commonly non-compete clauses, limitations on the customers that may be served by distributors/licensees, limits on the pricing policies of distributors/licensees, stocking obligations, advertising obligations and, with respect to IP licensing agreements, the grant back of improvements and no-challenge clauses.

In the 1970s, the Commission took a very strict line on such non-territorial restrictions, often prohibiting them unless a company could demonstrate the imperative need to include them in these agreements. This can be seen from the following cases.

Traditional approach by the Court and the Commission

AOIP-Beyrard[43]   Mr Beyrard granted to AOIP an exclusive license to use his patents in France. AOIP's market share in France of the relevant products was 7 per cent. The following clauses were considered to infringe Article 85 (1):

- exclusivity;
- obligation not to actively export to countries where other licences are granted, no-challenge clause;
- validity of licence extends to life of any improvement patents;
- obligation to pay royalties after expiration of most recent patent;
- non-competition clause;
- obligation to pay royalties on manufacture of relevant products even if licensed technology not used.

An exemption was refused, because the following clauses were considered to be unlikely to provide the requisite efficiencies: no-challenge, non-competition, post-term royalty payment.

Vaasen-Morris[44]   This case concerned the grant of a patent licence that included a no-challenge clause and an obligation to purchase certain supplies exclusively from the licensor. The market share of the parties was found to be below 5 per cent, the annual turnover of the licensor was considered to be 'very small', and its only income was from royalties and orders of the equipment, the subject of the exclusive purchasing obligation. The equipment and technology was used for the manufacture of square sausages – Saucissons de Boulogne. The licence was considered to fall under Article 85 (1) and was viewed as unexemptable, because of the no-challenge and exclusive purchasing clause.

However, when one considers the Commission's approach to competition policy as a whole over the previous few years, one notes a change in emphasis. A shift seems to have been occurring away from the model of competition policy based on an examination of limits on contractual freedom towards one which considers that the crucial issue when examining an agreement is an analysis of it in the context of the market in question and the contracting parties' position upon the market. Only where they have important market shares, or the market is oligopolistic, will an agreement be likely to appreciably restrict competition.

Although the Court has consistently followed this approach in general terms from the earliest days,[45] it has never provided clear guidance for its application, and no doubt partly as a consequence of this the Commission has traditionally adopted a more conservative approach. Nevertheless, the Court's continuing and perhaps even more committed adhesion to a market-based analysis of competition policy in general, and vertical restraints in particular, can be adduced from more recent case law. In *Delimitis*,[46] for example, the Court made it clear that an exclusive purchasing agreement must be assessed in the light of the market in question and the undertakings' market shares. Similar indications can be found in cases on patent licensing. In *Bayer v. Süllhöffer*, for example, the Court stated that a 'no-challenge clause in a patent licensing agreement may, depending on the legal and economic context, restrict competition within the meaning of Article 85 (1)'.[47] In *Ottung v. Klee and Weilbach*[48] the Court used similar language regarding a post-term obligation not to manufacture the licensed product. In *Erauw-Jacquery v. La Hesbignonne*, however, the Court decided that 'a provision in an agreement ... which obliges the grower to comply with minimum prices fixed by the other party falls within the prohibition set out in Article 85 (1) of the Treaty if it apparently affects trade between Member States'.[49]

It appears reasonable to conclude on the basis of these cases that the Court's approach in *Maize Seeds*, which is based on a careful and realistic approach of the agreement in its economic and factual context, is increasingly becoming the corner-stone of the Court's approach to competition policy in general, and to vertical restraints in particular.[50] Furthermore, there is increasing evidence that the Commission is increasingly, if not consistently, following this approach. In *Odin*,[51] for example, the Commission concluded that a JV fell outside the scope of Article 85 (1) because, on the basis of a comprehensive market analysis, the companies were not potential competitors. A similar approach can be seen in *GEC–Siemens/Plessey*,[52] where the Commission considered that a joint venture between companies with important market shares, but one that operated in a competitive market, did not appreciably restrict competition within the meaning of Article 85 (1).

Specifically in relation to IP licensing, in *Moosehead–Whitbread* the Commission found that on the facts of the case a trademark no-challenge clause fell outside the scope of Article 85 (1):

> Only where the use of a well-known trademark would be an important advantage to any company entering or competing in any given market and the absence of which therefore constitutes a significant barrier to entry, would this clause, which impedes the licensee to challenge the validity of the trademark, constitute an appreciable restriction of competition within the meaning of Article 85 (1).[53]

A more 'economic' approach to vertical restraints

Thus, if the approach of the Community to competition policy in general, and vertical restraints in particular, becomes concentrated on the effects of the agreements, what will be the basic elements on which this policy approach is translated into practical application?

First, the strict approach taken with respect to absolute territorial protection and passive territorial restrictions will not necessarily be relevant to other types of vertical restraints. The objectives underlying the two will be different. Regarding territorial restrictions, the Community will continue to apply a mixed Single Market/antitrust objective, resulting in absolute territorial restriction being considered a *per se* infringement of Article 85 (1). With respect to other clauses the aim is simply to ensure that markets are not foreclosed or that price parallelism is not facilitated. There is every reason to expect that the former test will be more difficult to satisfy than the latter.

Second, it is necessary to realize that the grant of a patent licence or distributorship is normally a pro-competitive, not an anti-competitive act. The conclusion of such agreements by definition usually increases, not decreases, the number of competitors present on the market. Not only does it spread the use of new technologies and new goods throughout the Community, thus intensifying interbrand competition, it can also act as a catalyst for intensified Community integration. An example of the latter factor can be seen from the following example. If company A, which operates exclusively in France, grants a patent licence to B, operating in Italy, the effect of the grant of the licence will be that both markets benefit from the use of the technology, deepening Community integration. This benefit that may accompany such agreements is particularly important with respect to SMEs, which may well lack the resources to exploit their inventions outside their own geographical sphere of activity, at least in the short to medium term. This factor must be fully taken into account in determining whether a vertical agreement appreciably restricts competition within the meaning of Article 85 (1), and, where Article 85 (1) is applicable, whether an exemption is possible.

Third, a number of clauses common to patent licensing or distribution arrangements can reinforce the existing foreclosure effect of exclusive licences, depending on the specific circumstances of the case in question. These clauses include the following: no-challenge clause, automatic extension of our IP licence through improvement patents, non-competition clauses, royalty extension clauses, quantity limitations, price limitations, customer limitations, obligatory assignments of improvements, tying, etc.

Such clauses raise entry barriers and, where they enable the undertakings in question to eliminate competition in respect of a substantial part of the products in question, should be prohibited (see *Windsurfing*).[54] However, where the undertakings concerned do not have significant/important market shares and operate on competitive markets, such clauses are largely neutral with respect to competition, and in such circumstances any prohibition of such restraints can only be justified on grounds of 'fairness' rather than the maintenance of open and competitive markets. Indeed, the blanket prohibition of these clauses between companies with low market shares can (and probably does) prejudice competition and therefore the competitiveness of Community industry. This is because a refusal to contemplate the inclusion of such clauses in patent licences or distribution agreements will lead to the deterrence of the grant of technology licenses or distributorships, or at least the limitation of the enthusiasm of licensees/distributors to properly invest in licences or distributors once granted and thus a limit on the effective diffusion of technology or goods throughout the Community.

An example might be the prospective grant of a licence by a small technology company to a larger firm. The patent licence would usually be accompanied by the transfer of know-how and specialized personnel. The small company will fear (and justifiably so) that the licensee will absorb the know-how, and then challenge the validity of the patent. Even if it is convinced that the patent is valid, the small firm would not have the resources to fight the action in court. The refusal to permit no-challenge clauses in such circumstances may well lead the small company to decide not to license the patent, but exploit it itself to a more limited extent, relying on slow organic growth.

Fourth, not all clauses in vertical agreements can be viewed as having an equally restrictive effect on competition. Certain clauses, such as limitations on the freedom of undertakings as to the prices that they may charge or the quantities they may sell, can cause particularly serious restrictions of competition. Agreements containing such clauses will always therefore be likely to attract the Commission's interest. The question whether any given market exhibits a sufficient level of interbrand competition to conclude that non-territorial vertical restraints will not appreciably raise entry barriers or assist price parallelism is a difficult one. There will always be cases where the answer to this question is affirmative and those where the market will be viewed as clearly non-competitive. There will, however, always be a large 'grey-zone'. In this area at least, where uncertainty prevails, there is every reason to expect that these 'hard-core' clauses will continue to be prohibited.

On this basis it seems logical to conclude that, at least in theory, in future the Commission should, in each case, where absolute territorial protection does not exist, carry out a detailed analysis of the market in question and the undertakings' position upon it to determine whether the agreement will be likely to raise entry barriers and thus significantly contribute to market foreclosure or pricing parallelism. If the answer to this question is that it will not, these aspects of a vertical agreement would benefit from a negative clearance. If doubt exists – it falls within the 'grey-zone' mentioned above – it is unlikely that the Commission would even grant a negative clearance or exemption to any of the 'hard core' clauses mentioned above, although with respect to the other, less inherently restrictive clauses, an exemption would be possible.

Practical limitations

However, it is not possible to base future policy options simply on the basis of these somewhat theoretical considerations. Two further issues, probably of at least equal importance to these economic-based arguments, concern (i) the need to provide a regulatory system that is effective from the enforcement viewpoint, and (ii) the need to maintain a system that, from the business viewpoint, provides legal security at minimum cost. In this respect a basic contradiction needs to be faced between these two latter objectives and those mentioned above: the greater the use of market/economic analysis in the Commission's approach to vertical agreements, the greater the resultant legal uncertainty.

The Commission's experience when considering the renewal of the IP Licensing Block Exemption Regulation illustrates this. The previous version, adopted in 1984, provided a long list of 'black' clauses, such as non-compete, no-challenge clauses, etc. If, however, an IP licence is concluded between two companies that have modest market shares on a competitive market, the inclusion of such clauses can only have a pro-competitive, not an anti-competitive effect. However, if included in agreements between companies with large market shares, or on oligopolistic markets, they can have signifi-cant foreclosure effects. Thus, the Commission proposed to adopt a new regulation, containing market share criteria, seeking to exclude from the scope of the regulation companies with large market shares, or significant market shares operating on oligopolistic markets. For those companies not meeting these criteria, however, the 'blacklist' was to be much reduced.

During the consultation period, fierce opposition to this approach came from industry and legal representatives on the grounds of the uncertainty that would result. Calculating market shares is a difficult exercise, and an uncertain one. Industry and the legal profession argued that because of this, the introduction of such market shares would lead companies, for security reasons, to notify large numbers of agreements. Given the disadvantages of individual notification, industry clearly preferred a more restrictive block exemption, but one that covered agreements irrespective of their market shares. And this, finally, was the type of Block Exemption Regulation that was adopted.[55] Thus, whilst the approach of the Commission made clear sense in economic terms, regulatory considerations prevailed.

The Green Paper options

Four different options are put forward in the Green Paper. These are preceded by a list of considerations relevant to all the options, the most important of which are the following:

- the *per se* policy regarding absolute territorial protection and parallel trade restrictions will continue;

- a non-opposition procedure is included in the Franchising Regulation, whereby agreements containing clauses figuring in neither the black nor white list are exempted provided that a notification is made, and the Commission raises no objections within six months. Comments are invited whether this approach should be extended;
- the Commission has already published a draft revised *de minimis* notice, stating that vertical agreements with a market share of 10 per cent or less can benefit from the notice, providing that no provision is made for absolute territorial protection or RPM. It is stated that this can be taken as a 'working hypothesis' when examining these options.

Option I is to maintain the current system. Option II is to widen the scope of the existing block exemptions. The following suggestions are raised.

283 Measures to increase flexibility in general could include one or more of the following:

- the block exemptions would cover not only the precise clauses listed, but also clauses which are similar or less restrictive;
- the inclusion of prohibited clauses might not deny the benefit of the exemption for the rest of the agreement;
- the block exemption could apply to agreements involving more than two parties;
- a block exemption or a Commission notice for selective distribution could be enacted.

284 Specific measures to increase flexibility could include one or more of the following:

- the block exemptions for exclusive distribution and exclusive purchasing could be extended to cover services or to permit the distributor to transform or process the contract goods. Distributors could be allowed to add significant value by changing the economic identity of the goods without losing the benefit of the block exemption;
- the block exemption for exclusive purchasing agreements could be extended to cover partial as well as exclusive supply;
- the block exemption for franchising agreement could be extended to cover maximum resale price maintenance as an exception to the general principle that resale price maintenance will not be exempted;
- associations of independent retailers could be permitted to benefit from block exemption regulations, provided that the independent retailers are small and medium-sized enterprises

and that the market share of the association remains below a certain threshold;

- an arbitration procedure could be set up for distributors denied admission to a selective distribution network.

Option III is to follow an approach similar to that originally proposed by the Commission when reviewing the IP Licensing Regulations. It is characterized by two of the elements outlined above:

286 This option stresses Community competition policy's market integration objectives. Territorial protection and vertical restraints are seen as a significant contributory factor to the maintenance of considerable price differentials between Member States. It is certainly the case that many markets are becoming more concentrated at the production and distribution level, while vertical restraints can foreclose markets and raise barriers to entry. The value added by distribution is an important element in its own right. Intrabrand competition can play an important role in promoting competition in markets where interbrand competition is not fierce.

287 The current block exemptions apply without any market share limits. They could be amended so as to apply only where each party has less than, for instance, 40 per cent market share of the relevant market in the contract territory. There would be no block exemption above that threshold, at least in respect of the following restrictions:

- protection against active sales from outside the territory
- protection for exclusive dealing (prohibition to sell competing products/services).

289 The suggestions made in Option II could be applied to agreements below the market share threshold.

290 Parties may have doubts about the correct definition of a market and calculation of their share thereof, which could lead them to notify agreements to the Commission in a search for legal certainty. There would also be notifications of agreements where the parties have market shares in excess of the threshold.

291 The Commission would appreciate estimates of the number and type of cases likely to be notified, and views on whether guidelines explaining the circumstances in which the Commission

would grant exemptions under Article 85 (3) could solve this problem. Possible grounds for exemption could include the condition that there will be no significant price discrimination to the detriment of customers.

Thus, it is based on market shares: any approach by the Commission that seeks to take economic reality more into account when dealing with vertical restraints will be based on market shares in some form or other, as this is the only way to differentiate between agreements operating in markets with strong and weak interbrand competition.

However, it should be noted that this option fails to take account of the basic premise that a vertical agreement between two companies that do not enjoy market power and which operate on a market in which interbrand competition is intense, will not restrict competition, but can only intensify it.[56] Thus, such agreements should, at least in theory, attract negative clearance. Agreements between companies where there is in question, either due to the significant market shares of the companies concerned, or the concentrated nature of the relevant market, must be examined carefully to determine whether the resultant efficiencies outweigh the potential anti-competitive effect: the test of Article 85 (3), or, in other competition policy systems, the rule of reason analysis.

Option III continues, to pursue in large part, the present system of *de facto* viewing all agreements that are most unlikely to be challenged as falling under Article 85 (1) but meriting exemption, rather than attracting negative clearance. An exception is the draft revised *de minimis* rules, which, if adopted, would lead to *de facto* negative clearance for agreements between companies with market shares below 10 per cent. This seems, however, a very low threshold when applied to vertical restraints.

Option IV seeks to address these issues:

293 The idea underlying this option is that economic analysis of vertical restraints should be implemented by legal instruments which give undertakings a considerable degree of legal certainty. The economic criteria designed to determine the market conditions in which Article 85 (1) would apply could be developed, in the first place, within the framework of a new Commission notice and subsequently, in the light of the experience acquired, within the framework of a negative clearance regulation.

294 This option would provide for more flexible treatment of vertical arrangements for agreements between parties with no significant market power. The alleged limiting effect of block exemptions and emphasis on the legal classification of different forms of distribution would be reduced.

295 For parties with less than, for instance, 20 per cent market share in the contract territory, there would be a rebuttable presumption of compatibility with Article 85 (1) ('the negative clearance presumption'). In other words, vertical restraints in such circumstances would not normally be caught by Article 85 (1). This presumption would cover all vertical restraints except those relating to minimum resale prices, impediments to parallel trade or passive sales, or those contained in distribution agreements between competitors.

296 This negative clearance presumption could be rebutted by the Commission on the basis of a market analysis that would take account of factors such as:

- market structure (e.g. oligopoly);
- barriers to entry;
- the degree of integration of the Single Market, evaluated on the basis of indicators such as the price differential existing between Member States and the level of market penetration in each Member State of products imported from other Member States, or;
- the cumulative impact of parallel networks.

297 Agreements which, as a result of this market analysis, were shown to fall within Article 85 (1) could benefit from a block exemption if they fulfilled the necessary conditions (see below variants I and II). The negative clearance presumption could be implemented by a Commission Notice and subsequently in the light of the experience acquired, within the framework of a negative clearance regulation that would require a new Council enabling Regulation under Article 87 of the Treaty.

298 For cases with market share above for instance 20 per cent, and for those below 20 per cent that fall within Article 85 (1), there could be two possibilities, as follows:

Variant I

299 All cases over 20 per cent could be covered by the block exemption described in *Option II* (wider block exemption).

Variant II

300 All cases over 20 per cent would be covered by the block

exemption described in *Option III* (i.e. inapplicability of block exemption to certain restrictions above 40 per cent market share).

Conclusions

For many years academics have criticized the Commission's policy on vertical restraints, on the grounds that it is too legalistic: it exempts where it should clear, the resultant block exemption system places industry in a clausal strait-jacket. What is clear, however, is that there is a balance between a more 'economic' approach and the simplicity of the Commission's regulatory approach. As was evidenced in the consultation on the IP Licensing Regulation, industry has a strong preference for a system that reduces regulatory costs and provides legal certainty.

NOTES

1 *Grundig–Consten*, Commission decision 23 September 1964, Case 56/64 and 58/64, 20 October 1964 OJ 2545, Court of Justice judgment, 13 July 1966, ECR (1966), 389.
2 In theory exceptional circumstances may permit exemption, and in *Distillers* such a (loose) ban was tolerated for a limited period, but no case exists where such a system was formally approved.
3 They were originally set to expire end 1997, but were extended by two years to permit the Commission to complete the Green Paper consultation.
4 *Green Paper on Vertical Restrains in EC Competition Policy*, 22 January 1977. Available from the Office of Publications of the EC, reference COM (96), 721. It can also be downloaded from DG IV's internet site: http: 158.167.37.38.8080/en/comm/dg04/entente/other.html.
5 Green Paper, § 32.
6 Green Paper, § 44.
7 The two concepts do not necessarily lead to the same result, as was demonstrated during the consultation undertaken by the Commission on the renewal of the IP licensing block exemption regulation. The Commission proposed to increase the 'economic element' in its revised regulation, by reducing the 'black' clauses that would lead an agreement to fall outside the scope of the Regulation, whilst intro-ducing market share criteria so that agreements between companies potentially enjoying market power would need to notify their agreement(s) individually. Although this makes at least more economic sense than the approach taken in the previous Regulation (all agreements could benefit from the old Regulation, irrespective of the potential level of market power enjoyed by its signataries, but must fit within the strait-jacket of a fairly restrictive regulation), industry strongly objected to the new proposal, on the grounds of regulatory cost.
8 Green Paper, § 10–13.
9 *Grundig–Consten, op. cit.*

10 Commission Decision, 21 December 1994, OJ (1994) C387/95.

11 Commission Decision, 15 July 1992, OJ (1992) L233/27.

12 Commission Decision, 15 March 1991 OJ (1992) L131/32.

13 Commission Decision, 4 June 1991, OJ (1991) L287/39.

14 Commission Decision, 22 June 1993, OJ (1993) L272/28.

15 *Nungesser v. Commission*, 258/78, 8 June 1982, ECL (1982), 2015.

16 *Ibid.*

17 *Ibid.*

18 Commission notice on agreement of minor importance, OJ C231/2, 12 September 1986, Revised OJ C386, 23 December 1994. Note that a revised draft has been published, OJ 29/3, 30 January 1997.

19 *Miller v. Commission*, 19/77, 1 February 1979, ECL (1978), 131.

20 6 May 1996, ABA Conference, Brussels.

21 Green Paper, § 39.

22 Commission Decision, 5 October 1973, OJ (1973), L293/40.

23 Commission Decision, 22 December 1976, OJ (1977), L16/8.

24 Judgment of the Court of Justice, 3 July 1985, ECR (1985), 2015.

25 Commission Decision, 12 December 1988, OJ (1989), L22/12.

26 6 May 1996, ABA Conference, Brussels.

27 *Technique Minière*, repeated and affirmed in subsequent cases, e.g. *L'Oréal v. De Nieuwe*, AMCK ECR (1980) 3775 at 3792.

28 *Danish Fur Breeders v. Commission*, Case T-61/89, 2 July 1992, ECR.

29 *Nungesser v. Commission, op.cit.*

30 I.e., those that impose territorial obligations on the licensee in addition to the obligation to limit exploitation of the patent to a particular geographic area ('a regional licence for part of the territory for which the patent is granted, or a licence limited to one place of exploitation or to a specific factory').

31 *Kabelmetal-Luchaire*, Commission Decision, dated 18 July 1975 OJ L222/34, 22 August 1975.

32 Regulation 1983/83, OJ (1983) L173/1, amended OJ (1983), L281/24.

33 Commission Notice on Regulations 1985/83 and 1984/83, OJ (1984), L101,2, amended OJ (1992), L121/2.

34 1996 IP Licensing Block Exemption Regulation, Art. 1 (1).

35 Preamble to the regulation.

36 Green Paper, § 22.

37 6 May 1996, ABA Conference, Brussels.

38 Green Paper, § 20.

39 Green Paper, § 21.

40 Art. 1 (3) reg. 1983/83, (1983) OJ 173/1, amended (1983) OJ, L281/24.

41 Art. 1 (5) reg. 2349/84, (1984) OJ L219/5, amended (1985) OJ L113/34 and reg. 151/93.

42 Patent Licensing Regulation, Art. 1 (b).

43 *AOIP-Beyrard*, Commission Decision of 2 December 1975, OJ (1976), L6/8.

44 *Vaasen-Morris*, Commission Decision of 10 January 1979 OJ (1979), L19/32.

45 See, e.g., *Technique Minière*, 56/65, 30 June 1966, ECL (1966), 235.

46 *Delimitis v. Henninger Bräu*, C-234/89, 28 February 1991, ECL (1991), 935.

47 Judgment of 27 September 1988.

48 Judgment of 12 May 1989.

49 Judgment of 19 April 1993.
50 The Court's judgments in *Coditel II* and *Pronuptia* also support this view.
51 Commission Decision, 13 July 1990, OJ, L209/15. See also Konsortium ECR 900. Commission Decision, 27 July 1990, OJ L225/31, where another JV was granted negative clearance.
52 *GEC-Siemens/Plessey*, OJ C239/2, 25 October 1990.
53 Commission Decision, 23 March 1990.
54 *Windsurfing v. Commission*, 193/83, 25 February 1986, ECL (1986), 611.
55 Regulation 240/96, OJ, L31/2, 9, 2, 96.
56 Subject to the inclusion of absolute territorial protection and RPM, in line with the Commission's approach in this area.

16

COMPETITION POLICY REGARDING VERTICAL TRADE RESTRAINTS

A Japanese view

Hideaki Kobayashi

Introduction

I shall first describe what is the current policy of the Fair Trade Commission of Japan (JFTC) on this question, and then explain how the JFTC implement such policy. I shall then express my views on the implication of such policy to international trade as well as on the need for international cooperation in this field.[1]

Competition rules regarding vertical trade restraints

The first topic is the current Japanese competition rules on VTRs. Here I wish to cover the following three topics. First, resale price maintenance (RPM); second, vertical non-price restraints; third, vertical mergers.

Resale price maintenance

In the JFTC's Ordinance on Unfair Trade Practice issued in accordance with section 2, item 9 of the Anti-Monopoly Act (AMA), RPM is listed as one of the acts that constitute unfair trade practice and thus is illegal.[2]

The JFTC published in 1991 a policy statement entitled *The Anti-Monopoly Act Guidelines concerning Distribution Systems and Business Practices* (the 'Distribution Guidelines'), which states as follows:

> In cases where, as a part of marketing activities, or as requested by distributors, a manufacturer restricts the sales price of distributors, it is in principle illegal as an unfair trade practice, because it reduces or eliminates price competition among distributors.[3]

There are mainly two exceptions to this rule. One is the exception regarding 'copyrighted works' (as prescribed in section 24–2 (4) of the AMA). Such works include books, magazines, newspapers, records, music tapes, and CDs.[4]

However, the JFTC has made it clear, as a part of the Japanese government's deregulation programme, that such an exception shall be thoroughly reviewed in order to clarify and reduce the scope of application of such exception.

The second category of exception concerns the items designated by the JFTC for that purpose based on section 24–2 (l) to (3) of the AMA. Presently, the designated items are fourteen kinds of cosmetics and fourteen kinds of medicines. However, it was announced in March 1996 in the government's declaration on the revised deregulation programme that all the exceptions on cosmetics and medicines were to be abolished by the end of March 1997.

Vertical non-price restraints

There are several types of vertical non-price restraints, such as (i) restrictions on distributors' handling of competing products, (ii) restrictions on the distributor's sales territory, (iii) restrictions on distributors' customers, and (iv) restrictions on retailers' sales methods.

The JFTC's Distribution Guidelines of 1991 clarify its position on each type of restriction.

Restrictions on distributors' handling of competing products

The Guidelines state that:

> In cases where a restriction on handling of competing products (such as exclusive dealing arrangements) is imposed by an influential manufacturer in a market, and if the restriction may result in making it difficult for new entrants or competitors to easily secure alternative distribution channels, such restriction is illegal as an unfair trade practice.[5]

The Guidelines also state that:

> whether a manufacturer is influential in a market or not is in the first instance judged by the market share of the manufacturer, that is, whether its market share is more than 10 per cent or its position is within the top three in the market.[6]

The Guidelines further note that 'whether or not a restriction may result in making it difficult for new entrants or competitors to easily secure alternative distribution channels'[7] is to be determined taking fully into account the following four factors:

1   market structure (market concentration, characteristics of the products, degree of product differentiation, distribution channels, difficulty in new market entry, etc.);[8]
2   the position in the market of the manufacturer (in terms of market share, rank, influence of brand name, etc.);
3   the number of distributors affected by the restriction, and their positions in the market; and
4   the impact of the restriction on business activities of the distributors.

Restrictions on distributors' sales territory

The Guidelines make it clear that the following types of restrictions are not illegal: (i) restrictions that assign a specific territory to each distributor as the area of primary responsibility, and (ii) those that restrict the area where a distributor may establish business premises.

Regarding a restriction that assigns a specific area to each distributor and prohibits the distributor from selling outside each area or selling to customers outside each area, the Guidelines state that, if it is imposed by an influential manufacturer,[9] and also if the price level of the product covered by the restriction is likely to be maintained,[10] such restriction is illegal as an unfair trade practice (Article 13 of the General Designation).

Restrictions on distributors' customers

According to the Guidelines, when a manufacturer imposes on wholesalers such restrictions as (i) requiring each wholesaler to supply only to certain retailers, or (ii) prohibiting wholesalers from buying or selling products among themselves, they are illegal as unfair trade practices (Article 13 of the General Designation) only if the price level of the product is likely to be maintained.

However, when a manufacturer prohibits wholesalers to sell to price-cutting retailers, it is in principle illegal as an unfair trade practice (Article 2 or 13 of General Designation), since the price level of the product is likely to be maintained.

Restrictions on retailers' sales methods

Such restrictions could take the form of manufacturers requiring various sales methods such as demonstration-sales, home delivery services, an exclusive shelf-space or display area, or certain measures for the maintenance of the quality of the product.

The Guidelines state that in cases where such restrictions are used as a means to restrict such elements as sales price, the handling of competing products, sales territories or customers, their legality is to be judged on the basis of the criteria I have just mentioned for each element.[11]

Vertical mergers

The JFTC's *Administrative Procedure Standards for Examining Mergers*, issued in July 1980, revised in August 1994, state that in examining vertical mergers, the JFTC would take into account not only market share after the merger and the situation of competition in the relevant markets, but also the following factors.

The extent of foreclosure of the relevant market

The degree of effect of the vertical merger on the business activities of competitors of the merging companies, including whether or not the merger would deprive the competitors of their important suppliers or customers, or of opportunities of doing business with them.

The degree of the heightening of entry barriers

Circumstances that would or would not result in significant increase in the minimum capital requirement for entry into the relevant market, on account of the merger or vertical integration triggered by the merger.

JFTC's law enforcement in the field of vertical trade restraints

The JFTC has been taking measures actively against anti-competitive vertical trade restraints. A recent example is its cease and desist order in June 1996 against the largest cosmetic company in Japan, which had been found to have maintained the prices of its commodities by preventing discount sales by supermarket chains (through offering to the supermarket chains samples to be attached to the cosmetics, or providing assistance for sales promotion campaigns). Because of the JFTC's action, prices of cosmetics of not only that company but also of most other makes started to fall appreciably.

As I have mentioned, VTRs could have both pro-competitive and anti-competitive effects, depending upon the nature of the restrictions as well as the condition of the market. We also have to bear in mind the possibility that the activity in question of a certain firm may be but an example of the widespread practice of firms in that market. Accordingly, in considering the application of competition laws to VTRs, one would have to grasp not only the concrete details of the restrictive actions in question but also the general condition of the market, such as the prevalent business practices of firms in the market, as well as the structure of the market.

It is from such a standpoint that the JFTC has been carrying out a series of comprehensive 'economic condition surveys', which consist of market-specific surveys as well as of cross-market surveys. Market specific surveys have been carried out in such sectors as plate glass, cars, car parts, paper, agricultural chemicals, synthetic rubber, rolled aluminium, construction machinery, and construction materials. Currently, surveys are going on in the photographic film and paper markets. As cross-market surveys, the JFTC has carried out a survey on six major industry groups in 1993–4, and another on independent industry groups in 1995.

The JFTC has made public the findings of all such surveys, together with its proposals to the firms concerned from the viewpoint of improving the competitive condition in the market and of preventing anti-competitive activities. The JFTC has also made follow-up surveys in some cases to find out how well such proposals have been accepted and put into practice.

Implication to international trade

In applying competition rules to the VTRs, the JFTC is fully cognisant of its implication to international trade. What is relevant here, for example, is the possibility of foreclosure of market by the long-standing trade relationships between firms, which is often referred to as *keiretsu* relationships in Japan. The 1991 Distribution Guidelines were compiled taking into account, among others, the concerns regarding such possibility of foreclosure expressed by our foreign trading partners. The Guidelines specifically refer to the possibility of various types of VTRs obstructing either foreign imports or new market entry by firms. In formulating the Guidelines, the JFTC solicited the opinions of foreign authorities concerned and took their views into account as much as possible.

Also in selecting the specific fields for the economic surveys I have just mentioned, the JFTC had taken into account the foreign claims that certain business practices in particular Japanese markets are hindering market access for foreign firms.

Implication to possible future international cooperation in the field of competition and trade policies

Since VTRs could work as obstacles to market access, it seems desirable that they be included as a subject in possible future global discussions on the relationships between competition and trade policies.

Although it is true that VTRs could be pro-competitive under certain circumstances and anti-competitive under others, most of the competition authorities of the world would agree that resale price maintenance normally obstructs competition and accordingly needs to be prohibited, possibly with very limited exceptions. Most of us would also agree that those types of non-price VTRs that are likely either to obstruct new market entry or to maintain price levels need to be prohibited or at least discouraged. Reaching a consensus on such matters among the world's competition authorities even in more or less abstract terms would be desirable from the viewpoint of not only enabling those authorities to implement competition policy with stronger confidence and vigour but also removing obstacles to free international trade. I know it is a difficult task, but why don't we try?

As I have mentioned, in applying competition laws to VTRs, one needs to have sufficient information on the business practice in question itself as well as on the market where it was carried out. One would also have to analyse such information properly from the competition point of view.

It would be most appropriate if each competition authority picks up a few markets where VTRs are considered to be causing competition problems, and carries out thorough surveys on the state of affairs of the business practices in question as well as on the structure of the market concerned. When competition authorities of several countries pick up the same products and carry out such surveys on their own markets, it would enable international comparison on the market structure and business practices regarding those particular products. It would also be useful to compare policies and regulations of each country regarding specific types of VTRs.

We have already seen the benefits of such international comparisons in some of the OECD–CLP round table discussions, such as those on cars and car-parts distribution.

I wish to conclude by stressing that coordination and cooperation regarding measures *vis-à-vis* VTRs among the competition authorities of the world would not only facilitate effective implementation of the competition policy but also help to remove obstacles against free trade.

NOTES

1 What I am going to say is basically my own view and does not always reflect the official position of the JFTC.

2 RPM was first declared illegal by the Supreme Court in its decision on 'the first powdered milk case' in 1975.

3 JFTC, *The Anti-Monopoly Act Guidelines concerning Distribution Systems and Business Practices*.

4 The justifications for such exceptions are (i) that such works have been traditionally traded on a 'quasi-consignment basis' under which returning goods to the seller has been allowed, and (ii) that since it is important, from the cultural point of view, for the shops to have as wide a variety of works as possible, it is desirable to lessen the shops' risk for carrying such a wide variety of works, by ensuring a certain profit margin.

5 *The Anti-Monopoly Act Guidelines concerning Distribution Systems and Business Practices*, General Designation, Article 11 or 13.

6 *Ibid.* Nevertheless, even if a firm falls in this category, the restriction by the manufacturer is not always illegal. Rather, they indicate a 'safe harbour' in which firms are free from competition law problems.

7 *Ibid.*
8 As an element of market structure, other manufacturers' behaviour is also to be considered. For example, in cases where other manufacturers also restrict the handling of competing products, it is more likely to result in making it difficult for new entrants to easily secure alternative distribution channels.
9 The criteria for determining whether a manufacturer is 'influential in a market' are similar to those in the case of restrictions on distributors' handling of competing products.
10 According to the Guidelines, whether or not 'the price level of the product covered by the restriction is likely to be maintained' is to be determined, taking comprehensively into account the following factors:

- actual conditions of interbrand competition (market concentration, characteristics of the product, degree of product differentiation, distribution channels, difficulty in new market entry, etc.);
- actual conditions of intrabrand competition for the products (degree of dispersion in prices, business types of distributors dealing in the products, etc.);
- the number of distributors affected by the restriction, and their positions in the market; and
- impact of the restriction on business activities of the distributors (extent, manner, etc. of the restriction).

11 When such restrictions are considered to have rational reasons for the purpose of ensuring proper sales of the products, such as assuring the safety of the product, preservation of its quality, the maintenance of the credibility of the trade mark, and also when they are applied to all the retailers on equal terms, such restrictions in themselves do not present any problem under the AMA.

17

VERTICAL RESTRAINTS OF TRADE AND NATIONAL COMPETITION LAWS IN AN INTEGRATED WORLD ECONOMY

Dieter Wolf

Treatment of vertical restraints of competition under German law

Contractual restraints of competition

Unlike Article 85 (1) of the EC Treaty, the German Act Against Restraints of Competition (ARC) makes a clear *a priori* distinction between vertical and horizontal restraints of competition. While the latter are prohibited in principle under German law, vertical restraints are largely assessed on the basis of the abuse principle.

Resale price maintenance

German law is at its most restrictive where resale price maintenance (RPM) is concerned. Section 15 of the ARC bans RPM in principle, although section 16 of the ARC exempts publications. In competition theory, RPM is not considered an altogether negative phenomenon. The Chicago School, for example, has justified RPM by arguing that it may increase distribution efficiency at the retail level. Speaking against RPM, on the other hand, is the experience that it tends to restrict price competition at the retail level by eliminating intrabrand competition.

However, those theoretical considerations were not crucial to the German legislator's decision, embodied in the 1973 ARC amendment, to prohibit RPM. Rather, that decision was primarily motivated by the realization that in practice, RPM systems faced pressure from two sources: on the one hand, large-scale forms of distribution increasingly had developed alongside the traditional medium-sized retail trade since the early seventies. Owing to a more favourable cost structure, those large-scale distributors considered that RPM curtailed their freedom to compete, and therefore often failed to comply. On the other hand, parallel imports from other EU member states, which benefited from the price differential within the EU, resulted in a situation where the requirement of a watertight RPM system was no longer met. The competition authorities took this as a starting point for subjecting RPM to abuse control.

While RPM is prohibited except as otherwise provided in section 16 of the ARC, firms are allowed under section 38a of the ARC to issue non-binding price recommendations for the resale of their branded goods. However, such recommendations are subject to abuse control by the competition authorities.

Treatment of distributional restraints and exclusive dealing under German law

The treatment of distributional restraints and exclusive dealing under German law is clearly more liberal than that of RPM. Generally, manufacturers may choose whatever distribution system they like for their goods or services. Distributional restraints and exclusive dealing arrangements are therefore allowed in principle under German law. Such vertical restraints are subject to abuse control, though. This system has proved successful, particularly in view of the growing economic importance of franchising.

Market-dominating and powerful enterprises, too, are free in principle to structure their distribution systems as they see fit. However, the structure and operation of their distribution systems is subject to the ban on discrimination.

Distributional restraints are often practised by manufacturers of branded goods to ensure that their products are sold exclusively by specialized retailers, to the exclusion of cheap dealers. The economic rationale provided for this type of restraint is that this is the only way of ensuring that customers get adequate advice from the specialized retailer while at the same time excluding free-riding by unqualified dealers. Thus selective distribution arrangements serve to protect product quality and brand image.

On the other hand there are also competitive arguments against selective distribution agreements. While the competitive importance of interbrand competition has been emphasized as an argument for selective distribution, the actual or potential role of intrabrand competition has been underrated. What is more, where selective distribution systems are operated, unilateral emphasis is placed on the manufacturer's interests, whereas the interests of third parties are disregarded, i.e. the interests of dealers that are excluded from the distribution of the particular products. This explains why abuse control is indispensable, even though selective distribution agreements may be beneficial.

In German law, the competitive effects of exclusive dealing are not considered to be negative in principle either. Restraints of this type may have positive effects on competition if they increase sales of a product and enable a dealer to thoroughly develop a market. To support exclusive dealing it may also be argued that in many cases the services rendered by retailers – sales promotion, after-sales service, stock-keeping – enable newcomers and small- and medium-sized firms to enter the market in the first place.

In spite of those positive competitive effects of exclusive dealing agreements, the negative sides must not be overlooked: competitors of the binding firms are deprived of the opportunity to enter into business relations with the binding firms' partners. Where exclusive dealing arrangements are practised on too large a scale, they may result in creating serious barriers to market entry. Thus exclusive dealing, too, is ambivalent as regards its competitive effects and is subject to abuse control under German law.

General abuse supervision of distributional restraints and exclusive dealing is laid down in section 18 of the ARC. On the basis of that section the competition authorities may challenge such restraints of competition, in particular, if:

- the restrictions cover a significant number of firms in a particular market and restrict their competitive freedom;
- the existing restraints unfairly restrict market entry by newcomers; or
- the extent of such restrictions in a market substantially impairs competition in the market or other markets.

Treatment of selective distribution systems operated by market-dominating or powerful firms

Section 26 (2) of the ARC provides for stricter standards to be applied to market-dominating or powerful firms. Those firms, too, may operate selective distribution systems, but only if the qualitative criteria for selecting their distributors are factually justified and non-discriminatory.

Selective distributional restraints are operated mainly by branded goods manufacturers who are in a powerful, but not dominant market position. 'Powerful' in this context means that firms at the retail level consider themselves dependent on the purchase of a particular branded product. For if they did not carry those items, their reputation would be compromised in the eyes of their customers. However, since the fifth ARC amendment in 1989, the protection against discrimination by merely powerful enterprises has been confined to small- and medium-sized buyers only. Thus manufacturers of well-known branded goods no longer have to supply large firms in the distributive trade, if doing so would run counter to their distributional concept.

Vertical mergers

It is generally held that vertical mergers may well have positive effects, as long as they increase efficiency in the purchase and/or sale of products. On the other hand, they raise competition problems if they result in competitors being driven or excluded from the market, or if they create or increase entry barriers. Under German law, vertical mergers have to be judged by the same criteria as horizontal mergers. The essential test therefore is whether a market-dominating position is created or strengthened as a result of the merger. Unlike horizontal mergers, vertical mergers do not result in an increase of market share. Whether a particular vertical merger is likely to create or strengthen a market-dominating position can thus be shown only by means of the other, less concrete structural criteria mentioned in section 22 (1) no. 2 of the ARC. These criteria include financial strength, access to the supply or sales markets as well as legal or actual barriers to market entry by other firms. As a rule, those qualitative criteria do not suffice to prove that a market-dominating position has been *created*; at best they may serve to prove that an already existing market-dominating position has been *strengthened*.

Market access

In applying the ARC provisions on non-price vertical restraints of competition – sections 18 and 26 (2) of the ARC – ensuring free market access is a major consideration. A firm's interest in free market access may possibly conflict with the manufacturer's interest in deciding for himself on the channels of distribution for his products.

Section 18 of the ARC assumes that as a rule, non-price vertical restraints do not lead to serious negative effects on competition and that – by reinforcing interbrand competition – they may in fact have a positive effect on competition. The possibility of agreeing exclusive dealership arrangements may possibly even make market entry easier for newcomers. On the other hand, German law is indeed aware of the danger that a comprehensive system of distributional restraints and exclusive dealership arrangements in a particular market virtually blocks third parties from gaining access to existing distribution channels. Therefore, the powers of the competition authorities under section 18 of the ARC are mainly aimed at preventing foreclosure of market access.

Free market access is also an important consideration in the context of applying the discrimination ban of section 26 (2) of the ARC to market-dominating and powerful firms. Under that section the manufacturer's interests and the interests in free market access of the firm seeking delivery have to be weighed up. In weighing up the parties' interests, the competition authority has to bear in mind that the central aim of this section of the ARC is to protect the freedom of competition.

Treatment of vertical restraints of competition at the European and International levels

The decision to treat vertical restraints differently from horizontal restraints of competition under German law has proved successful. Basically, the legal practice at the European level is in line with this assessment. The primary Community legislation does not make a distinction between horizontal and vertical restraints and prohibits both in principle (Article 85 (1) of the EC Treaty). However, the enforcement practice of the Commission and the secondary Community legislation has led to a more differentiated treatment. Many types of vertical restraints are now exempt from the ban laid down in Article 85 (1) of the EC Treaty, mainly as a result of the instrument of block exemption directives. To that extent, in practice growing convergence of German and European competition law is noticeable. The key points of a draft for the sixth amendment of the ARC indicate that it is not envisaged to abandon the tried and tested rules for the treatment of vertical restraints of competition under German law.

As far as an 'international antitrust code' is concerned, in my view, differentiated treatment of vertical restraints of competition according to their competitive effects would be appropriate as well. Resale price maintenance should be generally forbidden. As regards non-price vertical restraints, abuse control seems to be necessary, but also sufficient. If, however, market power is involved, as is the case with selective distribution systems operated by market-dominating companies, the effects on competition are naturally stronger and thus more likely to require action by the competition authority. The goal must be to safeguard free market access and protect competition originating from newcomers.

Especially in view of the trend towards globalization of competition it must be ensured that companies do not use vertical restraints of competition in order to redivide a world-wide or at least international market into national markets and block the free market access of third parties. The development of the European internal market has shown that such concerns are quite realistic. Particularly in the early stages after 1958 there were efforts by manufacturers to segment the evolving Common Market by selective and exclusive distributional restraints and to cordon-off the individual geographic sub-markets by re-import bans. It is therefore necessary to counteract such developments also in the international arena.

VI

BUSINESS PERSPECTIVES

18

INTERNATIONAL
COMPETITION LAW IN THE
1990s

A Canadian perspective

Calvin S. Goldman and Milos Barutciski

Introduction

Active enforcement of competition laws was, until fairly recently, limited to some of the member states of the Organization for Economic Cooperation and Development (OECD). This situation has changed dramatically over the last ten years. The rapid pace of globalization and trade liberalization in recent years has led to an increasing recognition by governments throughout the world that the efficient operation of markets requires an effective competition law to ensure that the benefits of privatization, deregulation and other market-opening initiatives are not undermined by anti-competitive conduct.

International business and legal advisers must now contend with the widespread proliferation of competition laws throughout the world, including Asia and the Pacific Rim,[1] Latin America and the Caribbean,[2] and the economies in transition of Eastern Europe and the former Soviet Union.[3]

In addition to the broader acceptance of competition law principles, globalization and trade liberalization have led to a growing recognition that effective enforcement of competition law in international markets requires greater cooperation between enforcement officials in different jurisdictions.

In the multilateral context, this trend is reflected by the adoption, in July 1995, of a revised OECD Recommendation concerning cooperation between member countries on anti-competitive practices affecting international trade. The 1995 Recommendation goes considerably beyond the previous 1986 OECD Recommendation[4] by incorporating extensive new provisions intended to promote greater coordination of investigations and mutual assistance among OECD member states.

In this regard, Canada has recently taken a number of steps to increase its ability to cooperate with foreign competition authorities. These will be considered in the first part of this paper, with a particular focus on enforcement cooperation in transborder criminal matters between Canada and the US.

The proliferation of competition laws has also meant that international mergers and acquisitions are now potentially subject to competition review in multiple jurisdictions. In the second part of this paper, we discuss the principal features of Canada's merger review process under the Competition Act, focusing on its impact on international transactions.

In addition, the growing recognition that effective competition laws are essential for the efficient operation of international markets has led to a renewed interest in the interface between competition policy and trade policy. In particular, it has been suggested that competition policy should be added to the World Trade Organization's agenda in the near future, with a view, perhaps, to the adoption of international norms and disciplines under the auspices of the WTO.[5] We review some of these recent developments concerning the trade and competition interface in the third part of this paper.

Finally, a further important development is the renewal of a more vigorous approach by the US antitrust authorities to the extra-territorial assertion of jurisdiction with respect to conduct abroad that injures either US consumers or US exporters.[6] In 1995, the US antitrust authorities issued new Antitrust Enforcement Guidelines for International Operations which, among other things, announced a two-pronged approach to anti-competitive conduct abroad whereby the US authorities would first seek cooperative enforcement in conjunction with foreign authorities, failing which US law may be applied unilaterally. In this regard, the former Deputy Assistant Attorney General in charge of International Antitrust made the following remarks in 1995:

> [T]he Guidelines note that if the conduct is unlawful under the importing country's antitrust laws as well, the Agencies are prepared to work with that country's authorities, if they are better situated to remedy the conduct, *and if they are prepared to take action pursuant to their own laws that will address the US concerns.*[7] (Emphasis added.)

International enforcement cooperation: the Canada/United States model

The increasing integration of the North American economy as a result of the North American Free Trade Agreement (NAFTA) which entered into force in January 1994, and the Canada–US Free Trade Agreement before it, gives rise to both economic benefits and an increased risk of anti-competitive conduct that spans borders. As a result, the governments of Canada and the US have taken several steps to enhance the level of cooperation and information-sharing between them. This increased cooperation has resulted in several joint investigations[8] as well as instances where the competition authorities of one country have assisted their counterparts in the other country to obtain criminal convictions under their respective competition laws.[9]

This increased cooperation has been made possible by a number of recent developments, including:

- the signing on 3 August 1995 of an Agreement between Canada and the US regarding the application of their competition and deceptive marketing practices laws (the '1995 Agreement');
- the extension in 1991 of the Extradition Treaty between Canada and the US to offences punishable by the laws of both countries by imprisonment for a term exceeding one year (which includes competition law offences);[10] and
- the entry into force on 14 January 1990 of the Treaty between the Government of Canada and the Government of the US on Mutual Legal Assistance in Criminal Matters (MLAT).[11]

Recent speeches by the heads of the Canadian Competition Bureau[12] and the US Antitrust Division have emphasized the joint accomplishments of the Canadian and US authorities. For example, the US Assistant Attorney General for Antitrust, Anne Bingaman, recently made the following remarks:

Our cooperative relationship with Canada offers [an] example of true joint prosecution to the mutual benefit of both the US and Canada, in the area of criminal antitrust enforcement. Our MLAT with Canada, which became effective in 1990, permits us to share evidence in criminal matters, and the recent thermal fax paper, plastic dinnerware, and ductal pipe cases show how cross-border cooperation has led to successful prosecution of international antitrust crimes.[13]

Enforcement cooperation is also occurring on a trans-Atlantic basis. As many of you are aware, the US and EU concluded an Agreement regarding the application of their competition laws on 23 September 1991. Although the European Court of Justice held in 1994 that the manner in which the Agreement was adopted did not comply with certain provisions of the Treaty of Rome, the status of the Agreement was regularized by its confirmation by the EU's Council of Ministers in 1995. The joint investigation of Microsoft by the US and EU antitrust authorities in 1994[14] is an important example of the closer ties between the European and North American authorities in the area. It also appears that the ongoing negotiations between Canada and the EU toward concluding a similar agreement have recently gained some momentum after several delays.

In addition, each of Canada and the US, in its own right, has announced recent initiatives which may lead to additional cooperation between them in the future.

In November 1994, President Clinton signed into law the International Antitrust Enforcement Assistance Act (IAEAA), which, among other things, allows the Antitrust Division of the US Department of Justice and the Federal Trade Commission (FTC) to enter into Antitrust Mutual Assistance Agreements (AMAAs) with foreign governments. The IAEAA expressly permits the US agencies to assist foreign competition authorities in investigations under foreign competition laws, including the use of compulsory investigative powers to obtain evidence from firms and individuals located in the US, as well as the communication to foreign competition authorities of certain confidential information obtained by the US antitrust agencies in the course of investigations under US antitrust laws.

Although the US has not yet entered into any AMAAs with foreign governments, the recent competition law amendments initiative announced by the Canadian Minister of Industry includes a proposal for greater information-sharing and mutual assistance between Canadian and foreign competition authorities.[15]

Although the Canadian proposal is not identical to the US IAEAA, it is to be expected that, in the event that the Canadian proposals are adopted into law, Canada and the US will rapidly take steps to conclude an antitrust mutual assistance agreement pursuant to their respective laws.

Overview of Canadian competition law and enforcement

The Competition Act (the 'Act') is the principal competition law in Canada. It is enforced by the Director of Investigation and Research (the 'Director') who is the head of the Competition Bureau (the 'Bureau').[16] The Bureau, like the US Antitrust Division and the FTC, employs staff with legal, economics and business training.

The Act applies to all business activity in all sectors of the Canadian economy, with certain limited exceptions. It contains a number of criminal offences, notably price-fixing and bid-rigging, which are among the Bureau's main enforcement priorities. The Act also contains certain non-criminal matters, referred to as 'reviewable matters', which may be the subject of a remedial order by the Competition Tribunal, a quasi-judicial tribunal composed of Federal Court judges and lay members.

With respect to criminal matters, the Bureau conducts investigations and, if it finds evidence of criminal conduct, the Director may refer the matter to the Attorney General of Canada for prosecution. The decision to lay criminal charges is ultimately made by the Attorney General. Similarly, the Director may recommend to the Attorney General that individuals or firms be granted immunity as a result of their cooperation in the detection and investigation of criminal offences. Ultimately, however, the decision to grant immunity is made by the Attorney General.[17]

The Act provides for fines of up to C$10 million and prison terms of up to five years for price-fixing and other conspiracies to unduly lessen competition, and unlimited fines and prison terms of up to five years for bid-rigging. In contrast to the US, Canada has a long history of a voluntary, compliance-oriented and less litigious enforcement approach to its competition laws. As such, there have been relatively fewer public and private proceedings, and, with very few notable exceptions, no one has gone to jail for a competition offence.[18]

It should be noted, however, that the Canadian enforcement environment is changing. The Bureau has recently indicated that there will be more recommendations for jail sentences in the future.[19]

Similarly, the Director and the Attorney General have sought increasing penalties to deter anti-competitive behaviour. Recent fines in conspiracy and bid-rigging cases have been the highest ever and the trend is upward.

Considerations arising from increased enforcement cooperation

As noted above, cooperation and coordination among the Canadian and US competition authorities have been increasing in recent years. The principal forms of cooperation between Canada and the US in criminal matters include information exchange and the use of compulsory investigative powers pursuant to the MLAT. Indeed, the extensive use of the MLAT by Canadian and US authorities in recent years may be viewed as a laboratory for the future development of international cooperation in the antitrust field. Some of the challenging issues that will arise in this area have already come up in the context of cooperation using the MLAT, as discussed below.

More generally, information-sharing between Canadian and US authorities can occur pursuant to the MLAT, the 1995 Agreement or through informal exchanges.[20]

The MLAT requires Canada and the US to provide assistance to each other in 'all matters relating to the investigation, prosecution and suppression of offences'. The MLAT applies in Canada to all indictable criminal offences, including conspiracy and bid-rigging under the Act. A request for assistance must be accompanied by any information that the other party requires to execute the request. The Director has indicated that, as of August 1995, there had been eleven MLAT requests in competition law matters – five by Canada and six by the US.[21]

The MLAT and the 1995 Agreement are subject to Canadian legislation prohibiting the disclosure of information except under certain conditions. In the competition law context, the most important statutory restriction on disclosure is section 29 of the Act.

Section 29 prohibits the Bureau from disclosing information gathered using compulsory process (e.g. through a search warrant or a section 11 order) or in a pre-merger notification filing, other than to a Canadian law enforcement agency or 'for the purposes of the administration or enforcement of the Act'. Although section 29 does not generally protect information that is voluntarily provided to the Bureau, the Director has publicly stated that non-section 29 information will be treated in the same manner as section 29 information.[22]

It is the Director's position that the phrase 'administration or enforcement of [the] Act' in section 29 permits disclosure to a foreign agency 'where the proposed communication is for the purpose of receiving the assistance or cooperation of that agency regarding a Canadian investigation'.[23]

The Director's position on the interpretation of section 29 has led to a vigorous debate in Canadian legal and business circles. In particular, the National Competition Law section of the Canadian Bar Association has stated that it disagrees with the Director's interpretation, and that currently the Director is not entitled to share information protected by section 29 with foreign agencies in any circumstances.[24]

The MLAT and the 1995 Agreement impose obligations on each party to maintain the confidentiality of information communicated under those agreements. Nevertheless, concerns arise because there may be situations where a party is unwilling or unable to preclude disclosure to third parties. It should be noted that the confidentiality provisions in the 1995 Agreement might also be waived.[25]

With respect to the treatment of confidential information under the Act, it should be noted that the National Competition Law Section of the Canadian Bar Association issued a commentary on the Director's amendments proposals of June 1995.[26] The CBA commentary included proposals for prior notice to information providers before confidential information is communicated to foreign authorities, an opportunity for judicial review of the proposed communication, the implementation of safeguards for the protection of confidential information communicated to a foreign authority and restrictions on the use of the information and downstream disclosure by the foreign authority. The Consultative Panel appointed by the Director subsequently adopted many of the CBA's recommendations in its report.[27] In particular, the Consultative Panel adopted many of the safeguards proposed in the CBA commentary. However, with respect to the issue of notice to information providers before confidential information is communicated to a foreign authority, the Consultative Panel could not reach a consensus. This remains an open issue at the present time.

Compelled testimony and immunity

As noted above, the Director may use certain compulsory powers to obtain evidence in the course of investigations under the Act. For example, section 15 allows the Director to obtain a search warrant from a court to enter into premises and seize evidence. Section 11 allows a court to order the examination of persons under oath, as well as the production of documents and other things. Although a person may not refuse to answer a question pursuant to an order under section 11, the Act provides a form of 'use immunity' by stipulating that no testimony given by a person in that regard will be used or received against him in any criminal proceedings, other than in the prosecution for perjury or for giving contradictory evidence.

As noted above, the Director takes the position that he is entitled to provide compelled testimony to the US antitrust authorities under the MLAT, the 1995 Agreement or on his own initiative where to do so would advance a Canadian investigation under the Act. Such disclosure could occur without notice to the person who gave the testimony. This is an open issue subject to legal debate in Canada, as noted above.

Likewise, compelled testimony can be gathered in the US using the grand jury process. Such information might be supplied to Canada either under the MLAT or pursuant to the 1995 Agreement. It appears that disclosure of grand jury information under either mechanism can occur without prior notice to the person whose testimony was so provided.

In addition to the possibility that compelled evidence pursuant to section 11 or 15 of the Act might be provided to the US antitrust authorities, the Canadian legislation implementing the MLAT or the Mutual Legal Assistance in Criminal Matters Act (MLAA), also provides a mechanism for Canadian authorities to use compulsory process to obtain evidence on behalf of the US antitrust authorities in criminal matters. However, the MLAA specifically provides that a judge may impose terms and conditions on the transmission of such evidence to a foreign authority after hearing representations from various parties.[28]

The MLAA also contemplates that, before compelled testimony can be transmitted to a foreign agency, the Minister of Justice must be satisfied that the foreign agency will comply with any terms and conditions imposed by the judge.

International Chamber of Commerce position on international cooperation

The International Chamber of Commerce (ICC) recently released a Statement on international cooperation between antitrust authorities.[29] Although the statement noted that there was some difference of opinion between ICC members in Europe and North America as to the appropriateness of greater cooperation and information exchange in the absence of further convergence of substantive competition laws, it also noted that, notwithstanding these differences, there was unanimous and grave concern among ICC members that information should be properly protected:

> The dangers of disclosing confidential information or trade secrets to foreign agencies derive from the fact that if such information falls into the hands of competitors of the company involved, the competitive position of the company may be adversely affected. . . . Furthermore, any erosion of the confidence that companies currently have that confidential information will not be disclosed to competitors is bound to limit the nature and extent of the data that companies are willing to supply voluntarily and to impair the open dialogue between such companies and antitrust agencies.[30]

Among other things, the ICC strongly recommended that legislative provisions for the exchange of confidential information should contain procedural safeguards, including:

- prior notification to information providers of any proposed exchange for information, unless doing so would be prejudicial to the investigation, whereupon notice would be given when it is no longer prejudicial, with a right of retroactive review;
- independent review of adverse decisions;
- substantial convergence and similarity in the laws protecting solicitor–client privilege between the jurisdictions exchanging information;
- the foreign (receiving) jurisdiction should provide competition law enforcement immunity of a similar or greater nature than that which would be available or which has been provided in the jurisdiction disclosing the information;
- the receiving party must agree to reciprocate; and
- exchanges of information should speed up investigations rather than lead to further delays.

The views set out in the ICC Statement are shared by many members of the Canadian business and legal communities and have led to extensive discussion of the appropriate standards for international enforcement cooperation in the context of the recent Canadian amendments initiative.[31]

International mergers and the Competition Act

Globalization and the proliferation of competition laws have also led to an increase in the number of mergers that are subject to merger review under the laws of two or more jurisdictions. When contemplating such a transaction, merging parties must take great care to coordinate their strategies for dealing with multi-jurisdictional review. It is important to consult competition counsel at an early stage to establish general guidelines and obtain preliminary advice with respect to a broad range of issues ranging from procedural matters, such as document creation and confidentiality agreements, to possible divestitures and other remedies that may be required by certain jurisdictions. These issues will often have a significant impact on the parties' negotiations and must therefore be addressed from the outset.

In addition, it is important to ensure that competition counsel in different jurisdictions cooperate closely in their efforts to steer a proposed transaction through their respective merger review processes. In this regard, it may, in some instances, be beneficial to consider the possibility of entering into a joint privilege agreement between the merging parties so as to facilitate close cooperation between counsel.

In the following remarks, we will provide a brief overview of the Canadian merger review process, while noting some of the key differences from US merger law. We will then review certain strategic issues to be considered in dealing with the Bureau. Finally, we will discuss some of the issues that arise in the context of multi-jurisdictional merger review.

The Canadian merger review process

There are two sets of merger provisions in the Act that must be assessed by parties contemplating a merger:

1 the substantive provisions in Part VIII; and
2 the pre-merger notification provisions in Part IX.

These provisions apply independently of each other. Thus, even if a transaction raises no substantive competition issues under Part VIII, the merging parties must nevertheless comply with the filing and waiting period requirements of the notification provisions in Part IX, if the applicable financial thresholds are met and no exemption applies. Conversely, an acquisition that does not meet the notification thresholds may still be subject to review under Part VIII of the Act.

A merger may be subject to a remedial order under Part VIII where the Competition Tribunal (the 'Tribunal') finds that the merger prevents or lessens, or is likely to prevent or lessen, competition substantially. However, no order may be made if the merging parties are able to satisfy the requirements of the efficiency exception in section 96 of the Act, by establishing that:

1 the merger has brought about or is likely to bring about gains in efficiency that will be greater than, and will offset, the likely anti-competitive effects of the merger; and

2   the efficiency gains would not likely be attained if the order in question
     were made.

The Tribunal's remedial powers include dissolution of the merger and
divestiture of assets, in the case of a completed merger, and a prohibition
order, in the case of a proposed merger.

   Only the Director may bring an application in respect of a merger before
the Tribunal. Unlike in the US, private parties have no ability to challenge
a merger before the Tribunal.

   The analytical framework adopted by the Director in his review of mergers
is similar to that which is adopted in the US, i.e., there is a market power
focus, a hypothetical monopolist approach to market definition and a broadly
similar approach to the analysis of barriers to entry and other qualitative
assessment criteria. The Director's approach to these and other issues is discussed in considerable detail in the 1991 Merger Enforcement Guidelines
(the 'MEGs').[32] However, two key differences in the Canadian and US
approaches are: (i) the above-noted exception for efficiencies set forth in
section 96 of the Act;[33] and (ii) the reduced weight given to high market
shares/concentration.[34]

Pre-merger notification

The pre-merger notification requirements of the Act do not apply unless two
thresholds, relating to the 'combined size of the parties and their affiliates'
and the 'size of the transaction', respectively, are exceeded.

   First, pre-notification will not be required unless the parties to the transaction, together with their affiliates, have gross revenues from sales in, from
or into Canada that exceed C$400 million; or have assets in Canada the
aggregate value of which exceeds this threshold.

   With respect to the 'size of the transaction', pre-notification will not be
required unless one of the following thresholds is met:

1   in the case of an asset acquisition, the value of the Canadian assets
     acquired or the annual gross revenues from sales in or from Canada
     generated by those assets exceeds C$35 million;
2   in the case of an acquisition of shares of a corporation, the value of the
     Canadian assets or the annual gross revenues from sales in or from
     Canada of the corporation and its subsidiaries exceeds C$35 million;
3   in the case of an acquisition of shares of a public company, the acquisi-
     tion results in the acquiror holding voting shares which carry more than
     20 per cent of the outstanding votes (or more than 50 per cent if the
     acquirer already holds 20 per cent or more) attached to all the voting
     shares of the corporation; and
4   in the case of an acquisition of shares of a private company, the

acquisition must result in the acquirer holding voting shares which carry more than 35 per cent of the outstanding votes (or more than 50 per cent if the acquirer already holds 35 per cent or more) attached to all the voting shares of the corporation.

Generally, the most recent audited financial statements are used as the measure of the value of assets and sales, although detailed regulations under the Act should be consulted in the context of each particular transaction. Other specific thresholds apply to amalgamations and other combinations.

Filing requirements

A 'proposed transaction' must be notified to the Director by the person or persons proposing the transaction. Unlike the US Hart-Scott-Rodino Act, there is no requirement that all parties to a transaction notify separately. The general practice in Canada is that counsel for the acquirer prepares the formal filing, although in many cases counsel for the acquiree separately submits all or some of the information required in respect of the acquiree.

A notifier has the option of submitting a 'short-form' or 'long-form' filing. However, where a short-form filing is made, the Director may at any time within the required short-form waiting period (discussed below) elect to require a long-form filing. Although this power has rarely been exercised, the possibility that it may be exercised strongly mitigates in favour of making a long-form filing where a transaction is on a 'short fuse' (i.e., less than thirty days).

Where a short-form filing has been made and the Director has not elected to require a long-form filing, a proposed transaction cannot be completed until the expiration of seven days after the required information has been received by the Director.

Where a long-form filing has been made, a proposed transaction cannot be completed until the expiration of twenty-one days after the required information has been received by the Director.

Where the proposed transaction is an acquisition of voting shares that is to be effected through the facilities of a stock exchange in Canada, the proposed transaction cannot be completed until after the expiration of ten trading days, or such longer period of time, not exceeding twenty-one days, as may be allowed by the rules of the stock exchange before the shares must be taken up.

As a practical matter, when the Director has not completed his review of the merger by the end of the statutory waiting period and he has significant preliminary concerns regarding the potential effect of the transaction on competition, he either informs the merging parties that if they close they will do so at their own risk, or he requests parties to (i) postpone their transaction pending his review or (ii) provide an acceptable undertaking to hold the two businesses in question separate and apart pending the conclusion of his review. In the absence of such cooperation, he may file an application for an interim injunction pursuant to section 100 of the Act.

Failure to pre-notify 'without good or sufficient cause, the proof of which lies on the person', constitutes a criminal offence subject to a fine of up to $C5,000, imprisonment for up to two years, or both. Any officer, director or agent of a corporation who directed, authorized, assented to, acquiesced in or participated in the offence is deemed to be a party to the offence and subject to the same penalties.

Advance Ruling Certificates (ARC)

The Act also provides for the issuance of an ARC by the Director where he is satisfied that he would not have sufficient grounds on which to apply to the Tribunal for a remedial order with respect to a proposed transaction. The issuance of an ARC:

1   provides an exemption from the pre-notification provisions of Part IX of the Act; and
2   prevents the Director from applying to the Tribunal in respect of the transaction solely on the basis of information that is substantially the same as the information on the basis of which the certificate was issued, if the transaction is substantially completed within one year after the certificate is issued.

A request for an ARC should be accompanied by sufficient information to enable the Director to ascertain that the transaction will not prevent or lessen competition substantially in any of the affected markets.

Initial approach to the Bureau

Broadly speaking, the Canadian approach to merger enforcement under the Act, like the approach of the EU Merger Task Force, is more consultative, cooperative and less litigious than the typical US practice.

This can have significant practical implications. For example, it is common practice in Canada to discuss a proposed notifiable merger with the Bureau on a confidential basis in advance of filing, and perhaps in advance of when US authorities might otherwise be approached.

Where a merger exceeds the pre-merger notification thresholds in Part IX of the Act, such a consultation can be very helpful to confirm whether the Bureau is likely to require a long- form filing or would be satisfied with a short-form filing. Furthermore, such informal consultations with the Bureau can assist in determining what information can be omitted from the formal filing, for example, on the basis that it is not relevant, and whether there is a good chance of an ARC being granted if sought.

288

The Director has also come to expect informal notification of mergers which do not exceed the formal pre-merger notification thresholds, where such mergers would result in market shares or concentration levels in excess of the levels set forth in the MEGs.[35] A former Director has suggested that if firms do not provide such notice, they can expect to be subjected to a more formalized process in the Bureau's review of the transaction in question.[36]

Early contact with the Bureau can provide an important indication of the input that the US or EU authorities are likely to receive from the Bureau in any discussions between the agencies. This can be a particularly significant consideration where the key issues are likely to be similar in the merger reviews of Canadian, US and EU antitrust authorities.

As one of the authors indicated in his Statement to the US FTC's hearings on the Changing Nature of Competition in a Global and Information-Driven Age,[37] confidential guidance from a competition authority with respect to a proposed transaction, such as that provided by the Director through his Programme of Compliance, including confidential Advisory Opinions, is an extremely useful vehicle to promote compliance with competition laws. Similarly, the ongoing dialogue that an effective compliance-oriented approach engenders reduces costs to both merging parties and enforcement authorities by allowing the authorities to obtain key information more quickly, thus putting them in a position to be able to reach an informed decision without unnecessary delay, as might be occasioned by extensive and open-ended information requests.

In addition, early contact can provide a good sense of what is likely to be required to get the merger through the Bureau as well as the amount of time likely to be required to complete the Bureau's review. This can be a helpful barometer of the approach likely to be taken by US and EU authorities.

In short, early consultation usually puts counsel in a more knowledgeable position than they would have been in had they not sought that guidance, and avoids the substantial time and effort that could be required to deal with one or more information requests or other difficulties that could very well arise if a cooperative approach is not adopted with the Bureau. Unlike the DOJ's business review programme, there is no public announcement of advisory opinions issued by the Director.

Coordination of international submissions

Given the similarity between the Canadian and US substantive approach to merger review, as well as the increasing level of enforcement cooperation, close attention needs to be paid to coordinating the content of submissions.

Inconsistent submissions in different jurisdictions, if they come to the knowledge of the respective authorities, can create mistrust and perhaps delay approvals. However, given the nuances in the approaches that are taken to various issues, there is nothing wrong with placing differing levels of emphasis on various matters in briefs to the US, Canadian and EU antitrust authorities. For example, the Bureau's more liberal approach to exiting firms that are not yet failing, as well as to efficiencies, would suggest that these issues be given much greater emphasis in Canadian filings than in filings elsewhere.

Similarly, the Bureau may be prepared to place greater weight than its US and EU counterparts on the degree of innovation and change in the market in deciding not to challenge a merger. This is a consideration that was highlighted in the Bureau's recent press releases relating to the Rogers–Maclean Hunter and Telus–Ed Tel mergers. In addition, the recent decision in respect of the SmithBooks–Coles merger suggests that the Bureau may be more willing than other authorities to permit a finding of low barriers to trump what it believes to be an otherwise problematic merger.

Similarly, there is nothing wrong with taking different positions on issues such as market definition or ease of entry where there are objectively sound reasons for doing so. For example, from time to time it can be objectively established that the geographic market is North America, when viewed from a Canadian perspective, because lower-cost US suppliers would clearly continue to be able to constrain the merged entity's ability to increase prices; whereas from a US perspective, the geographic market may be limited to the US because higher-cost Canadian suppliers would not be able to constrain pricing behaviour in the US.

Where foreign counsel have not had an opportunity to finalize their views on critical issues such as market definition, it may be that the best strategy to adopt in Canada is to take a very low key approach, and, in any initial consultations with the Bureau, simply outline the transaction and its underlying rationale and ask the Bureau what information it will require while the parties continue to prepare the pre-merger notification filing (if applicable) or written submissions.

This will leave flexibility for counsel in the various jurisdictions to continue refining their positions while ensuring that any submissions to the Canadian authorities will not be inconsistent with the positions that are ultimately developed by such foreign counsel.

Confidentiality in the merger review process

Confidentiality is a particularly sensitive issue in the merger review context. This is especially the case with respect to exchanges of information with foreign competition authorities. Although the 1995 Canada–US Agreement is expressly subject to the parties' confidentiality laws, it is important to ensure that the two countries' authorities refrain from open-ended exchanges of information until the confidentiality issue is resolved by appropriate legislative safeguards.

Competition policy and world trading system

The rapid pace of globalization and trade liberalization has brought renewed international attention to the interaction between competition and trade policies. In this regard, it is important to note that the 1948 Havana Charter for an International Trade Organization contained a Chapter V on 'Restrictive Business Practices'. The Havana Charter provided for an international complaints and investigation procedure under the authority of the International Trade Organization with respect to an open-ended list of restrictive business practices, including price-fixing, customer and territorial market allocations, price discrimination and abuse of intellectual property rights. The Havana Charter did not come into force due, primarily, to the unwillingness of the US Congress to ratify it. As a result, competition policy has not figured prominently in the multilateral trading system established in 1947 under the provisional General Agreement on Tariffs and Trade (GATT).

The important role of competition policy in fostering an open trading system was subsequently recognized by the European communities with the adoption of Articles 85 and 86 of the Treaty of Rome. To date, the EU's competition law remains the only substantive supranational competition law in the world. It is perhaps not surprising that the success of the EU's competition law in promoting market integration has prompted a renewed interest in the adoption of competition policy provisions in other international trade arrangements.

For example, Chapter 15 of the NAFTA requires the parties to 'adopt or maintain measures to proscribe anti-competitive business conduct and take appropriate action with respect thereto, recognizing that such measures will enhance the fulfilment of the objectives of [the] Agreement'.[38] Chapter 15 also encourages the Parties to cooperate in the enforcement of their respective competition laws.

With a view to expanding the role of competition policy in the North American free trade area, Chapter 15 establishes a Working Group on Trade and Competition pursuant to Article 1504 with a mandate to make recommendations on relevant issues concerning the relationship between competition laws and policies and trade in the free trade area by the end of 1998. In this regard, the 1994 Report of the American Bar Association's Section of Antitrust Law Task Force on the Competition Dimension of NAFTA provided one of the first substantive treatments of this issue in a trilateral context.

Similarly, the relationship between competition and trade policies has been targeted for further work by the members of the Asia–Pacific Economic Cooperation Forum with a view to concluding a broad trade liberalization agreement to be implemented within the next fifteen years. Likewise, the Cartagena Declaration issued on 21 March 1996 by trade ministers representing thirty-four nations participating in the Free Trade Area of the

Americas initiative established a working group on competition policy to make specific recommendations on how to proceed in the construction of the FTAA in this area.

Although the WTO Agreements that were concluded at the end of the Uruguay Round in 1994 do not include general provisions in relation to competition policy, such provisions are included in several of the WTO Agreements dealing with specific subject matters (e.g., the Agreement on Trade-Related Intellectual Property Rights, the Agreement on Technical Barriers to Trade, the Agreement on Pre-shipment Inspection, the General Agreement on Trade and Services and the Agreement on Government Procurement). Furthermore, certain WTO Agreements[39] contain provisions calling for further examination of the competition policy aspects of those agreements.

In this regard, it is noteworthy that there have been increasing calls to add competition policy to the WTO agenda at the Singapore Ministerial Conference in December 1996.[40]

It should be noted, however, that the addition of competition policy to the WTO agenda is not uncontroversial. There are many among the international business and legal communities who believe that multilateral negotiation on competition policy within the WTO framework are premature. For example, the 24 April 1996 statement of the International Chamber of Commerce prepared for the WTO Singapore Ministerial Conference states:

> The ICC welcomes the analytical work begun in several fora to increase the understanding of the linkages between trade and competition policy. But that work – to which business is contributing its views – has a long way to go before it can be determined how the issues involved might be tackled in a multilateral negotiation. Meanwhile, we suggest that the WTO Ministerial Meeting in Singapore should take the opportunity to examine how and to what extent this complex subject should be included in the WTO's future work program.[41]

With a view to preparing an international business position on the relationship between competition and international trade policies, the International Chamber of Commerce established a Joint Working Party on Competition and International Trade in 1995. The Joint Working Party, which includes representatives of the business and legal communities from Europe, the Americas and Japan, under the chairmanship of one of the authors of this paper, will issue its report in 1997. Some of the issues that the Joint Working Party may examine include:

- potential conflicts between competition and trade policies;
- prospects for harmonization and convergence of competition and trade policies;

- trade laws that restrain competition, notably anti-dumping laws;
- the role of competition law in promoting market access; and
- the potential role of international dispute resolution in relation to competition policy.

Other initiatives studying the relationship between competition and trade policies include the OECD's ongoing work under the auspices of the Competition Law and Policy Committee and the Trade Committee, the Institute for International Economics in Washington DC and the American Bar Association's Joint Task Force on Antitrust and the Global Economy.

Although it remains to be seen whether the interface between competition and trade policies is ripe for multilateral negotiations within the WTO context, the gradual convergence of national competition laws and the trend toward greater international enforcement cooperation demand increased attention from the international business and legal communities to ensure that competition laws continue to allow international markets to operate in a fair and efficient manner and on the basis of the fundamental principle of national treatment. Much work remains to be done in the context of these interesting and important issues.

NOTES

1 For example, India, Pakistan, Korea, Sri Lanka, Taiwan and Thailand.
2 For example, Argentina, Brazil, Chile, Colombia, El Salvador, Jamaica, Mexico, Peru and Venezuela.
3 For example, Bulgaria, the Czech Republic, Hungary, Kazakhstan, Latvia, Lithuania, Poland, Romania, Russia, the Slovak Republic, Ukraine and Uzbekistan.
4 Revised Recommendation of the Council concerning cooperation between member countries on restrictive business practices affecting international trade, adopted by the OECD Council on 21 May 1986.
5 See R. Ruggiero, Director General, World Trade Organization, 'Antitrust: Rules, institutions and international relations', Rome, 20–1 November 1995; see also R. Ruggiero, 'The road ahead: International trade policy in the era of the WTO', Ottawa, Canada, 28 May 1996.
6 In 1993, the US Supreme Court reasserted an expansive approach to the 'effects doctrine' with respect to conduct abroad that has a substantial effect on US consumers, in *Hartford Fire Insurance Co. v. California*, 113 S. Ct. 2891. Also, in 1992, the US Antitrust Division reversed its earlier policy with respect to conduct abroad that injures US exports by announcing that it would henceforth enforce the US antitrust laws with respect to such conduct. This policy was reaffirmed in the 1995 Antitrust Enforcement Guidelines for International Operations.
7 D. P. Wood, 'The 1995 antitrust enforcement guidelines for international operations: An introduction', Address to the American Bar Association Antitrust Section Spring Meeting, 5 April 1995, pp. 14–15. Reprinted with permission.

8 For example, a joint investigation by the Canadian Competition Bureau and the US Antitrust Division which commenced in 1992 led to convictions under both Canadian and US law in relation to the North American thermal fax paper market (see G. N. Addy, 'Address to the Canadian Bar Association', Competition Law Section, 30 September 1994). Another joint investigation by the Canadian Competition Bureau and the US Antitrust Division led to a conviction under the Competition Act with respect to an agreement to lessen competition in Canada unduly in the supply and sale of iron pipe on 27 September 1995 (Competition Bureau, News Release, 'Canada Pipe Company Ltd. pleads guilty and pays record $2.5 million fine for conspiracy offence under the Competition Act').

9 For example, in 1994, the US Antitrust Division obtained convictions with respect to a price-fixing conspiracy in the plastic dinnerware industry. The investigation included a US request for assistance pursuant to which Canadian authorities searched the premises of a company in Canada to obtain evidence in support of the US investigation. (A. K. Bingaman, 'Cooperative antitrust enforcement', Address to the American Bar Association, Antitrust Section, 7 April 1995.)

10 Treaty of Extradition, 22 March 1976, US–Canada, 1976 Can. T. S., No. 3 (as amended by an exchange of Notes on 28 June and 29 July 1974 and a Protocol dated 11 January 1988).

11 1990 Can. T. S., No. 19, signed 18 March 1985.

12 See note 6; see also G. N. Addy, Address to the Canadian Bar Association 1995 Annual Competition Law Conference, 29 September 1995.

13 A. K. Bingaman, 'International cooperation and the future of US antitrust enforcement', Address to the American Law Institute, 72nd Annual Meeting, 16 May 1996.

14 The Microsoft investigation is also important in the context of international information-sharing. Although the US–EU Agreement does not allow the sharing of confidential information, Microsoft agreed to waive confidentiality protections in order to arrive at a single coordinated remedy in both the EU and the US.

15 *Industry Canada*, News Release, 'Industry Minister Manley announces consultations on Competition Act amendments', 28 June 1995. Concurrently with Minister Manley's announcement, the Director issued a Discussion Paper setting out an outline of proposed amendments ('Competition Act Amendments', June 1995). The Canadian Bar Association subsequently issued a commentary on the proposed amendments ('Response to Proposed Changes to the Competition Act', November 1995). On 6 March 1996, the Consultative Panel appointed by the Director to consider the amendment proposals issued its report (*Report of the Consultative Panel on Amendments to the Competition Act*).

16 For a more extensive review of Canada's competition laws, see C. S. Goldman and J. D. Bodrug (eds), *Competition Law of Canada*, Juris Publishing Inc.

17 For a discussion of the Director's Immunity Policy, see H. I. Wetston, Director of Investigation and Research, 'Notes for an address to the Canadian Corporate Council Association', Calgary, 19 August 1991; and H. S. Chandler, Deputy Director of Investigation and Research, 'Getting down to business: The strategic direction of criminal competition law enforcement in Canada', Address to the Insight and Globe and Mail Conference on Emerging Issues in Competition Law,

10 March 1994. See also C. S. Goldman and P. S. Crampton, 'The Director's immunity program: Some policy and practical considerations', Insight Conference on Competition Law – Compliance in an Aggressive Marketplace, 11 May 1993.

18 Although there have been a number of individuals convicted on indictments over the years, jail sentences have been imposed in only two cases: one for bid-rigging and one for misleading advertising.

19 See H. S. Chandler, *op. cit.*; and G. N. Addy, Director of Investigation and Research, Address to the Canadian Bar Association National Competition Law Conference, 30 September 1994.

20 The Director recently noted that his office takes advantage of the 'ample' opportunities for increased cooperation by way of informal contacts to discuss common issues at a general level. See G. N. Addy, Address to the American Bar Association, Section of Antitrust Law, Chicago, 6 August 1995, p. 2.

21 *Ibid.*, p. 12.

22 See Director of Investigation and Research, 'Communication of confidential information under the *Competition Act*', Information Statement, May 1995, p. 3.

23 *Ibid.*

24 National Competition Law section of the Canadian Bar Association, 'Commentary on the draft information bulletin of the Director of Investigation and Research respecting confidentiality of information under the Competition Act', December 1994, p. 29 *et seq.*

25 For a detailed discussion of the mechanisms for enforcement cooperation between Canada and the US, see C. S. Goldman and J. T. Kissack, 'Current issues in cross-border criminal investigations: A Canadian perspective', Fordham Corporate Law Institute, 26–7 October 1995; see also J. F. Rill and C. S. Goldman, 'A US and Canadian perspective on Canadian international antitrust enforcement', *International Business Lawyer*, 1995, vol. 23.

26 *Response to Proposed Changes to the Competition Act*, November 1995.

27 *Report of the Consultative Panel on Amendments to the Competition Act*, March 1996.

28 Subsection 20(2) of the MLAA contemplates that representations may be made by, among others, the person who produced a record or a thing pursuant to an order under the MLAA. Thus, if a person providing compelled testimony under the MLAA was also compelled to produce records or things, he would have an opportunity to make representations.

29 Commission on Law and Practices Relating to Competition, International Chamber of Commerce, 'Statement on international cooperation between antitrust authorities', 28 March 1996.

30 *Ibid.*

31 See note 15.

32 For a detailed discussion of the MEGs, see P. S. Crampton, 'Canada's new merger enforcement guidelines: A "nuts and bolts" review', *Antitrust Bulletin*, 1991, vol. 36, p. 883.

33 For a detailed discussion of the Canadian approach to efficiencies, see P. S. Crampton, 'The efficiency exception for mergers: An assessment of early signals from the Competition Tribunal', *Canada Business Law Journal*, 1993, vol. 21, s. 371. See also C. S. Goldman, 'The merger review process: The Canadian experience', Remarks before the Federal Trade Commission hearings on the

changing nature of competition in a global and information-driven age, Washington DC, 13 December 1995.

34 For a comparative review of the Canadian and US merger guidelines, see P. S. Crampton, 'The DOJ/FTC 1992 horizontal merger guidelines: A Canadian perspective', *Antitrust Bulletin*, 1993, vol. 38, p. 665.

35 In this regard, the MEGs provide, at §4.2.1:

> [T]he Director generally will not challenge a merger on the basis that the merging parties will be able to unilaterally exercise greater market power than in the absence of the merger, where the post-merger market share of the merged entity would be less than 35 per cent. Similarly, the Director generally will not challenge a merger on the basis that the interdependent exercise of market power by two or more firms in the relevant market will be greater than in the absence of the merger, where:
>
> (i) the post-merger share of the market accounted for by the four largest firms in the market would be less than 65 per cent, or (ii) the post-merger market share of the merged entity would be less than 10 per cent.

36. 'Competition cop threatens crackdown on firms withholding merger information', *The Globe & Mail*, 25 May 1990, quoting H. I. Weston, the Director from October 1989 to June 1993.

37 C. S. Goldman, *op. cit*, note 33.

38 NAFTA, Chap. 15, Art. 1501 (1).

39 E.g., Agreement on Trade-Related Investment Measures, Art. 9; Agreement on Trade-Related Intellectual Property Rights, Art. 8 (2).

40 For example, see R. Ruggiero, note 5; see also the Trans-Atlantic Business Dialogue draft Progress Report of 18 April 1996 on Competition Policy.

41 WTO Singapore Ministerial Conference, Statement of the International Chamber of Commerce, 24 April 1996.

19

INTERNATIONAL
COMPETITION POLICIES:
A BUSINESS PERSPECTIVE

Furthering effective procedures within Europe[1]

P. M. A. L. Plompen

An efficient application of European competition rules is essential for the competitiveness of business. The Commission has recognized this and is working on improvement of its rules and procedures both in the area of merger control and in the area of agreements having effect on competition. Business organizations like the Union of Industrial and Employers' Confederations of Europe (UNICE) and ICC have made substantial proposals on this to the Commission.

In the field of merger control one of the most urgent changes to be made is the introduction of exclusive Commission jurisdiction in case of multi-member state jurisdiction over mergers below the European turnover thresholds. Also the way Article 85 of the Treaty is applied calls for urgent change. Hereafter I will concentrate on that.

I cannot describe the problem regarding the application of Article 85 (3) better than the editor of the *Common Market Law Review*, who wrote recently:

> Enforcement of EC competition law has been characterized by a paradox ever since Regulation 17 was adopted in 1962: though the Commission lacked the administrative resources to deliver more than twenty decisions a year, an expansive reading of Article 85 (1) EC, concerning the notions of restriction of competition and the effect on trade between the Member States, taken together with the exclusive exemption power of the Commission according to Article 9 (1), Regulation 17/62, has 'created an absurd discrepancy between the Commission's theoretical jurisdiction and its capacity to generate the decisions called for by its overbroad interpretation of Article 85 (1)'.[2] Parties who apply for an exemption under Article 85 (3) EC still have

to wait for years to be granted such an exemption if they are not satisfied with a 'comfort letter', the precise legal status of which is a topic of some discussion. In the perspective of an integral application of Article 85 (1) and (3) EC the length of these proceedings is plainly unacceptable. For a Community based on the rule of law, the length is nothing less than an outright scandal. As far as the relevant contracts fulfil the criteria of Article 85 (3) EC, the undertakings have a right to be granted an exemption. Such a right is nothing other than the general right to trade; it is hard to see how the Community can justify an intrusion into this right by its everlasting lack of resources. It is from this perspective that the pros and cons of a decentralized enforcement of EC competition law, and especially the competence to grant exemptions, have to be discussed.[3]

In its recent discussion paper 'Modernizing EU competition policy, refocusing the scope and administration of Article 85',[4] UNICE complained that EC competition law and regulations impose significant compliance costs on business. The complexity of the rules requires extensive expert advice from specialized in-house and/or outside legal counsel. A substantial portion of the compliance costs, however, has little to do with safeguarding effective competition. Costs are often incurred to ensure compliance with formalistic rules and cumbersome administrative procedures that do not provide legal certainty.

Competition law is a priority area for administrative simplification – the removal of unnecessary burdens and the limiting of regulation to matters of genuine economic importance. It is an area where actual implementation of the recommendation of the European Commission for 'modernizing the role of public administration' with a view to enhancing the competitiveness of European businesses should be given high priority. The EU must arrange a legal environment that allows businesses to take the necessary decisions with a minimum of uncertainty and delay.

The UNICE paper points out that the ability of national competition authorities to apply their national rules despite the presence of a comfort letter of the European Commission, and the increasing trend towards enforcement of competition laws through private party litigation, highlights the importance of providing more legal certainty more effectively.

UNICE believes that the time has come to question which basic changes in the rules and procedures and in the interpretation of Article 85 should be introduced in order to achieve competition regulation which is appropriate to the requirements of a modern economy.

UNICE proposes that a first part of the Commission's initiative should be to adopt a more realistic approach to the issue of whether the effect of an agreement on competition is 'appreciable', as defined by the Court of First Instance.[5] The Commission should issue further guidelines in this connection.

Also the Notice on Agreements of Minor Importance should be changed, in that the turnover test and market-share test should be alternative rather than cumulative. The present market-share threshold of 5 per cent should be considerably increased (compare the 15 per cent threshold in Form A/B for the provision of data regarding competitors in the relevant market). Furthermore, UNICE proposes that Commission intervention in vertical agreements should be limited to situations where the businesses involved abuse their dominant position on the relevant market, or hinder the access of new market entrants. UNICE also proposes a broadening of the scope of block exemptions, in a less clause-oriented approach, and to include in all block exemption regulations a severance rule providing that a block exemption is not automatically lost if a clause which is not listed in the block exemption regulation concerned should be found to infringe Article 85 (1). UNICE also advocates simplification of the procedural rules concerning clearance of individual notified agreements: the accelerated procedure adopted for the clearance of cooperative structural joint ventures should be applied more broadly.

The above proposals seem to be possible without any formal changes having to be made to Regulation 17.

UNICE, however, also proposes to broaden the scope of Article 4 (2) of Regulation 17 (e.g. to include the agreements mentioned in the 1968 Notice on Cooperation and in the 1979 Subcontracting Notice); the agreements concerned should be presumed to be exemptible under Article 85 (3) EC. The effect of such provision would be that a national judge or national authority which has to decide on the applicability of Article 85 (1) EC or national competition law to such an agreement has to take into account the probability that the agreement concerned, if notified, would be granted an exemption with retroactive effect as from the date of the contract.

UNICE is of the opinion that decentralization of the power to exempt under Article 85 (3) to the competition authorities of the member states could lead to unacceptably divergent policies in different member states, and could seriously hurt the broader and more efficient application of the one-stop-shop principle within the Community which UNICE advocates. Personally I hope that also in this area some improvement might be achievable, as I will explain below.

The Commission has stated that it intends to direct its scarce resources to cases and questions with a Community interest. Less important cases will either be handled by way of comfort letters, or be left to the initiative of private parties before the national courts. The Court of First Instance has endorsed this position.[6] Dr Ehlermann even advocates that it would be perfectly legitimate for the Commission to establish for requests for exemptions under Article 85 (3) an order of priority which takes into account the degree of probability of a favourable (or unfavourable) decision.[7] Requests for exemption which have no or only a very small chance of succeeding, in his opinion can be attributed a lower priority than those which raise no or probably very few problems. I fail to see how the probability of an exemption in itself can be decisive with a view to the Community interest. I would suggest that an assessment of the exemptibility of 'difficult' cases often should be given high priority by the Commission.

In this respect it might be instructive to quote the 24th Competition Report of the Commission:

> It sometimes happens that a firm whose agreement is threatened with prohibition by a national authority tries to protect itself by notifying the agreement to the Commission and asking it to exempt the agreement under Article 85 (3). If the Commission then had to formally initiate proceedings as provided for in Article 9 (3) of Regulation 17, the national authority would lose its power to prohibit the agreement under Article 85 (1). It was decided in such cases to follow a procedure similar to that proposed for national courts confronted with the same situation.
>
> At the request of the national authority, the Commission departments, having received for exemption purposes a notification which in all probability seems likely to block action by the national authority, will give a provisional opinion of the likelihood of an exemption. If it appears prima facie that the agreement is not eligible for exemption, the Commission will indicate that, in view of the circumstances, it does not intend to initiate proceedings in respect of the agreement.
>
> This approach would be used in the case of agreements that have no community relevance in particular those whose impact was mainly within one and the same member state.[8]

What I miss here painfully is an additional statement that the competition authorities of the member states agree that if the Commission indicates that the agreement concerned prima facie is indeed eligible for exemption, the national authorities will not initiate proceedings under their national laws. Such statement being absent, notifying parties still have to be concerned about (the length of the) proceedings necessary to obtain legal certainty: as long as the Commission has not formally initiated proceedings their agreement might still be vulnerable to attack under national legislation or national implementation of Article 85 (1).

Another problem of this Commission working procedure is that for an unknown period of time the way their case is going to be dealt with by which authority will not be known to the parties involved. Of course, they might receive general and informal indications about the prima facie opinion of the national authority and/or the European Commission officials involved, but their case may be pending, and therefore also the legal certainty with respect to the validity of the agreement may be lacking, for a rather long period of time. I sincerely hope that I don't have to live through another experience like *Philips–Osram Lampglass components JV*.[9]

Informal prenotification discussions with both authorities took place since August 1991 (Brussels) and February 1992 (Berlin). Both the Commission and the Bundeskartellamt were notified of that JV in March 1992. Various extensive requests for information had to be answered. In October 1993 DG IV wrote a preliminary Article 85 (3) comfort letter. In November 1993 the Bundeskartellamt informed the parties that it would reopen its own investigation as the Commission apparently would not take a formal exemption decision, and requested further information. In January 1994 the Commission gave formal notice of its favourable intention in the *Official Journal*. The notification then had to be converted to encompass the whole of the EEA. The Commission in May 1994 decided that in view of the position of the Bundeskartellamt it really had to issue a formal decision, which it managed to adopt in December 1994. Concluding, it took Brussels and Berlin some two years to sort out a problem of jurisdiction concerning a case where they had known they had a substantive difference of opinion already after only a few months. This was not an extremely important business transaction, but to the parties who have to decide on investments and prepare their various stakeholders for important changes, such procedural delays are always damaging.

The inadequacy of jurisdictional procedures, especially with respect to joint ventures, sometimes obliges legal advisers to explain to their management that they had better not structure their activities the way they would prefer, but if possible construct a 'concentration' type of transaction in order to obtain speedy legal certainty under the Merger Control Regulation. The same, *mutatis mutandis*, applies also to the contract 'moulds' provided by block exemption regulations.

This situation clearly is unacceptable. Even if changing Regulation 17 were not possible, further improvement as to the application of Article 85 (3) in a way efficiently providing a real European level playing field must take place. This would remain necessary even if the current Merger Control Regulation review should lead to making joint ventures of a structural character subject to the Merger Control Regulation procedure, and even if future block exemption regulations are broader and include a severance provision as described above.

Possible improvement of the existing jurisdictional situation should also be explored, e.g. along the following lines:

> The Commission and the member state competition authorities enter into a working arrangement regarding all notified agreements the competitive effects whereof have their centre of gravity within one member state. The Commission within a period of two weeks

after notification of an agreement will decide whether or not it will deal with the notification itself, or request the national authority of the member state where the centre of gravity of the competitive effects of the agreement is located to provide the Commission with its prima facie opinion as to the compatibility of the agreement with Article 85. The Commission will give prior notification of such request to the parties. Of course such request only can be made to a national authority that pursuant to national legislation is empowered to adequately investigate whether the transaction prima facie should be prohibited under Article 85 (1) or prima facie would be exemptible under Article 85 (3). The national authority will send its prima facie opinion to the Commission within two months. The Commission on the basis of that opinion then within two weeks decides whether it will initiate proceedings itself (prohibition, 'informal' or 'formal' comfort letter, Article 85 (3) decision) or not (leaving the matter to be decided by the national authorities under its national law or under Article 85 (1)). If the national authority does find prima facie exemptibility, and the Commission agrees, or if the national authority's prima facie opinion is not favourable, but the Commission's opinion is, the Commission will initiate proceedings and write a comfort letter (formal or informal) to the parties involved, and the national authority (and the other member state authority) will refrain from further action. (Also national courts will refrain from action that might run counter to possible future exemption by the Commission).

A member state authority can within two weeks after receiving copy of a notification filed with the Commission also take the initiative and propose the Commission to request for its prima facie opinion as to the application of the European competition rules. If a national authority is confronted with an agreement which in its prima facie opinion is outside the scope of a block exemption regulation it will allow the parties to file a notification to the European Commission. After that again the above working arrangement will apply.

Under the working arrangement between the Commission and the national authorities described above, the Commission would retain its legal monopoly to apply Article 85 (3). Of course in all these situations the parties involved could also opt for not notifying to the European Commission, but instead ask for an exemption under national law, if possible. Such national exemption, however, would only have effect on the national territory of the member state concerned. Normally that would mean that in cases having transnational effect the parties will opt for notification to the Commission. The above approach leaves discretion with the Commission with regard to reference to national authorities and would, at the same time allow the Commission to take the degree of national experience into account.

I would like to make two further suggestions to minimize the costs of implementation of European competition rules for business. Where application of competition rules is increasingly dependent on economic analysis of the effects of certain arrangements on dynamic and expanding relevant markets, it is unacceptable to force enterprises to incur often high legal costs for advice which can more appropriately and more readily be given by experienced and qualified in-house counsel. I cannot stress enough the importance of in-house legal counsel for creating improved awareness of and compliance with competition rules within the enterprises involved. This advice should be 'privileged' if the in-house legal counsel is a member of a professional organization guaranteeing the objectivity and independency of its members' professional advice. This is all the more necessary in view of any exchange of information that might be agreed upon by Brussels and competition authorities of countries which provide for such legal privilege.

Another improvement of the working practice of the Commission would be to acknowledge on an informal basis a central contact point within groups of enterprises. In case questions arise, requests for information have to be sent, etc. The Commission should not only inform the legal entities involved, but should also send a copy to that group contact person. This would enhance the efficiency of the communications between the Commission and the relevant group of enterprises enormously. If necessary, such a working arrangement could be based on a letter from the top company of such a group, also on behalf of the companies belonging to the group, partly waiving potential confidentiality restrictions applicable to the Commission concerning such group companies.

NOTES

1 A part of the following remarks has earlier been presented to the Workshop on Implementation of Antitrust Rules in a Federal Context, organized by the European University Institute in Florence in April 1996.
2 Forrester and Norall, 'Competition Law', 1991, *Yearbook of European Law*, pp. 407–9.
3 'Editional comments', *Common Market Law Review*, vol. 32, 1995, p. 2.
4 UNICE Discussion Paper of September 1995.
5 Case T-7/93 (*Langnese*).
6 Case T-24/90 (*Automec II*).
7 Implementation of EC competition law by national antitrust authorities, Treviso, 1995, p. 12.
8 24th Competition Report, 1994, point 41.
9 *Philips–Osram Lampglass components JV*, Case IV/34.252, *Official Journal* of 31 December 1994, No. L378, 37.

20

MERGER CONTROL IN THE EU AND THE TREATMENT OF STRATEGIC ALLIANCES

Michael J. Reynolds

MERGER CONTROL IN THE EC

The EC Merger Control Regulation (4064/89) (MCR) entered into force on 21 September 1990 and provides procedures for Commission notifications and investigations which are applicable specifically to concentrations. The main advantage of transactions falling within the MCR is that it provides a 'one-stop shop': the European Commission is the only European antitrust authority with competence to examine the transaction; the national authorities have no jurisdiction. The Commission is obliged to make its appraisal of the merger within fixed time limits and must issue a formal reasoned decision either approving or prohibiting the transaction, which provides legal certainty for the parties involved.

The disadvantage of the MCR, however, is that all transactions which fall within the scope of the MCR must be notified in a specified and very detailed format, before they come into effect. Companies need to be aware of when notification under the MCR is necessary, because failure to notify or supply the correct information to the Commission can lead to the imposition of heavy fines, periodic payments and even an expensive unravelling of the merged entities. Regulatory requirements and the consequences of failure to comply with those requirements are the subject of this paper.

Review of the MCR

Following the publication of a Green Paper on the subject in January 1996, the Council of Ministers have discussed proposals for the first major review of the MCR since its adoption in 1989, focusing on amendments proposed by the Commission in July and September 1996. In November 1996 the progress of the first of those amendments, that concerning a reduction of the 'Community dimension' turnover thresholds in the Regulation, suffered a serious setback as the Council voted against it by qualified majority. The proposal proved to be highly controversial, not least because of the considerable increase in the scope of the Commission's powers that it entailed, and almost half the member states expressed their opposition to it. It would have lowered the world-wide turnover thresholds from Ecu 5 billion to Ecu 3 billion, and the Community turnover thresholds of at least two of the enterprises from Ecu 250 million to Ecu 150 million. The proposal is now off the agenda for the foreseeable future.

The Council's decision on the second major issue, that of establishing a mechanism which would resolve the problem of multiple national notifications, was adopted by the European Council of Foreign Affairs Ministers on 27 June 1997. Under the present system, transactions which fall outside the scope of the MCR may have to satisfy conditions imposed by a number of national authorities, of which there will soon be fourteen, including eight which have a mandatory notification requirement. A system of multiple national notifications increases the risk of legal uncertainty in transactions as well as the possibility of inconsistent decisions and places extra financial burdens on the companies involved. The Council was keen to adopt a less complex system and it worked on a proposal by the Commission by which a 'one-stop shop' would be introduced for transactions which have significant transnational effects but which fall below the thresholds of the MCR.

Under the amended Regulation, the existing Community dimension thresholds will remain. However, where those thresholds are not satisfied, the Commission's competence will be extended to concentrations which satisfy the following new thresholds:

1   the combined aggregate worldwide turnover of all the undertakings concerned is more than Ecu 2,500 million;
2   in each of at least three member states, the combined aggregate turnover of all the undertakings concerned is more than Ecu 100 million;
3   in each of the three member states included for the purpose of (2), the aggregate turnover of each of at least two of the undertakings concerned is more than Ecu 25 million; and
4   the aggregate Community-wide turnover of each of at least two of the undertakings concerned is more than Ecu 100 million;

unless each of the undertakings concerned achieves more than two-thirds of its aggregate Community-wide turnover in one and the same member state.

Under proposed amendments to the Regulation, the obligation to notify transactions falling below the existing thresholds and above new lower thresholds would have depended also upon the transaction in question falling within the scope of at least three national merger control regimes. That proposal, which would have presented considerable practical difficulties, has been abandoned in favour of a purely turnover-based approach.

The introduction of the new turnover thresholds will mean that, in the case of a transaction involving a number of parties active in several member states or across the whole Community, the number of combinations of turnover which it may be necessary to analyse could be considerable. A detailed breakdown of the parties' Community turnover by member state, calculated in accordance with the provisions of the Regulation, will be required to enable a view to be reached on whether a transaction potentially falling within the new thresholds will be subject to notification under the Merger Regulation. For those companies which do not maintain turnover information on a country by country basis, it will be necessary to ensure that means exist of generating that information. As this will generally be confidential information, the new rules will create an added complication for a company mounting a hostile take-over bid.

The Regulation will apply in its amended form to 'full function' joint ventures, rather than, as at present, only to 'concentrative' ones. A major advantage of the new rules is, therefore, that the assessment of the 'co-operative' aspects of full function joint ventures satisfying the Community dimension thresholds will have to be completed within the strict time limits laid down by the Merger Regulation.

The distinction between concentrative and co-operative joint ventures (which has to date governed whether transactions are subject to Article 85 or to the MCR) has been one of the most problematic aspects of the present regime. Under the amended Regulation, the focus of attention will shift to whether or not a joint venture satisfies the requirement of 'performing on a lasting basis all the functions of an autonomous economic entity' and is therefore to be regarded as a concentration.

The amendments which have been agreed include a number of other welcome changes and clarifications. These include:

- amendments to the method by which turnover of financial institutions is calculated, so that it is based on gross income rather than assets;
- the provision of a legal basis for acceptance of modifications to concentration plans in the course of a first phase inquiry, and for the attachment of undertakings and conditions to first phase decisions;
- extension of the suspension period after notification of a transaction from the present three weeks to the conclusion of the enquiry. This has been accompanied by a slight broadening of the scope for derogations.

Earlier proposals to introduce fees in respect of review mergers under the Regulation were rejected.

The new turnover tests and application of the Merger Regulation to the co-operative aspects of full function joint ventures will introduce additional complexity into the process of determining whether certain proposed transactions fall within the scope of the Merger Regulation. Both of these changes seem likely in practice to result in significantly more transactions falling within the scope of the Regulation. This should be welcome to those merging parties to whom the benefits of the 'one stop shop' will be available, and who are able to avoid the complications of multiple notifications. There are no indications yet as to whether the Merger Task Force will secure additional resources to handle the new volume of work. For notifying parties, completion of the Form CO will continue to require a considerable amount of work, necessitating preparation well in advance. Close liaison with the Merger Task Force prior to notification will be even more important than at present.

Notification requirements

When does the Merger Control Regulation apply?

Until the amendments to the MCR come into force, a merger or 'concentration' under the MCR arises where two or more previously independent undertakings merge, or one or more undertakings acquire control of the whole or part of another undertaking, or two or more undertakings form a third undertaking as a joint venture.

The key issue is whether or not the possibility of exercising decisive influence over strategic commercial behaviour has been conferred. The acquisition of property rights and the terms of any shareholders' agreements are important, but regard will also be had to long-term supply agreements or other arrangements that give rise to economic dependence. A minority shareholding can confer control, particularly if the bulk of the remaining shares in the company concerned are widely dispersed amongst the public.

Even if there is a concentration, the MCR will only apply if certain specified quantitative criteria or thresholds are reached which give the merger a Community dimension. A merger, acquisition or joint venture that qualifies as a concentration within the meaning of the Regulation will come within the exclusive jurisdiction of the Commission if it has a Community dimension. If it does not, then the Commission has no jurisdiction over the case and it falls to be assessed according to the laws of the member states concerned (see below).

If the operation is a concentration within the meaning of the Regulation, but it does not have a Community dimension, the Commission does not have the jurisdiction to consider the case.

The thresholds for a Community dimension are met when:

- the aggregate world-wide turnover of all the undertakings concerned exceeds Ecu 5,000 million *and*:

- each of at least two of the undertakings concerned has Community-wide turnover in excess of Ecu 250 million; *unless*
- all of the undertakings concerned achieve more than two-thirds of their Community-wide turnover in one and the same member state.

Where an undertaking concerned is part of a group of companies, the turnover of the whole group must be taken into account in determining whether these thresholds are met. A group relationship exists where one company has the right to manage the affairs of another undertaking, by virtue of shareholdings, voting rights or management appointment powers. These powers may be deduced from the past behaviour of the undertakings concerned. Where only part of an undertaking is acquired, only the turnover relating to the part of the business acquired will be taken into account as far as the seller is concerned.

The Commission has long held the view that the thresholds above which transactions fall to be regulated by the MCR should be reduced. However, with the recent rejection of its proposals to this effect by the Council of Ministers, it is now unclear as to whether or not the reduction of the thresholds is a realistic possibility.

Merger procedure

Mergers with a Community dimension

Mergers, including concentrative joint ventures, with a Community dimension have to be notified to the Commission within one week and cannot be put into effect before notification or within three weeks thereafter without the consent of the Commission. Notification must be made on the prescribed form (Form CO) which entails the submission of very detailed market and economic information. The time limit of one week starts from the conclusion of an agreement or the acquisition of a controlling interest, and cannot be extended. In practice, notifying parties will, however, normally have held confidential informal pre-notification meetings with the Commission's Merger Task Force (MTF) as provided for in the implementing regulations, to present the proposed transaction, verify that it is indeed a merger with a Community dimension, and to explore any possible competition concerns. Once notified, the Commission publishes a notice to that effect in the EC *Official Journal* inviting comments from third parties.

If the Commission finds that the transaction has a Community dimension, it has one month from notification in which to decide whether to approve the transaction (which happens in over 80 per cent of cases) or open in-depth, so-called 'Phase II', proceedings, which it will do wherever there are serious doubts as to the compatibility of the transaction with the Common Market. If not, the Commission will have to adopt a decision stating the grounds on which the case does not have a Community dimension. This will be either because it is not a concentration, as defined by the Regulation, or because it does not meet the threshold criteria. In the former case any agreement may still be considered under Article 85 of the EC Treaty, which prohibits agreements which restrict competition, unless it can be shown, on the basis of the criteria for exemption laid down by Article 85 (3), that the economic benefits outweigh the anti-competitive effects. In the latter situation only the national authorities will have jurisdiction under the one-stop rule if the deal is still a concentration, as defined in the Regulation.

Phase II proceedings (opened in under 7 per cent of cases) must be concluded within a maximum of four months, at the end of which the Commission must either approve or prohibit the merger. During this time the Commission will seek the further views of industry and customers, request further information from the parties and call for in-depth market and economic analysis. At the beginning of this period the Commission will issue a Statement of Objections to the parties, to which they have the right to make a written reply and, if they wish, to present their case orally at a formal hearing in the presence of representatives of the member states. The Commission may also hear other interested parties.

During the Phase II proceedings, the parties also have the opportunity to enter into negotiations and to offer undertakings or changes to the notified transaction to meet the Commission's concerns. Such undertakings should be structural rather than purely behavioural. For example, companies can agree to divest assets, change distribution systems or grant intellectual property licences to resolve competition issues. It is up to the notifying parties to make such proposals to the Commission as the MTF does not have any authority to force changes, although it is empowered in its final Decision to impose conditions and obligations if the proposals are accepted. Examples of the types of conditions that the Commission has required in the past in order to approve a merger are discussed further below. The parties must table undertakings at least one month before the end of the Phase II proceedings in order to permit third parties to comment and for the opinion of the Advisory Committee to be obtained.

Mergers without a Community dimension

Any merger, acquisition or joint venture which is a concentration as defined in the Regulation, but which does not meet the thresholds laid down by the Regulation, does not have Community dimension and therefore falls within the jurisdiction of the national authorities of the member states (see below). The Commission has no jurisdiction to deal with these cases, either under the MCR or under the other rules on competition except in very restricted circumstances and, even then, it has declared that it does not, in principle, intend to apply the rules to such mergers.

This means that these mergers fall to be examined under the laws of each and every member state in which the merger has an effect.

The Commission's investigation

The Commission is granted sweeping powers of investigation under the MCR, as well as the right to require information to be provided. In carrying out the duties assigned to it the Commission may, under Article 11, request the parties in writing to supply it, by a particular date, with specified information. Requests may also be served on third parties. The request for information will state the legal basis and purpose of the request, together with details of the penalties for supplying incorrect information – a fine of between Ecu 1,000 and 50,000.

If the information requested is not provided within the period fixed by the Commission, or incomplete or incorrect information is provided, the Commission will fix a date by which the information must be provided. This decision will state the penalties for non-compliance, which could consist of a fine and a periodic penalty payment of up to Ecu 25,000 per day of default.

Commission officials are also empowered to examine a company's books or business records, take copies, ask for oral explanations on the spot, and enter premises, land and vehicles of undertakings in pursuance of their investigations.

Having conducted its enquiries the Commission decides whether or not the concentration will create or strengthen a dominant position as a result of which effective competition is likely to be impeded in the common market or in a substantial part of it.

In previous years, the Merger Task Force has adopted a very dynamic view of the market, especially in the face of emerging competition, or potential competition from outside the Community, and in several cases has looked favourably on the creation of high market shares. However, more recently, the Commissioner for Competition, Karel van Miert, has taken a tougher enforcement line. Six of the eight prohibitions under the Merger Regulation have taken place since 1995, and the sixth and seventh prohibitions were announced in rapid succession in November and December 1996.

Sanctions

Fines and penalties for failure to comply with regulatory requirements

The Commission can enforce the notification requirements under the MCR by means of powerful sanctions. A notifiable transaction may not be put into effect before it is notified or within the three weeks following notification.

Article 7 of the Regulation also provides for the extension, where necessary, of this period of suspension. Negligent or intentional failure to notify lays an acquiring company opens to the possibility of fines. The Commission may fine undertakings between Ecu 1,000 and 50,000 if they fail to notify a concentration, supply incorrect or misleading information in a notification, or if they produce the required books or other business records in incomplete form during investigations or they refuse to submit to an investigation. The Commission may also decide to impose fines of up to 10 per cent of group turnover where undertakings either intentionally or negligently put into effect a concentration before its notification or before the period of suspension has expired. Therefore if the parties fail to notify a merger at all, heavy fines may well follow. In setting the amount of a fine, the Commission will take into account the nature and gravity of the infringement in the particular case.

A notifiable transaction that is put into effect without proper notification will not be valid unless cleared by the Commission under the MCR. If the concentration has already been implemented, the Commission may, as well as imposing heavy fines, order the divestiture of parts of the business, the cessation of joint control or any other action that may be appropriate in order to restore conditions of effective competition. The Commission is therefore empowered to order the parties to do anything that might be required to restore the competitive status quo. In addition, the Commission can revoke decisions of compatibility where the decision was based on incorrect information or where a condition to the decision has been breached. However, transactions in securities on recognized stock exchanges may nevertheless be deemed valid, unless the buyer and seller knew or ought to have known that the transaction was carried out in breach.

In conclusion therefore, under the MCR severe sanctions can be imposed for breaches of procedural requirements, such as the implementation of a merger without prior notification.

Examples of merger cases

Mergers prohibited under the MCR

The following eight cases are the only occasions on which the Commission has prohibited mergers outright under the MCR. The cases illustrate how the Commission may decide on a restrictive product market definition, the effect of which is to give rise to a proportionately high market share for the merged parties.

Aérospatiale–Alenia/de Havilland (1991)

The first ever prohibition under the MCR concerned the ATR joint venture between the French company Aérospatiale and Alenia of Italy, which was proposing to acquire the Canadian turbo-prop aeroplane manufacturer, de Havilland, from Boeing. The Commission decided that the merger would create a dominant position on the world market for turbo-prop 'commuter' aircraft, which would have the effect of forcing existing competitors out of the market and of discouraging potential market entrants.

The geographical market was considered to be the world-wide one, excluding China and Eastern Europe, on the basis that there are no major costs or other barriers to world trade in commuter aircraft. The Commission decided that there was sufficient evidence of significant market penetration to support this analysis.

In defining the product market, jet aircraft were excluded because they are considerably more expensive to buy and operate, and are consequently used on higher-density or longer distance flights than turbo-prop planes. According to the Commission, the concentration would have given the merged venture around a 50 per cent share of the overall world-wide commuter plane market, the nearest competitor, Saab, having only around 19 per cent. More controversially, the Commission further sub-divided the market into planes with around thirty, fifty and seventy seats, on the basis of differing production and purchasing patterns for each type, and found that in the relevant product market of forty to fifty-nine seats, the new entity would obtain about 64 per cent of the world market.

Media Service GmbH (1994)

The Commission's second prohibition decision related to the proposed creation of a joint venture, Media Service GmbH (MSG), between Bertelsmann, Deutsche Bundespost Telekom and the Kirch Group to provide technical, business and administrative handling of digital pay-TV and other communications services. After second-phase proceedings, the Commission concluded that the joint venture would produce or aggravate a dominant position on three markets: the provision of technical and administrative services to the pay-TV market; the German-speaking pay-TV market; and the cable infrastructure. The Commission considered it unlikely that competitors would be able to enter the pay-TV market, since MSG would have held a monopolistic position in the supply of programmes and services, such as the distribution of decoders and the administration of customer base. The Commission rejected proposed undertakings offered by the parties late in the second stage of proceedings. It considered that these were either conditional or mere declarations of intent and were not structural, so were not likely to modify the initial analysis. It was the structural features of MSG which would lead to a protection of the market for services and for digital pay-TV.

However, some months after the prohibition, the Commission approved a revised deal between UFA, Bertelmann's holding company, for its film, television and radio activities, and Compagnie Luxembourgeoise de Télédiffusion. The Commission found that this new deal would not have a dominant position on the German market for free-access TV, given the strong position of channels linked to the rival Kirch Group.

Nordic Satellite Distribution (1995)

In the *Nordic Satellite Distribution* case, the Commission, again after undertaking a second-phase in-depth investigation, declared the proposed joint venture between Norsk Telekom, TeleDanmark and Kinnevik to be incompatible with the Common Market and the EEA Agreement. The joint venture would create or strengthen a dominant position in three markets: the provision of satellite TV transponder capacity to the Nordic region; the Danish market for the operation of cable TV networks; and the market for distribution of satellite pay-TV and other encrypted TV channels direct-to-home. The vertically integrated nature of the operation meant that the market positions downstream (cable TV operations and pay-TV) would reinforce the positions upstream (satellite transponders and provision of programmes) and vice versa. The Commission considered that the parties together would be able to foreclose the Nordic market for satellite TV.

The Commission saw similarities between this case and the MSG merger prohibition involving the German pay-TV market. However, it invited the present joint venture to be presented in a modified form, and acknowledged that joint ventures, particularly where they are of a transnational nature, can be instrumental in the development of the media and telecommunications sectors to their full potential. It indicated that new developments would be taken into account in considering any amended proposals.

Holland Media Group (1995)

The fourth ever Commission prohibition under the MCR occurred in September, 1995 in relation to the Holland Media Group which is the proposed joint venture between RTL, Veronica Omroeporganisatie and Endemol Entertainment Holding B.V. The Commission voiced the concern that HMG would lead to the creation of a dominant position on the TV advertising market in the Netherlands and the strengthening of Endemol's existing dominant position on the Dutch TV production market. The Commission was also concerned that HMG would become the largest broadcaster in the Netherlands, and would be free from competitors.

In July 1996, the Commission approved a modified version of the proposal. The parties submitted certain amendments to the joint venture in order to address the Commission's objections to the joint venture when it was prohibited in 1995. First, in order to allay the Commission's fears that the HMG joint venture would lead to the creation of a dominant position on the TV advertising market in the Netherlands and the strengthening of Endemol's already existing dominant position on the Dutch TV production market, Endemol withdrew completely its participation in HMG. Secondly, HMG undertook to transform RTL5, the commercial TV channel, into a news channel and to operate only two commercial channels with coordinated programme schedules. In particular, it undertook not to use RTL5 as a 'fighting channel' which could directly counteract the programming of competing channels. The withdrawal of Endemol from HMG has removed the structural link between the largest Dutch TV producer and the leading commercial broadcaster in the Netherlands. Endemol's departure also means that HMG will no longer have preferential access to Endemol's productions, and has allowed Endemol to set up together with other partners a new sports channel in the Netherlands.

Gencor–Lonrho (1996)

Following a second-phase (four month) investigation, the Commission prohibited the proposed merger of Impala Platinum, controlled by the South African company Gencor, and Lonrho's platinum division.

The Commission's principal reason for prohibiting the merger was a concern that it would lead to the creation of a duopoly consisting of Gencor–Lonrho, which, as a result of the merger, would have a combined share of 28 per cent of the platinum market world-wide, and Amplats (Anglo American Platinum Corporation), which currently enjoys a share of 35 per cent of the platinum market.

The Commission's concern was based on the following factors: 80 per cent of the platinum trade is sold on the basis of long-term contracts; there is no product which is readily substitutable for platinum in its major uses, namely jewellery, motor car catalytic converters and catalysis applications in industry; the recent fall in the price of platinum has been, in addition to the effect of the liquidation of the Russian platinum stock, a result of Lonrho's presence in the market which would be removed if the planned merger was approved; and finally, the purchaser's choice of suppliers and therefore scope for negotiation, is already very limited, since South African companies hold 90 per cent of the world reserves. The other 10 per cent held by Russia is likely to be exhausted by the end of the century.

Tuko–Kesko (1996)

The Commission announced the sixth ever prohibition under the MCR in November 1996. This concerned the acquisition of Tuko by Kesko. The enterprises involved were two Finnish companies active in the sale of general consumer goods in Finland. The Commission believed that the Kesko group was a centrally planned organization, and that Tuko retailers would be integrated into this organization as a result of the acquisition.

The Kesko group consists of Kesko Oy and related companies, together with 'K-retailers', of which the latter are independent legal entities, varying considerably in the size of their operations. The Commission has stated that the following considerations led it to consider that it was a centrally planned group: the group's sourcing, marketing operations and joint presentation of logos, the ownership by Kesko Oy of retailing premises, and the financial commitments made by K-retailers to Kesko Oy.

Kesko and Tuko retailers offer a one-stop shopping service for a range of both fresh and 'dry' food products, and non-food products such as toiletries and cleaning agents. The combined retail market share of Kesko and Tuko is at least 55 per cent, whether assessed at local, regional or national level. This position on the market is further enhanced by the large size of their retail outlets, their customer loyalty schemes, private label products, distribution systems and the purchasing power of Kesko Oy as buyer of the goods from the manufacturers.

The Kesko group is also active in the cash and carry market, where customers are smaller companies, such as restaurants, which cannot use traditional wholesaling networks. The Commission considered that in this market the acquisition would create a monopolistic supply, since combined market shares would vary regionally from 50 per cent to 100 per cent.

Saint-Gobain/Wacker–Chemie/Nom (1996)

In December 1996, the Commission announced its opposition to the Saint-Gobain/Wacker–Chemie/Nom joint venture in the silicon carbide sector. The parties to the joint venture were Société Européenne des Produits Refractaires (SEPR), which belongs to the French group Saint-Gobain; Nom, owned by the Dutch state; and Elektroschmelzwerk Kempten (ESK), part of the German Wacker-Chemie group.

The Commission identified five relevant markets: the world market for silicon carbide of metallurgical quality; the world market for crude silicon carbide; the European market for silicon carbide for abrasive applications; the European market for heat-resistant applications; and the (undefined) market for silicon carbide intended for other industrial applications.

In the markets for silicone carbide for abrasive and heat-resistant applications, the joint venture would have resulted in a 60 per cent market share for the parties, whilst the three remaining competitors in Europe would have shares of less than 10 per cent. Furthermore, the parties to the joint venture are the technological leaders and the only providers of the whole range of silicon carbide grades for abrasives and refractories.

In an attempt to gain the Commission's approval of the transaction, the parties proposed to withdraw their support for the anti-dumping measures affecting imports of silicon carbide from Russia, the Ukraine and China which are in force until April 1999. However, the Commission decided that this undertaking would not solve the competition problems raised by the proposed joint venture.

Blokker/Toys 'R' Us (1997)

Following an in-depth investigation, in June 1997 the Commission prohibited the proposed acquisition by Blokker of Toys 'R' Us. Blokker is one of the major retail operators in the Netherlands, selling toys through its chains of specialised toy outlets, and Toys 'R' Us is the wholly owned subsidiary of Toys 'R' Us Inc., which is one of the world's biggest toy retailers.

The Commission initiated its investigation at the requst of the Dutch Government under Article 22 of the MCR, as it had previsouly done in the *Holland Media Group* case (1995) and in the Tuko-Kesko case (1996). In the absence of this request, the Commission would not have had jurisdiction to deal with the case as the requisite turnover thresholds set out in the MCR were not attained by the parties.

The Commission concluded that the relevant market was the market for retail outlets selling toys throughout the year in the Netherlands. Blokker already enjoyed a dominant position in the market for specialised toy outlets, with a market share almost four times bigger than that of its nearest competitor. Its retail formulae also gave it a substantial advantage over its competitors, strengthening its gatekeeper position *vis à vis* suppliers with regard to access to the retail market. The proposed acquisition would only have led to a small increase in the market, but it would have further entrenched Blokker's dominant position, granting it access to the important market segment of large-scale suburuban retailing in which, prior to the acquisition, only Toys 'R' Us was active.

Commission intervention under Articles 85 and 86

There are a number of other cases in which Commission has intervened to prevent or impose conditions on mergers under Articles 85 and 86. Most of the following cases were dealt with by the Commission prior to the entry into force of the MCR, but they illustrate the Commission's willingness to prohibit mergers that it considers to be anti-competitive by any means which it has at its disposal.

Philip Morris–Rembrandt/Rothmans

This case illustrates how the Commission will consider proposals made by the parties to amend their agreements, even at a late stage in the proceedings, in order to facilitate a settlement. In May 1982, the Commission issued a statement of objections in respect of certain agreements concluded between Philip Morris Inc (PM) and Rembrandt Group Ltd, part of the Rothmans group. The PM and Rothmans groups form part of the small group of multinational conglomerates which dominate world cigarette markets. Two agreements were under investigation: first, that concerning the sale by Rembrandt to PM of half of its wholly-owned subsidiary, Rothmans Tobacco Holdings Ltd, which in turn controlled Rothmans International plc (RI), and secondly, a partnership agreement providing for cooperation in the conduct of RI's affairs in areas such as joint distribution, manufacturing, technical know-how and research.

In its investigation, the Commission had particular regard to the influence that PM had over its direct competitor, RI. In particular, PM had a right of veto over RI by virtue of its control of the holding company. The overall effect of the agreements was that the investment and commercial strategies of RI could only be determined jointly by PM and Rembrandt. The Commission found that the transfer of equity involved in this case fell within Article 85 (1), and also considered that the agreements infringed Article 86 since the agreements had neutralized PM as a significant competitor in a narrowly oligopolistic market, bringing about an abusive strengthening of the dominant positions held.

In 1984 therefore PM and Rembrandt drew up new agreements by which Rembrandt retained full ownership of the holding company and control over the affairs of RI. The Commission accepted the revised agreements, subject to a number of undertakings from the parties, including the obligation on PM to obtain clearance from the Commission for any amendments to the new agreements, in particular (i) any increase in its shareholdings, or (ii) any circumstance by which PM would obtain 25 per cent or more of the voting rights in Rothmans International.

British Airways–British Caledonian

In this 1987–8 investigation, the first to involve Community airlines, the Commission examined the effects of the British Airways/British Caledonian merger on receipt of a complaint by British Midland. The case is instructive in that it shows how the Commission has allowed a merger to proceed on receipt of undertakings from the parties involved. In this case, the Commission was concerned that the merger would strengthen the already strong position of British Airways in the scheduled air services market in Europe. Some of the most important undertakings offered by the merged airline included the giving up of routes which would otherwise have been granted to British Caledonian; the limiting of its share of take-off and landing slots at London (Gatwick) to 25 per cent of the total available for four years from 1989; and the granting of the Gatwick–Rome route to a smaller airline.

Continental Can

This was the first occasion on which the Commission applied Article 86 to a concentration. Continental Can, a packaging manufacturer, had a controlling interest in a West German packaging manufacturer called SLW. Continental Can signed an agreement to take over a company called TDV, which made the same products as SLW, although TDV held a strong position on the Benelux, as opposed to the German, market.

The Commission opened an investigation of the TDV acquisition under Article 86 and reached a decision which was that essentially Continental Can held a dominant position through SLW. By obtaining a controlling interest in TDV, Continental was abusing that dominant position by 'practically eliminating' competition in Benelux and West Germany, which together constituted a substantial part of the common market. In the Commission's view the strengthening of a dominant position by a merger could, in itself, constitute an abuse where, as a result of the merger, the competition which would have existed, actually or potentially, prior to the merger would in practice be eliminated for the products in question in a substantial part of the common market.

Continental Can subsequently appealed to the European Court of Justice for annulment of the Commission Decision. The Court supported the Commission's position on the applicability of Article 86 to concentrations, although in fact it annulled the Commission Decision because of the Commission's assessment of the relevant product market. This case (and the *Gillette* case – see below) illustrate, however, the Commission's willingness to intervene where the parties to a merger hold a dominant position.

Mergers cleared under the MCR subject to conditions

Although outright prohibition by the Commission of a notified concentration under the MCR is rare, merger clearance is often subject to the receipt of undertakings from the parties, or the imposition of conditions by the Commission. Under the MCR the Commission may attach to its decisions conditions and obligations intended to ensure that the companies concerned comply with the commitments they have entered into to modify the original planned concentration. The following cases illustrate some of the conditions that have been imposed by the Commission in the past prior to the approval of a merger decision.

Crown Cork & Seal–CarnaudMetalbox

In October 1995 the Commission cleared under the MCR the acquisition of the French company CarnaudMetalbox by the US company Crown Cork & Seal by way of a public share offer for an estimated $5.2 billion. The merger, which created the world's largest packaging company, raised serious doubts as to its compatibility with EC competition laws, particularly in the market for tinplate aerosol cans, where the aggregated market share of the two companies reached approximately 65 per cent of the market in the European Economic Area (EEA) in 1994. The Commission conducted an in-depth investigation, and the approval was eventually granted on condition that the two companies divest five plants in Europe, which represented approximately 22 per cent of the EEA market. In relation to the food can market the Commission considered that the operation would not create a single dominant position in view of the competitive features of this market. The Commission also decided that no significant anti-competitive effects would occur in the upstream steel markets or the markets for beverage closures.

Kimberly-Clark–Scott Paper

After five months of extensive investigation the Commission approved the merger between two US companies, Kimberly-Clark and Scott Paper, on the basis of substantial modifications agreed by the parties. Under the terms of the modifications made, the parties would not combine Kimberly-Clark's Kleenex brand and Scott Paper's Andrex brand consumer tissue businesses in the UK or Ireland. Other modifications to the merger with respect to Ireland and the UK included divestiture of various branded products, coupled with certain limitations on the use by the parties of the Kleenex and Andrex trademarks. In spite of these measures, the merged businesses still created the largest tissue paper producer in the world and Europe.

BP–Mobil

In 1996, BP and Mobil secured the Commission's approval for the proposed combination of their fuels and lubricants operations in Europe. The structure of the joint venture involved BP acting as 'Fuels Operator' (with a 70 per cent equity stake in the fuels operations, Mobil having a 30 per cent stake) and Mobil acting as 'Lubricants Operator' (with a 51 per cent stake in the lubricants operations, BP having a 49 per cent stake), with both parties acting under the authority of a jointly controlled Supervisory Committee. The cooperation extended to numerous post-refinement product markets, including retail and non-retail sale of fuels, automobile and industrial lubricants and various other oil-based products. However, the companies' other core businesses and international operations remained separate.

The joint venture had a European market share of about 10 per cent for retail motor fuels (making it Europe's third largest supplier) and about 18 per cent for lubricants. However, the competitors in all the markets affected were other large multinational petrochemical companies and in some countries strong local competitors also existed. Furthermore, the increasing trend of entry by supermarket chains into the retail motor fuels market provided competition for the joint venture. Another common feature was a significant and widespread over-capacity in the product markets. Even in countries where the combined market share was high, the Commission considered that the joint venture was not likely to create or strengthen a dominant position in a substantial part of the Common Market.

Ciba-Geigy–Sandoz

Following a second-phase investigation, in 1996 the Commission approved the planned merger between Sandoz AG and Ciba-Geigy AG into the company Novartis AG. However, the approval was granted only after the parties agreed to undertakings in the area of animal health as competition concerns existed in the market for products for the treatment of parasites, such as fleas or ticks in small animals. The parties had a very strong position in one of the crucial products in this market: the growth inhibitors that interrupt the reproductive cycle of parasites. Ciba-Geigy and Sandoz control three out of the five active substances available in the world. To overcome this potential competition problem, the parties undertook to grant non-exclusive licences for methroprene, one of the active substances, and to supply the licensees with this active substance until the commencement of their own production.

The Commission also examined carefully the R&D activities of the two companies, noting that the merger would result in a significant combined R&D potential. However, it was considered that there were enough other companies having the necessary 'critical mass' in this field. Novartis will continue to face competition in all areas from a number of major competitors such as Glaxo-Wellcome, Upjohn Pharmacia, Bayer, BASF, Rhone-Poulenc and others.

TELECOMMUNICATION SERVICES AND COMPETITION LAWS IN EUROPE

The development of competition rules in the telecommunications sector

The Commission perceives the telecommunications sector as vital to the emerging information society and to the economic wellbeing of the Community and its citizens as a whole. Moves towards the achievement of a single market in telecommunications started in earnest in 1987 when the Commission issued its Green Paper on telecommunications, providing an outline of the initiatives that the Commission intended to take. Full liberalization of EU telecoms is now scheduled for 1 January 1998. The majority of EU member states have entered into a commitment to lift government restrictions on the provision of telecommunications infrastructure and services by that date. Liberalization will be accompanied by a new regulatory framework which is designed to ensure that the same rules apply throughout the EU, guaranteeing fair competition between all operators, as well as universal access for all citizens, regardless of location or revenue. Within the Commission, responsibility for telecommunications is split between DGXIII, which deals with telecommunications as an industry, and DGIV, which deals with competition, Directorate C.2 being the division with specific responsibility for the telecommunications sector, whose head of unit, Mr Ungerer, was previously with DGXIII.

The Commission has had to overcome reluctance on the part of certain member states which traditionally viewed their state-owned public telecommunications operators (TOs) as national champions, and has used its powers under Article 90 as the legal basis both for liberalizing telecommunications markets and for establishing a new regulatory framework. Article 90 recognizes that member states may accord special or exclusive rights to undertakings charged with the fulfilment of tasks in the general economic interest. However, Article 90 also provides that the member states may not enact or maintain in force any provisions which are contrary to the Treaty rules, and in particular, the competition rules must be applied to such entities in so far as the application of those rules does not prevent them from carrying out their assigned tasks. Most importantly, Article 90 also provides for the Commission to issue directives of general application requiring the abolition of monopoly rights. The Commission has reached political agreement with the Council to consult it before adopting further Article 90 directives. In practice, this has meant that the Commission has circulated draft Article 90 directives for comments from the Council and the European Parliament as well as any interested third parties, and amendments to the drafts have been agreed by the Commission in conjunction with the Council agreeing to progress various draft Council directives.

The Commission has also been able to coerce the member states into adopting various Council directives in the telecommunications field on the basis of Article 100A, which is the main legal basis for harmonization measures.

Strategic alliances – tools to achieve liberalization

The telecoms sector requires cooperation agreements between telecoms operators in order to ensure network and services interconnectivity, one-stop shopping and one-stop billing, so that a satisfactory service is provided for users. Strategic alliances are arrangements between companies which do not reach the level of a full merger of all their activities, but go beyond a limited agreement to undertake some activities in common. Strategic alliances allow TOs to adapt quickly and effectively to the progressive, substantial and rapid changes in the markets within which they operate, particularly in terms of technologies available, scale of operations and geographic coverage available or required.

There have been several mergers in the telecoms sector, most of which have involved a large operator acquiring a smaller operator in another country in order to expand into that country – for example, the joint venture between Cable & Wireless and the German Group VEBA, in which the new enterprise consolidated the two groups' telecommunication activities in Germany. This presented no competition problems, since strong competition already existed in the German market. Furthermore, with the German market due to liberalize in 1998, the new joint venture would provide potentially strong competition to existing national monopoly telecommunications providers. As a result the joint venture was approved by the Commission under the MCR. In December 1996, the Commission cleared a merger bringing together the UK interests of Videotron, Cable & Wireless, Nynex, BCE and Mercury Communications to form a new cable television/telecommunications group, known as Cable and Wireless Communications. In approving this merger, the Commission had particular regard to the dominant position currently held by British Telecom in these areas and the stimulus to future competition that would be provided by the new group. Similarly, a joint venture between GEC of the UK and Finmeccania of Italy to produce certain communication products, including military products, was cleared under the MCR. This was because in that particular market there was already such a large range of other potential suppliers of these products, leading the Commission to take the view that the new joint venture would not prejudice effective competition.

By contrast, all of the international strategic alliances involving national TOs have been subject to intense scrutiny by regulators which on the one hand, wish to promote alliances in the interests of encouraging information superhighways and business efficiency, while on the other hand being keen to prevent infringement of competition rules. The Commission also has jurisdiction over mergers in the telecommunications sector where the turnover thresholds of the MCR are met. The Commission examines all aspects of strategic alliances on their own merits. Some recent cases illustrate the tension that exists between the competing Commission policy requirements.

BT–MCI

In July 1994 the Commission cleared the joint venture between BT and MCI, known as Concert, making it the first of the planned joint ventures in the telecommunications sector to have cleared all the regulatory procedures around the world. The new joint venture company was formed to address the emerging market for value added and enhanced services to large multi-national corporations, extended enterprises and other intensive users of telecommunications services provided over international intelligence networks. The joint venture was originally notified to the Commission under the MCR in August 1993, but the Commission ruled it was not a concentration and converted the notification to an Article 85 proceeding.

The Commission attached two conditions, with the agreement of the parties, to the exemption under Article 85 (3) of the EC Treaty. First, any user in the EEA must be able to obtain the alliance's services through MCI instead of BT, even though BT is appointed exclusive distributor in Europe. Secondly, a limit of five years' duration has been placed on a provision under which MCI will be prevented from using certain intellectual property rights if it seeks to enter BT's core business market, and once that period has expired, MCI will regain its rights in the EEA. The joint venture was granted a seven-year exemption, until November 2000, at which time the parties may seek a renewal.

In November 1996 the parties announced their intention to merge to form Concert plc. The proposed transaction would be the largest ever acquisition by a UK company. The parties view the merger as the natural progression of the Concert Communications venture and cited as justification for the merger customers' desire to satisfy all their communications needs through one supplier. The new entity would have annual revenues of over £25 billion and would serve all related product markets including local, long distance and international, mobile, multimedia and Internet services and network-based services. The merged company will bring together the financial resources to enable it to pursue growth, including acquisitions and joint ventures.

In May 1997, after holding an in-depth investigation into the proposed merger, the Commission granted its approval. The Commission found that the merger, as notified, would create or reinforce a dominant position in the markets for international voice telephony services between the UK and the US and in the audioconferencing market, but cleared the concentration on the basis of the undertakings offered by the parties.

The Commission considered in detail the question of access to transatlantic cable capacity. Both BT and MCI have significant capacity entitlement to transatlantic submarine cable between the UK and the US. The Commission found that, after the merger, BT/MCI would be able to internalise the payments for UK/US traffic, while competitors would have to pay a foreign correspondent carrier in the country of destination. Moreover, the merger would restrict the possibility of entry into the market for new operators. However, the Commission cleared this aspect of the merger after having accepted the undertakings proposed by the parties, which included obligations to make available cable capacity to new entrants to the market and to sell BT's capacity on the UK–US route currently leased to other operators. The Commission's concerns in relation to the audioconferencing market were allayed by MCI undertaking to divest its audioconferencing business in the UK.

Atlas–GlobalOne

The *Atlas–GlobalOne* case presented the Commission with the opportunity to ensure adherence to the EU liberalization timetable in two of the most significant member states with state-owned operators. The French and German governments agreed to liberalize alternative infrastructure by 1 July 1996 and public voice telephony by 1 January 1998. This was the price for the Commission taking a favourable view of the creation of Atlas, the joint venture between France Telecom (FT) and Deutsche Telekom (DT) and GlobalOne, the joint venture between Atlas and the US carrier Sprint in which FT and DT each bought a 10 per cent stake for a total investment of about US$4bn. The Commission also required various changes to be made by the parties to ensure that the monopoly positions of FT and DT would not stifle competition, in particular by imposing obligations and conditions to prevent discrimination and cross-subsidies and requiring access to be granted to third parties.

Uniworld

The other major alliances seeking to compete in the emerging market for seamless global corporate services, Unisource/Telefonica and Uniworld, were not voluntarily notified to the Commission, leading to the opening of proceedings on the Commission's own initiative and a request to the parties to provide details. Unisource is an alliance between PTT Telecom of the Netherlands, Telia of Sweden and Swiss PTT, which is being joined by Telefonica of Spain. Uniworld is an alliance between Unisource and AT&T. In December 1996, the Commission published notices indicating that it would take a favourable view of the alliance. However, the final decision has not yet been published. This is probably due to the fact that Telefonica has withdrawn from the alliance and that the Commission is now re-examining the alliance in the light of these developments. These alliances have given the Commission the chance to require commitments on liberalization in two further member states, the Netherlands and Spain, as well as in a non-EU state, Switzerland. The governments of each of these countries have confirmed that they will meet the EU deadline for market liberalization of 1 January 1998. The Commission had particular leverage over Spain, since Telefonica's membership of Unisource required Commission approval. Spain had to agree to forgo its right to postpone the introduction of full competition for up to five years past the 1 January 1998 deadline that it had negotiated in the Council. Full liberalization of the Spanish telecommunications market is now to take place by 30 November 1998, with three licences being granted by 1 January 1998 plus limited licences for the cable TV companies to offer telecoms within their areas. Since the domestic market of the fourth Unisource member, Telia, is already open to competition, Sweden has simply been asked to provide a progress report on the state of competition. In respect of the Uniworld transaction, AT&T offered undertakings including keeping the Commission informed should any complaint on access or interconnection be filed against it in the US, as well as offering cost-based accounting at certain rates to operators with international facilities licences in the EEA and Switzerland.

Conclusions

Alliances affect the definitions of markets that are vast and developing rapidly, and competition authorities are keen to ensure the effective application of competition rules to such markets. However, they also acknowledge that markets must restructure in order to provide modern telecoms services in a global market. These cases demonstrate the readiness and ability of the Commission to use all the tools at its disposal to open the telecommunications market to competition. In doing so, the Commission has been able to extract undertakings to enhance competition not only from the parties concerned, but also from various member states to ensure that the EU timetable for liberalization is met. The Commission views this as an important step towards its ultimate goal of the setting up of a European, and indeed global, information society.

COORDINATION AND COOPERATION BETWEEN COMPETITION AUTHORITIES

Regulation of international mergers has been greatly assisted by the increased cooperation that exists both within the Community, and between the Commission and the regulatory authorities in third countries. This cooperation can take the form of both formal and informal agreements. The significance of this cooperation for notifying parties is that merger notification must be consistent in all jurisdictions or else the notifying parties will lack credibility.

International antitrust agreements

In April 1995 the Council, following a proposal from the Commission, decided to approve a new antitrust cooperation agreement with the US concerning the application of competition rules. The new agreement provides for the exchange of information on general matters relating to the implementation of competition rules, as well as cases handled by both parties. Under the agreement the respective competition authorities on both sides of the Atlantic are still required to maintain the confidentiality of information gathered during respective investigations. Under an earlier 1991 agreement with the US, which was declared void for procedural reasons, 173 cases were the subject of notification: sixty-one from the EC to the US, of which forty-five related to mergers, and 112 from the US to the EC, of which seventy-seven concerned mergers.

In addition to the US agreement, the Council recently gave the Commission a negotiating brief to conclude a similar cooperation agreement between the EC and Canada. An agreement with Australia is also anticipated. Even where no formal agreement is in place the Community expects to cooperate with the competition authorities in third countries. The Commission's strategy has been to push for the development of international principles, such as the revival of the 'positive comity' principle. This rule provides that a party whose important interests are affected by the anti-competitive practices in another party's territory may request the latter to examine those practices. There are also frequent exchange visits such as, for example, the exchanges of staff that have taken place between the Commission and the American Department of Justice and the Federal Trade Commission. In addition, seminars are held to discuss common problems that different competition authorities share.

Liaison with the authorities of the member states

The Commission also liaises with the competition authorities of the various member states as regards merger control. Under the MCR the Commission is required to transmit to the competent authorities of member states copies of notifications within three working days. There is an Advisory Committee consisting of representatives of the competition authorities of member states which must be consulted before any decision is taken as to whether a notified concentration is compatible with the Common Market or any fines or periodic penalty payments are imposed. The Commission produces a draft decision on which the Advisory Committee delivers its opinion and the Commission is required to take account of this opinion.

The Commission may also refer cases to be decided by the regulatory authorities of member states. Although the purpose of the 'one-stop shop' for merger control within the Community was to avoid the need for transactions to obtain approval from each national competition authority in the EC in which the merger produces effects there are exceptions to this principle. There are cases where, although the Commission may have jurisdiction, a case will be dealt with by national competition authorities, and vice versa. The following exceptions were inserted into the Regulation at the request of particular member states and as a result they have become known as the German, English and Dutch clauses, respectively.

The German clause (Article 9)

Within three weeks of receiving its copy of a notification, a member state may notify the Commission that a concentration threatens to create or strengthen a dominant position as a result of which effective competition would be significantly impeded on a distinct market within that member state. If the Commission agrees that there is such a distinct market or that such a threat exists it may either deal with the case itself or refer it to the competent authorities of the member state concerned, with a view to the application of the state's national competition laws.

The Commission must decide whether to refer a particular case within six weeks of notification if the Commission has not initiated an in-depth investigation, or within three months of notification where proceedings have been initiated. If the Commission has not taken any decision on referral within three months of notification, the matter is deemed to have been referred to the member state.

In late 1993, in the case of the proposed creation of a herb and spice joint venture between the food companies CPC, McCormick and Rabobank, and again in 1997, concerning the acquisition by Southern/Bayernwerk/PreussenElektra of BEWAG, the Commission agreed to the request of a member state for referral of a merger to its national competition authorities under Article 9 of the MCR.

The English clause (Article 21)

Article 21 of the MCR enables member states to take appropriate measures to protect legitimate interests other than those that are taken into consideration by the MCR, provided that those interests are compatible with the general principles and other provisions of Community law.

'Legitimate interests' are defined by the MCR as including public security, plurality of the media and prudential rules. Any other public interest on the basis of which a member state wishes to review a transaction which falls within the scope of the Regulation must be communicated by the member state concerned to the Commission, which will decide whether it should be so recognized. The most recent example of this was in 1995 when the UK government applied to the Commission requesting that the provisions of the 1991 Water Industry Act be considered a 'legitimate interest' under Article 21, which would enable the Commission to investigate the French water company Lyonnaise des Eaux's bid to buy Northumbrian Water.

The Dutch clause (Article 22)

Under Article 22 of the MCR a member state is allowed to ask the Commission to act under the Regulation in relation to a transaction which, although it has no Community dimension, creates or strengthens a dominant position as a result of which effective competition would be significantly impeded within that State's territory. The clause was designed to protect member states with no effective merger control provisions of their own. In 1995, it was used by the Dutch government to refer to the Commission a case involving TV advertising and production (the *Holland Media Group* case). It has most recently been used in the 1997 *Blokker/Toys 'R' Us* case, in which, following a request from the Dutch competition authorities, the Commission examined and subsequently prohibited the acquisition of a subsidiary of the world's largest toy retailer.

Future possibilities for greater cooperation

The coexistence of many different merger control authorities can give rise to various difficulties, especially as regards transnational mergers and acquisitions, frustration over the collection of information and conflicting resolutions where one authority approves and another blocks the same deal. The drawbacks of the present system include duplication of checks on compliance with the competition rules and associated costs, as well as the risk of divergent decisions and the possibility of firms 'shopping around' for authorities they believe may be favourable to their case. Regulatory authorities have in the past disagreed with each other over the scope of their jurisdiction, and for businesses, the multiplicity of jurisdictions can lead to greater uncertainty over the legality of an agreement where more than one approval is necessary.

Subsidiarity in policing competition rules

The Commission has for some years been promoting its aim of giving a more active regulatory role in competition matters to the authorities of the various member states, although its efforts have so far not met with a great deal of success. Following its 1993 notice on cooperation with national courts, the Commission published in October 1997 a notice on cooperation between national competition authorities and the Commission in the handling of cases falling within Articles 85 and 86 of the Treaty. The Commission is encouraging these authorities to directly apply Community law themselves instead of requiring firms to refer the Community law aspects of their cases to the Commission. The Commission argues that national authorities are closer to the activities that require monitoring and are often in a better position than the Commission to perform the role of 'watchdog'.

It is proposed that national competition authorities should in future be able to deal with matters relating to conduct which has an appreciable effect on trade between member states, either at their own initiative or at the Commission's request. However, the notice makes it clear that the Commission should remain the only body that has the power to grant the exemption to the ban on restrictive practices in individual cases under Article 85 (3) of the Treaty, or to deal with matters arising from the exemption, for example a complaint against a decision to withdraw it. Furthermore, the Commission has suggested that where a case involves businesses located in several member states, the Commission should usually deal with it, since it would be difficult for a national authority to conduct investigations outside its borders.

OECD – *case study of the Gillette acquisition*

In 1993 the Organization for Economic Cooperation and Development (OECD) produced a report on merger control cooperation between member countries. The OECD report analysed the procedures employed by competition authorities, identifying procedural differences impeding cooperation between regulatory authorities and areas for potential convergence and cooperation. The method employed by the OECD was the use of case studies that had involved two or more different authorities reviewing the same transaction.

One such case study was the purchase by Gillette of Stora's consumer products division (which included the Wilkinson Sword wet-shaving business) by means of a leveraged buy-out company called Eemland. The transaction was reviewed by various regulatory bodies around the world, including those in the UK, France, the US and Australia, as well as by the European Commission.

In the UK, the case was transferred to the MMC for a detailed investigation under UK merger control legislation. The MMC decided that as a result of the merger Gillette had become a significant shareholder in the parent of Wilkinson Sword, Gillette's only substantial competitor in the UK razor blade market. The MMC were unable to identify significant benefits from the transaction that would offset its detrimental competitive effect and therefore recommended that Gillette should divest itself of certain equity and debt interests.

The Commission investigation took place before the implementation of the MCR, but the Commission found that Gillette had abused its dominant position under Article 86 of the EC Treaty and ordered divestiture of Gillette's equity and debt interests in Eemland. Gillette tried to reach an amicable settlement with the Commission (as it had done by means of a consent decree with the US Department of Justice). However, in June 1991 the Commission issued a Statement of Objections, which was followed by a formal Decision in November 1992. The Commission expressed the concern that Gillette might be abusing its dominant position in the wet-shaving market by holding a substantial equity stake in Eemland and by becoming one of its creditors. The Commission also found that agreements between Gillette and Eemland, relating to the geographical separation of the

Wilkinson Sword trademark between the Community and neighbouring countries, would have involved commercial cooperation between the respective owners of the Wilkinson Sword trademarks in breach of Article 85. The Commission Decision required Gillette to reassign to Eemland the Wilkinson Sword businesses and trademarks in the EFTA countries and various Central and Eastern European countries.

In the UK proceedings, Gillette made an application to the High Court of Justice for judicial review of the case, and as regards the Commission Decision, it intended to bring an appeal to the European Court of First Instance. However, both these steps became irrelevant following the 1993 disposal by Eemland of its Wilkinson Sword business to Warner Lambert, by virtue of which the regulatory authorities' concerns about the equity and shareholding links between Gillette and Eemland were removed.

In analysing the degree of cooperation between the regulatory authorities in this case the OECD found that as different authorities completed different stages of their investigations in this transaction, agencies in other countries had the benefit of published reports analysing the transaction. For example, the MMC report was available to the Australian Trade Practices Commission in their investigation, and the report by the French authorities reviewed the actions taken by the US, the UK and the German authorities as well as the EC Commission. In investigating this case the Merger Task Force used staff seconded from the German FCO and the UK's OFT, thereby ensuring personal contacts with the national competition authorities from which they had been seconded. It is thought that at one point the case workers from the FCO visited Brussels and held informal meetings with DGIV. Gillette had in certain cases encouraged those contacts in order to reach a settlement, although this had proved difficult because of the different objectives of some of the authorities.

The OECD report recommends that in the future improved cooperation between competition authorities should take place including coordination of timetables, a cooperative approach and discussion of issues such as relevant market or method of analysis. Encouragement should also be given to negotiation of further bilateral and multilateral agreements on cooperation in competition cases. In some cases the idea of waiver by the parties of their confidentiality rights may also be beneficial and could be encouraged.

WTO

More recently, Ministers meeting at the World Trade Organization (WTO) Singapore conference, which took place in December 1996, agreed to set up a working group which would study issues relating to the interaction between trade and competition policy, including anti-competitive practices, in order to identify areas that may be considered further in the WTO framework. However, the WTO is not yet ready to negotiate rules in this area and any future negotiations will only take place by explicit consensus decision among WTO members. The Commission's view is that the absence of clear principles at global level hinders access by European firms to foreign markets, and that development of such principles would reduce the disparity between national competition rules with a corresponding reduction in compliance costs for companies, and an increase in their security against competitors who have been protected by lax competition rules.

The Commission has suggested the gradual development of a framework for international competition rules. Although eventually all WTO countries could adopt and enforce their own competition rules along common agreed principles, initially the framework may be limited to those countries which already have competition rules. Other aspects that should be developed would include the procedures for exchanging information; notifying other countries of investigations to avoid legal disputes on cross-border problems; and requesting action in relation to foreign markets. The Commission proposed that the WTO should set up a compliance mechanism for competition policy, similar to its trade disputes settlement procedures, so that common rules could be enforced. The WTO working group's programme is to be kept under review over the next two years.

NATIONAL MERGER CONTROL

UK

The Fair Trading Act 1973 applies to acquisitions of control, including those which have 'material influence'. The transaction may be referred by the Secretary of State for Trade and Industry to the Monopolies and Mergers Commission (MMC) if either the transaction results in the creation or increase of a market share of 25 per cent or more, or the gross value of the world wide assets being acquired exceeds £70 million. A merger situation meeting either of the above criteria is said to 'qualify for investigation'. The task of the MMC when a merger reference is made is to investigate and report upon whether it operates or may be expected to operate against the public interest.

Two procedures are now in use regarding pre-notification. First, an informal application to the Office of Fair Trading (OFT) for a decision by the Secretary of State not to refer a merger to the MMC may be made either before or after the merger has been completed. There are no fixed time limits in respect of an informal application, but non-binding timetable targets for handling mergers have been announced. In 90 per cent of cases a decision will be reached within forty-five working days of receipt of sufficient information. Second, the bidder (or in the case of an agreed merger, both parties) may pre-notify the merger proposal to the OFT in a prescribed form by way of a 'merger notice'. Once the merger notice has been given, if a period of thirty-five working days (twenty working days and a possible fifteen-day extension) elapses without a reference to the MMC, no reference can be made in relation to that transaction. In other words, the merger is deemed to have been cleared.

Confidential guidance may be sought from the OFT before public announcement or completion of the transaction, in order to obtain a non-binding indication as to whether the Secretary of State is likely to refer the transaction to the MMC. Guidance may be sought at any time before the announcement. The OFT has a non-binding target of providing guidance in 90 per cent of cases within twenty-five working days. Usually, however, the announcement is made within twenty days. The transaction will either be cleared or will be referred to the MMC.

If a merger or proposed merger is referred to the MMC, the MMC will be given a time limit not exceeding six months (but at present usually three months) in which to produce their report, with the possibility of a further three months' extension. When a reference is made the Secretary of State has power to prohibit action which might prejudice the reference.

Should the MMC conclude that a merger may be expected to operate against the public interest, the Secretary of State may forbid its consummation (or order divestiture) or may accept undertakings from the companies concerned to avoid the adverse effects on the public interest which would otherwise be expected.

France

Under French law, a merger may be subject to control if the parties to the transaction, in the year prior to the merger, either had a combined market share exceeding 25 per cent of the French market or a substantial part of it, or had a combined turnover in France exceeding FFr 7 billion, provided that at least two parties each had a turnover in France exceeding FFr 2 billion.

Mergers that meet the required conditions may be voluntarily notified to the Minister of the Economy either before or within three months of the effective date of the transaction. The Minister must decide whether to approve a notified transaction or to refer it to the Competition Council for an advisory opinion within two months of the date of notification. If a transaction is referred to the Competition Council then the Minister has six months from the date of the notification within which to approve or prohibit the transaction.

The test for merger control on initial investigation is whether or not there has been a creation or strengthening of a dominant position. On further investigation, the test is whether or not the contribution to economic progress will compensate for the loss of competition. In reaching its decision, the

Competition Council is required to consider whether the proposed merger would lead to the companies being competitive on international markets.

Germany

There are stringent merger control provisions in Germany. The definition of a merger for these purposes is very broad. It includes the acquisition of shares, which, together with any already held by the offeror or its associates, confers either (i) 25 per cent or more of the capital or voting rights; or (ii) 50 per cent or more of the capital or voting rights; or (iii) a majority participation in the target. The occurrence of each of these three events is regarded as a new merger to which the merger control provisions apply afresh. The rules will also apply where there are common directorships, or dominating or material influence.

Notification of a merger must be given to the Federal Cartel Office (FCO) before its consummation if either one of the parties had a turnover of DM 2 billion world-wide in the year prior to the merger, or if two of the parties had a turnover of DM 1 billion in that period. In the case of a pre-merger notification, the FCO must, within one month from the receipt of the notification, notify the parties that the merger will be investigated if such is the case. If notice is given, the FCO has four months from receipt of the notification in which to prohibit the proposed merger. If the FCO prohibits a transaction it may not be consummated and contracts concluded disregarding the prohibition order are considered null and void. Disregarding the order can also lead to the imposition of fines.

Consummated mergers must be notified to the FCO without delay where the participating enterprises collectively had at any one time during the year preceding the merger sales of at least DM 500 million. Except in certain defined cases where the economic effect of the merger is small, the FCO has power to prohibit a merger within one year after the notification.

Belgium

The Law for the Protection of Economic Competition sets out the MCRs of Belgium. Concentrations must be notified to the Competition Service if the parties' combined market share exceeds 25 per cent of the relevant Belgian market and the companies have had a combined world-wide turnover in the previous business year exceeding BFr 3 billion.

The Competition Service will then investigate the facts and send a reasoned opinion to the Competition Council which must, within one month of the receipt of the notification, either approve the concentration unconditionally or open a further investigation in respect of it. If an in-depth investigation is opened, the Council must decide within a further seventy-five days whether to prohibit the concentration or to approve it. Approval may be conditional on the parties complying with the conditions imposed by the Competition Service.

Until the Competition Council has reached a decision in a particular case, or until either deadline has elapsed without a decision by the Council, the parties to the concentration may not take any steps that would permanently modify the structure of the market or make it impossible for the transaction to be subsequently reversed.

Austria

The Austrian Cartel Act 1988, as amended, sets out the Austrian competition regulations. The application of the Act has recently changed as a result of a January 1997 ruling by the Austrian Supreme Court.

Under the Cartel Act, pre-merger notification is mandatory for enterprises with world-wide turnover of (i) in aggregate AS 3.5 billion, and (ii) in the case of at least two of them, at least AS 5 million each. Austrain case law until recently required that the transaction have a structural link with Austria (for example, the existence of a subsidiary, branch or significant asset of one or more of the parties there) and that the transaction have an appreciable impact on a market in Austria. The structural link requirement has recently been rejected by the Austrian Supreme Court, which has ruled that the turnover test in the Cartel Act relates to sales in Austria.

Post-merger notification is mandatory for enterprises with an aggregate turnover of at least AS 150 million, but with a turnover less than the pre-notification threshold.

Prior to clearance by the Cartel Court, there is a compulsory waiting period before the transaction can go ahead. The initial waiting period is four weeks, and there will be deemed approval if no investigation has opened within that period. If the Cartel Court does open an investigation, this should not extend beyond five months from the filing. The test applied is whether or not the transaction results in the creation or strengthening of a dominant position.

Failure to notify is a criminal offence, the parties may be subject to fines, and the transaction may be declared a nullity.

Italy

The Italian Anti-Trust Law No. 287 of 10 October 1990 applies to concentrations, including mergers, indirect acquisitions, and concentrative joint ventures.

Pre-notification is mandatory in Italy where either the aggregate domestic turnover of the undertakings involved exceeds L 671 billion, or the domestic turnover of the undertaking to be acquired exceeds L 67.1 billion. These thresholds are linked to inflation and change annually.

The Competition Authority has an initial period of thirty days after receiving a notification to decide whether the notified transaction may result in the creation or strengthening of a dominant position on the Italian market. This is reduced to fifteen days if there is a take-over bid. If the Authority decides to open an investigation, this must be completed within a further forty-five days.

Failure to notify may result in the imposition of fines of up to 1 per cent of each undertaking's turnover for the previous year.

Spain

The Defence of Competition Law 1989 applies to proposals for more concentrations of undertakings or take-overs that may affect the Spanish market. A merger or acquisition may be challenged when either a market share of 25 per cent or more in Spain (or a substantial part of it) has been created or strengthened as a result of the transaction, or where the parties to the transaction have a combined turnover in Spain exceeding Pta 20 billion in the most recent financial year.

Notifications are voluntary, and the initial investigation period is one month, after which the transaction may be referred to the Court for the Defence of Competition, which has up to three months to reach a decision. The test that will be applied is whether or not a dominant position has been created or strengthened.

Poland

Poland passed its first comprehensive antitrust law in the form of the Antimonopoly Law on Counteracting Monopolistic Practices of 24 February 1990. The Antimonopoly Law deals, *inter alia*, with the control of mergers. Under Article 11 of the Act, any proposed merger or privatization of an undertaking, and any proposals to create a business which will have a dominant position on a market or where one party already holds a dominant position, must be notified to the Competition and Consumers' Protection Office (CCPO).

The Polish Antimonopoly Law relating to mergers has recently been expanded. Prior notification of the following types of mergers will in future have to be given to the CCPO:

- A merger between undertakings if their total annual turnover during the year preceding the year of notification exceeds Ecu 5 million.
- An acquisition of a collective group of assets from an undertaking if the total value of the group assets exceeds Ecu 2 million. Such an acquisition must be notified to the Antimonopoly Office whether it was carried out as one transaction or as a series of transactions within a twelve-month period.

- A subscription or acquisition of shares in another undertaking subsequent to which the subscriber or acquirer holds a share of the voting rights greater than or equal to one of the following thresholds: 10 per cent, 25 per cent, 33 per cent, or 50 per cent, but only if the total annual turnover of both undertakings during the year preceding the year of notification exceeds Ecu 5 million.

- A subscription or acquisition of shares by a financial institution professionally involved in trading in securities subsequent to which the financial institution holds a share in the voting rights greater than or equal to one of the following thresholds: 10 per cent, 25 per cent, 33 per cent or 50 per cent; but only if the total annual turnover of the target during the year preceding the year of notification exceeds Ecu 5 million. However, notification is not required where there is an intention to dispose of shares within twelve months, and the purchaser does not exercise any rights attached to the shares, other than the right to dividends and the right of disposal of the shares.

- Where the same person becomes a director or a deputy director or a chief accountant in or a member of the management, supervisory or audit board of competing undertakings, if the total value of the annual turnover in the year preceding the year of notification exceeds Ecu 5 million.

- An acquisition of the control of another undertaking in a manner other than those set out above, either directly or indirectly, where the total annual turnover in the year preceding the year of notification exceeds Ecu 5 million.

- The requirement of prior notification of intended mergers does not apply to the acquisition of publicly traded shares. The intention to merge must be notified to the CCPO within fourteen days of the event that gives rise to the obligation of notification. Following a notification, the CCPO has two months within which to take a decision. If no decision is given within this period the notified transaction is deemed to have been authorized. Article 12 of the Antimonopoly Law gives the CCPO power to order the division or liquidation of a business holding a dominant position if it restricts competition or the conditions for its creation. The CCPO can also specify the terms for any such division or liquidation. If a merger takes place without proper notification the CCPO can unravel it. Under Article 15 of the Act, if a business does not obey a decision of the CCPO, it can be obliged to pay a fine for each month of non-compliance with the CCPO's decision. The fine will equal 1 per cent of the company's revenue, less turnover tax, for the month in which the revenues were the highest in a given year.

INDEX